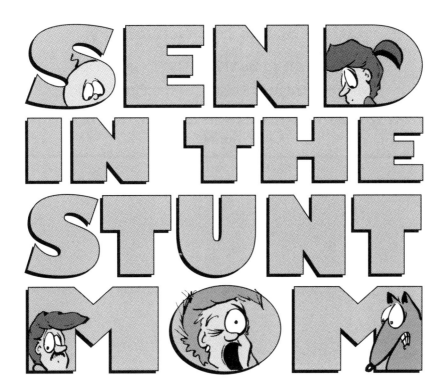

SEND IN THE STUNT MOM

Other books by Michael Fry

What I Want to Be When THEY Grow Up
Over the Hedge 3: Knights of the Picnic Table
Over the Hedge 2
Over the Hedge

THE SECOND COLLECTION OF Committed

SEND IN THE STUNT MOM

BY MICHAEL FRY

Andrews McMeel
Publishing

Kansas City

Committed is distributed internationally by United Feature Syndicate, Inc.

www.andrewsmcmeel.com

ISBN: 0-8362-3663-7

Library of Congress Catalog Card Number: 97-71635

Committed and **Over the Hedge** may be viewed on the World Wide Web:
www.unitedmedia.com

Send Michael Fry e-mail at:
Fry1@flash.net

To Sarah and Emily, my daughters, who so generously signed that prenatal agreement that keeps them from suing me for exploiting their childhood.

Frequently Asked Questions about *Committed*

1. What is *Committed*?

It's a rum-tum-tumbling-rolly-polly-universal-parallelogram-o-fun.
It's also got some kids and parent stuff and a dog and a *lot* of dense lettering.

2. What's with that screwy panel at the top with the aardvark or dog or whatever it is?

Amateurs borrow, professionals steal. Way back, many, many moons ago, when I was just a glimmer in my great-great-grandparents neocortex, there used to be a kool komic called *Krazy Kat*. *Krazy Kat* started as a small panel that ran underneath a bigger panel about some now-forgotten family. *Krazy Kat* went on to become an incredible artistic success and Final *Jeopardy* question. I'm not that ambitious. I'll settle for being Urkel's favorite comic strip.

3. What are the names of the characters?

Joe and Liz are the parents. Joe's the guy. Liz is the one who's not a guy. They're named after my dear departed grandparents who were married forever and lovingly washed the dishes together every night . . . twice . . . before putting them in the dishwasher.

Tracy is the four-year-old daughter. Zelda is the baby daughter. Bob is the dog. John is the Egg-Man. Koo-koo-ka-choo.

4. Just what exactly *is* the point?

It started out that I had this grandiose idea of redefining the family comic and bringing it from the '40s up to the '90s. This proved too fast a transition for the *Family Circus* crowd. So, I'm thinking of instituting Cute Mondays—every Monday one of the kids does something incredibly, nauseatingly cute and we all say, "Ahhhhh . . ." Don't worry though, Cute Mondays will be followed by Sarcastic Tuesdays, Cynical Wednesdays, Avant-Garde Thursdays, Dadaist Fridays, Representational Saturdays, and Corrupting-the-Youth-of-America Sundays.

5. How can I get *Committed* in my local paper?

Call them. Beg them. Plead with them. But under no circumstances stand outside their offices screaming, "SIMPLE, HUMAN JUSTICE! IT'S JUST A MATTER OF SIMPLE HUMAN JUSTICE!" It doesn't work. I tried.

6. What other stuff do you do?

I like to keep busy. When I'm not doing *Committed*, I like to keep my curling form from getting too rusty. Oh yeah, I also do *Over the Hedge* with T Lewis and *Out the Window* for *Windows Sources* magazine. I have this thing for prepositional phrases.

7. Can I suggest ideas?

Only really, really funny ones. But not ones that are funnier than what I can think up on my own. Because then I'll get insecure and we all know what happened the last time I got insecure....Whoa, Nelly!!

8. Do you have kids of your own?

I think they're mine. At least I'm pretty sure they're mine. Why, have you heard something?

9. Do they speak to you?

They speak a language that is strange to me. It sounds like English, but it's at a volume and frequency that causes my ears to bleed. I tend to work with them through an intermediary—their mother.

10. Why are your cartoons so dense?

Volume! Volume! Volume! The more stuff there is, the more there is to like. Unless of course you don't bother to read it. But that never happens.

11. How can I be a neurotic, anxious, desperate for validation, slave to cartooning like yourself?

Forget it. It takes years of dedication to perfect the sort of whiny anxious note of pathetic desperation for approval that we cartoonists have. It's not just a job, it's a paranoid excursion in hell!

12. Are you educated?

I've read all the great books: *Hop on Pop, One Fish, Two Fish, Red Fish, Blue Fish, Green Eggs and Ham* in the original Greek....

13. What kind of dog is Bob?

He's half Pit-Poodle and half Irish Wolf-Dachsund and half German-Chihuahua.

14. Why can't Bob be in the big panel and that ingratiatingly subfunctional family be in the small panel?

Bob is agoraphobic. He is afraid of white space.

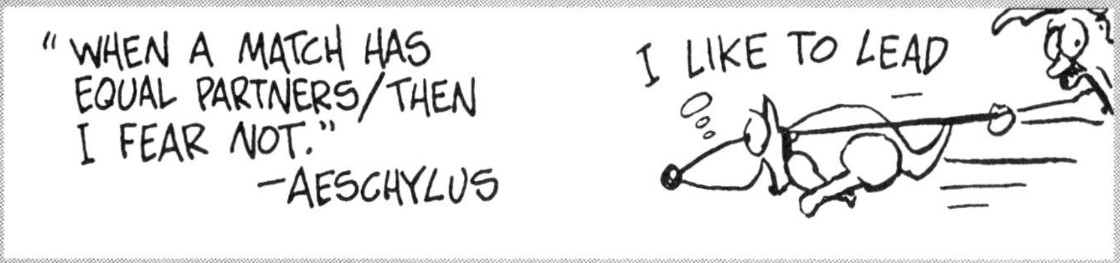
"WHEN A MATCH HAS EQUAL PARTNERS/THEN I FEAR NOT."
—AESCHYLUS
I LIKE TO LEAD

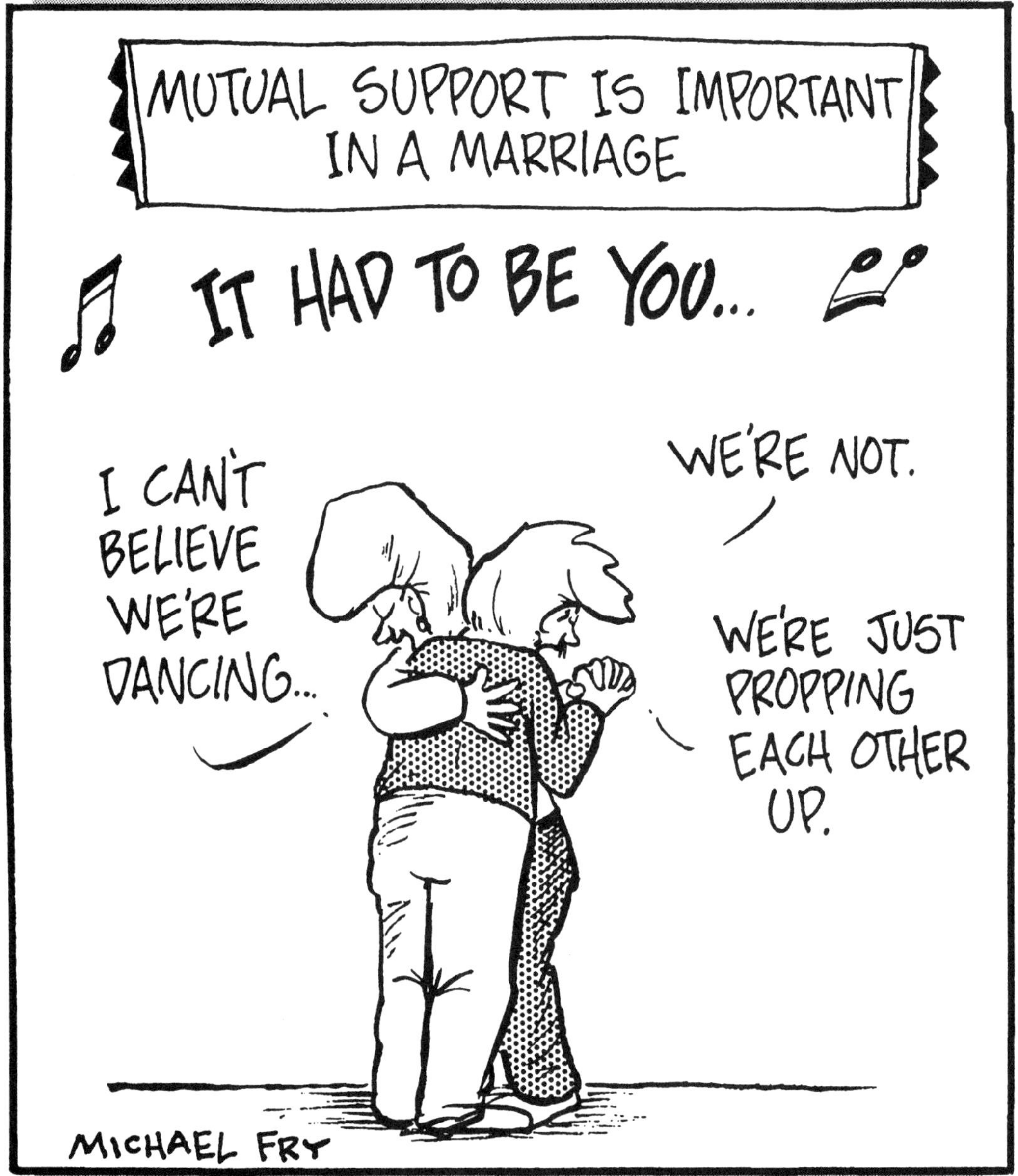
MUTUAL SUPPORT IS IMPORTANT IN A MARRIAGE
IT HAD TO BE YOU...
I CAN'T BELIEVE WE'RE DANCING...
WE'RE NOT.
WE'RE JUST PROPPING EACH OTHER UP.
MICHAEL FRY

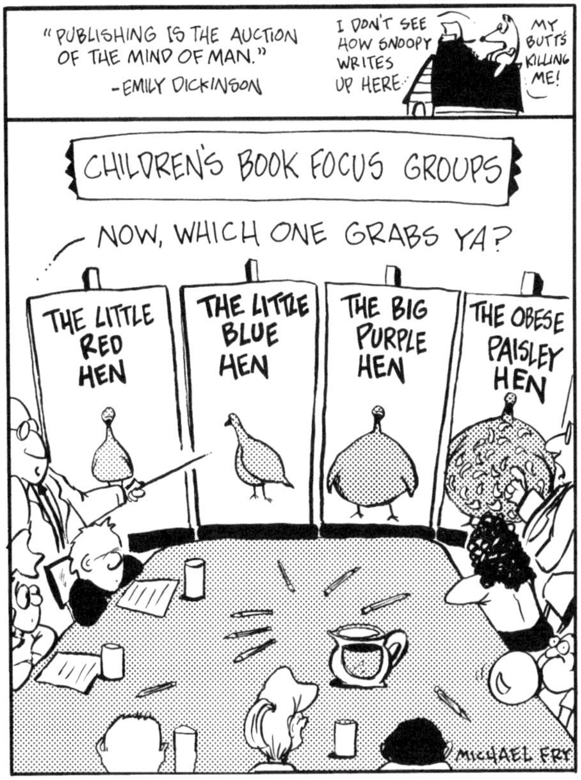
"PUBLISHING IS THE AUCTION OF THE MIND OF MAN." -EMILY DICKINSON
I DON'T SEE HOW SNOOPY WRITES UP HERE
MY BUTT'S KILLING ME!
CHILDREN'S BOOK FOCUS GROUPS
NOW, WHICH ONE GRABS YA?
THE LITTLE RED HEN
THE LITTLE BLUE HEN
THE BIG PURPLE HEN
THE OBESE PAISLEY HEN
MICHAEL FRY

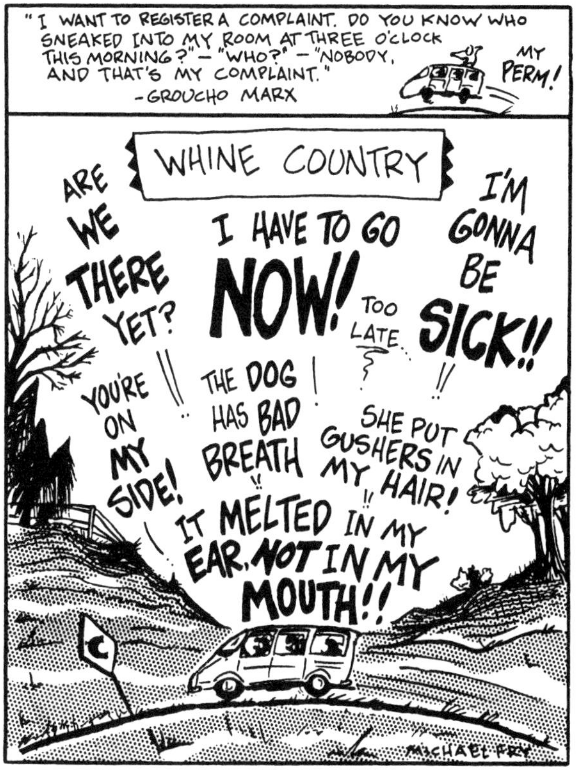
"I WANT TO REGISTER A COMPLAINT. DO YOU KNOW WHO SNEAKED INTO MY ROOM AT THREE O'CLOCK THIS MORNING?" - "WHO?" - "NOBODY, AND THAT'S MY COMPLAINT." -GROUCHO MARX
MY PERM!
WHINE COUNTRY
ARE WE THERE YET?
I HAVE TO GO NOW!
I'M GONNA BE SICK!!
TOO LATE...
YOU'RE ON MY SIDE!
THE DOG HAS BAD BREATH
SHE PUT GUSHERS IN MY HAIR!
IT MELTED IN MY EAR. NOT IN MY MOUTH!!
MICHAEL FRY

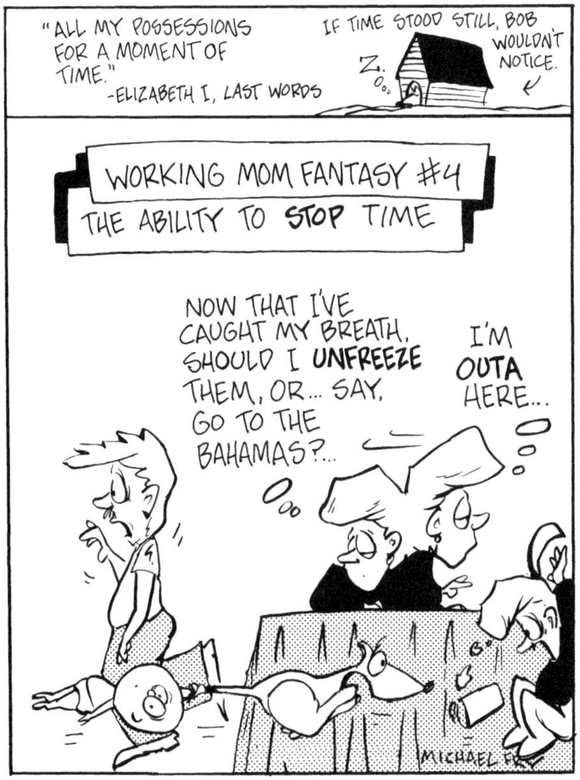
"ALL MY POSSESSIONS FOR A MOMENT OF TIME." -ELIZABETH I, LAST WORDS
IF TIME STOOD STILL, BOB WOULDN'T NOTICE.
Z.
WORKING MOM FANTASY #4
THE ABILITY TO STOP TIME
NOW THAT I'VE CAUGHT MY BREATH, SHOULD I UNFREEZE THEM, OR... SAY, GO TO THE BAHAMAS?...
I'M OUTA HERE...
MICHAEL FRY

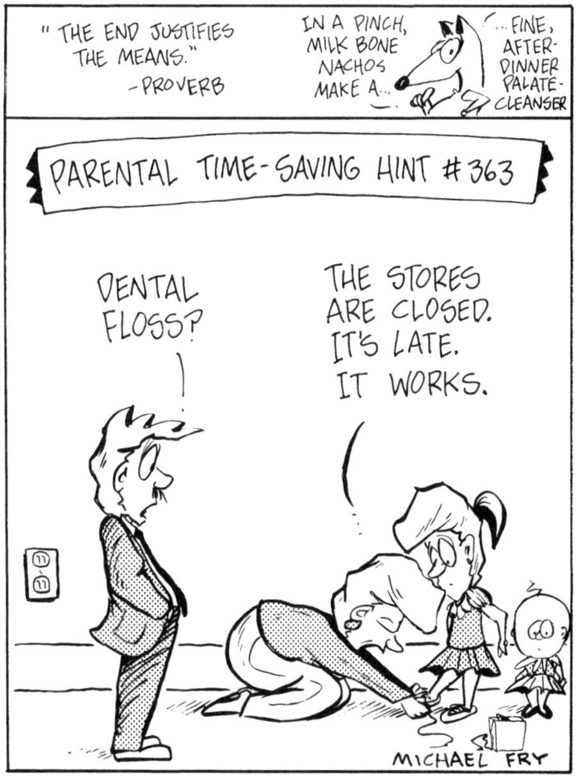
"THE END JUSTIFIES THE MEANS." -PROVERB
IN A PINCH, MILK BONE NACHOS MAKE A...
...FINE, AFTER-DINNER PALATE-CLEANSER
PARENTAL TIME-SAVING HINT #363
DENTAL FLOSS?
THE STORES ARE CLOSED. IT'S LATE. IT WORKS.
MICHAEL FRY

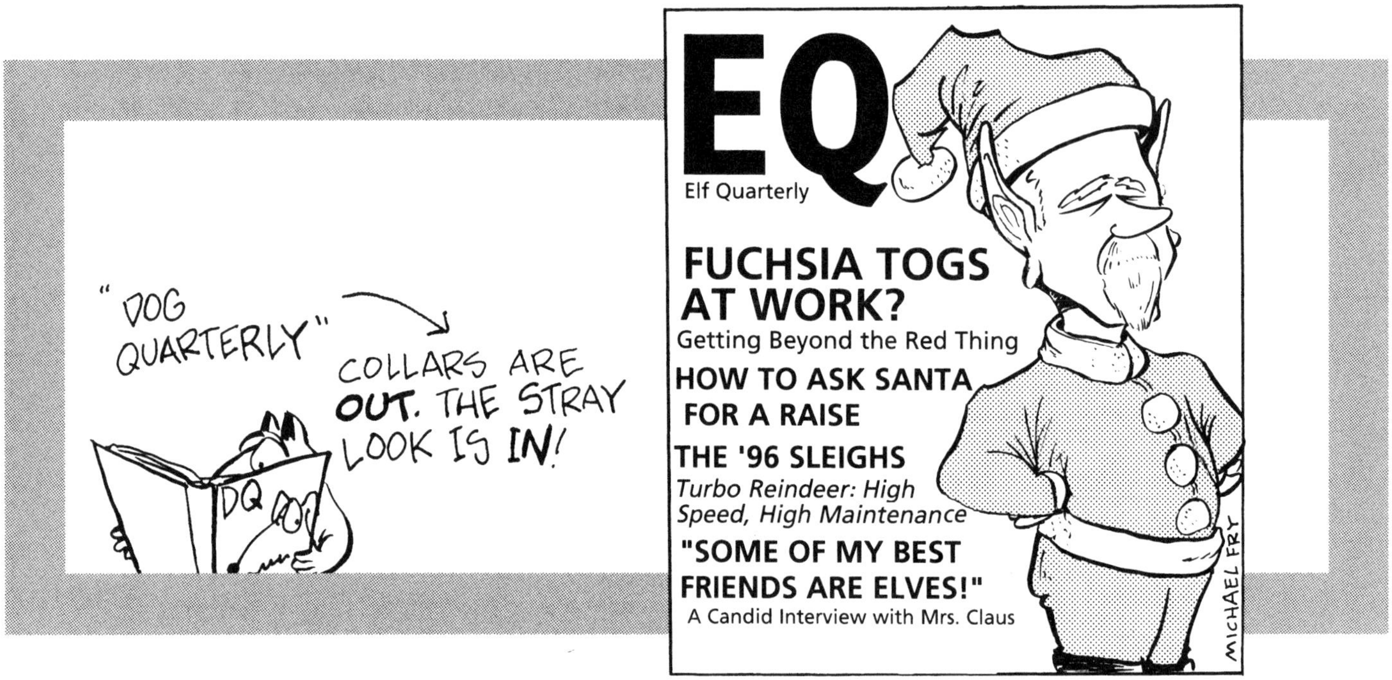
"DOG QUARTERLY"
COLLARS ARE OUT. THE STRAY LOOK IS IN!
DQ
EQ
Elf Quarterly
FUCHSIA TOGS AT WORK?
Getting Beyond the Red Thing
HOW TO ASK SANTA FOR A RAISE
THE '96 SLEIGHS
Turbo Reindeer: High Speed, High Maintenance
"SOME OF MY BEST FRIENDS ARE ELVES!"
A Candid Interview with Mrs. Claus
MICHAEL FRY

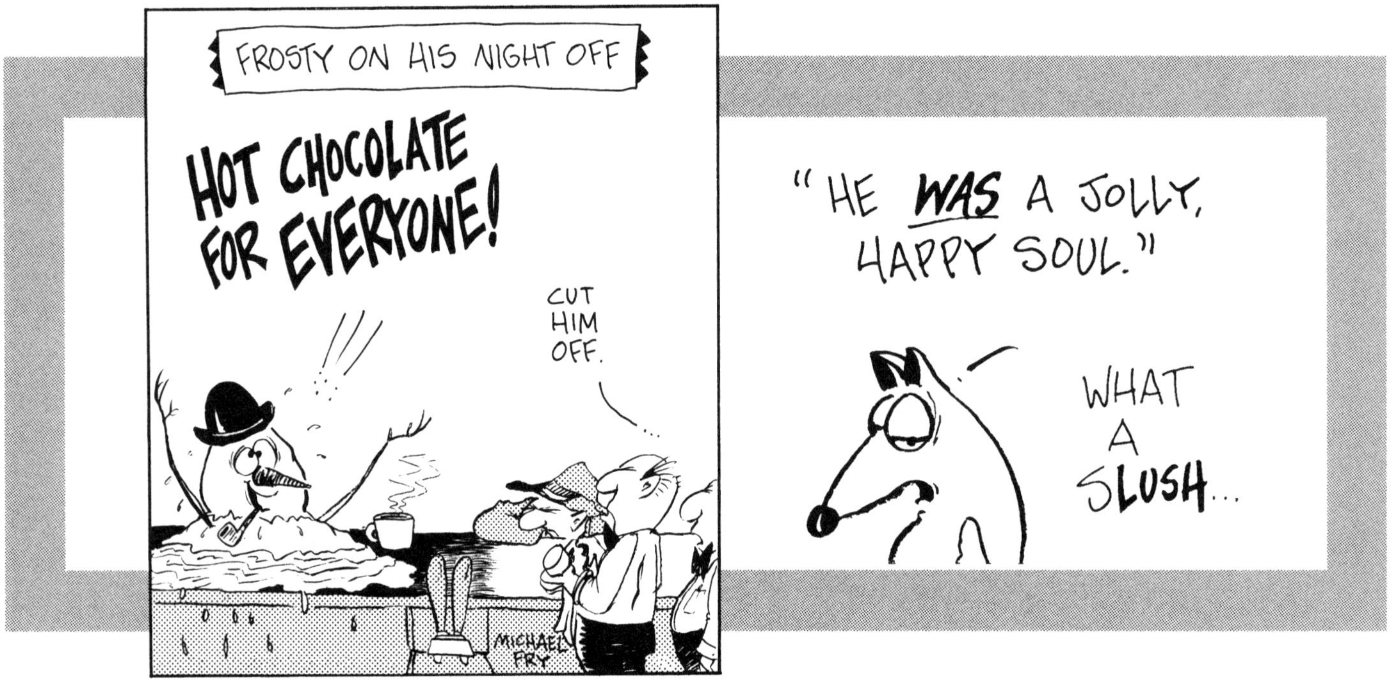
FROSTY ON HIS NIGHT OFF
HOT CHOCOLATE FOR EVERYONE!
CUT HIM OFF.
MICHAEL FRY
"HE WAS A JOLLY, HAPPY SOUL."
WHAT A SLUSH...

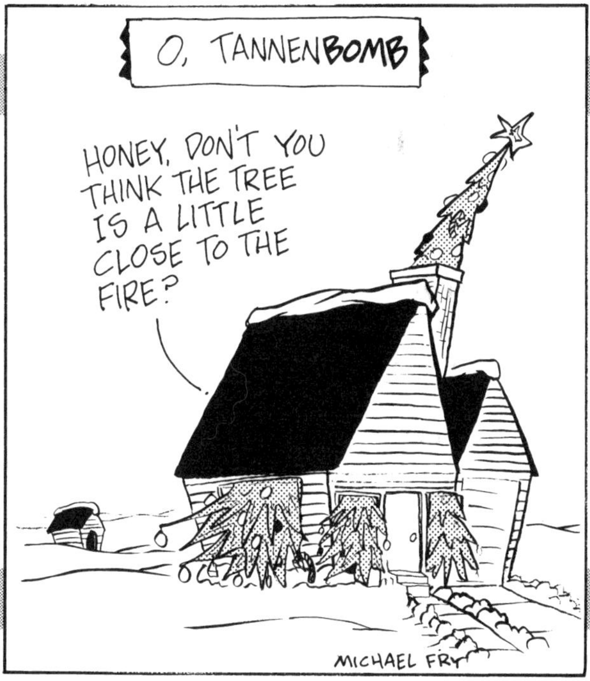
O, TANNENBOMB
HONEY, DON'T YOU THINK THE TREE IS A LITTLE CLOSE TO THE FIRE?
MICHAEL FRY

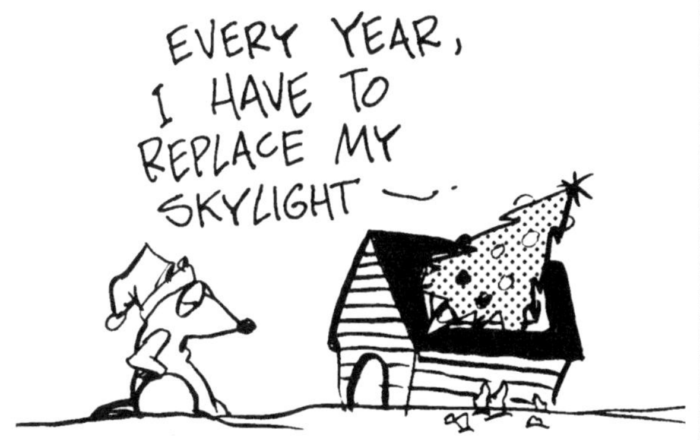
EVERY YEAR, I HAVE TO REPLACE MY SKYLIGHT

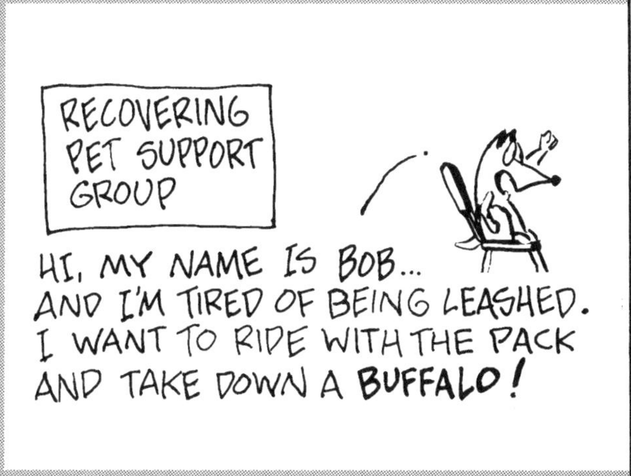
RECOVERING PET SUPPORT GROUP
HI, MY NAME IS BOB... AND I'M TIRED OF BEING LEASHED. I WANT TO RIDE WITH THE PACK AND TAKE DOWN A BUFFALO!

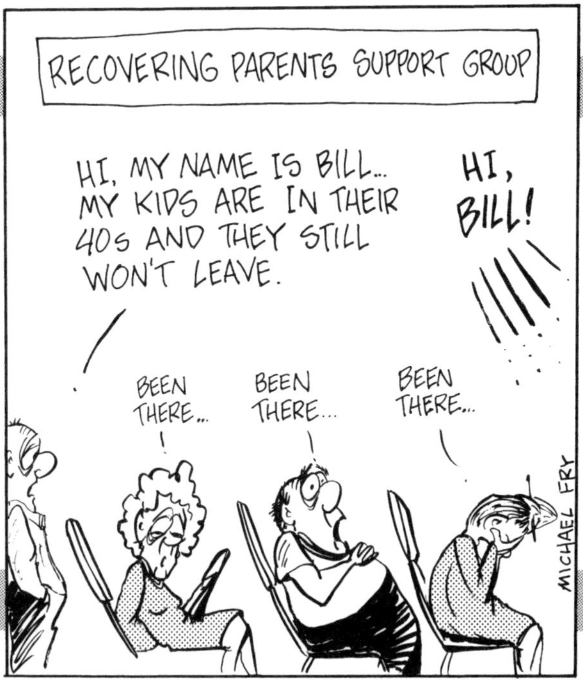
RECOVERING PARENTS SUPPORT GROUP
HI, MY NAME IS BILL... MY KIDS ARE IN THEIR 40s AND THEY STILL WON'T LEAVE.
HI, BILL!
BEEN THERE...
BEEN THERE...
BEEN THERE...
MICHAEL FRY

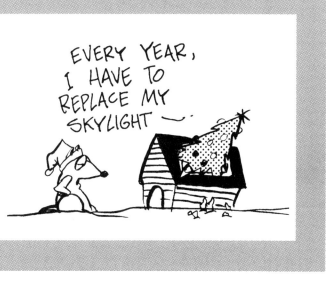

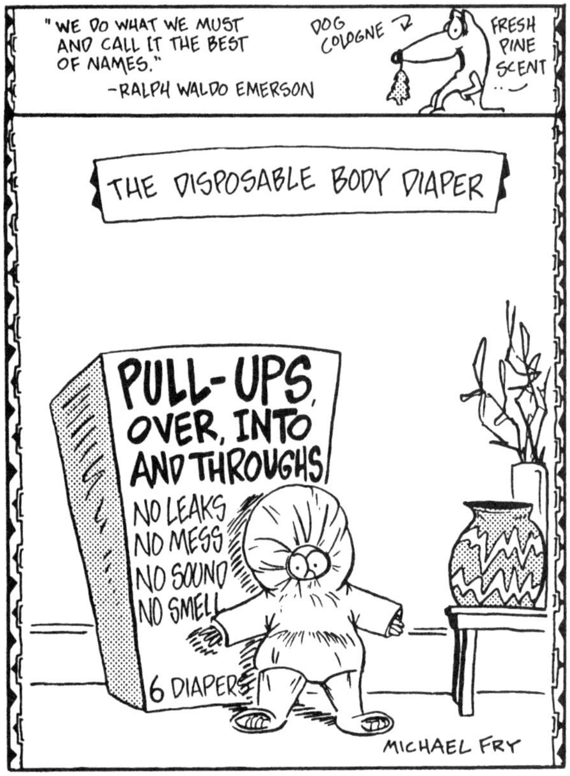
"WE DO WHAT WE MUST AND CALL IT THE BEST OF NAMES."
-RALPH WALDO EMERSON
DOG COLOGNE
FRESH PINE SCENT
THE DISPOSABLE BODY DIAPER
PULL-UPS, OVER, INTO AND THROUGHS
NO LEAKS
NO MESS
NO SOUND
NO SMELL
6 DIAPERS
MICHAEL FRY

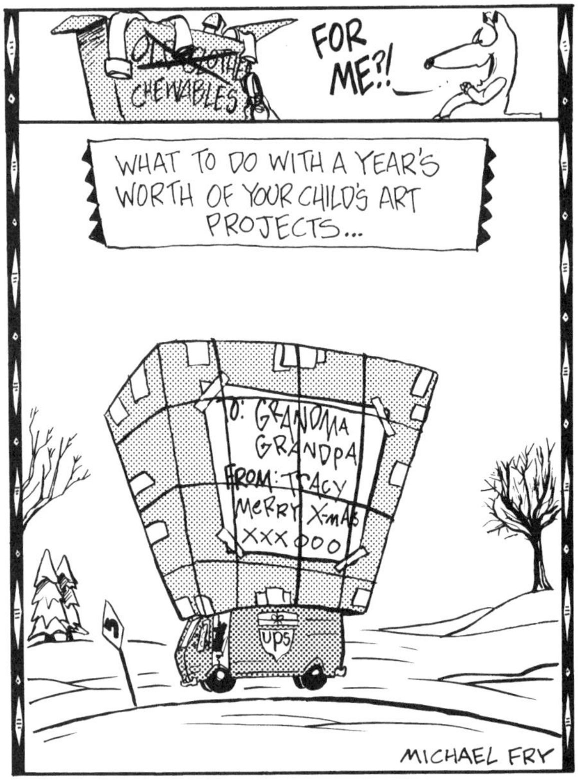
CHEWABLES
FOR ME?!
WHAT TO DO WITH A YEAR'S WORTH OF YOUR CHILD'S ART PROJECTS...
TO: GRANDMA GRANDPA
FROM: TRACY
MERRY X-MAS
XXX OOO
UPS
MICHAEL FRY

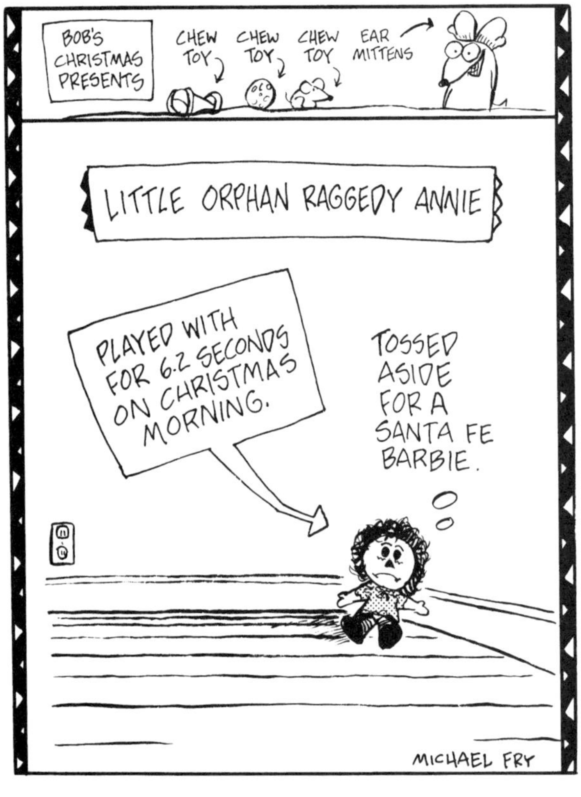
BOB'S CHRISTMAS PRESENTS
CHEW TOY
CHEW TOY
CHEW TOY
EAR MITTENS
LITTLE ORPHAN RAGGEDY ANNIE
PLAYED WITH FOR 6.2 SECONDS ON CHRISTMAS MORNING.
TOSSED ASIDE FOR A SANTA FE BARBIE.
MICHAEL FRY

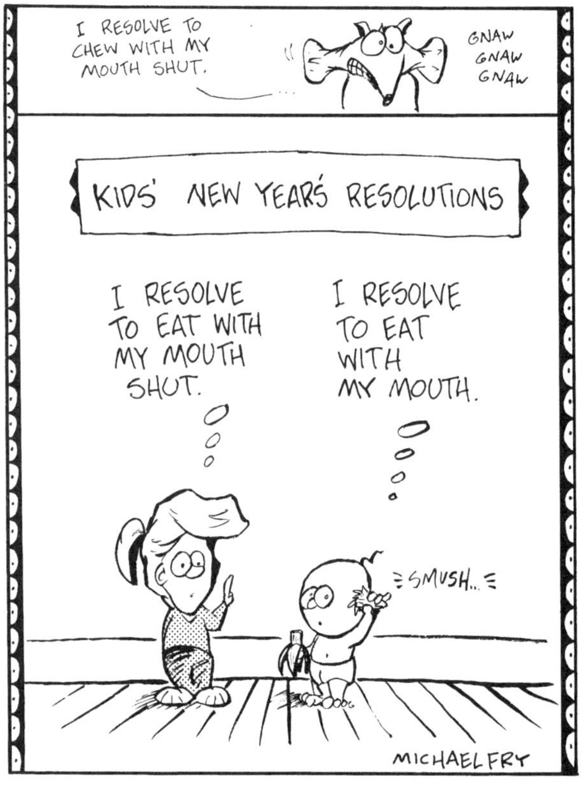
I RESOLVE TO CHEW WITH MY MOUTH SHUT.
GNAW GNAW GNAW
KIDS' NEW YEAR'S RESOLUTIONS
I RESOLVE TO EAT WITH MY MOUTH SHUT.
I RESOLVE TO EAT WITH MY MOUTH.
SMUSH...
MICHAEL FRY

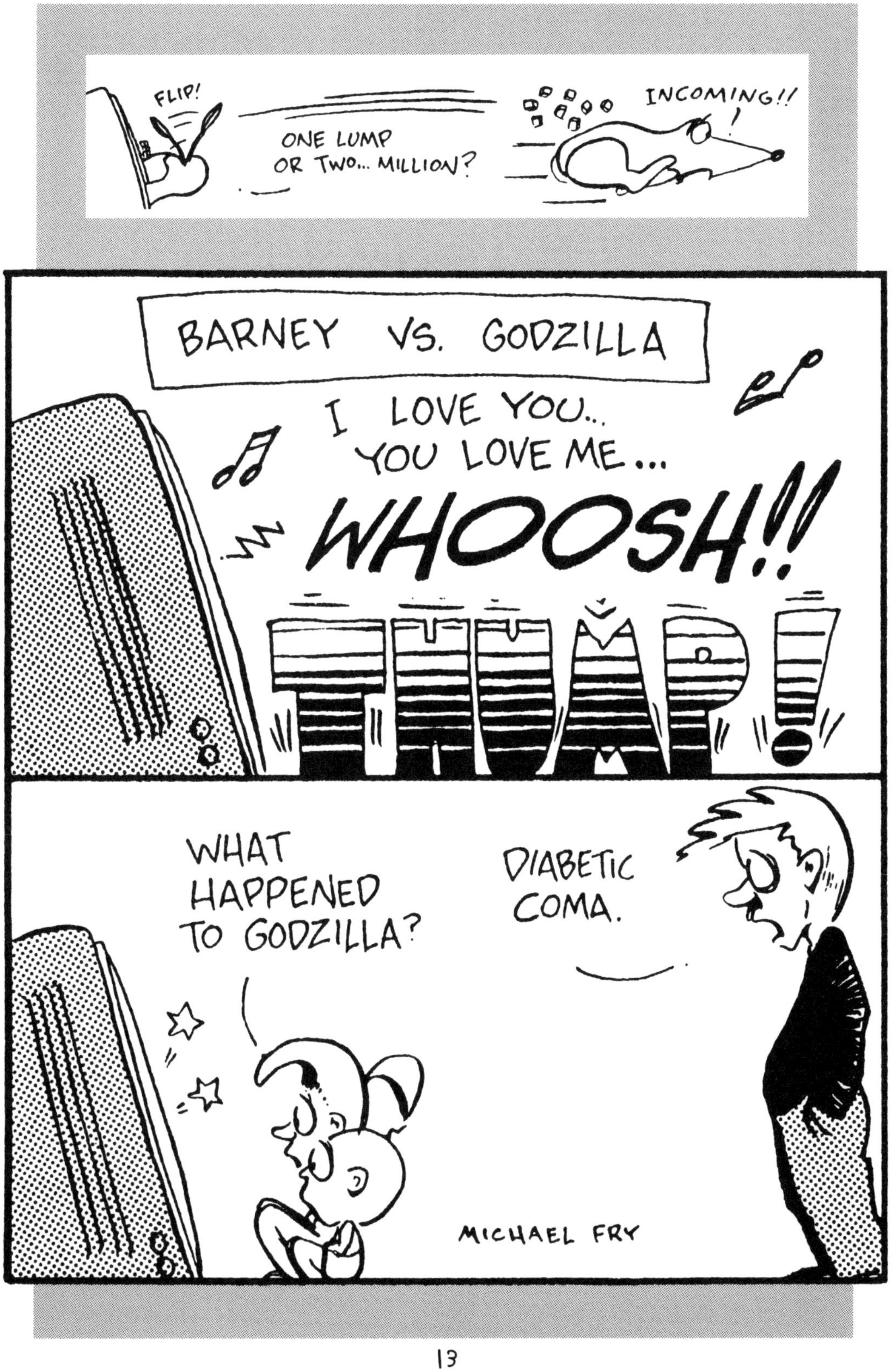
FLIP!
ONE LUMP OR TWO... MILLION?
INCOMING!!
BARNEY VS. GODZILLA
I LOVE YOU... YOU LOVE ME...
WHOOSH!!
THWAP!
WHAT HAPPENED TO GODZILLA?
DIABETIC COMA.
MICHAEL FRY

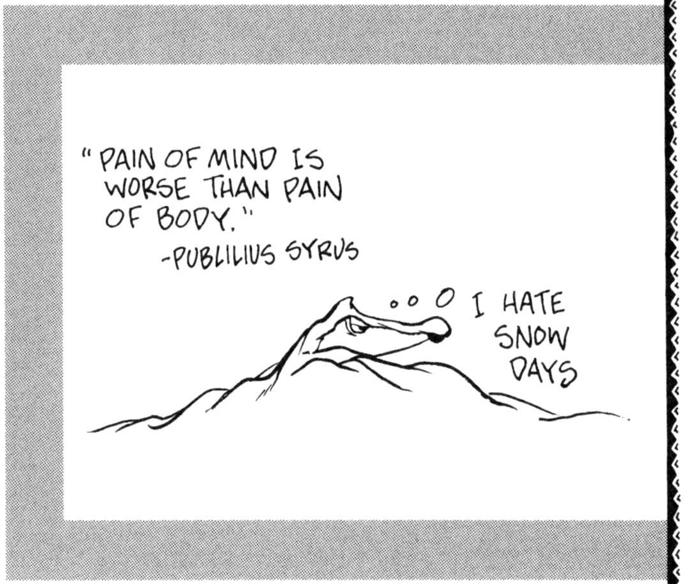
"PAIN OF MIND IS WORSE THAN PAIN OF BODY."
-PUBLILIUS SYRUS
I HATE SNOW DAYS

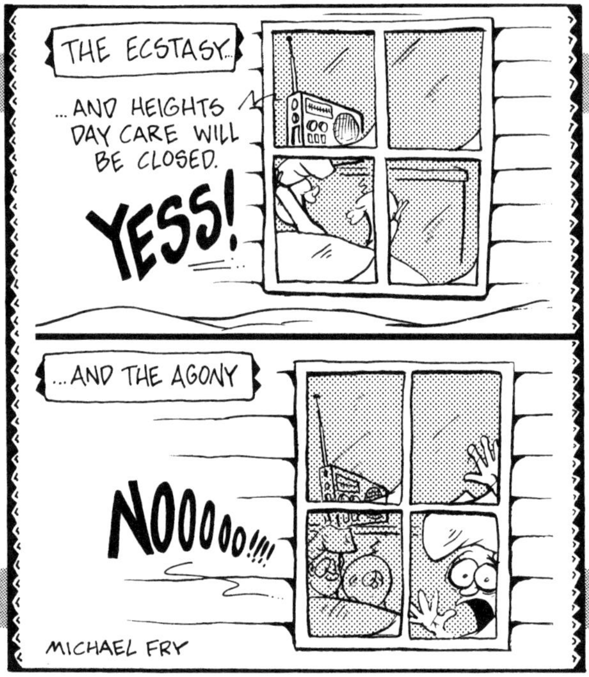
THE ECSTASY...
...AND HEIGHTS DAY CARE WILL BE CLOSED.
YESS!
...AND THE AGONY
NOOOOO!!!!
MICHAEL FRY

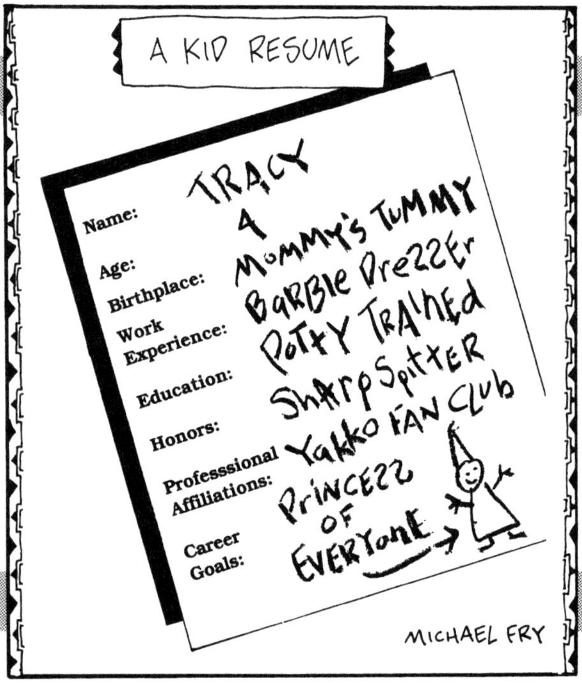
A KID RESUME
Name: TRACY
Age: 4
Birthplace: MOMMY'S TUMMY
Work Experience: BARBIE DREZZER
Education: POTTY TRAINED
Honors: SHARP SPITTER
Professional Affiliations: YAKKO FAN CLUB
Career Goals: PRINCEZZ OF EVERYONE
MICHAEL FRY

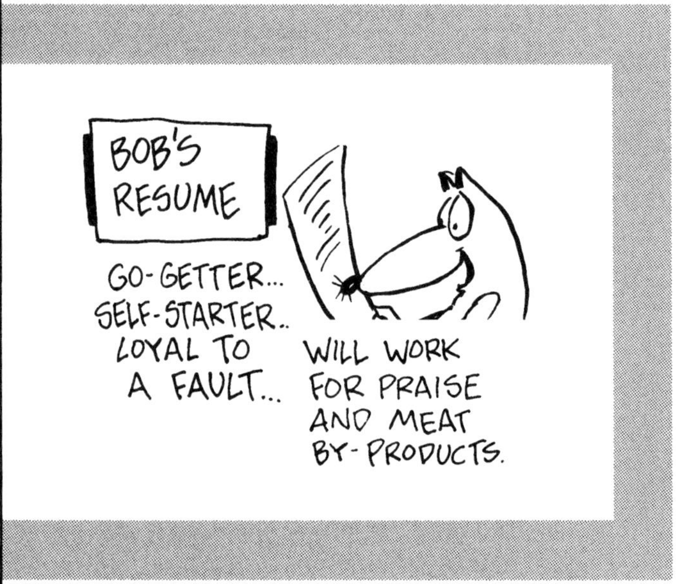
BOB'S RESUME
GO-GETTER... SELF-STARTER.. LOYAL TO A FAULT...
WILL WORK FOR PRAISE AND MEAT BY-PRODUCTS.

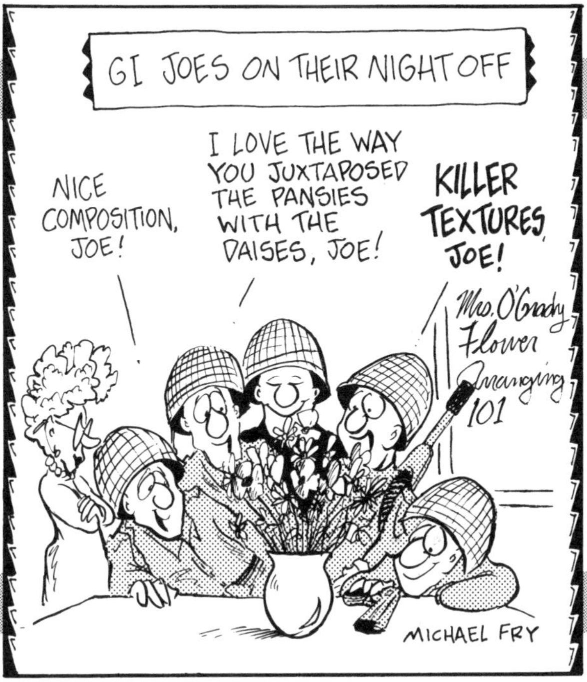
GI JOES ON THEIR NIGHT OFF
NICE COMPOSITION, JOE!
I LOVE THE WAY YOU JUXTAPOSED THE PANSIES WITH THE DAISES, JOE!
KILLER TEXTURES, JOE!
Mrs. O'Grady Flower Arranging 101
MICHAEL FRY

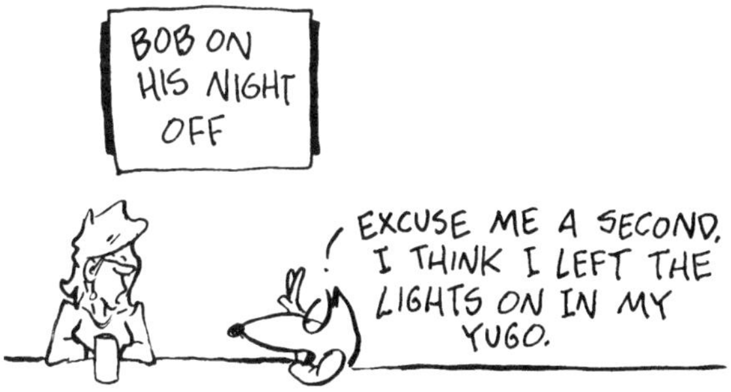
BOB ON HIS NIGHT OFF
EXCUSE ME A SECOND, I THINK I LEFT THE LIGHTS ON IN MY YUGO.

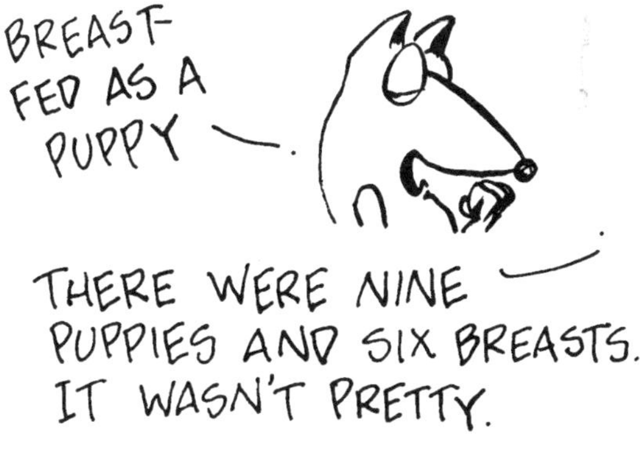
BREAST-FED AS A PUPPY
THERE WERE NINE PUPPIES AND SIX BREASTS. IT WASN'T PRETTY.

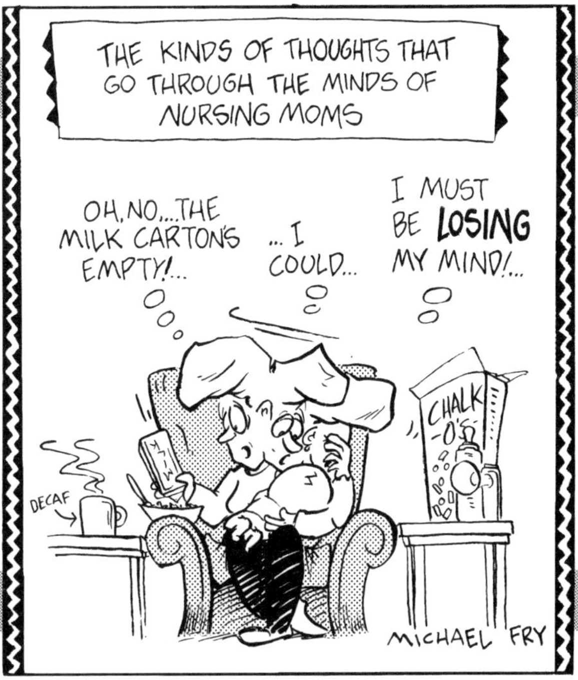
THE KINDS OF THOUGHTS THAT GO THROUGH THE MINDS OF NURSING MOMS
OH, NO,...THE MILK CARTON'S EMPTY!...
...I COULD...
I MUST BE LOSING MY MIND!...
DECAF
CHALK-O'S
MICHAEL FRY

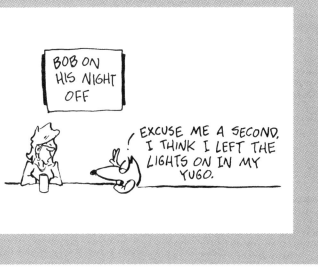

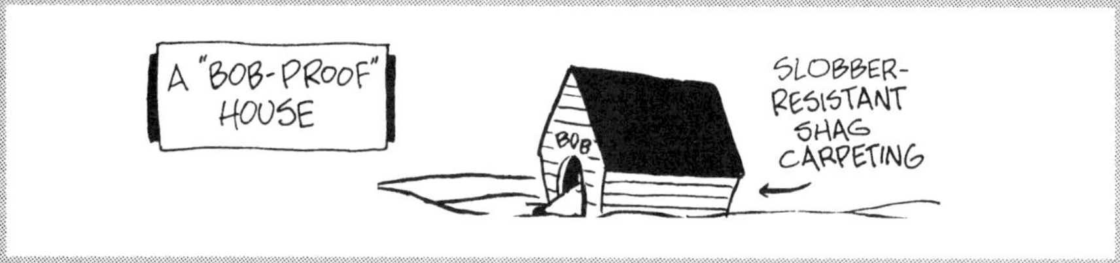
A "BOB-PROOF" HOUSE
BOB
SLOBBER-RESISTANT SHAG CARPETING

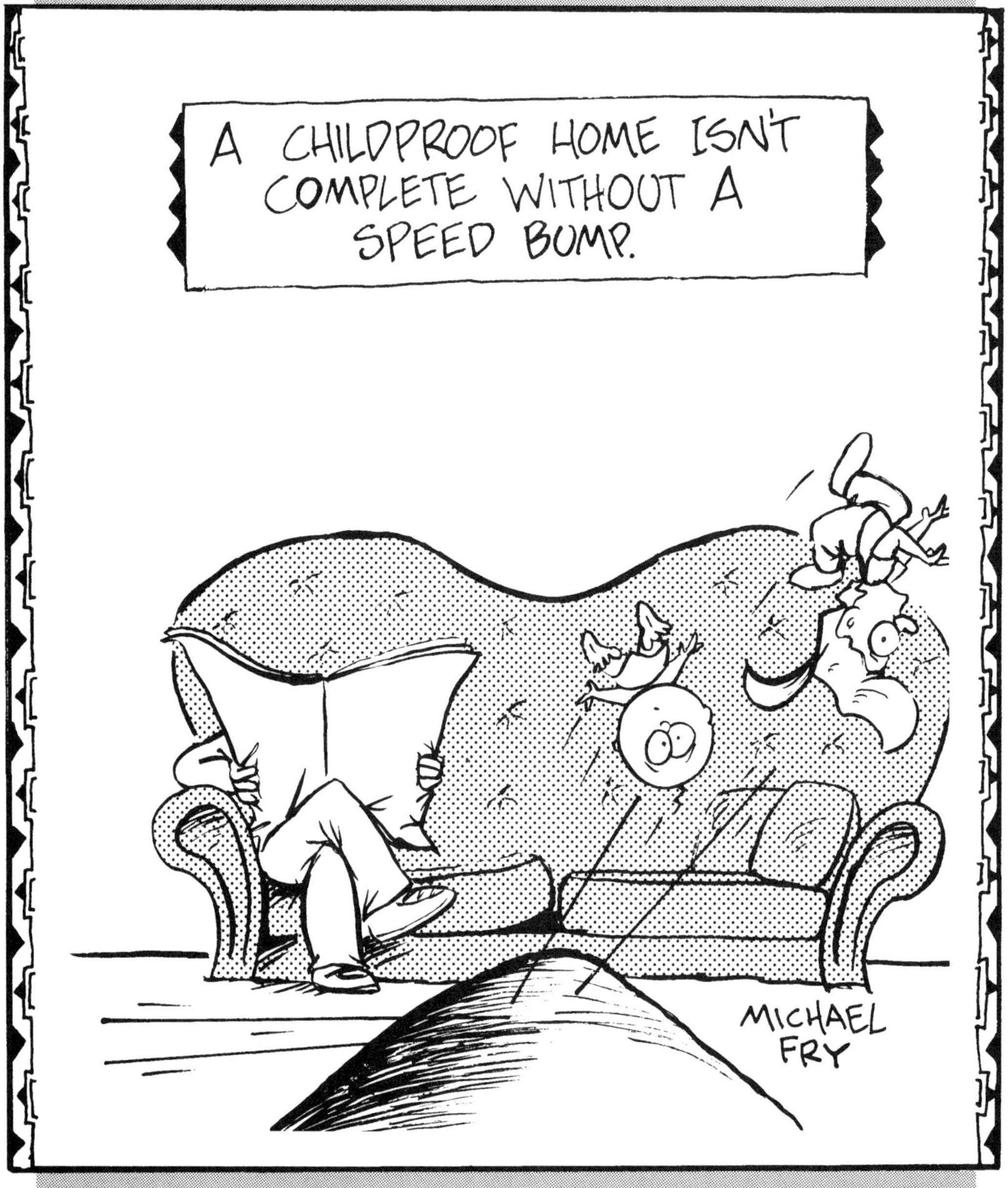
A CHILDPROOF HOME ISN'T COMPLETE WITHOUT A SPEED BUMP.
MICHAEL FRY

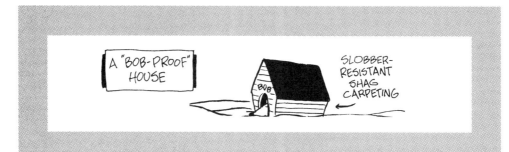

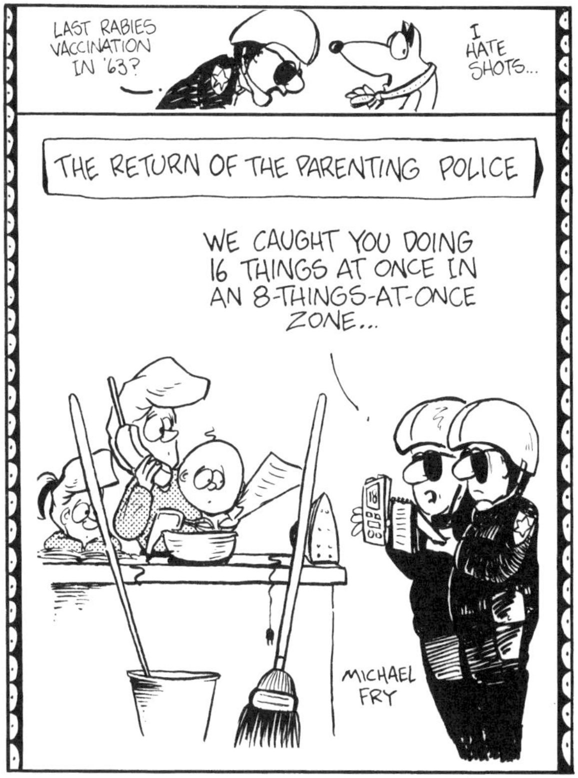
LAST RABIES VACCINATION IN '63?
I HATE SHOTS...
THE RETURN OF THE PARENTING POLICE
WE CAUGHT YOU DOING 16 THINGS AT ONCE IN AN 8-THINGS-AT-ONCE ZONE...
MICHAEL FRY

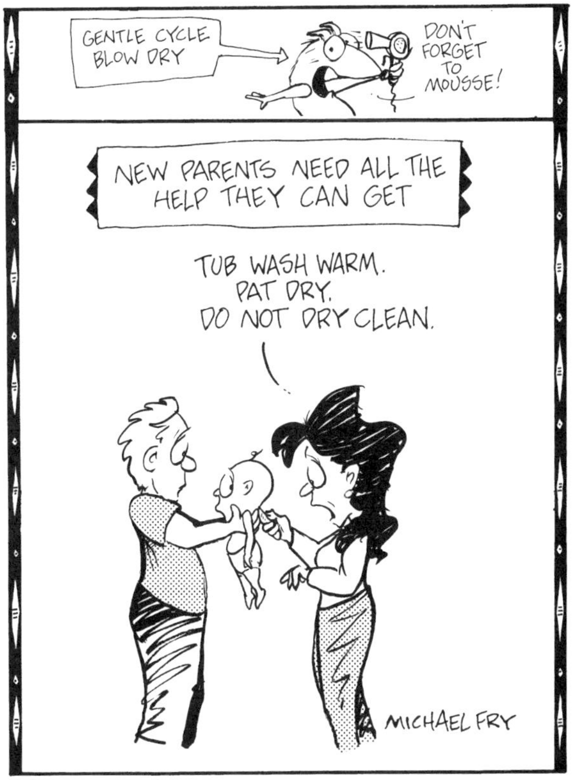
GENTLE CYCLE BLOW DRY
DON'T FORGET TO MOUSSE!
NEW PARENTS NEED ALL THE HELP THEY CAN GET
TUB WASH WARM. PAT DRY. DO NOT DRY CLEAN.
MICHAEL FRY

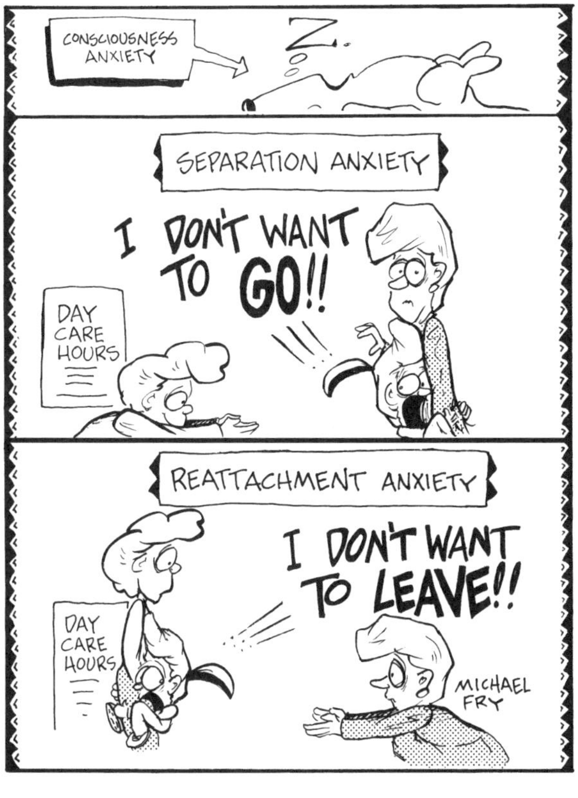
CONSCIOUSNESS ANXIETY
Z
SEPARATION ANXIETY
I DON'T WANT TO GO!!
DAY CARE HOURS
REATTACHMENT ANXIETY
I DON'T WANT TO LEAVE!!
DAY CARE HOURS
MICHAEL FRY

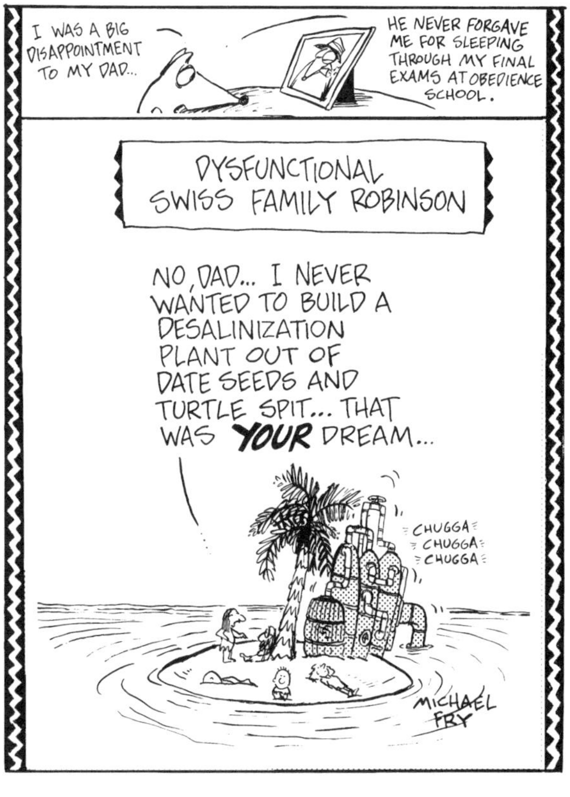
I WAS A BIG DISAPPOINTMENT TO MY DAD...
HE NEVER FORGAVE ME FOR SLEEPING THROUGH MY FINAL EXAMS AT OBEDIENCE SCHOOL.
DYSFUNCTIONAL SWISS FAMILY ROBINSON
NO, DAD... I NEVER WANTED TO BUILD A DESALINIZATION PLANT OUT OF DATE SEEDS AND TURTLE SPIT... THAT WAS YOUR DREAM...
CHUGGA CHUGGA CHUGGA
MICHAEL FRY

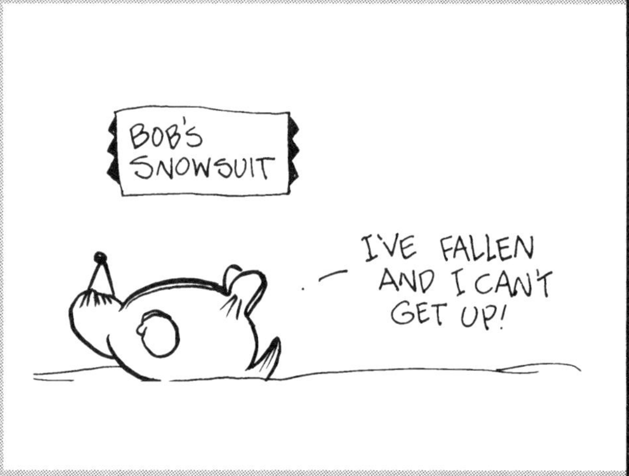
BOB'S SNOWSUIT
I'VE FALLEN AND I CAN'T GET UP!

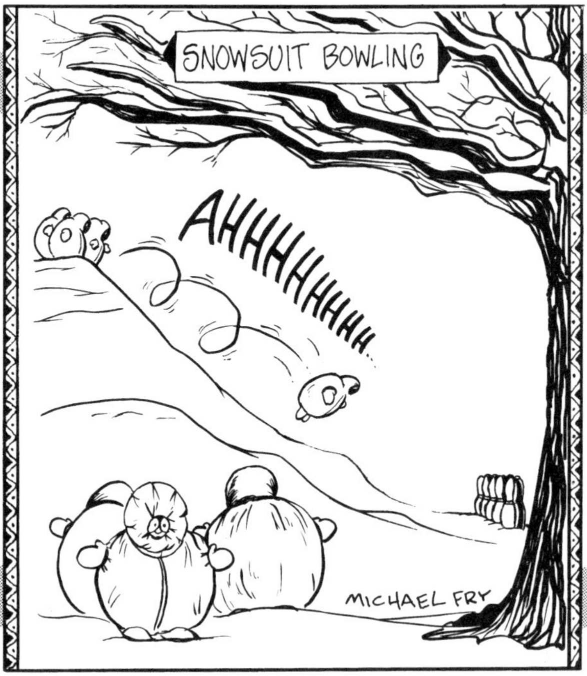
SNOWSUIT BOWLING
AHHHHHHHH...
MICHAEL FRY

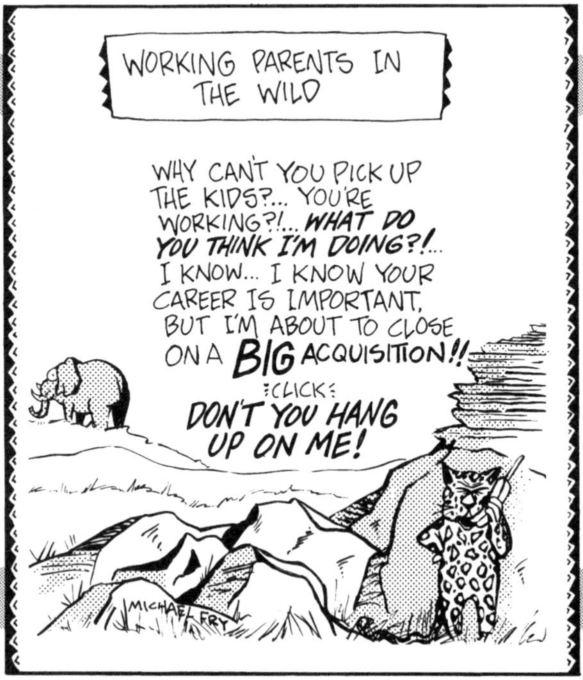
WORKING PARENTS IN THE WILD
WHY CAN'T YOU PICK UP THE KIDS?... YOU'RE WORKING?!... WHAT DO YOU THINK I'M DOING?!... I KNOW... I KNOW YOUR CAREER IS IMPORTANT, BUT I'M ABOUT TO CLOSE ON A BIG ACQUISITION!!
CLICK
DON'T YOU HANG UP ON ME!
MICHAEL FRY

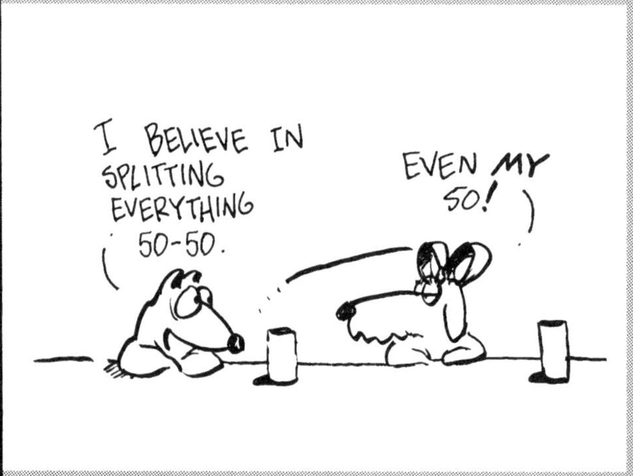
I BELIEVE IN SPLITTING EVERYTHING 50-50.
EVEN MY 50!

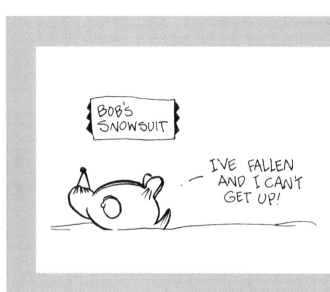

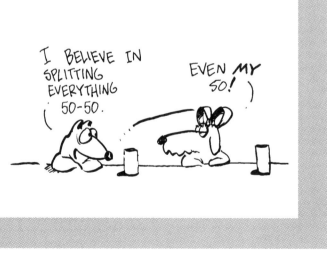

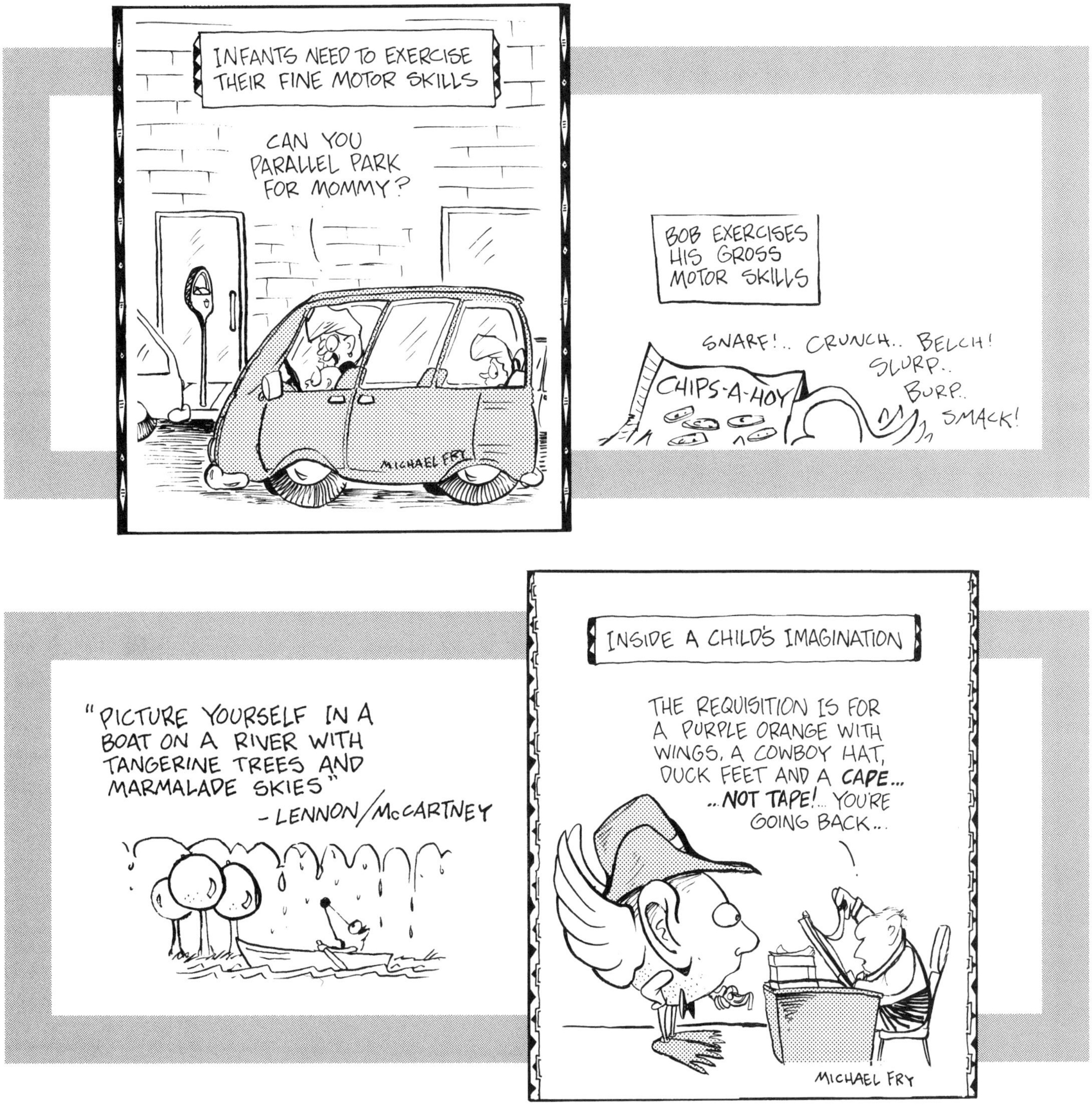
INFANTS NEED TO EXERCISE THEIR FINE MOTOR SKILLS
CAN YOU PARALLEL PARK FOR MOMMY?
MICHAEL FRY
BOB EXERCISES HIS GROSS MOTOR SKILLS
CHIPS-A-HOY
SNARF!.. CRUNCH.. BELCH! SLURP.. BURP. SMACK!
"PICTURE YOURSELF IN A BOAT ON A RIVER WITH TANGERINE TREES AND MARMALADE SKIES"
- LENNON/McCARTNEY
INSIDE A CHILD'S IMAGINATION
THE REQUISITION IS FOR A PURPLE ORANGE WITH WINGS, A COWBOY HAT, DUCK FEET AND A CAPE... ...NOT TAPE!... YOU'RE GOING BACK...
MICHAEL FRY

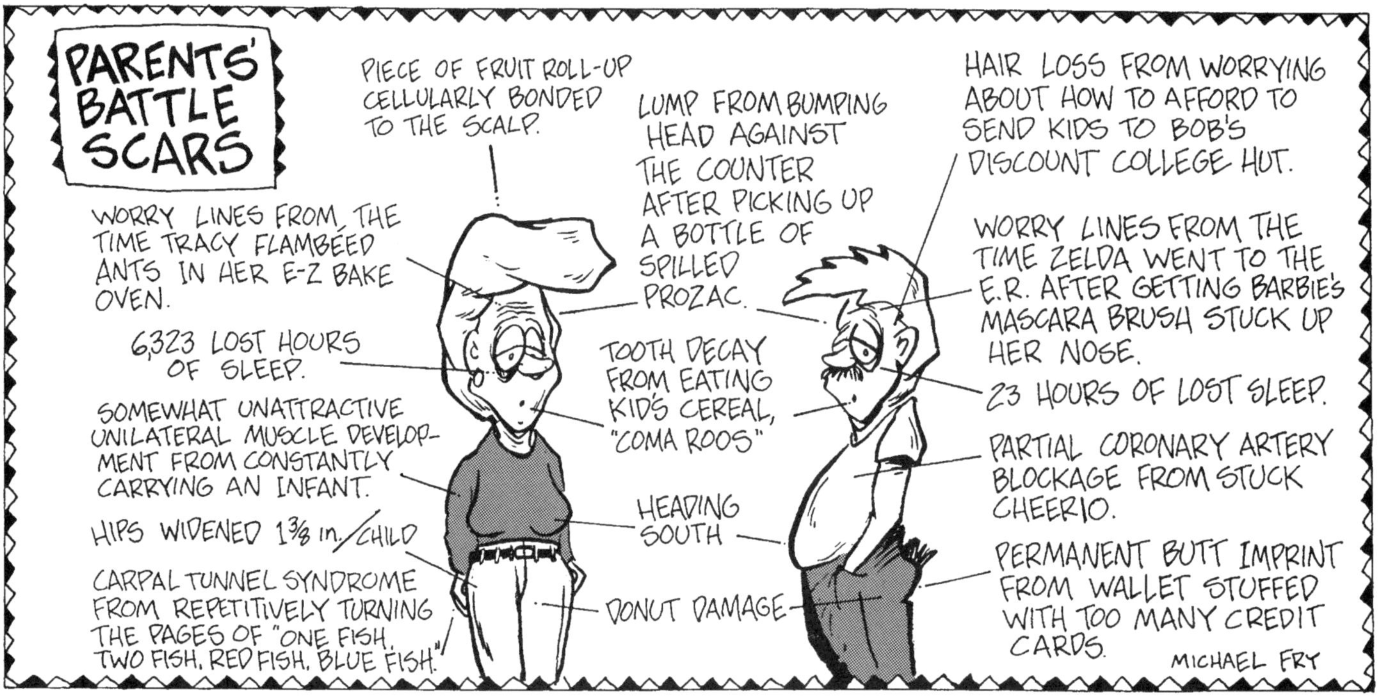
PARENTS' BATTLE SCARS
PIECE OF FRUIT ROLL-UP CELLULARLY BONDED TO THE SCALP.
LUMP FROM BUMPING HEAD AGAINST THE COUNTER AFTER PICKING UP A BOTTLE OF SPILLED PROZAC.
HAIR LOSS FROM WORRYING ABOUT HOW TO AFFORD TO SEND KIDS TO BOB'S DISCOUNT COLLEGE HUT.
WORRY LINES FROM THE TIME TRACY FLAMBÉED ANTS IN HER E-Z BAKE OVEN.
WORRY LINES FROM THE TIME ZELDA WENT TO THE E.R. AFTER GETTING BARBIE'S MASCARA BRUSH STUCK UP HER NOSE.
6,323 LOST HOURS OF SLEEP.
TOOTH DECAY FROM EATING KID'S CEREAL, "COMA ROOS"
23 HOURS OF LOST SLEEP.
SOMEWHAT UNATTRACTIVE UNILATERAL MUSCLE DEVELOPMENT FROM CONSTANTLY CARRYING AN INFANT.
PARTIAL CORONARY ARTERY BLOCKAGE FROM STUCK CHEERIO.
HEADING SOUTH
HIPS WIDENED 1 3/8 in./CHILD
CARPAL TUNNEL SYNDROME FROM REPETITIVELY TURNING THE PAGES OF "ONE FISH, TWO FISH, RED FISH, BLUE FISH."
DONUT DAMAGE
PERMANENT BUTT IMPRINT FROM WALLET STUFFED WITH TOO MANY CREDIT CARDS.
MICHAEL FRY

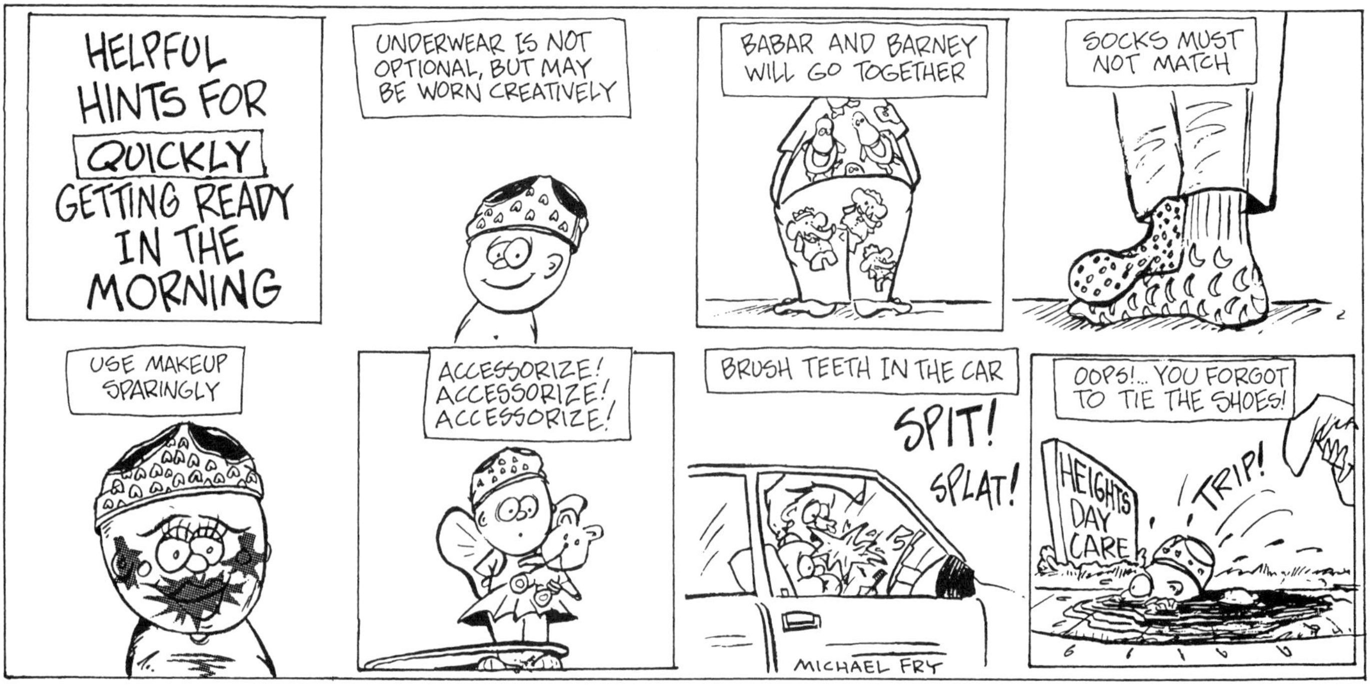
HELPFUL HINTS FOR QUICKLY GETTING READY IN THE MORNING
UNDERWEAR IS NOT OPTIONAL, BUT MAY BE WORN CREATIVELY
BABAR AND BARNEY WILL GO TOGETHER
SOCKS MUST NOT MATCH
USE MAKEUP SPARINGLY
ACCESSORIZE! ACCESSORIZE! ACCESSORIZE!
BRUSH TEETH IN THE CAR
SPIT!
SPLAT!
MICHAEL FRY
OOPS!... YOU FORGOT TO TIE THE SHOES!
HEIGHTS DAY CARE
TRIP!

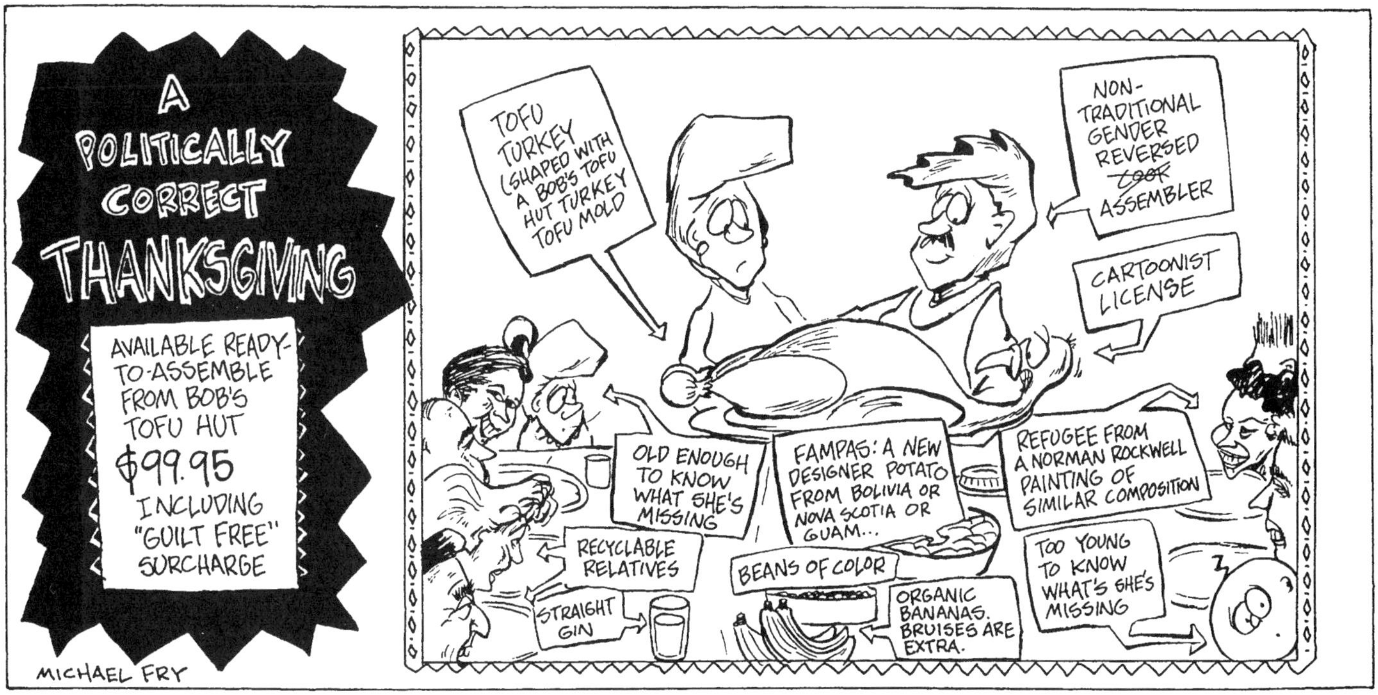
A POLITICALLY CORRECT THANKSGIVING
AVAILABLE READY-TO-ASSEMBLE FROM BOB'S TOFU HUT $99.95 INCLUDING "GUILT FREE" SURCHARGE
TOFU TURKEY (SHAPED WITH A BOB'S TOFU HUT TURKEY TOFU MOLD
NON-TRADITIONAL GENDER REVERSED ~~COOK~~ ASSEMBLER
CARTOONIST LICENSE
OLD ENOUGH TO KNOW WHAT SHE'S MISSING
FAMPAS: A NEW DESIGNER POTATO FROM BOLIVIA OR NOVA SCOTIA OR GUAM...
REFUGEE FROM A NORMAN ROCKWELL PAINTING OF SIMILAR COMPOSITION
RECYCLABLE RELATIVES
BEANS OF COLOR
TOO YOUNG TO KNOW WHAT'S SHE'S MISSING
STRAIGHT GIN
ORGANIC BANANAS. BRUISES ARE EXTRA.
MICHAEL FRY

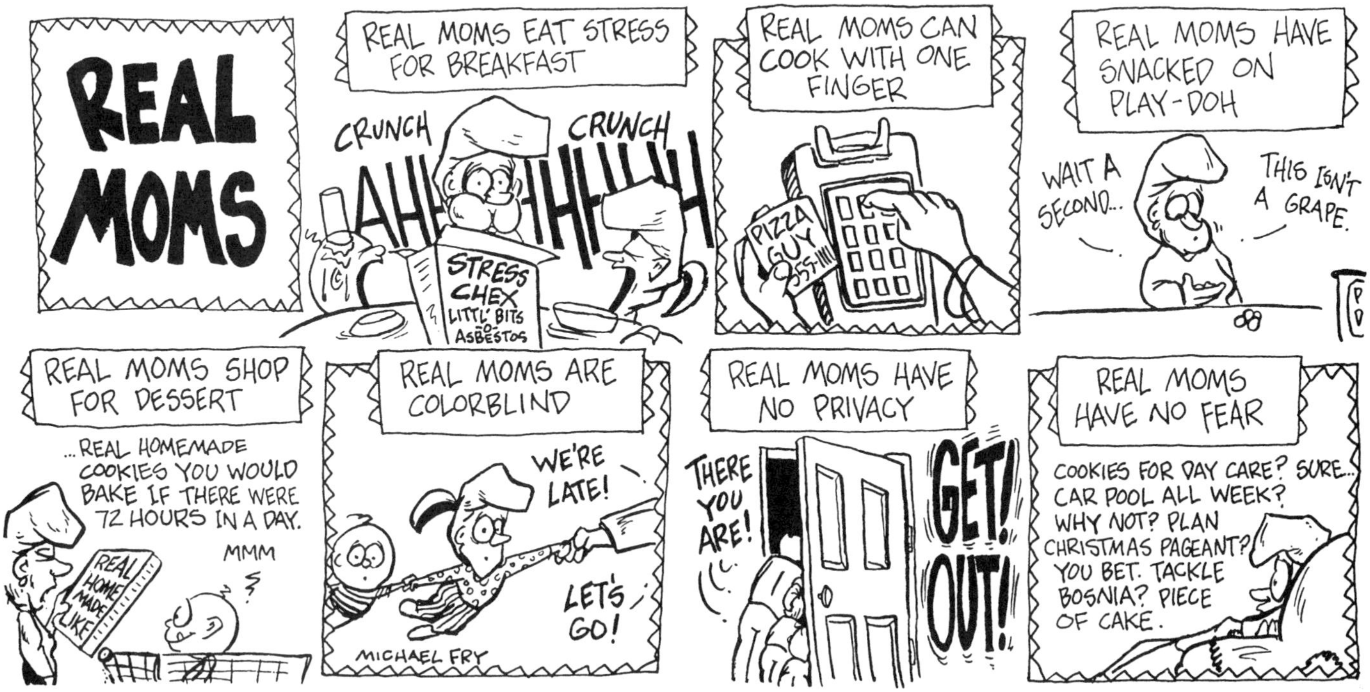
REAL MOMS
REAL MOMS EAT STRESS FOR BREAKFAST
CRUNCH
CRUNCH
AHHHHHHH
STRESS CHEX
LITTL' BITS O' ASBESTOS
REAL MOMS CAN COOK WITH ONE FINGER
PIZZA GUY 555-1111
REAL MOMS HAVE SNACKED ON PLAY-DOH
WAIT A SECOND...
THIS ISN'T A GRAPE.
REAL MOMS SHOP FOR DESSERT
...REAL HOMEMADE COOKIES YOU WOULD BAKE IF THERE WERE 72 HOURS IN A DAY.
REAL HOME MADE LIKE
MMM
REAL MOMS ARE COLORBLIND
WE'RE LATE!
LET'S GO!
MICHAEL FRY
REAL MOMS HAVE NO PRIVACY
THERE YOU ARE!
GET! OUT!
REAL MOMS HAVE NO FEAR
COOKIES FOR DAY CARE? SURE... CAR POOL ALL WEEK? WHY NOT? PLAN CHRISTMAS PAGEANT? YOU BET. TACKLE BOSNIA? PIECE OF CAKE.

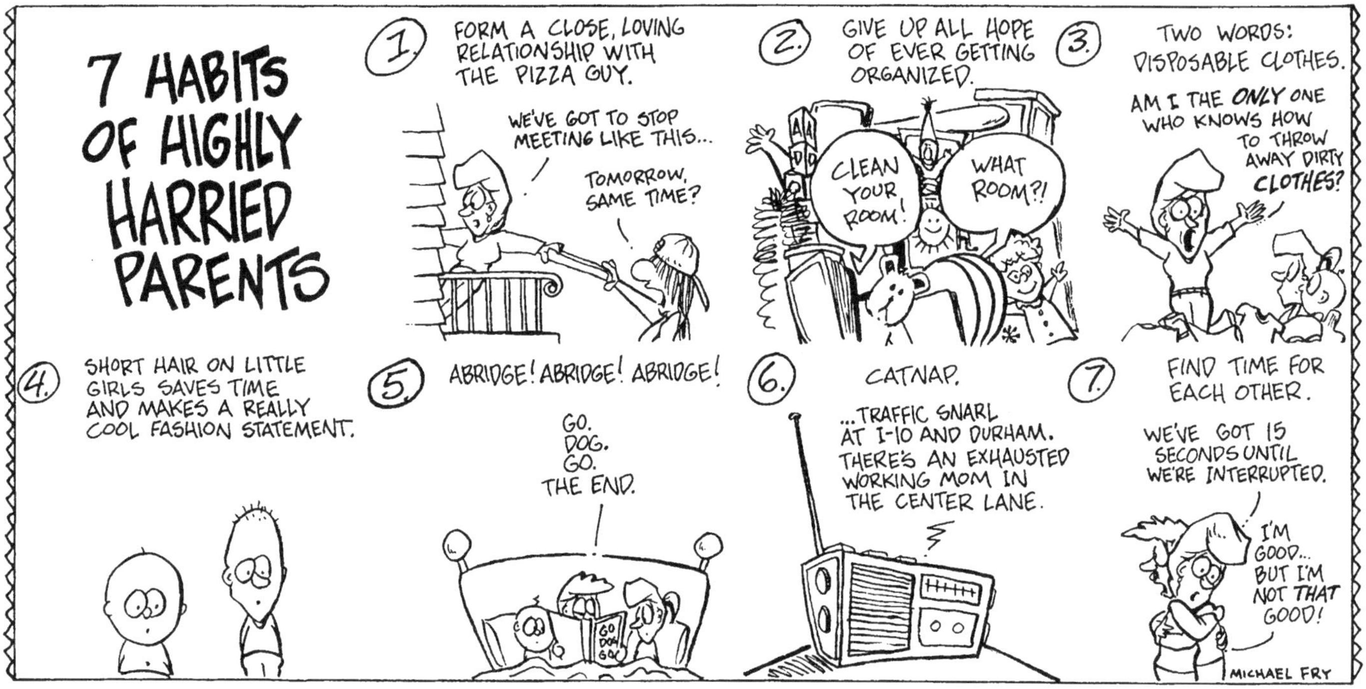
7 HABITS OF HIGHLY HARRIED PARENTS
1. FORM A CLOSE, LOVING RELATIONSHIP WITH THE PIZZA GUY.
WE'VE GOT TO STOP MEETING LIKE THIS...
TOMORROW, SAME TIME?
2. GIVE UP ALL HOPE OF EVER GETTING ORGANIZED.
CLEAN YOUR ROOM!
WHAT ROOM?!
3. TWO WORDS: DISPOSABLE CLOTHES.
AM I THE ONLY ONE WHO KNOWS HOW TO THROW AWAY DIRTY CLOTHES?
4. SHORT HAIR ON LITTLE GIRLS SAVES TIME AND MAKES A REALLY COOL FASHION STATEMENT.
5. ABRIDGE! ABRIDGE! ABRIDGE!
GO. DOG. GO. THE END.
6. CATNAP.
...TRAFFIC SNARL AT I-10 AND DURHAM. THERE'S AN EXHAUSTED WORKING MOM IN THE CENTER LANE.
7. FIND TIME FOR EACH OTHER.
WE'VE GOT 15 SECONDS UNTIL WE'RE INTERRUPTED.
I'M GOOD... BUT I'M NOT THAT GOOD!
MICHAEL FRY

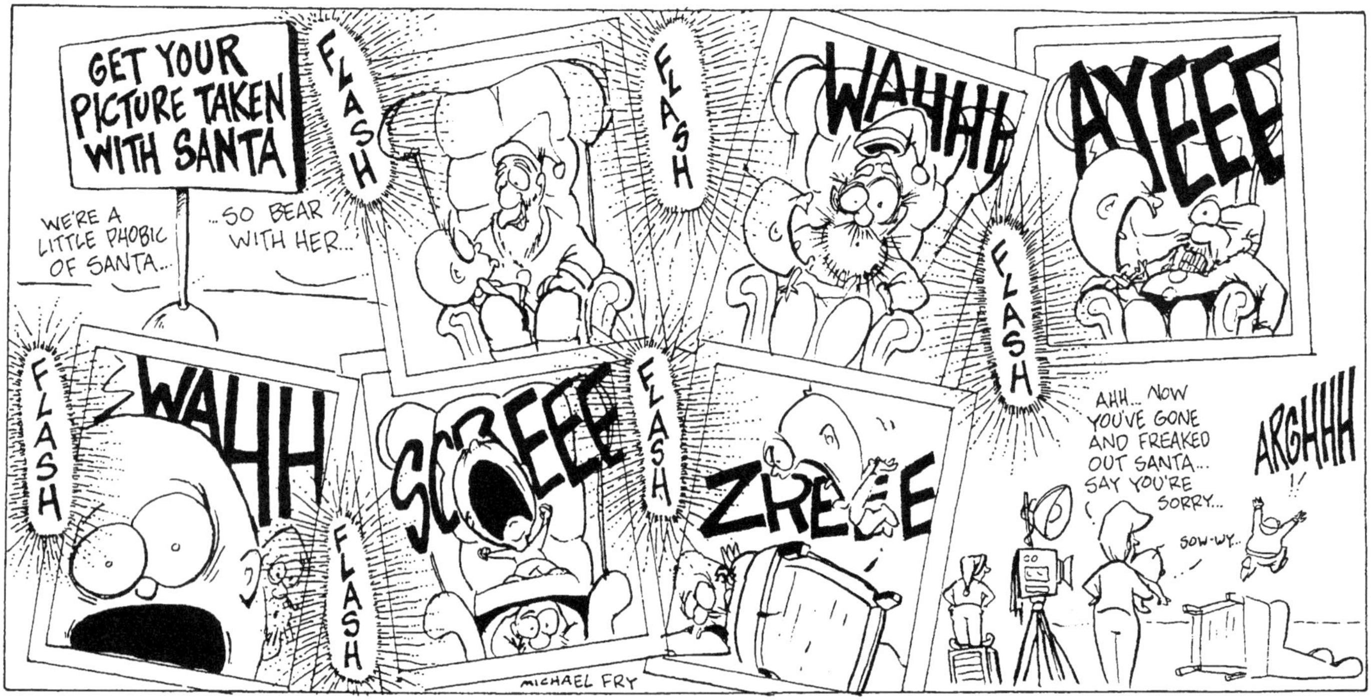
GET YOUR PICTURE TAKEN WITH SANTA
WE'RE A LITTLE PHOBIC OF SANTA...
...SO BEAR WITH HER...
FLASH
WAHHH
FLASH
AYEEE
FLASH
WAHH
FLASH
SCREEE
FLASH
ZREEE
FLASH
AHH... NOW YOU'VE GONE AND FREAKED OUT SANTA... SAY YOU'RE SORRY...
SOW-WY...
ARGHHH!!
MICHAEL FRY

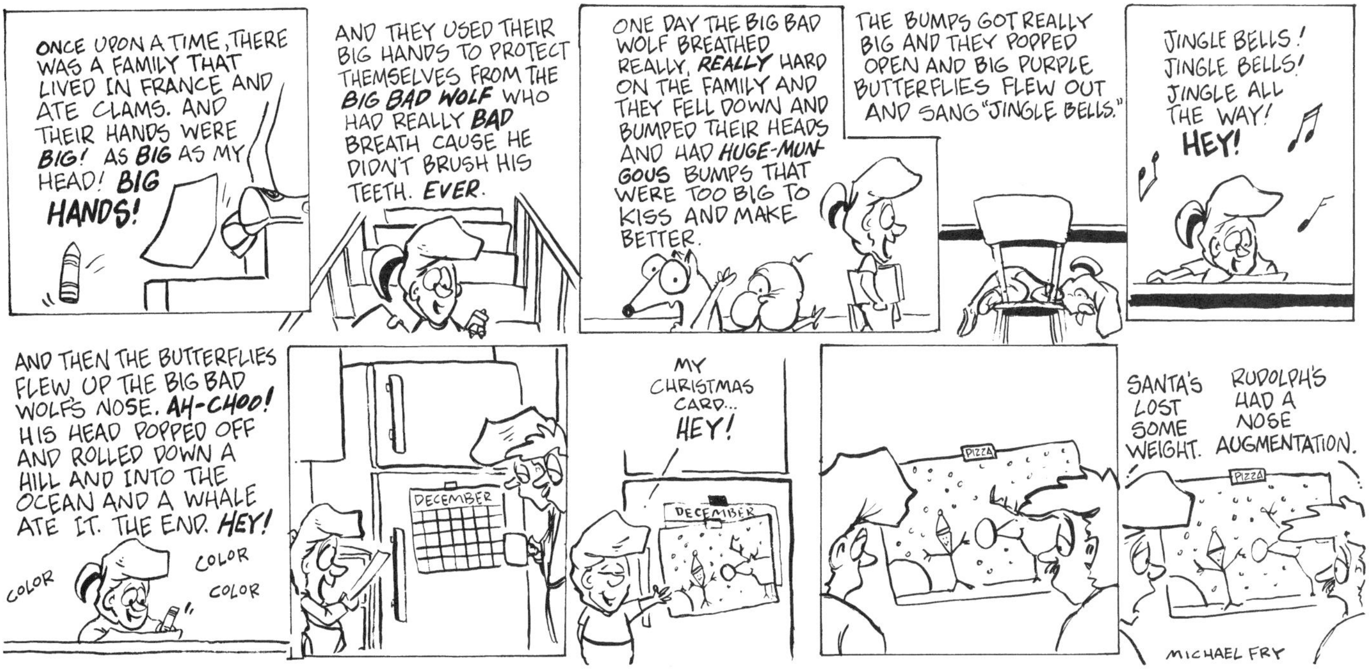
ONCE UPON A TIME, THERE WAS A FAMILY THAT LIVED IN FRANCE AND ATE CLAMS. AND THEIR HANDS WERE BIG! AS BIG AS MY HEAD! BIG HANDS!
AND THEY USED THEIR BIG HANDS TO PROTECT THEMSELVES FROM THE BIG BAD WOLF WHO HAD REALLY BAD BREATH CAUSE HE DIDN'T BRUSH HIS TEETH. EVER.
ONE DAY THE BIG BAD WOLF BREATHED REALLY, REALLY HARD ON THE FAMILY AND THEY FELL DOWN AND BUMPED THEIR HEADS AND HAD HUGE-MUNGOUS BUMPS THAT WERE TOO BIG TO KISS AND MAKE BETTER.
THE BUMPS GOT REALLY BIG AND THEY POPPED OPEN AND BIG PURPLE BUTTERFLIES FLEW OUT AND SANG "JINGLE BELLS."
JINGLE BELLS! JINGLE BELLS! JINGLE ALL THE WAY! HEY!
AND THEN THE BUTTERFLIES FLEW UP THE BIG BAD WOLF'S NOSE. AH-CHOO! HIS HEAD POPPED OFF AND ROLLED DOWN A HILL AND INTO THE OCEAN AND A WHALE ATE IT. THE END. HEY!
COLOR
COLOR
COLOR
DECEMBER
MY CHRISTMAS CARD... HEY!
DECEMBER
PIZZA
SANTA'S LOST SOME WEIGHT.
RUDOLPH'S HAD A NOSE AUGMENTATION.
PIZZA
MICHAEL FRY

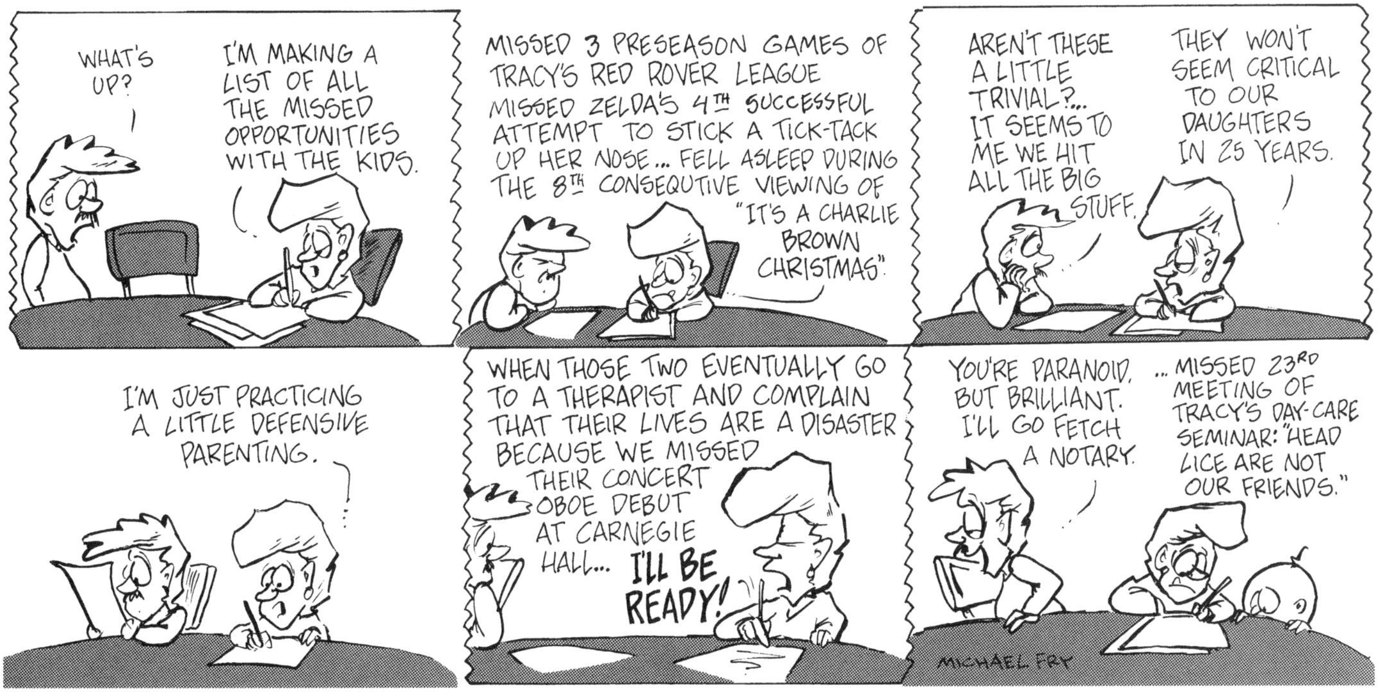
WHAT'S UP?
I'M MAKING A LIST OF ALL THE MISSED OPPORTUNITIES WITH THE KIDS.
MISSED 3 PRESEASON GAMES OF TRACY'S RED ROVER LEAGUE MISSED ZELDA'S 4TH SUCCESSFUL ATTEMPT TO STICK A TICK-TACK UP HER NOSE... FELL ASLEEP DURING THE 8TH CONSEQUTIVE VIEWING OF "IT'S A CHARLIE BROWN CHRISTMAS".
AREN'T THESE A LITTLE TRIVIAL?... IT SEEMS TO ME WE HIT ALL THE BIG STUFF.
THEY WON'T SEEM CRITICAL TO OUR DAUGHTERS IN 25 YEARS.
I'M JUST PRACTICING A LITTLE DEFENSIVE PARENTING.
WHEN THOSE TWO EVENTUALLY GO TO A THERAPIST AND COMPLAIN THAT THEIR LIVES ARE A DISASTER BECAUSE WE MISSED THEIR CONCERT OBOE DEBUT AT CARNEGIE HALL... I'LL BE READY!
YOU'RE PARANOID, BUT BRILLIANT. I'LL GO FETCH A NOTARY.
...MISSED 23RD MEETING OF TRACY'S DAY-CARE SEMINAR: "HEAD LICE ARE NOT OUR FRIENDS."
MICHAEL FRY

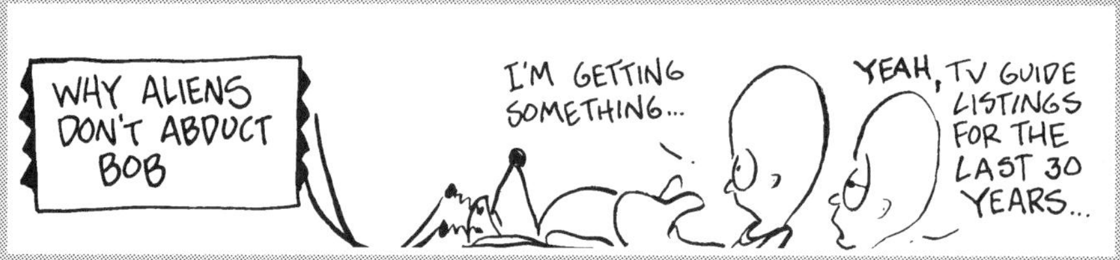
WHY ALIENS DON'T ABDUCT BOB
I'M GETTING SOMETHING...
YEAH, TV GUIDE LISTINGS FOR THE LAST 30 YEARS...

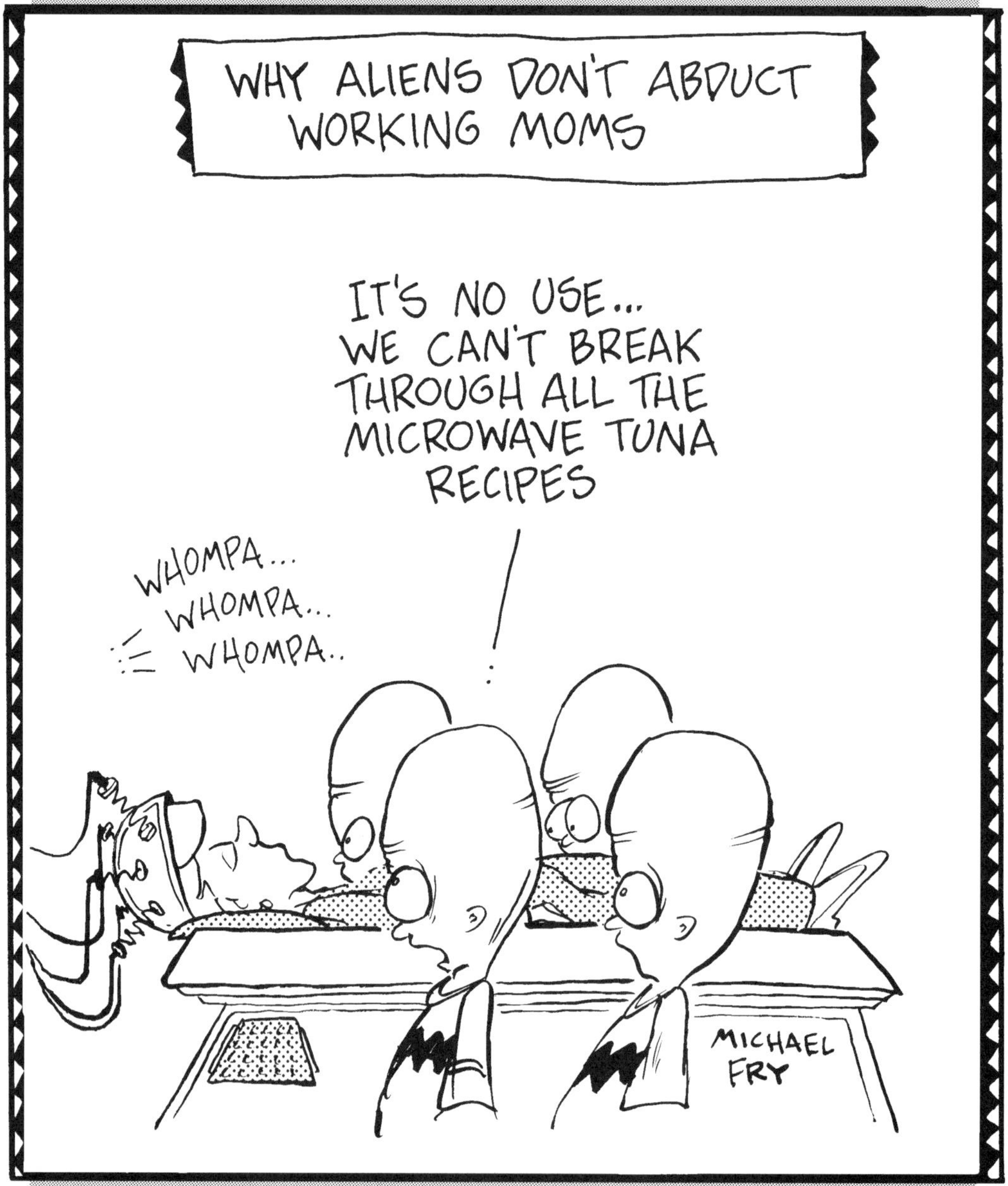
WHY ALIENS DON'T ABDUCT WORKING MOMS
IT'S NO USE... WE CAN'T BREAK THROUGH ALL THE MICROWAVE TUNA RECIPES
WHOMPA... WHOMPA... WHOMPA..
MICHAEL FRY

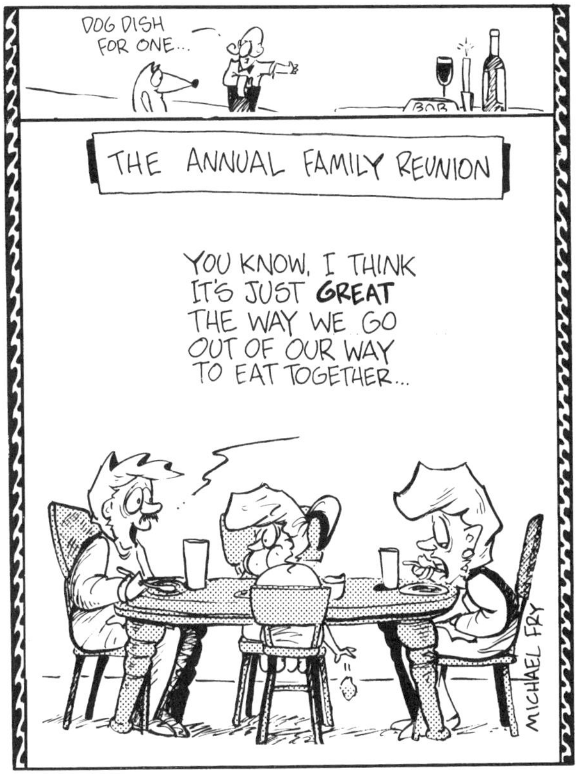
DOG DISH FOR ONE...
BOB
THE ANNUAL FAMILY REUNION
YOU KNOW, I THINK IT'S JUST **GREAT** THE WAY WE GO OUT OF OUR WAY TO EAT TOGETHER...
MICHAEL FRY

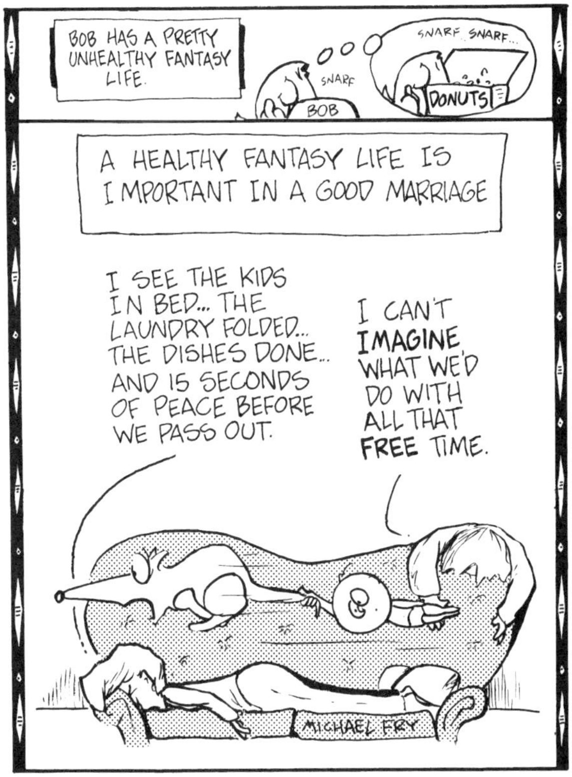
BOB HAS A PRETTY UNHEALTHY FANTASY LIFE.
SNARF
SNARF SNARF...
DONUTS
BOB
A HEALTHY FANTASY LIFE IS IMPORTANT IN A GOOD MARRIAGE
I SEE THE KIDS IN BED... THE LAUNDRY FOLDED... THE DISHES DONE... AND 15 SECONDS OF PEACE BEFORE WE PASS OUT.
I CAN'T **IMAGINE** WHAT WE'D DO WITH **ALL THAT FREE** TIME.
MICHAEL FRY

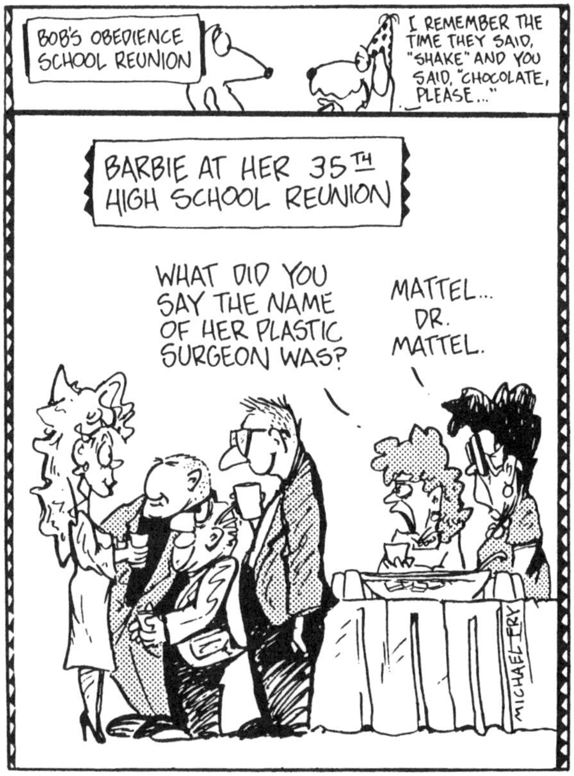
BOB'S OBEDIENCE SCHOOL REUNION
I REMEMBER THE TIME THEY SAID, "SHAKE" AND YOU SAID, "CHOCOLATE, PLEASE..."
BARBIE AT HER 35TH HIGH SCHOOL REUNION
WHAT DID YOU SAY THE NAME OF HER PLASTIC SURGEON WAS?
MATTEL... DR. MATTEL.
MICHAEL FRY

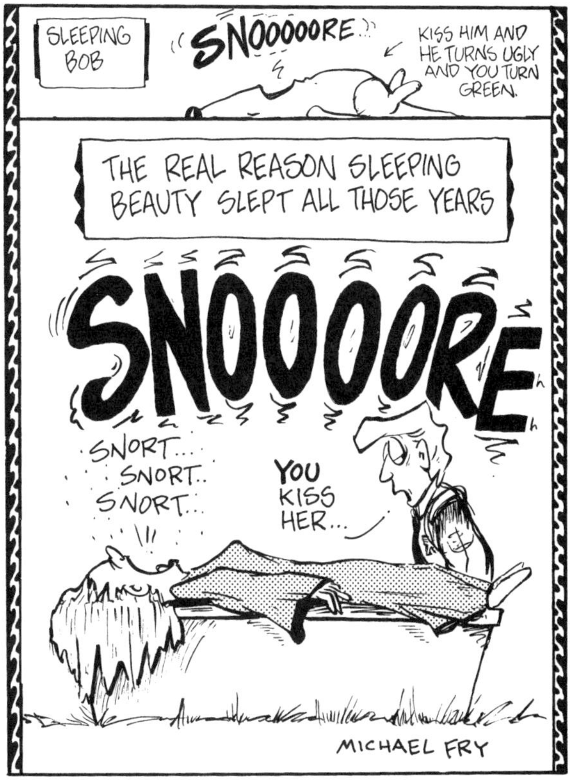
SLEEPING BOB
SNOOOOORE
KISS HIM AND HE TURNS UGLY AND YOU TURN GREEN.
THE REAL REASON SLEEPING BEAUTY SLEPT ALL THOSE YEARS
SNOOOORE
SNORT... SNORT.. SNORT..
YOU KISS HER...
MICHAEL FRY

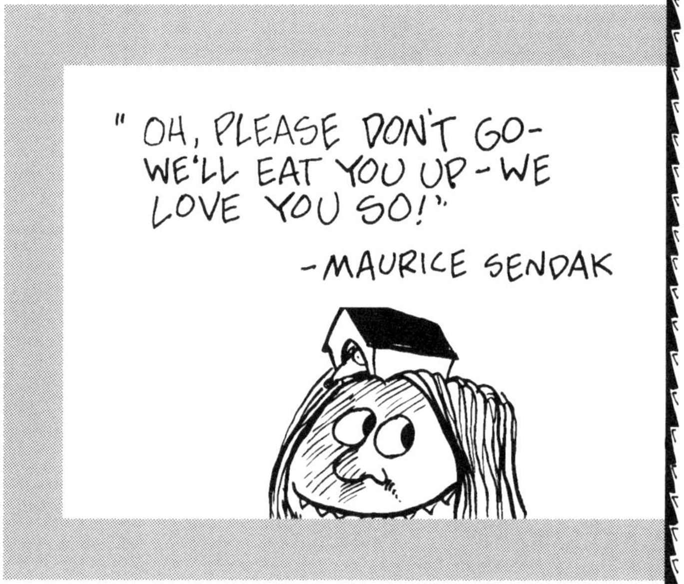
" OH, PLEASE DON'T GO-
WE'LL EAT YOU UP-WE
LOVE YOU SO!"
-MAURICE SENDAK

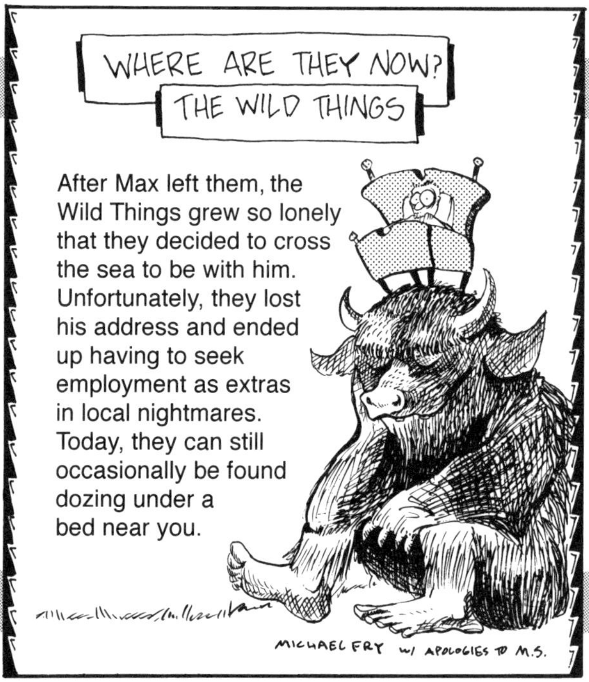
WHERE ARE THEY NOW?
THE WILD THINGS
After Max left them, the Wild Things grew so lonely that they decided to cross the sea to be with him. Unfortunately, they lost his address and ended up having to seek employment as extras in local nightmares. Today, they can still occasionally be found dozing under a bed near you.
MICHAEL FRY W/ APOLOGIES TO M.S.

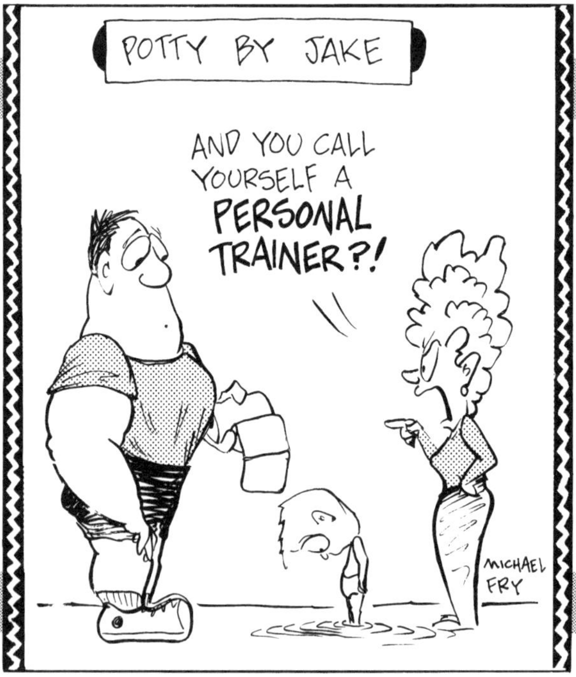
POTTY BY JAKE
AND YOU CALL YOURSELF A PERSONAL TRAINER?!
MICHAEL FRY

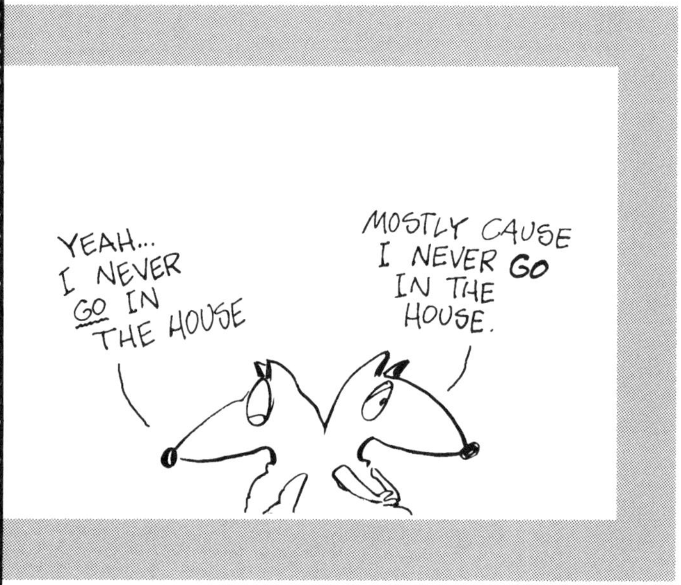
YEAH... I NEVER GO IN THE HOUSE
MOSTLY CAUSE I NEVER GO IN THE HOUSE.

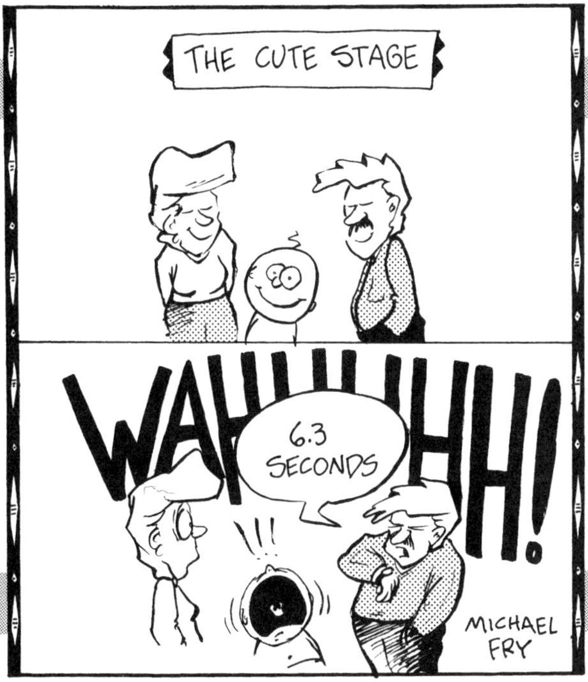
THE CUTE STAGE
WAHHHHHH!
6.3 SECONDS
!!!
MICHAEL FRY

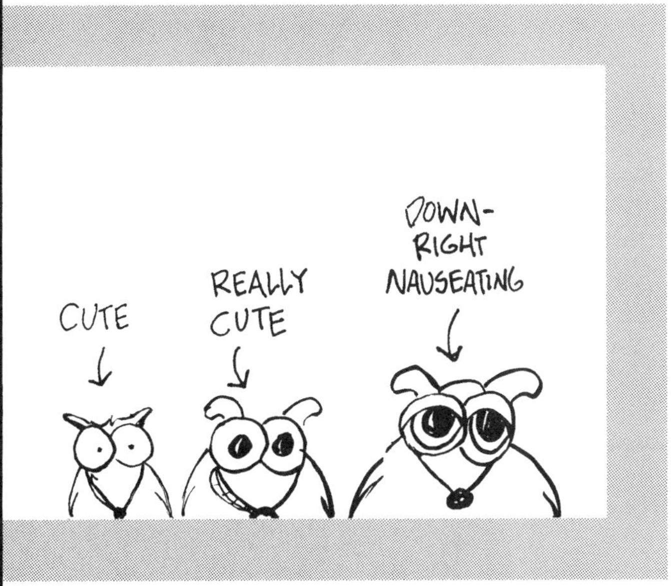
CUTE
REALLY CUTE
DOWN-RIGHT NAUSEATING

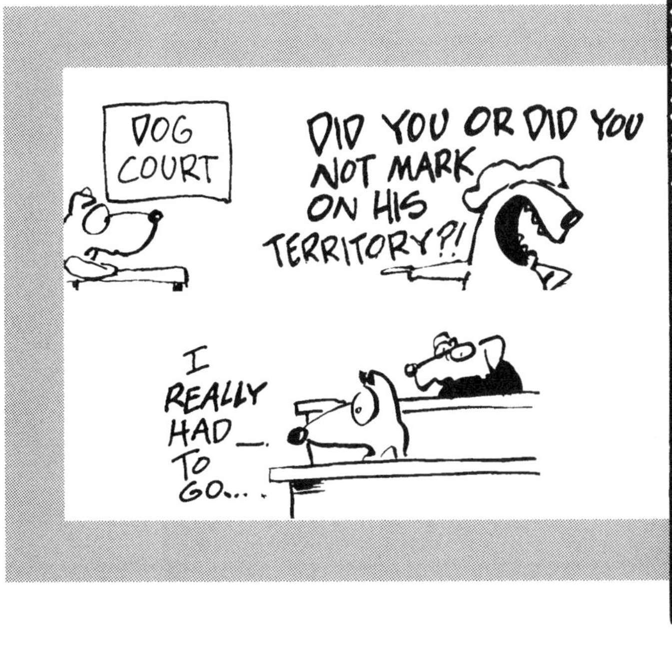
DOG COURT
DID YOU OR DID YOU NOT MARK ON HIS TERRITORY?!
I REALLY HAD TO GO...

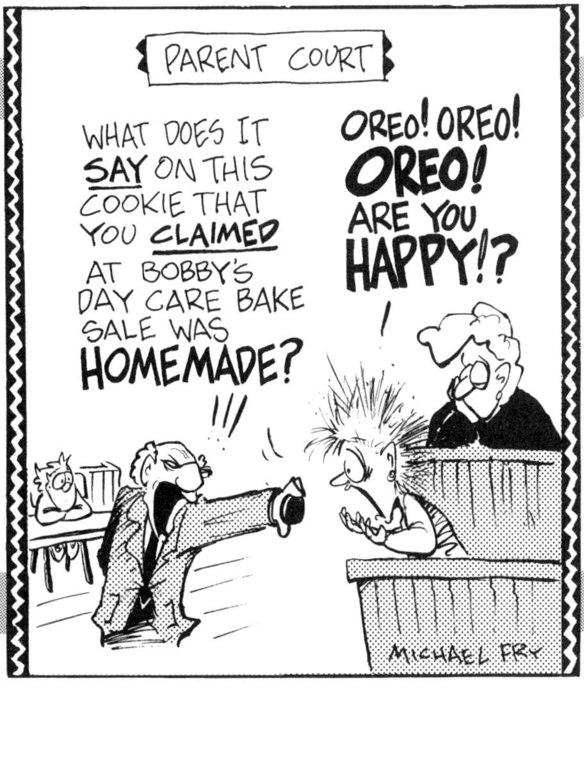
PARENT COURT
WHAT DOES IT SAY ON THIS COOKIE THAT YOU CLAIMED AT BOBBY'S DAY CARE BAKE SALE WAS HOMEMADE?
OREO! OREO! OREO! ARE YOU HAPPY!?
!!!
MICHAEL FRY

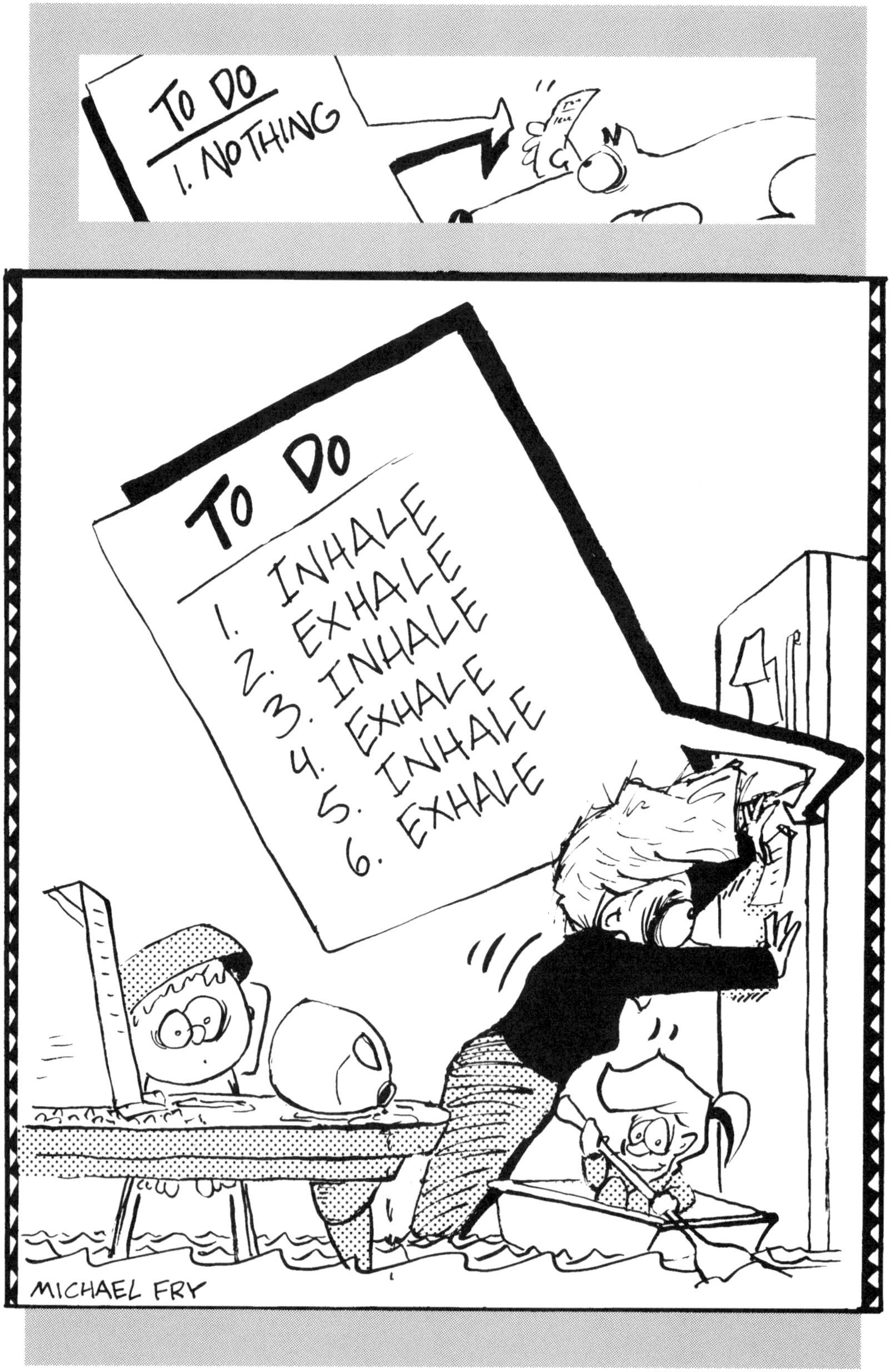
TO DO
1. NOTHING
TO DO
1. INHALE
2. EXHALE
3. INHALE
4. EXHALE
5. INHALE
6. EXHALE
MICHAEL FRY

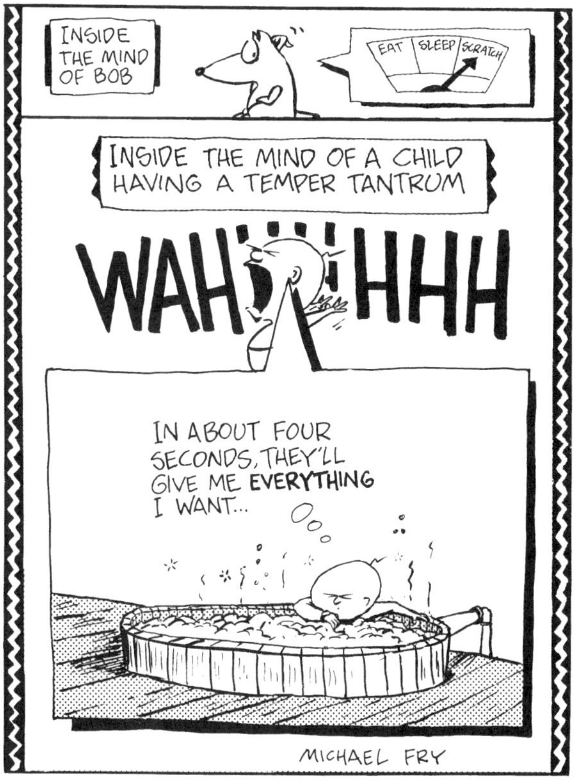
INSIDE THE MIND OF BOB
EAT SLEEP SCRATCH
INSIDE THE MIND OF A CHILD HAVING A TEMPER TANTRUM
WAHHHH
IN ABOUT FOUR SECONDS, THEY'LL GIVE ME EVERYTHING I WANT...
MICHAEL FRY

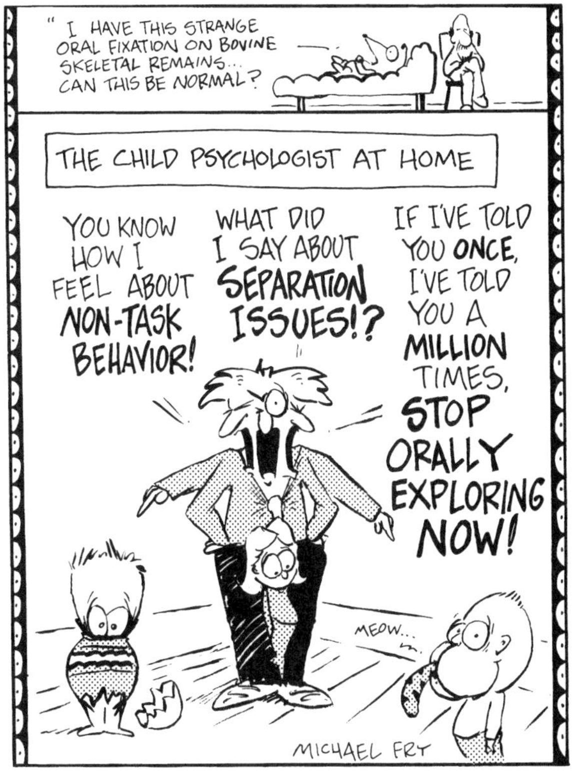
"I HAVE THIS STRANGE ORAL FIXATION ON BOVINE SKELETAL REMAINS... CAN THIS BE NORMAL?
THE CHILD PSYCHOLOGIST AT HOME
YOU KNOW HOW I FEEL ABOUT NON-TASK BEHAVIOR!
WHAT DID I SAY ABOUT SEPARATION ISSUES!?
IF I'VE TOLD YOU ONCE, I'VE TOLD YOU A MILLION TIMES, STOP ORALLY EXPLORING NOW!
MEOW...
MICHAEL FRY

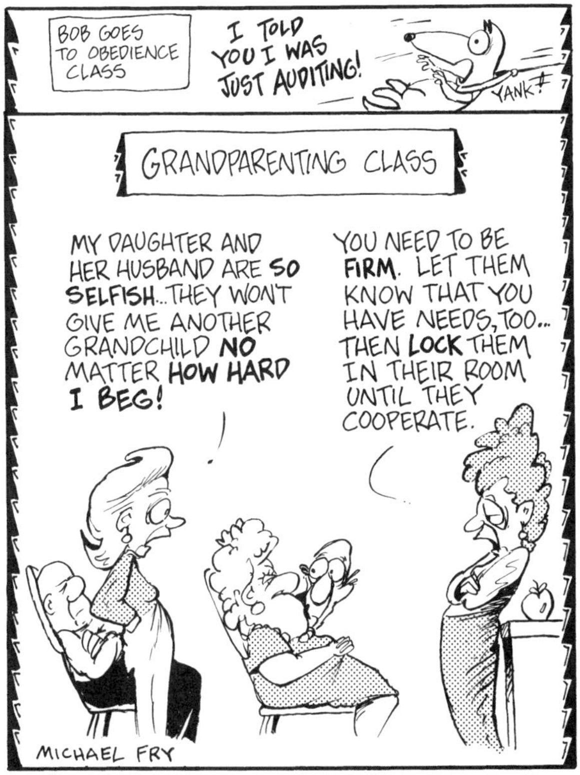
BOB GOES TO OBEDIENCE CLASS
I TOLD YOU I WAS JUST AUDITING!
YANK!
GRANDPARENTING CLASS
MY DAUGHTER AND HER HUSBAND ARE SO SELFISH...THEY WON'T GIVE ME ANOTHER GRANDCHILD NO MATTER HOW HARD I BEG!
YOU NEED TO BE FIRM. LET THEM KNOW THAT YOU HAVE NEEDS, TOO... THEN LOCK THEM IN THEIR ROOM UNTIL THEY COOPERATE.
MICHAEL FRY

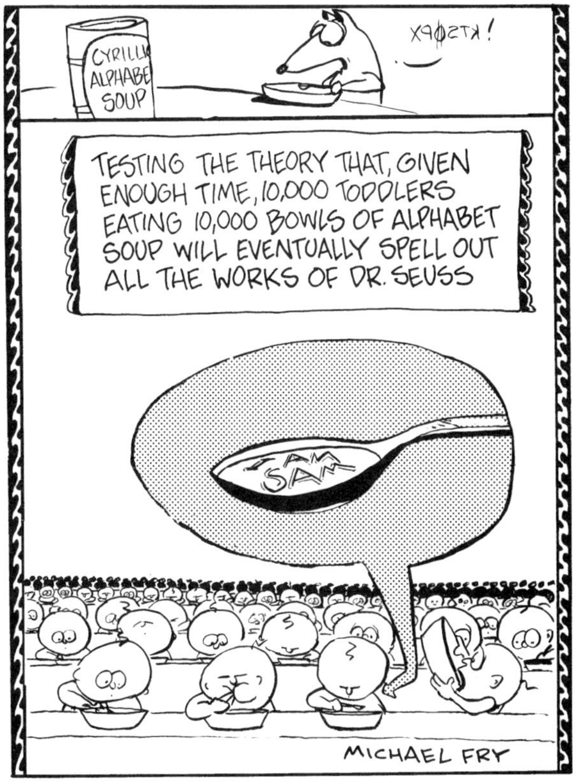
CYRILLIC ALPHABET SOUP
TESTING THE THEORY THAT, GIVEN ENOUGH TIME, 10,000 TODDLERS EATING 10,000 BOWLS OF ALPHABET SOUP WILL EVENTUALLY SPELL OUT ALL THE WORKS OF DR. SEUSS
I AM SAM
MICHAEL FRY

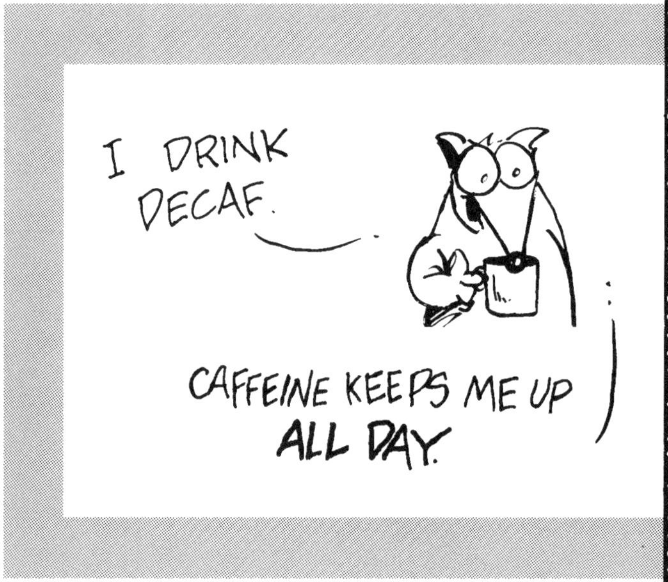
I DRINK DECAF.
CAFFEINE KEEPS ME UP ALL DAY.

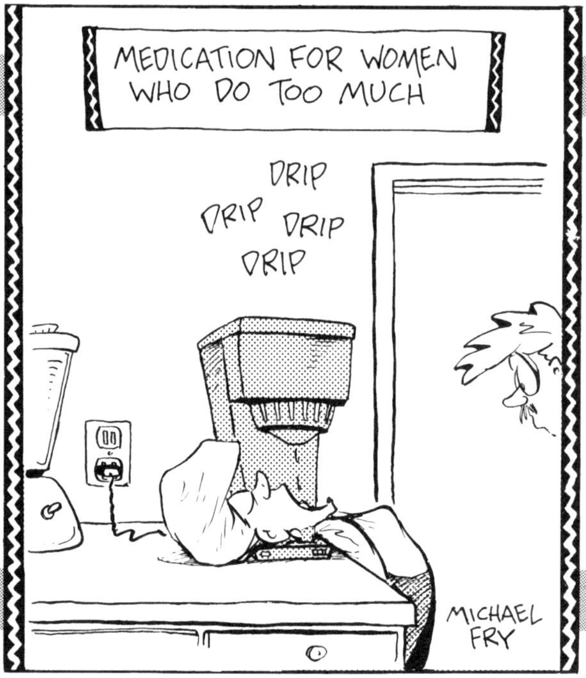
MEDICATION FOR WOMEN WHO DO TOO MUCH
DRIP
DRIP
DRIP
DRIP
MICHAEL FRY

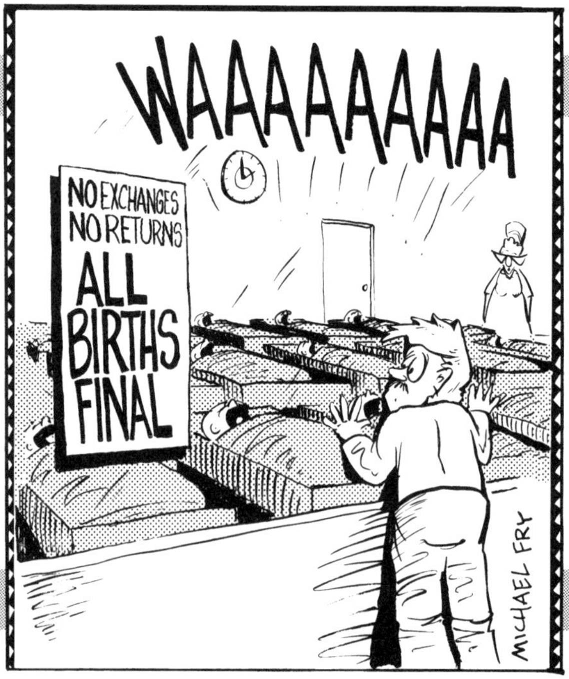
WAAAAAAAAA
NO EXCHANGES
NO RETURNS
ALL BIRTHS FINAL
MICHAEL FRY

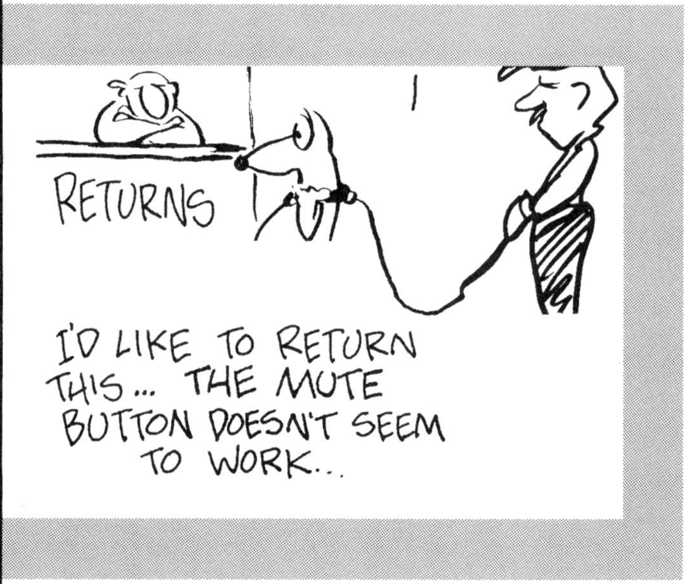
RETURNS
I'D LIKE TO RETURN THIS... THE MUTE BUTTON DOESN'T SEEM TO WORK...

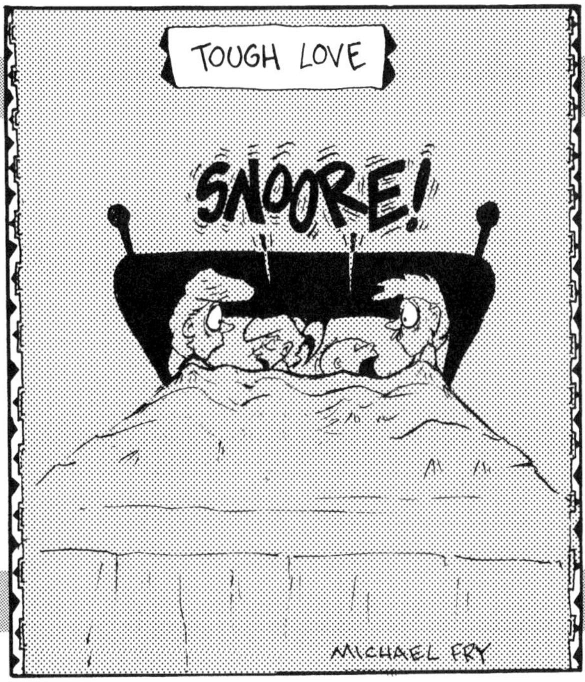
TOUGH LOVE
SNORE!
MICHAEL FRY

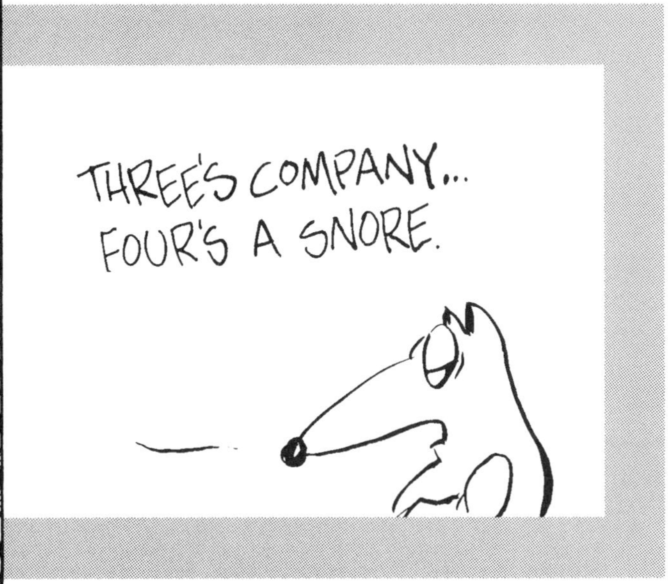
THREE'S COMPANY...
FOUR'S A SNORE.

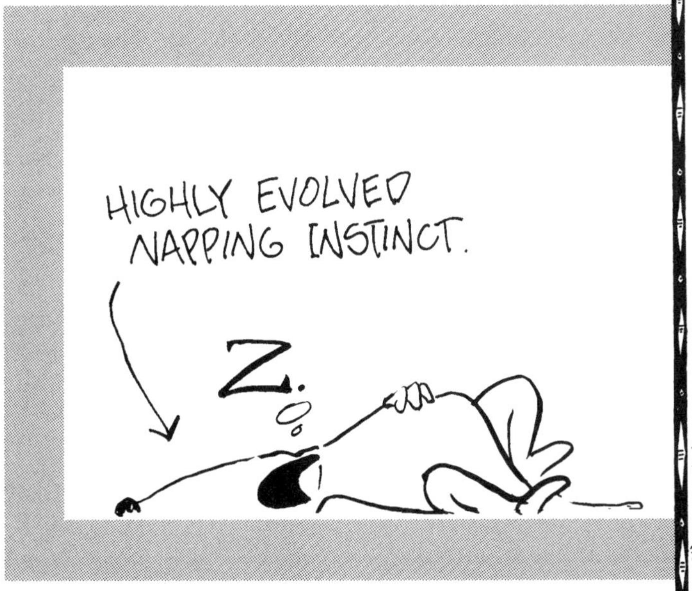
HIGHLY EVOLVED
NAPPING INSTINCT.
Z.

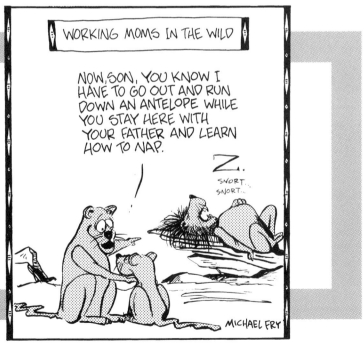

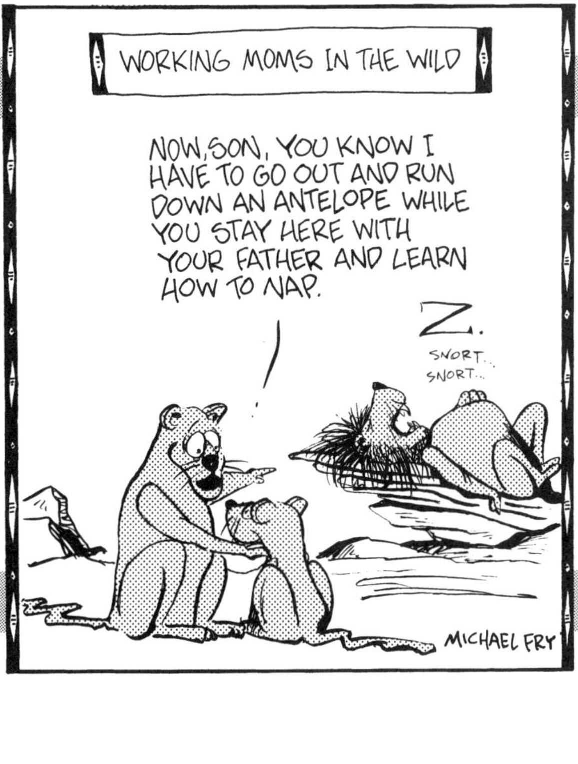
WORKING MOMS IN THE WILD
NOW, SON, YOU KNOW I HAVE TO GO OUT AND RUN DOWN AN ANTELOPE WHILE YOU STAY HERE WITH YOUR FATHER AND LEARN HOW TO NAP.
Z.
SNORT...
SNORT...
MICHAEL FRY

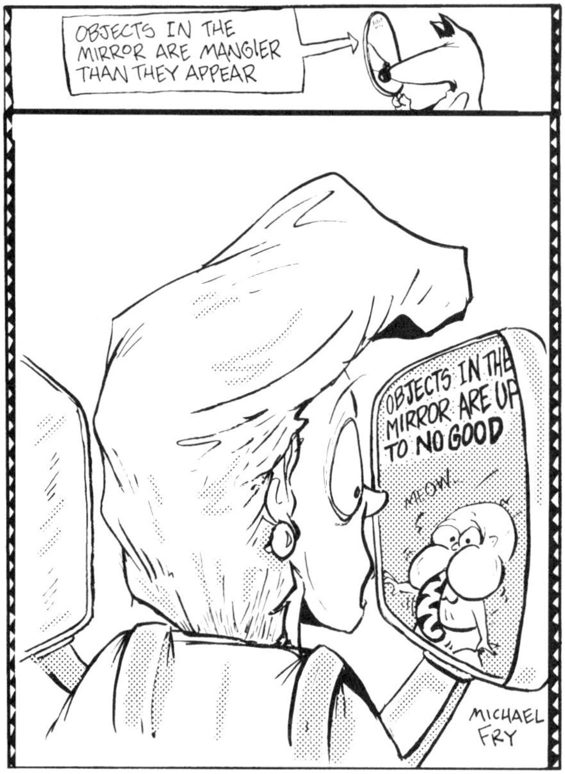
OBJECTS IN THE MIRROR ARE MANGIER THAN THEY APPEAR
OBJECTS IN THE MIRROR ARE UP TO NO GOOD
MEOW
MICHAEL FRY

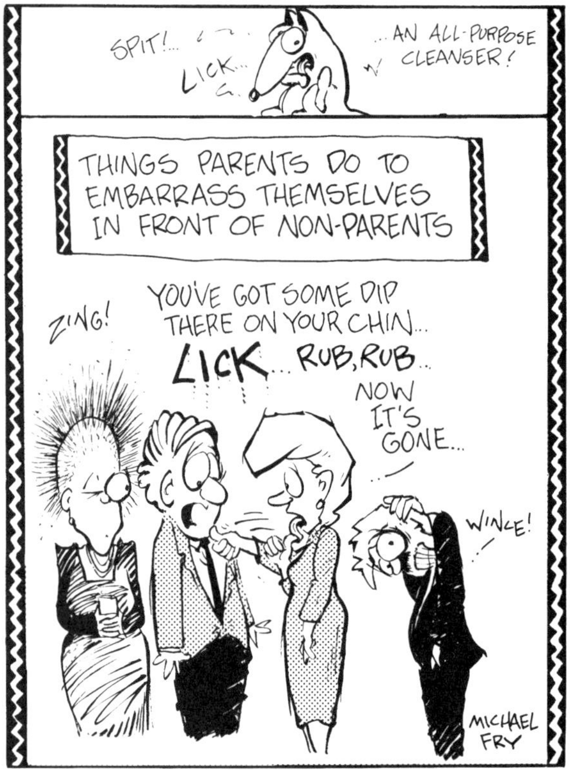
SPIT!...
LICK...
...AN ALL-PURPOSE CLEANSER!
THINGS PARENTS DO TO EMBARRASS THEMSELVES IN FRONT OF NON-PARENTS
ZING!
YOU'VE GOT SOME DIP THERE ON YOUR CHIN...
LICK... RUB, RUB...
NOW IT'S GONE...
WINCE!
MICHAEL FRY

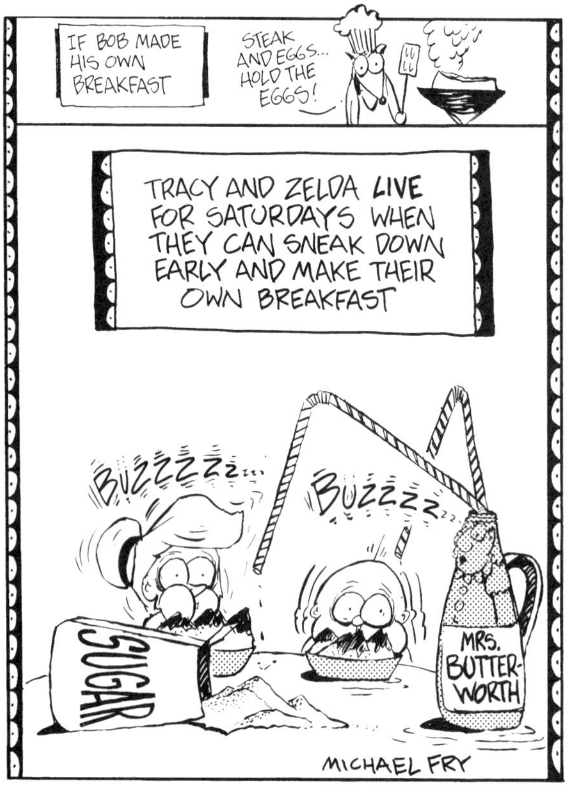
IF BOB MADE HIS OWN BREAKFAST
STEAK AND EGGS... HOLD THE EGGS!
TRACY AND ZELDA LIVE FOR SATURDAYS WHEN THEY CAN SNEAK DOWN EARLY AND MAKE THEIR OWN BREAKFAST
BUZZZZZz...
BUZZZZz
SUGAR
MRS. BUTTER-WORTH
MICHAEL FRY

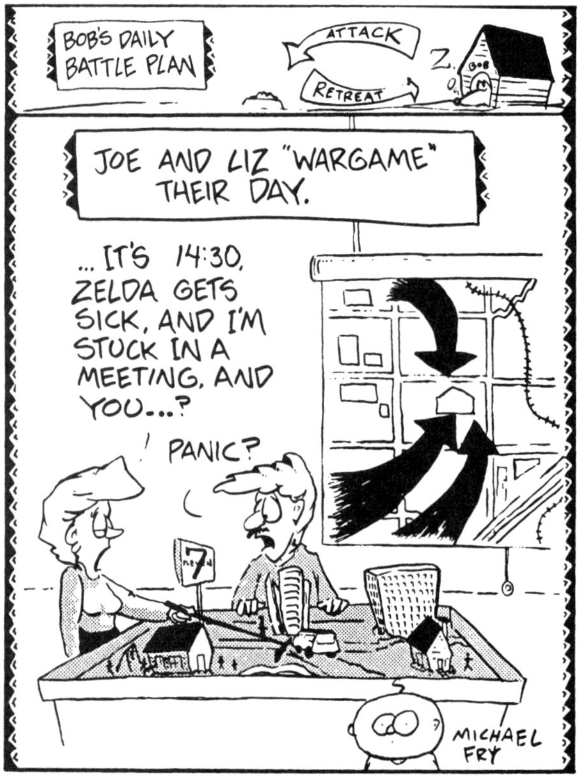
BOB'S DAILY BATTLE PLAN
ATTACK
RETREAT
Z
BOB
JOE AND LIZ "WARGAME" THEIR DAY.
...IT'S 14:30, ZELDA GETS SICK, AND I'M STUCK IN A MEETING, AND YOU...?
PANIC?
7
MICHAEL FRY

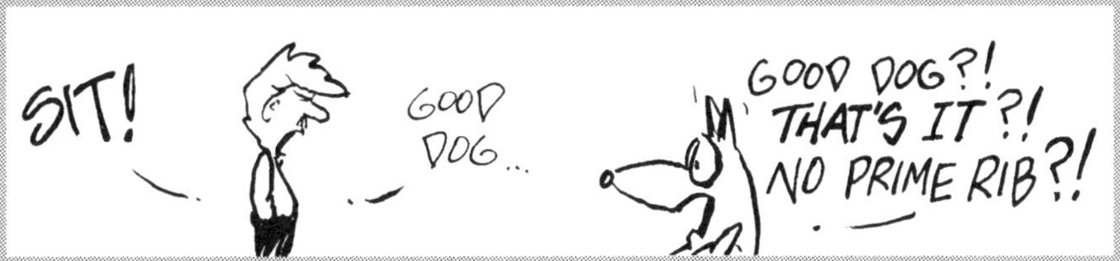
SIT!
GOOD DOG...
GOOD DOG?! THAT'S IT?! NO PRIME RIB?!

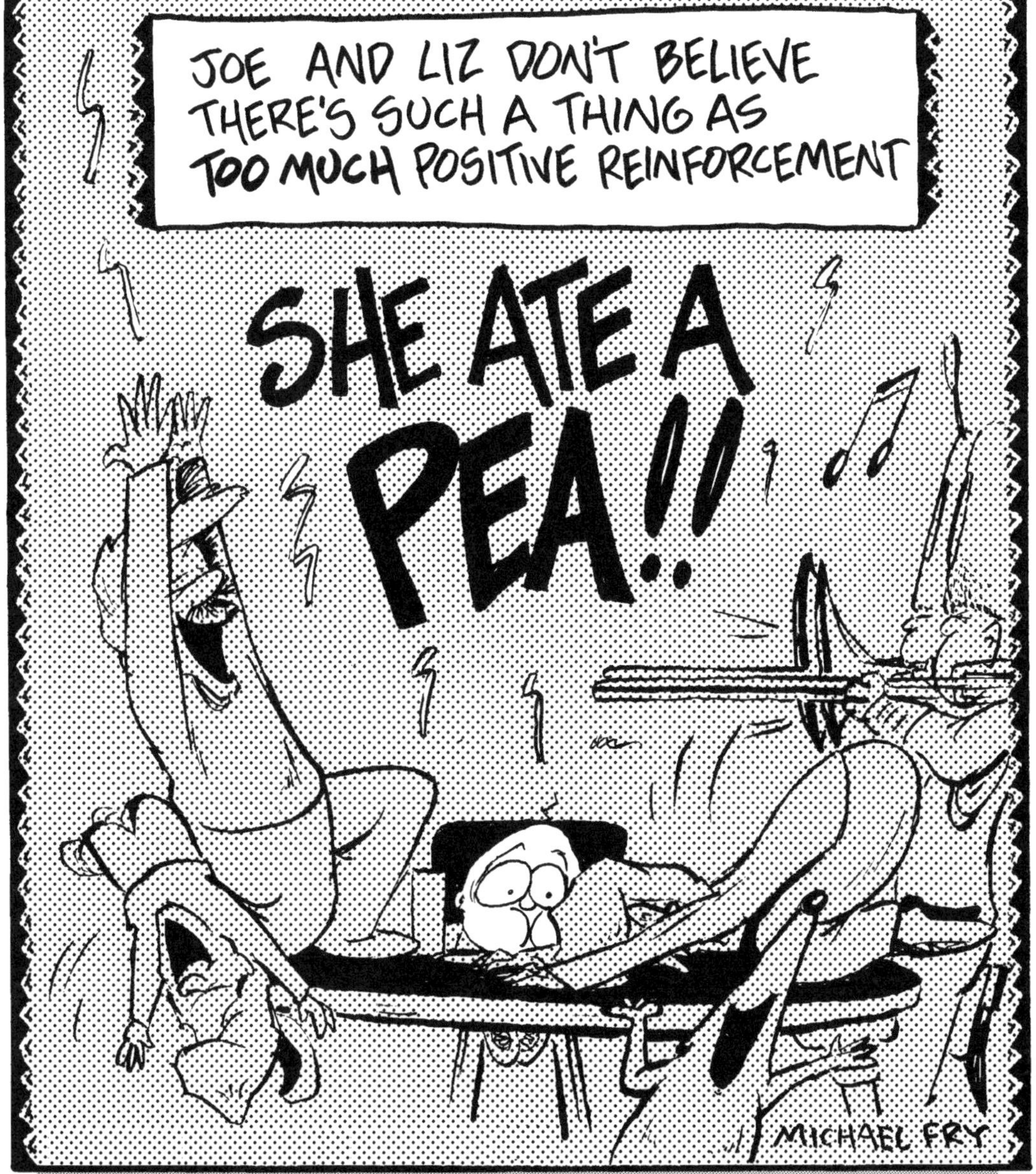
JOE AND LIZ DON'T BELIEVE THERE'S SUCH A THING AS TOO MUCH POSITIVE REINFORCEMENT
SHE ATE A PEA!!
MICHAEL FRY

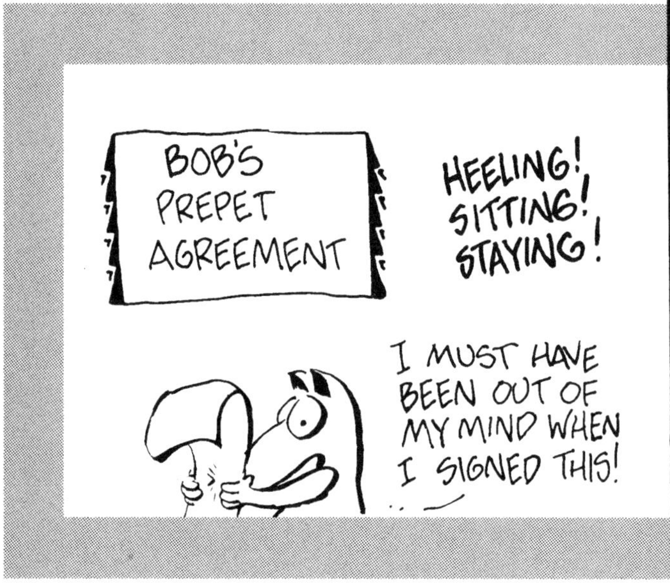
BOB'S PREPET AGREEMENT
HEELING! SITTING! STAYING!
I MUST HAVE BEEN OUT OF MY MIND WHEN I SIGNED THIS!

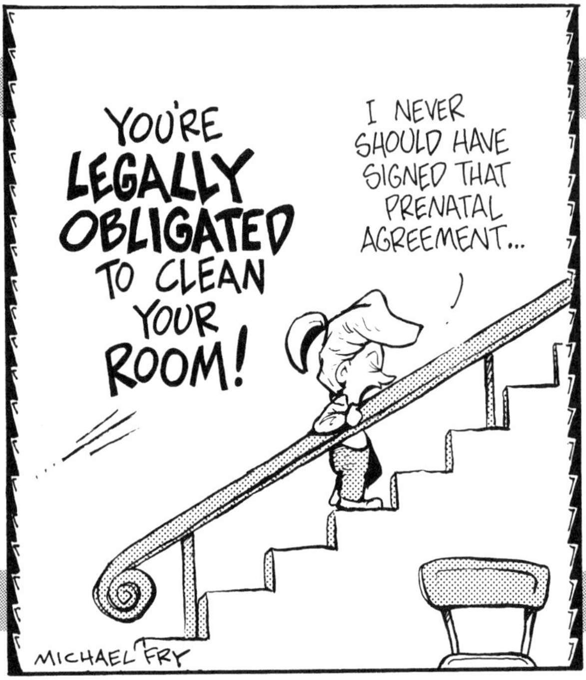
YOU'RE LEGALLY OBLIGATED TO CLEAN YOUR ROOM!
I NEVER SHOULD HAVE SIGNED THAT PRENATAL AGREEMENT...
MICHAEL FRY

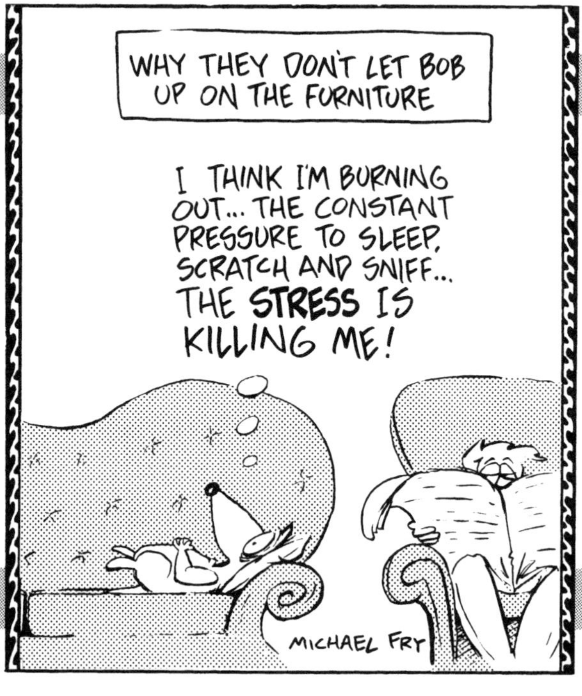
WHY THEY DON'T LET BOB UP ON THE FURNITURE
I THINK I'M BURNING OUT... THE CONSTANT PRESSURE TO SLEEP, SCRATCH AND SNIFF... THE STRESS IS KILLING ME!
MICHAEL FRY

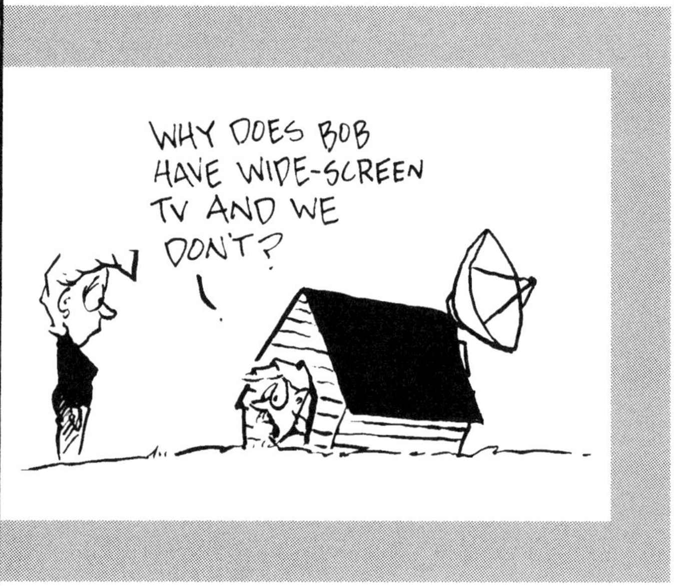
WHY DOES BOB HAVE WIDE-SCREEN TV AND WE DON'T?

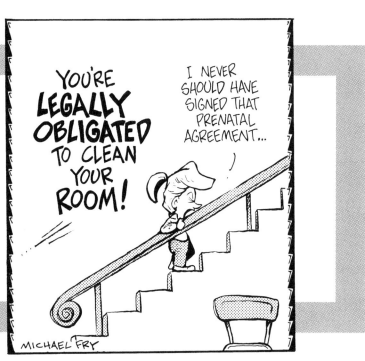

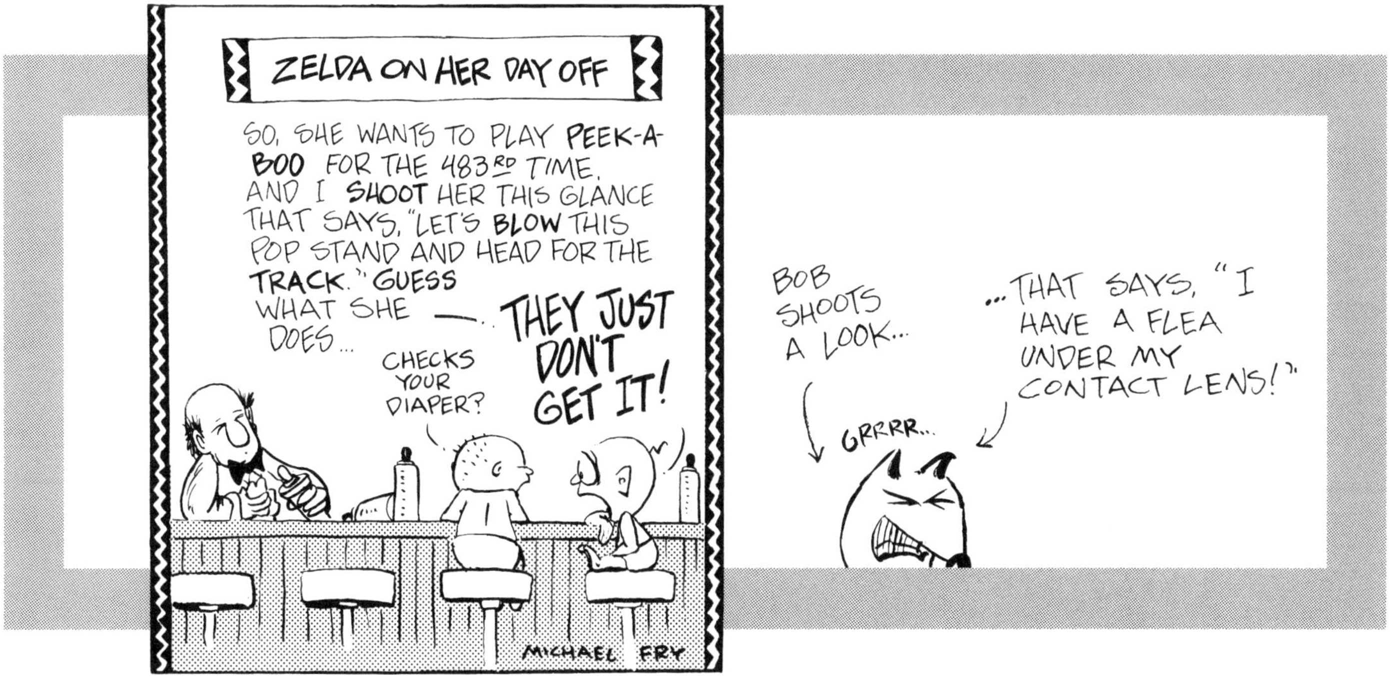
ZELDA ON HER DAY OFF
SO, SHE WANTS TO PLAY PEEK-A-BOO FOR THE 483RD TIME, AND I SHOOT HER THIS GLANCE THAT SAYS, "LET'S BLOW THIS POP STAND AND HEAD FOR THE TRACK." GUESS WHAT SHE DOES...
CHECKS YOUR DIAPER?
THEY JUST DON'T GET IT!
MICHAEL FRY
BOB SHOOTS A LOOK...
...THAT SAYS, "I HAVE A FLEA UNDER MY CONTACT LENS!"
GRRRR...

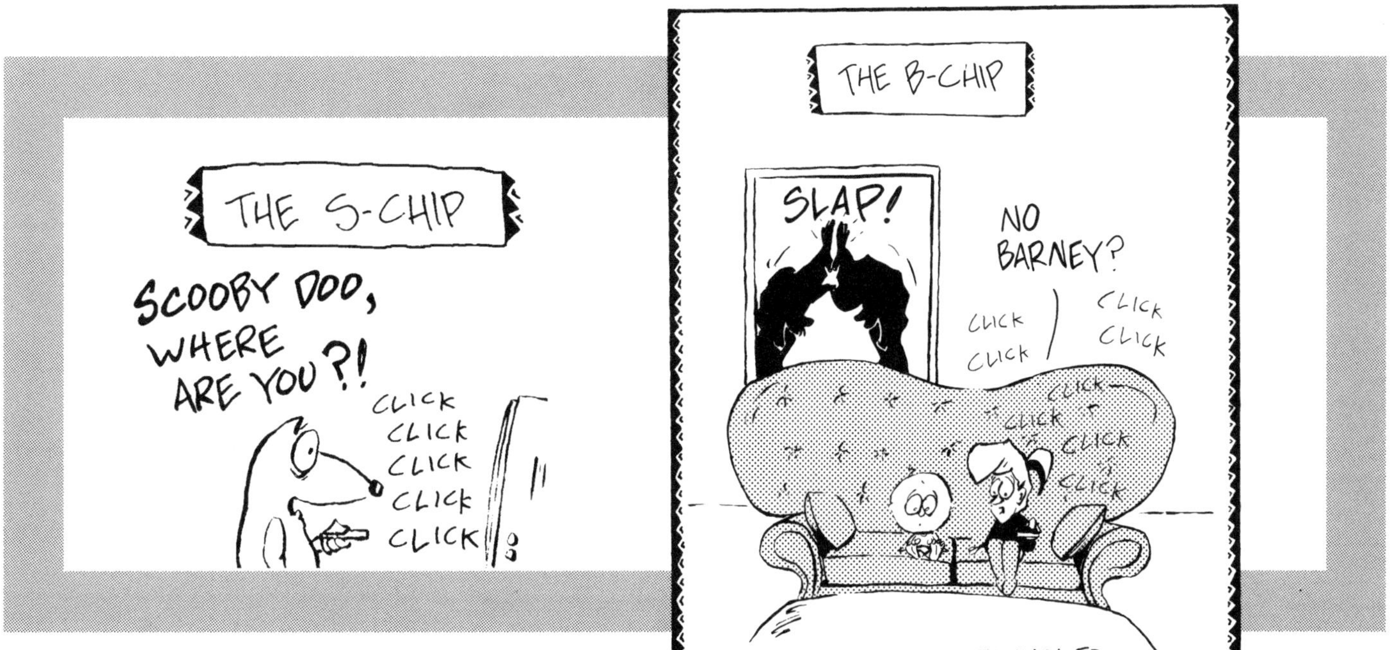
THE S-CHIP
SCOOBY DOO, WHERE ARE YOU?!
CLICK
CLICK
CLICK
CLICK
CLICK
THE B-CHIP
SLAP!
NO BARNEY?
CLICK
CLICK
CLICK
CLICK
CLICK
CLICK
CLICK
CLICK
MICHAEL FRY

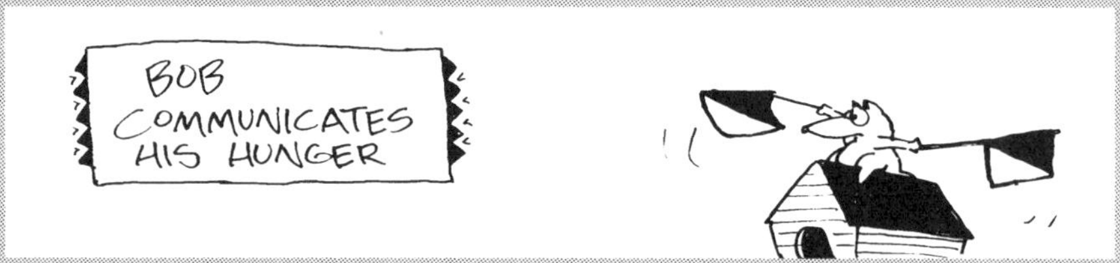

BOB COMMUNICATES HIS HUNGER

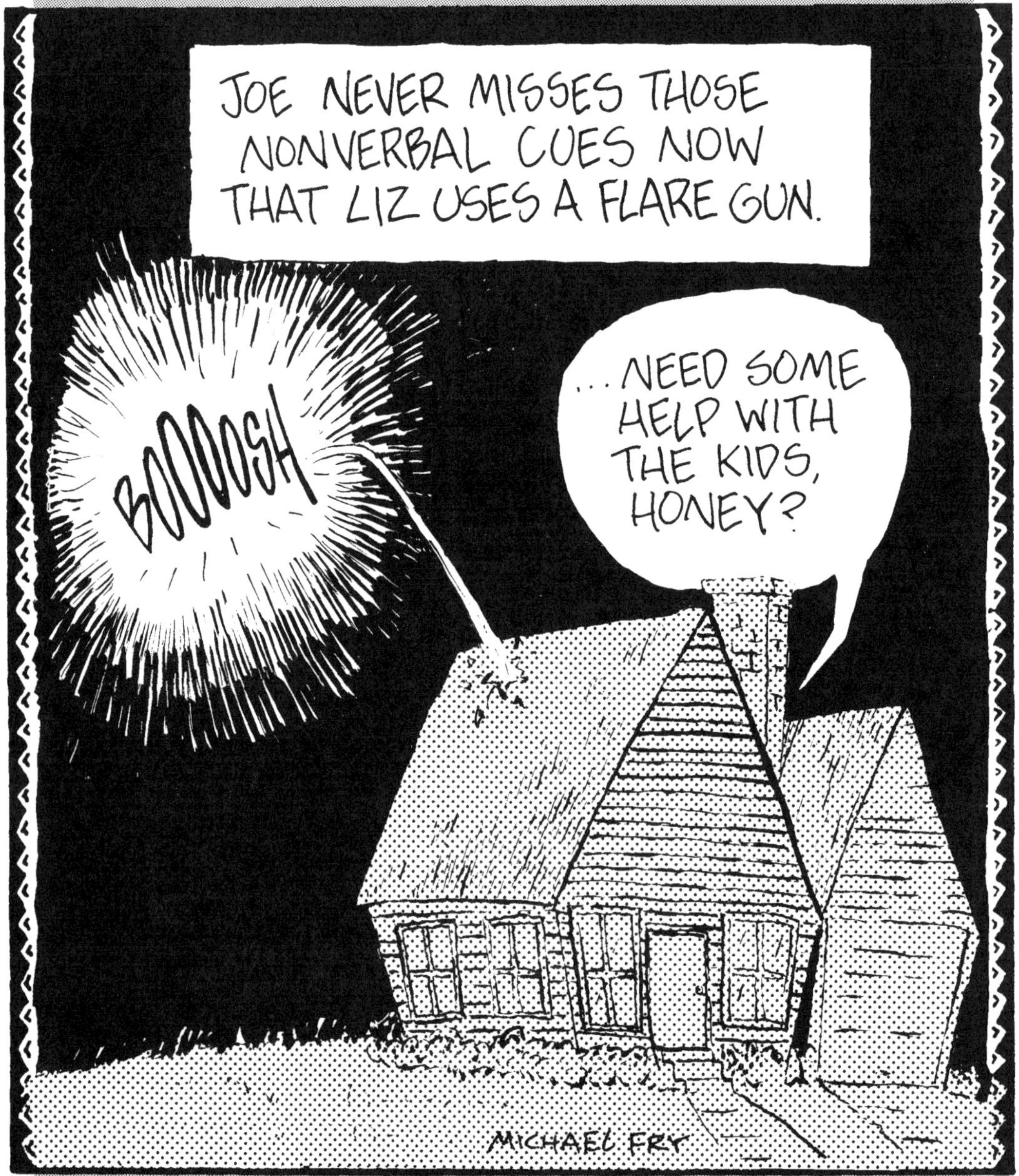

JOE NEVER MISSES THOSE NONVERBAL CUES NOW THAT LIZ USES A FLARE GUN.
BOOOOSH
...NEED SOME HELP WITH THE KIDS, HONEY?
MICHAEL FRY

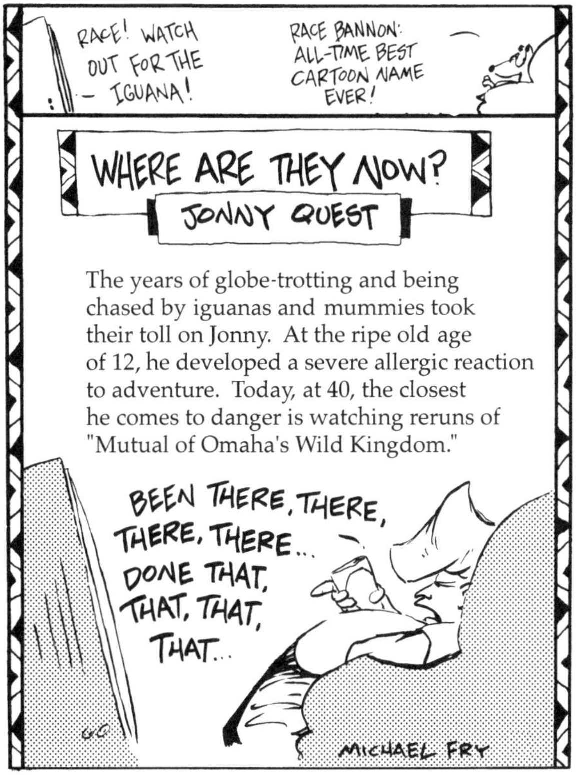

RACE! WATCH OUT FOR THE IGUANA!
RACE BANNON: ALL-TIME BEST CARTOON NAME EVER!
WHERE ARE THEY NOW?
JONNY QUEST
The years of globe-trotting and being chased by iguanas and mummies took their toll on Jonny. At the ripe old age of 12, he developed a severe allergic reaction to adventure. Today, at 40, the closest he comes to danger is watching reruns of "Mutual of Omaha's Wild Kingdom."
BEEN THERE, THERE, THERE, THERE... DONE THAT, THAT, THAT, THAT...
MICHAEL FRY

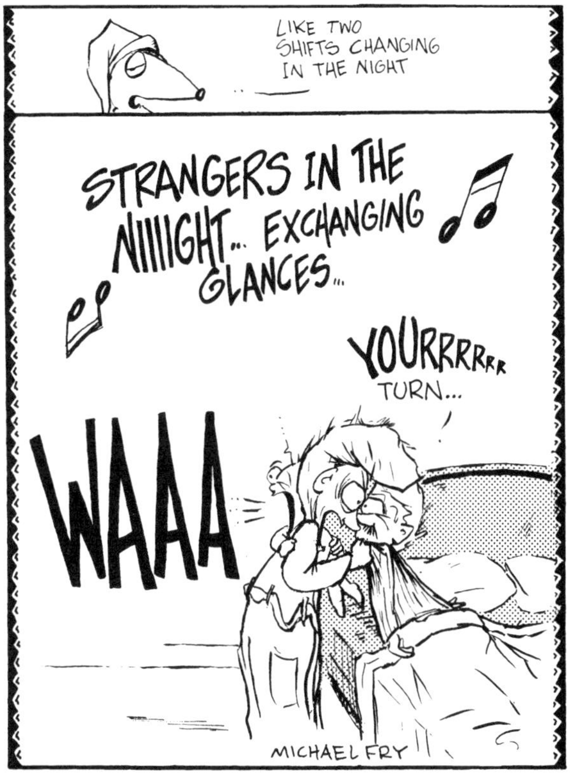

LIKE TWO SHIFTS CHANGING IN THE NIGHT
STRANGERS IN THE NIIIIGHT... EXCHANGING GLANCES...
YOURRRRRR TURN...
WAAA
MICHAEL FRY

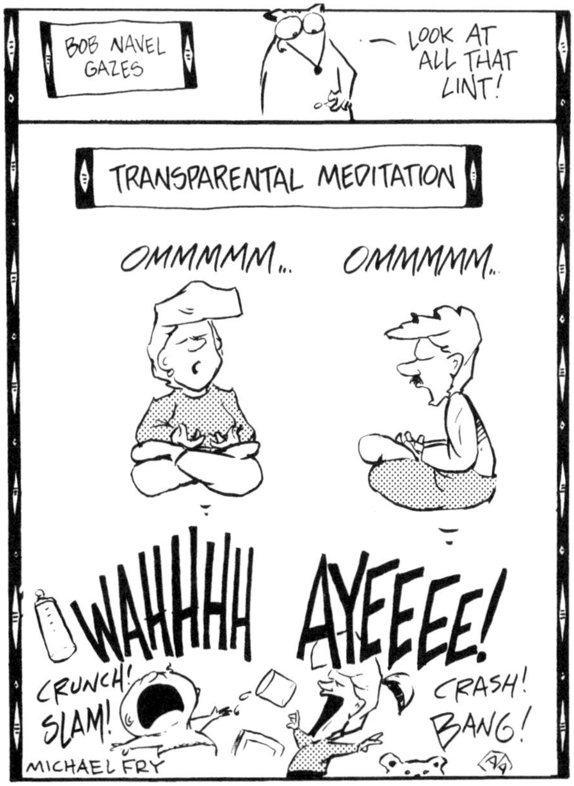

BOB NAVEL GAZES
LOOK AT ALL THAT LINT!
TRANSPARENTAL MEDITATION
OMMMMM...
OMMMMM...
WAHHHH
AYEEEE!
CRUNCH! SLAM!
CRASH! BANG!
MICHAEL FRY

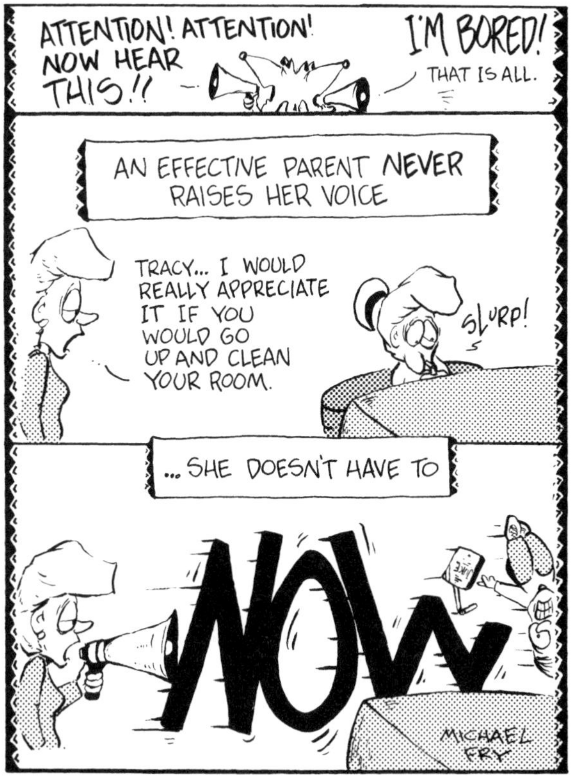

ATTENTION! ATTENTION! NOW HEAR THIS!!
I'M BORED! THAT IS ALL.
AN EFFECTIVE PARENT NEVER RAISES HER VOICE
TRACY... I WOULD REALLY APPRECIATE IT IF YOU WOULD GO UP AND CLEAN YOUR ROOM.
SLURP!
...SHE DOESN'T HAVE TO
NOW
MICHAEL FRY

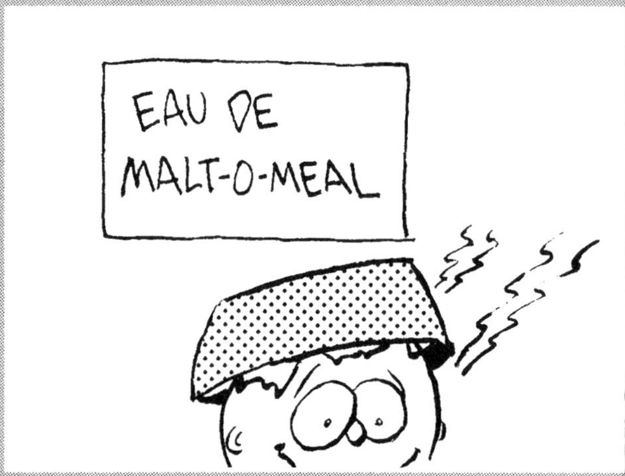
EAU DE MALT-O-MEAL

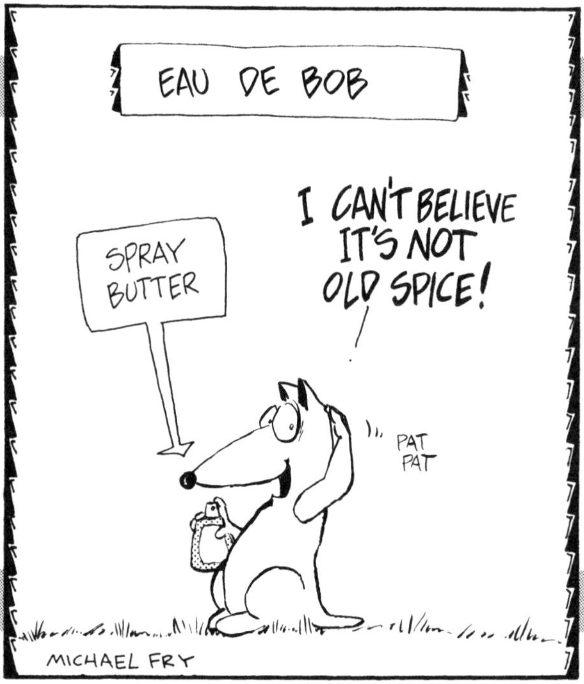
EAU DE BOB
SPRAY BUTTER
I CAN'T BELIEVE IT'S NOT OLD SPICE!
PAT PAT
MICHAEL FRY

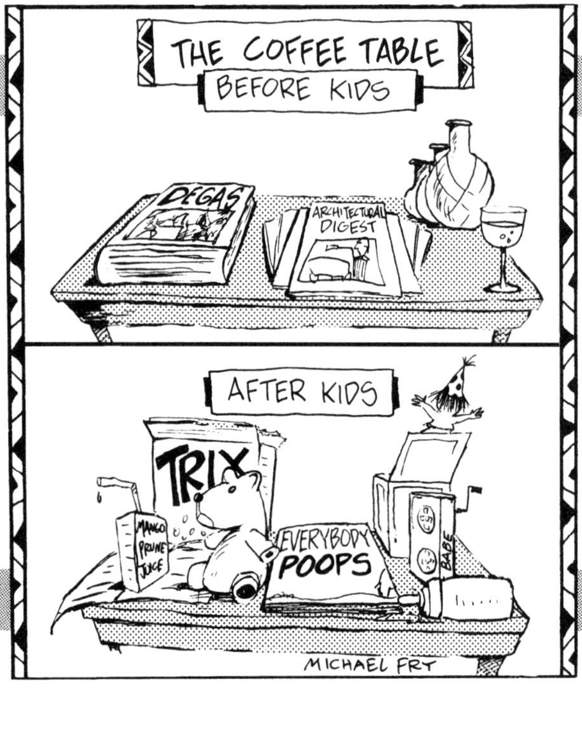
THE COFFEE TABLE
BEFORE KIDS
DEGAS
ARCHITECTURAL DIGEST
AFTER KIDS
TRIX
MANGO PRUNE JUICE
EVERYBODY POOPS
BABE
MICHAEL FRY

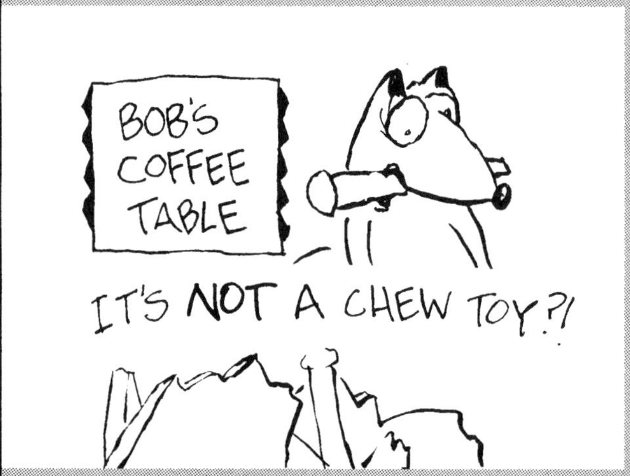
BOB'S COFFEE TABLE
IT'S NOT A CHEW TOY?!

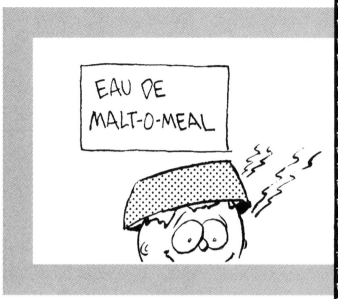

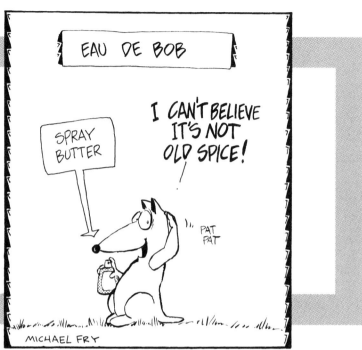

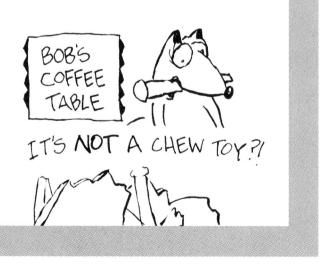

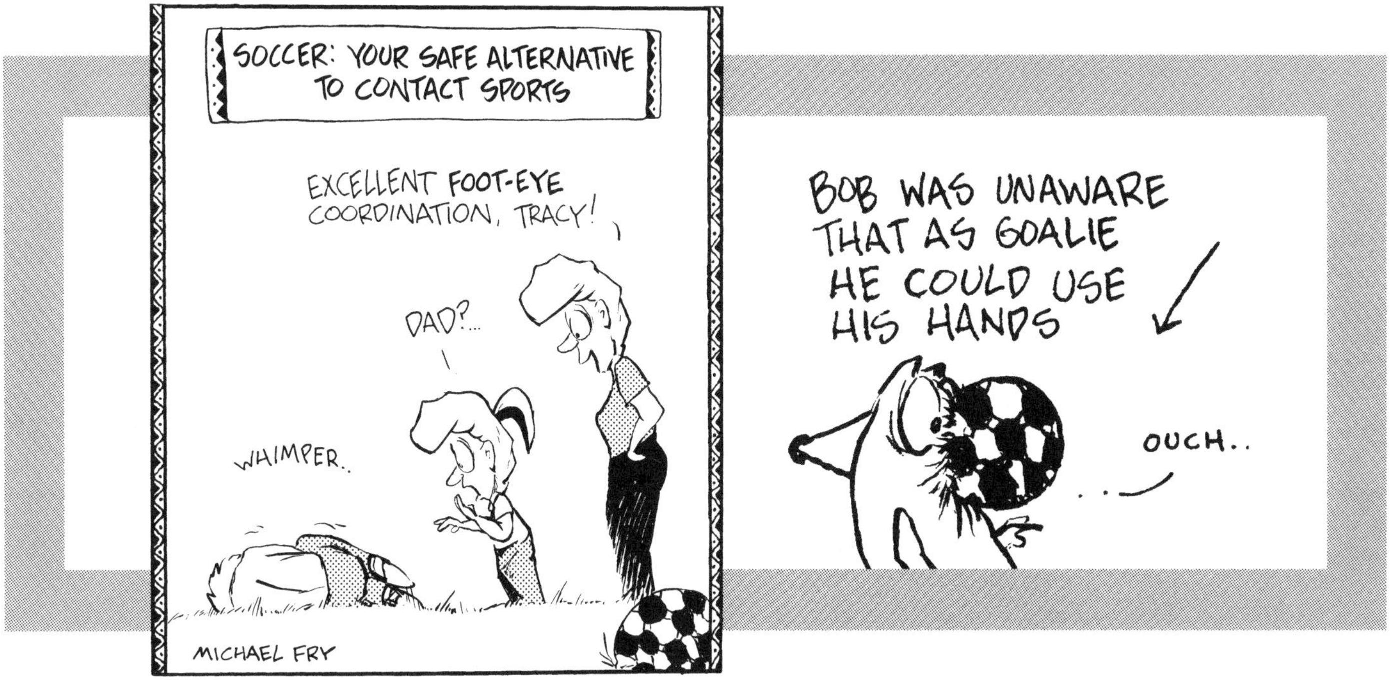
SOCCER: YOUR SAFE ALTERNATIVE TO CONTACT SPORTS
EXCELLENT FOOT-EYE COORDINATION, TRACY!
DAD?...
WHIMPER..
MICHAEL FRY
BOB WAS UNAWARE THAT AS GOALIE HE COULD USE HIS HANDS
OUCH..

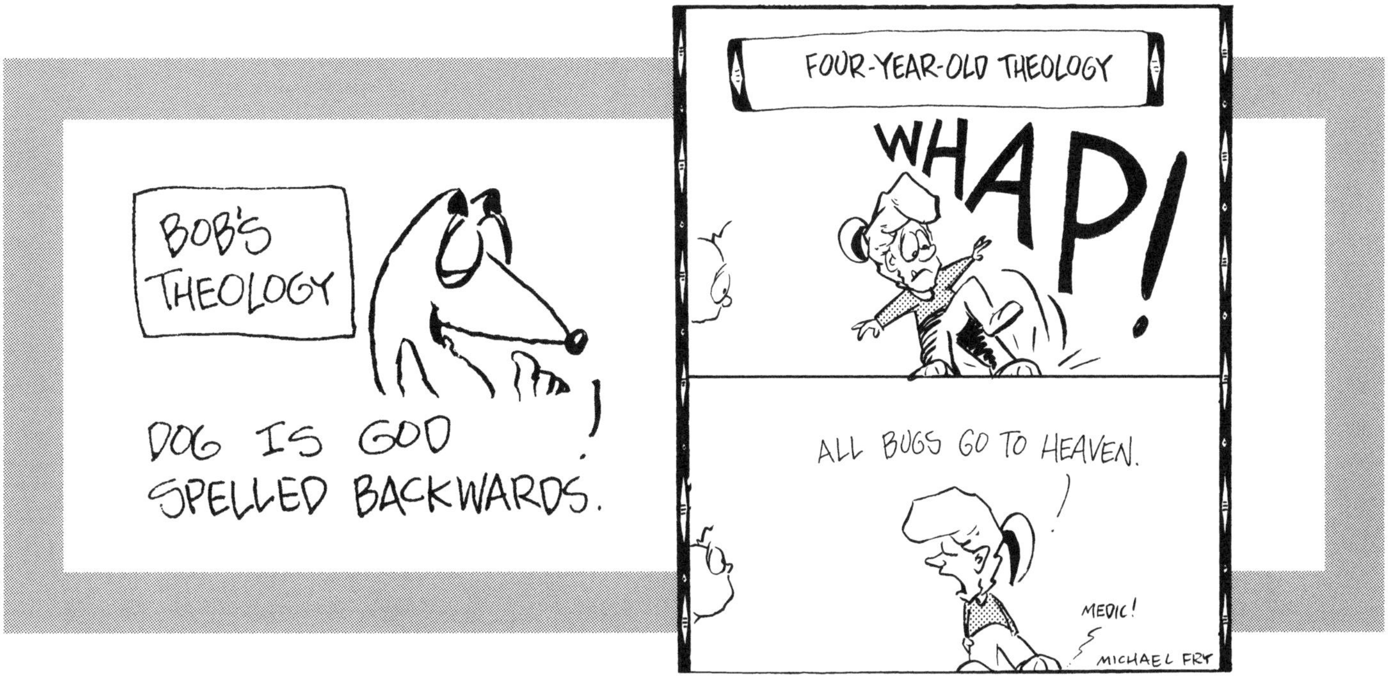
BOB'S THEOLOGY
DOG IS GOD SPELLED BACKWARDS.
FOUR-YEAR-OLD THEOLOGY
WHAP!
ALL BUGS GO TO HEAVEN.
MEDIC!
MICHAEL FRY

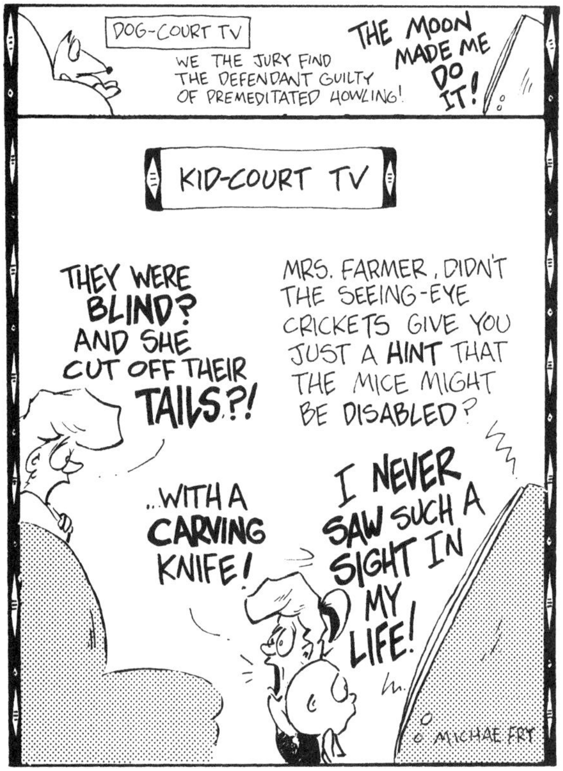
DOG-COURT TV
WE THE JURY FIND THE DEFENDANT GUILTY OF PREMEDITATED HOWLING!
THE MOON MADE ME DO IT!
KID-COURT TV
THEY WERE BLIND? AND SHE CUT OFF THEIR TAILS?!
MRS. FARMER, DIDN'T THE SEEING-EYE CRICKETS GIVE YOU JUST A HINT THAT THE MICE MIGHT BE DISABLED?
...WITH A CARVING KNIFE!
I NEVER SAW SUCH A SIGHT IN MY LIFE!
© MICHAEL FRY

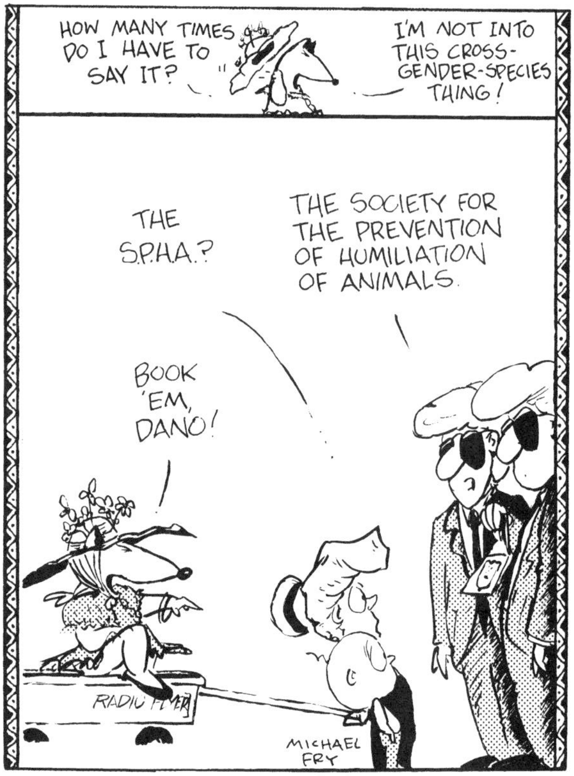
HOW MANY TIMES DO I HAVE TO SAY IT?
I'M NOT INTO THIS CROSS-GENDER-SPECIES THING!
THE S.P.H.A.?
THE SOCIETY FOR THE PREVENTION OF HUMILIATION OF ANIMALS.
BOOK 'EM, DANO!
RADIO FLYER
MICHAEL FRY

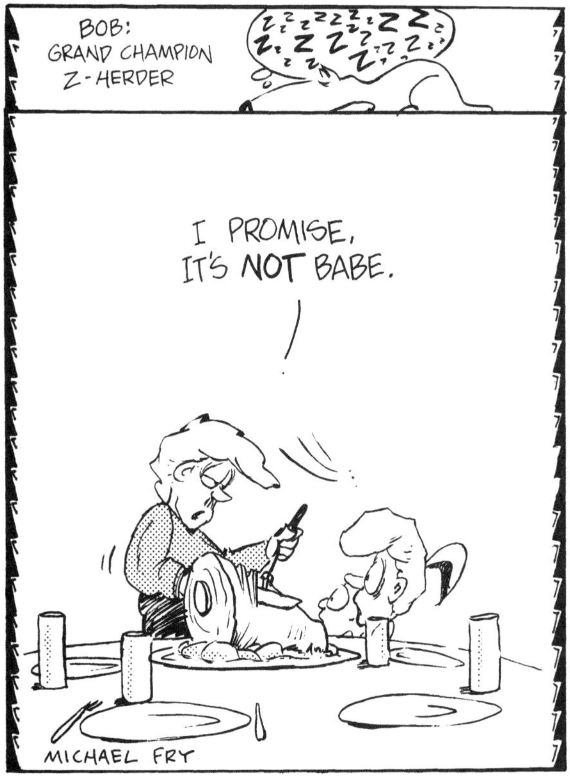
BOB: GRAND CHAMPION Z-HERDER
I PROMISE, IT'S NOT BABE.
MICHAEL FRY

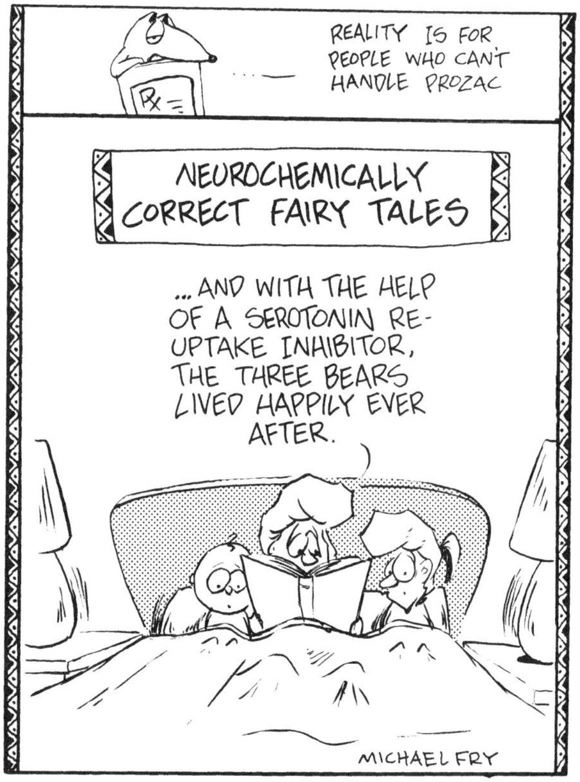
REALITY IS FOR PEOPLE WHO CAN'T HANDLE PROZAC
NEUROCHEMICALLY CORRECT FAIRY TALES
...AND WITH THE HELP OF A SEROTONIN RE-UPTAKE INHIBITOR, THE THREE BEARS LIVED HAPPILY EVER AFTER.
MICHAEL FRY

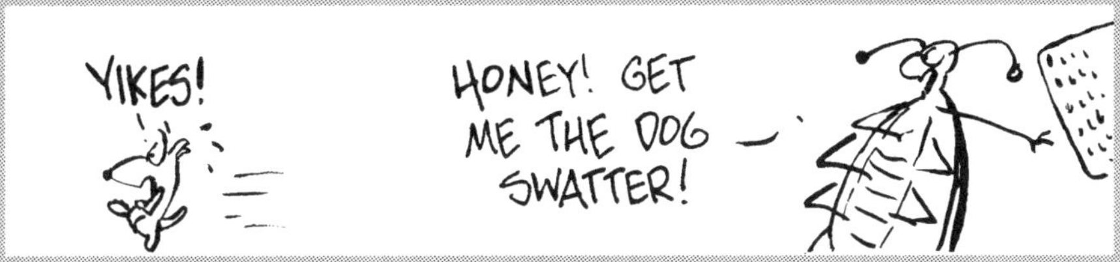
YIKES!
HONEY! GET ME THE DOG SWATTER!

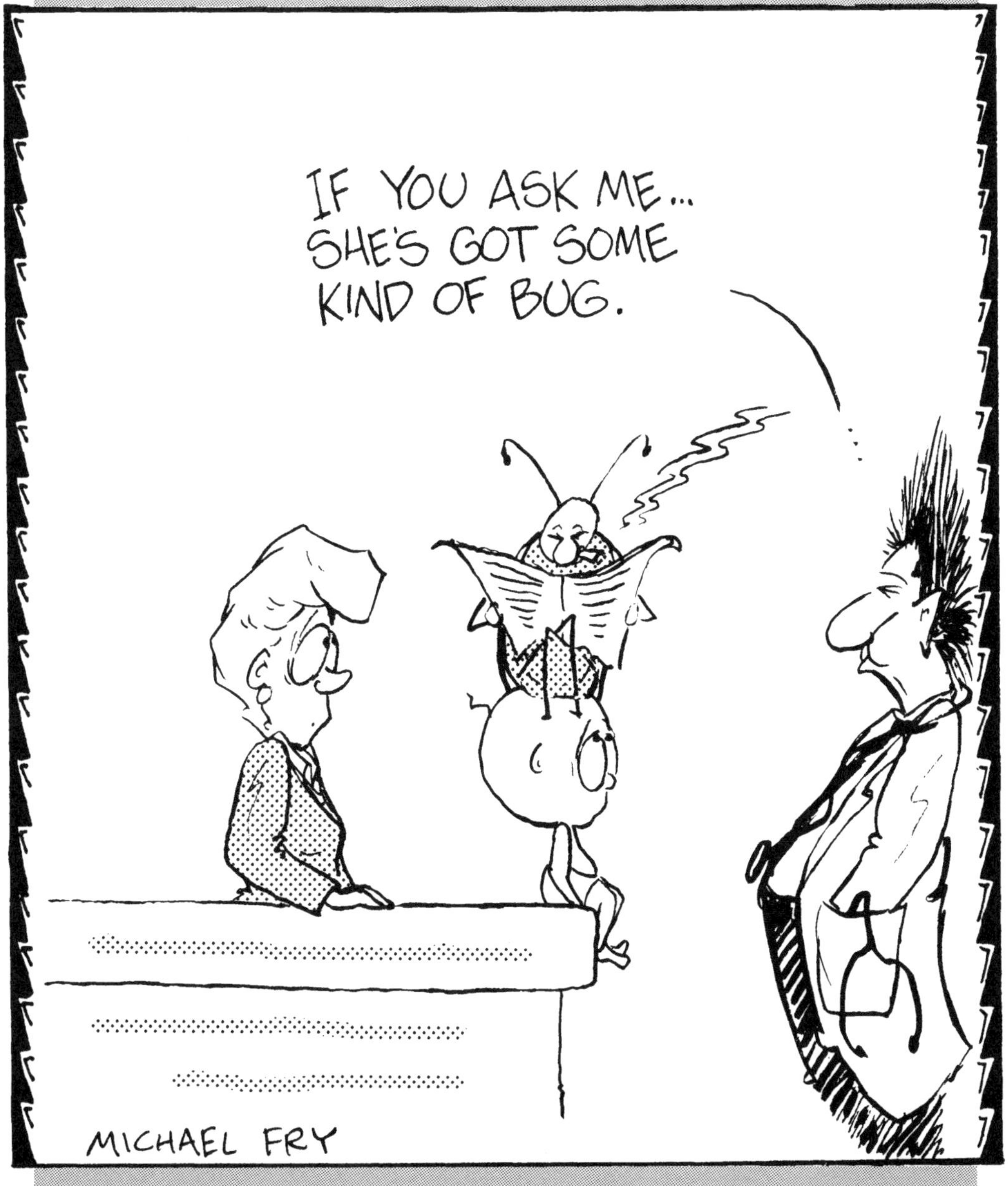
IF YOU ASK ME... SHE'S GOT SOME KIND OF BUG.
MICHAEL FRY

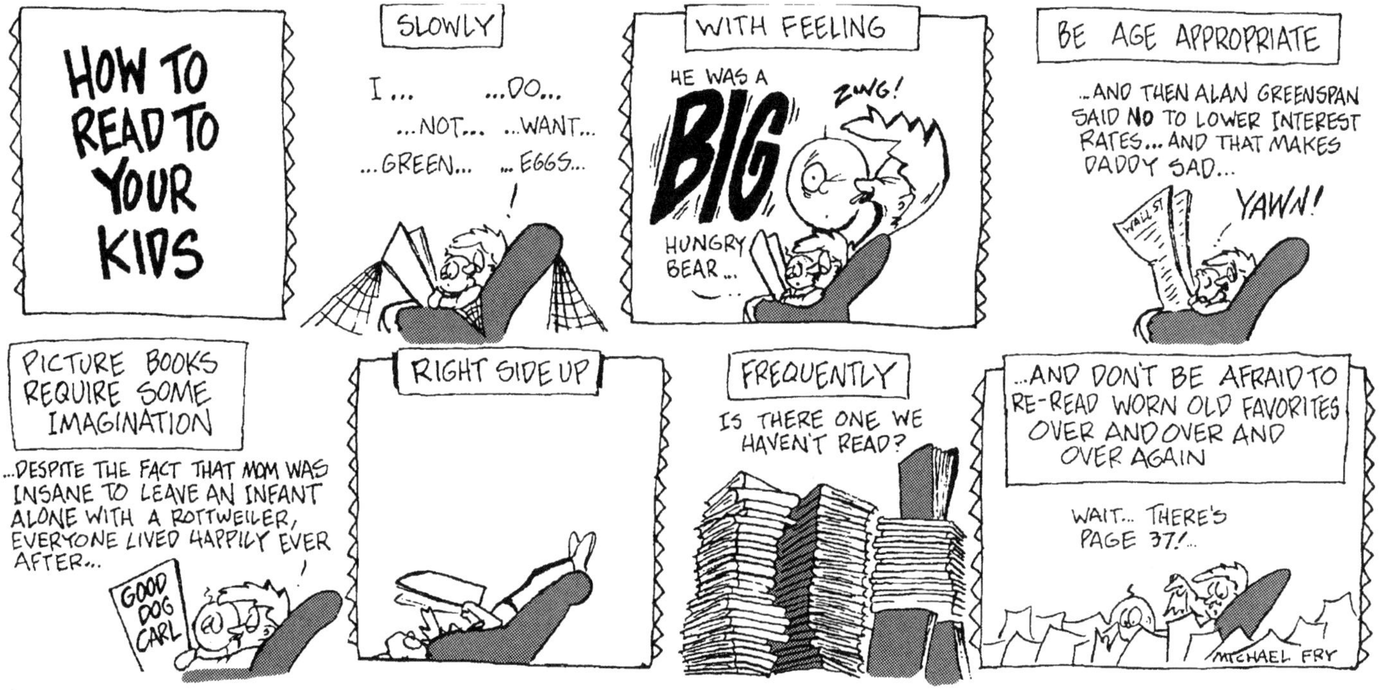
HOW TO READ TO YOUR KIDS
SLOWLY
I... ...DO... ...NOT... ...WANT... ...GREEN... ...EGGS...
WITH FEELING
HE WAS A BIG HUNGRY BEAR...
ZWG!
BE AGE APPROPRIATE
...AND THEN ALAN GREENSPAN SAID NO TO LOWER INTEREST RATES... AND THAT MAKES DADDY SAD...
YAWN!
PICTURE BOOKS REQUIRE SOME IMAGINATION
...DESPITE THE FACT THAT MOM WAS INSANE TO LEAVE AN INFANT ALONE WITH A ROTTWEILER, EVERYONE LIVED HAPPILY EVER AFTER...
GOOD DOG CARL
RIGHT SIDE UP
FREQUENTLY
IS THERE ONE WE HAVEN'T READ?
...AND DON'T BE AFRAID TO RE-READ WORN OLD FAVORITES OVER AND OVER AND OVER AGAIN
WAIT... THERE'S PAGE 37!...
MICHAEL FRY

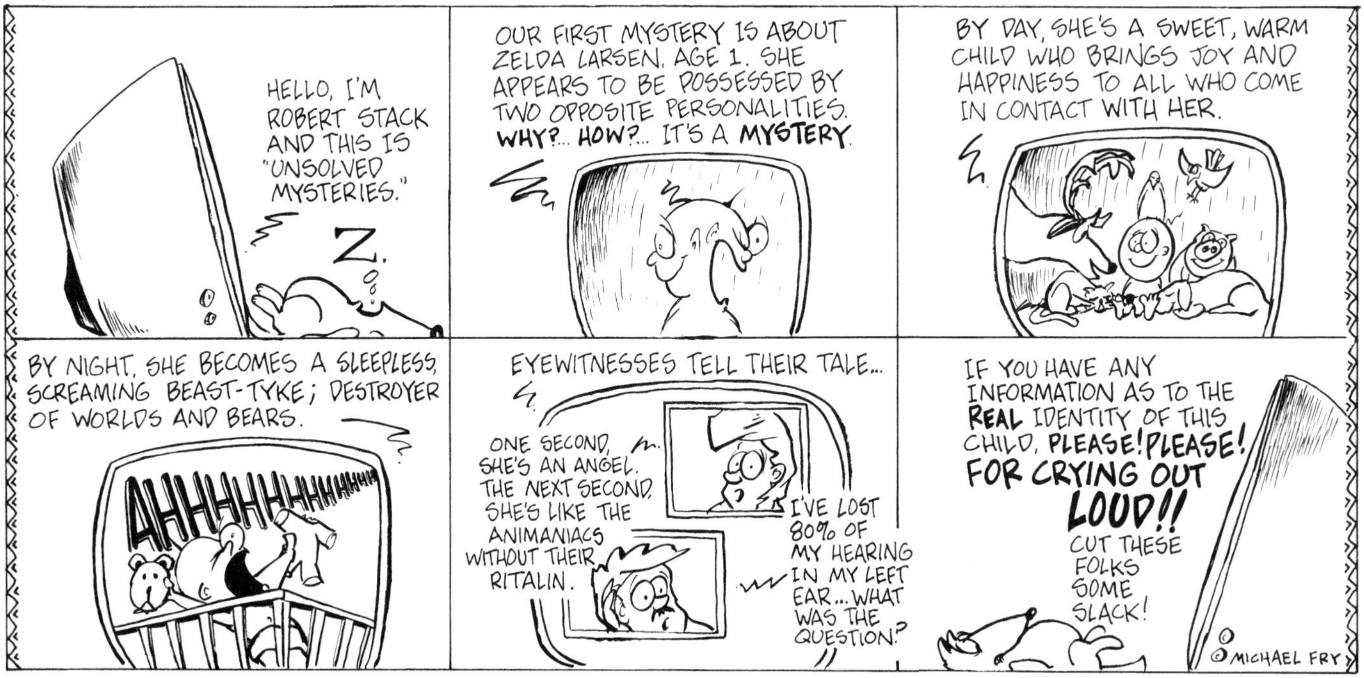
HELLO, I'M ROBERT STACK AND THIS IS "UNSOLVED MYSTERIES."
Z
OUR FIRST MYSTERY IS ABOUT ZELDA LARSEN, AGE 1. SHE APPEARS TO BE POSSESSED BY TWO OPPOSITE PERSONALITIES. WHY?... HOW?... IT'S A MYSTERY.
BY DAY, SHE'S A SWEET, WARM CHILD WHO BRINGS JOY AND HAPPINESS TO ALL WHO COME IN CONTACT WITH HER.
BY NIGHT, SHE BECOMES A SLEEPLESS, SCREAMING BEAST-TYKE; DESTROYER OF WORLDS AND BEARS.
AHHHHHHHHHHHH
EYEWITNESSES TELL THEIR TALE...
ONE SECOND, SHE'S AN ANGEL. THE NEXT SECOND, SHE'S LIKE THE ANIMANIACS WITHOUT THEIR RITALIN.
I'VE LOST 80% OF MY HEARING IN MY LEFT EAR... WHAT WAS THE QUESTION?
IF YOU HAVE ANY INFORMATION AS TO THE REAL IDENTITY OF THIS CHILD, PLEASE! PLEASE! FOR CRYING OUT LOUD!!
CUT THESE FOLKS SOME SLACK!
© MICHAEL FRY

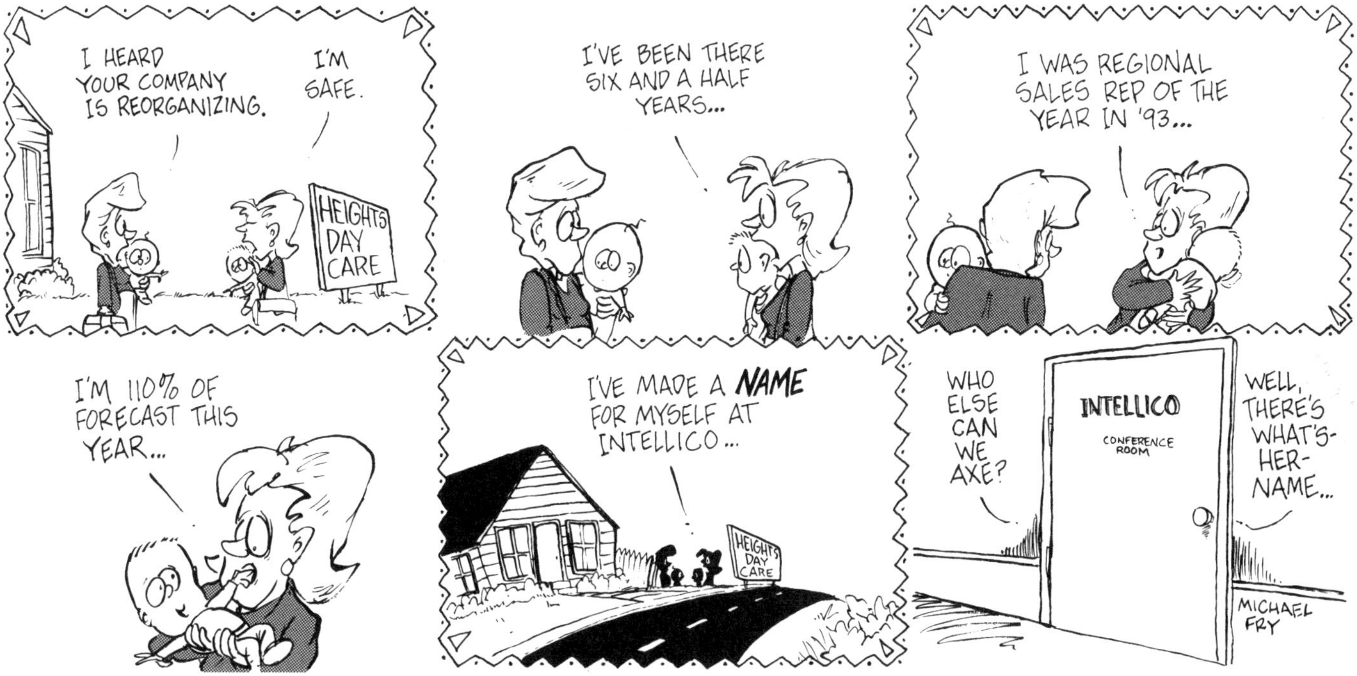
I HEARD YOUR COMPANY IS REORGANIZING.
I'M SAFE.
HEIGHTS DAY CARE
I'VE BEEN THERE SIX AND A HALF YEARS...
I WAS REGIONAL SALES REP OF THE YEAR IN '93...
I'M 110% OF FORECAST THIS YEAR...
I'VE MADE A **NAME** FOR MYSELF AT INTELLICO...
HEIGHTS DAY CARE
WHO ELSE CAN WE AXE?
INTELLICO
CONFERENCE ROOM
WELL, THERE'S WHAT'S-HER-NAME...
MICHAEL FRY

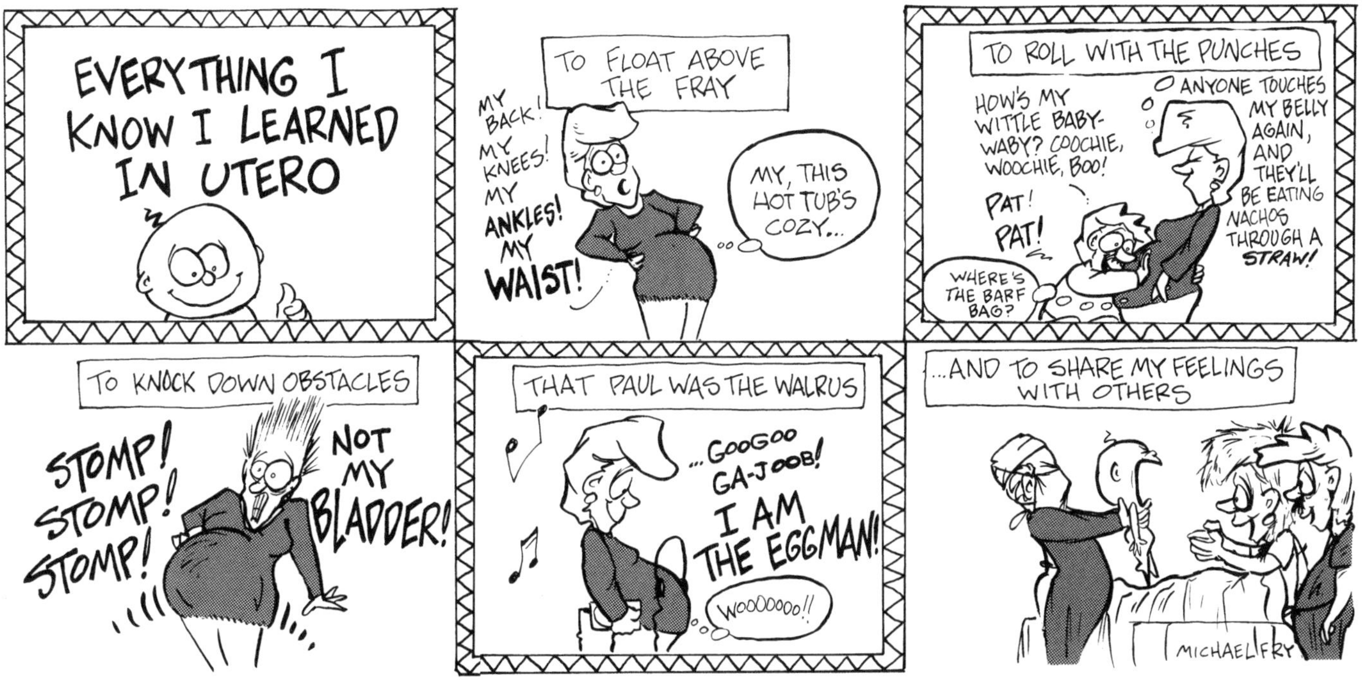
EVERYTHING I KNOW I LEARNED IN UTERO
TO FLOAT ABOVE THE FRAY
MY BACK! MY KNEES! MY ANKLES! MY WAIST!
MY, THIS HOT TUB'S COZY...
TO ROLL WITH THE PUNCHES
HOW'S MY WITTLE BABY-WABY? COOCHIE, WOOCHIE, BOO!
PAT! PAT!
ANYONE TOUCHES MY BELLY AGAIN, AND THEY'LL BE EATING NACHOS THROUGH A STRAW!
WHERE'S THE BARF BAG?
TO KNOCK DOWN OBSTACLES
STOMP! STOMP! STOMP!
NOT MY BLADDER!
THAT PAUL WAS THE WALRUS
...GOOGOO GA-JOOB! I AM THE EGGMAN!
WOOOOOOO!!
...AND TO SHARE MY FEELINGS WITH OTHERS
MICHAEL FRY

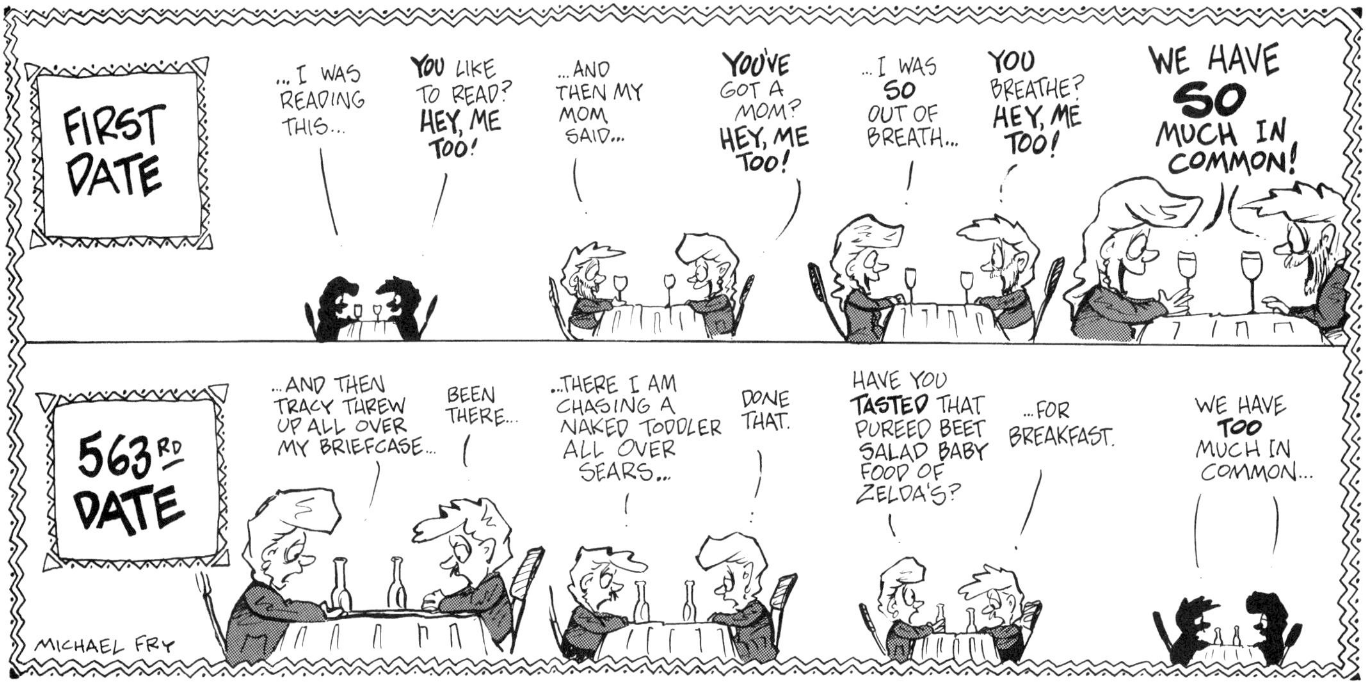
FIRST DATE
...I WAS READING THIS...
YOU LIKE TO READ? HEY, ME TOO!
...AND THEN MY MOM SAID...
YOU'VE GOT A MOM? HEY, ME TOO!
...I WAS SO OUT OF BREATH...
YOU BREATHE? HEY, ME TOO!
WE HAVE SO MUCH IN COMMON!
563RD DATE
...AND THEN TRACY THREW UP ALL OVER MY BRIEFCASE...
BEEN THERE...
...THERE I AM CHASING A NAKED TODDLER ALL OVER SEARS...
DONE THAT.
HAVE YOU TASTED THAT PUREED BEET SALAD BABY FOOD OF ZELDA'S?
...FOR BREAKFAST.
WE HAVE TOO MUCH IN COMMON...
MICHAEL FRY

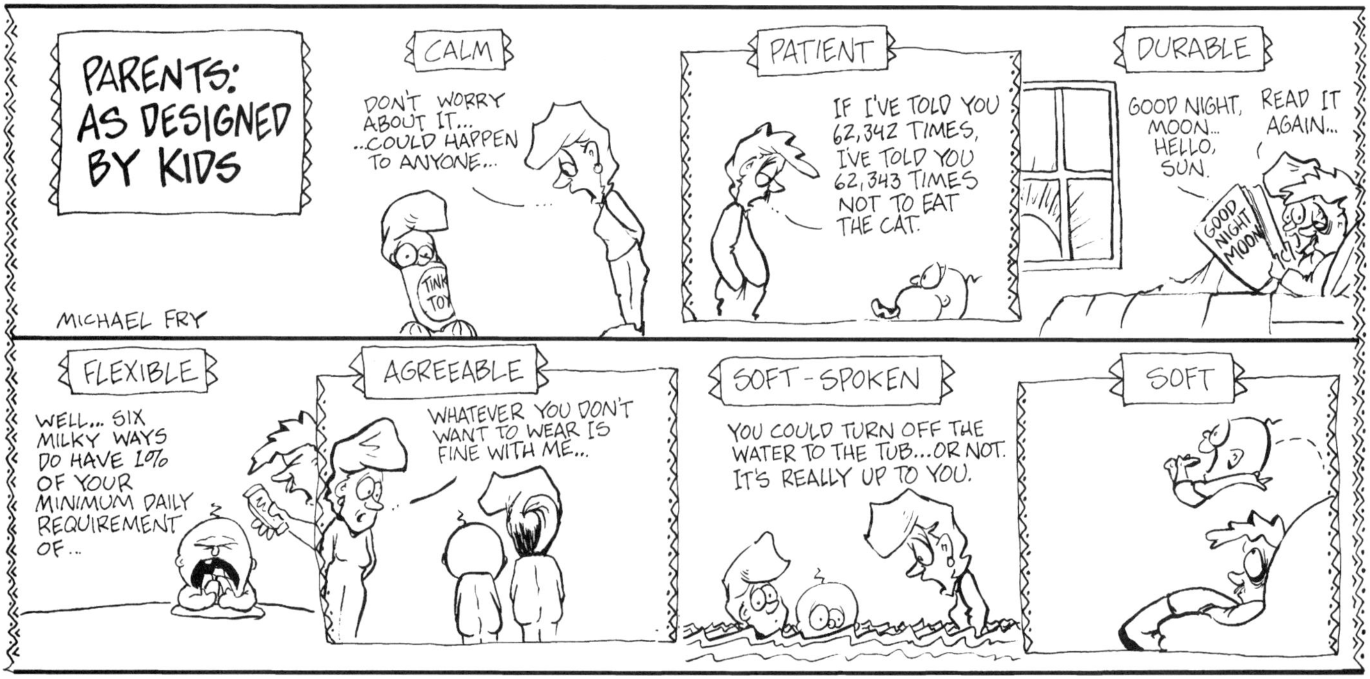
PARENTS: AS DESIGNED BY KIDS
MICHAEL FRY
CALM
DON'T WORRY ABOUT IT... ...COULD HAPPEN TO ANYONE...
TINK TOY
PATIENT
IF I'VE TOLD YOU 62,342 TIMES, I'VE TOLD YOU 62,343 TIMES NOT TO EAT THE CAT.
DURABLE
GOOD NIGHT, MOON... HELLO, SUN.
READ IT AGAIN...
GOOD NIGHT MOON
FLEXIBLE
WELL... SIX MILKY WAYS DO HAVE 1% OF YOUR MINIMUM DAILY REQUIREMENT OF...
AGREEABLE
WHATEVER YOU DON'T WANT TO WEAR IS FINE WITH ME...
SOFT-SPOKEN
YOU COULD TURN OFF THE WATER TO THE TUB...OR NOT. IT'S REALLY UP TO YOU.
SOFT

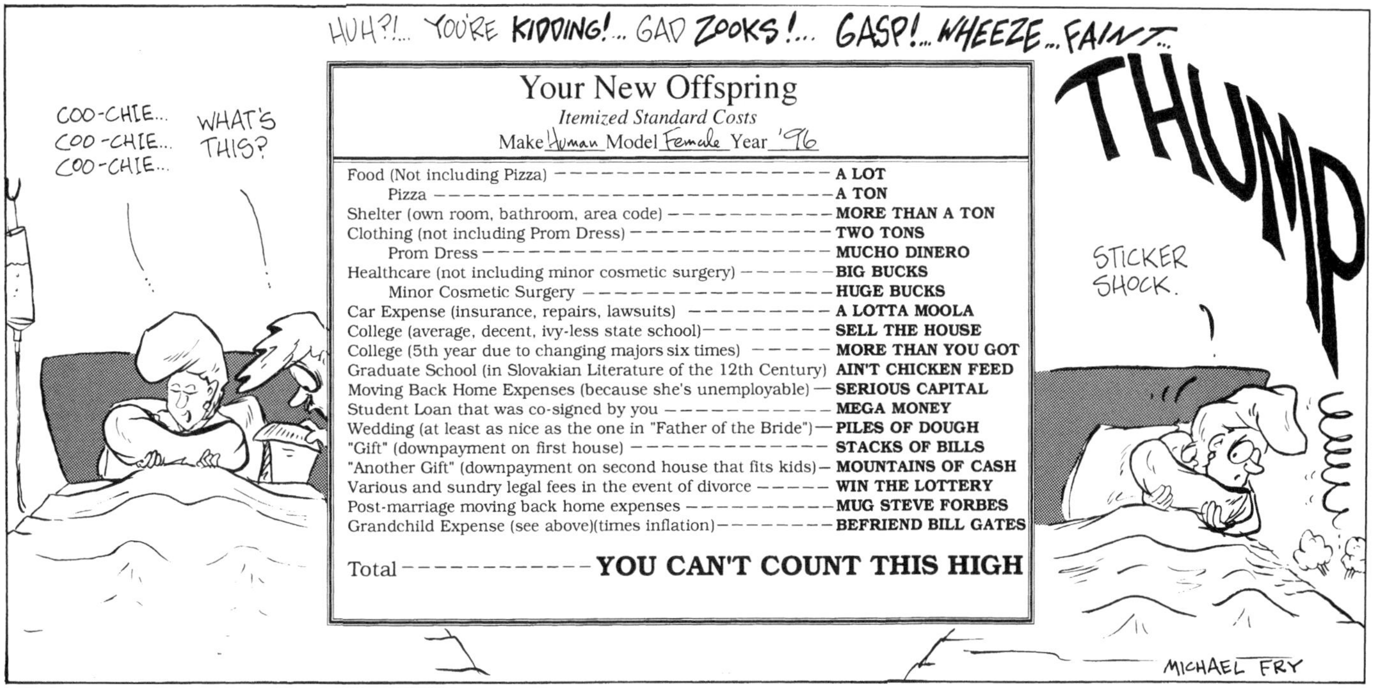
HUH?!... YOU'RE KIDDING!... GAD ZOOKS!... GASP!... WHEEZE... FAINT...
COO-CHIE... COO-CHIE... COO-CHIE...
WHAT'S THIS?
Your New Offspring
Itemized Standard Costs
Make Human Model Female Year '96
Food (Not including Pizza) — A LOT
Pizza — A TON
Shelter (own room, bathroom, area code) — MORE THAN A TON
Clothing (not including Prom Dress) — TWO TONS
Prom Dress — MUCHO DINERO
Healthcare (not including minor cosmetic surgery) — BIG BUCKS
Minor Cosmetic Surgery — HUGE BUCKS
Car Expense (insurance, repairs, lawsuits) — A LOTTA MOOLA
College (average, decent, ivy-less state school) — SELL THE HOUSE
College (5th year due to changing majors six times) — MORE THAN YOU GOT
Graduate School (in Slovakian Literature of the 12th Century) AIN'T CHICKEN FEED
Moving Back Home Expenses (because she's unemployable) — SERIOUS CAPITAL
Student Loan that was co-signed by you — MEGA MONEY
Wedding (at least as nice as the one in "Father of the Bride") — PILES OF DOUGH
"Gift" (downpayment on first house) — STACKS OF BILLS
"Another Gift" (downpayment on second house that fits kids) — MOUNTAINS OF CASH
Various and sundry legal fees in the event of divorce — WIN THE LOTTERY
Post-marriage moving back home expenses — MUG STEVE FORBES
Grandchild Expense (see above)(times inflation) — BEFRIEND BILL GATES
Total — YOU CAN'T COUNT THIS HIGH
THUMP
STICKER SHOCK.
MICHAEL FRY

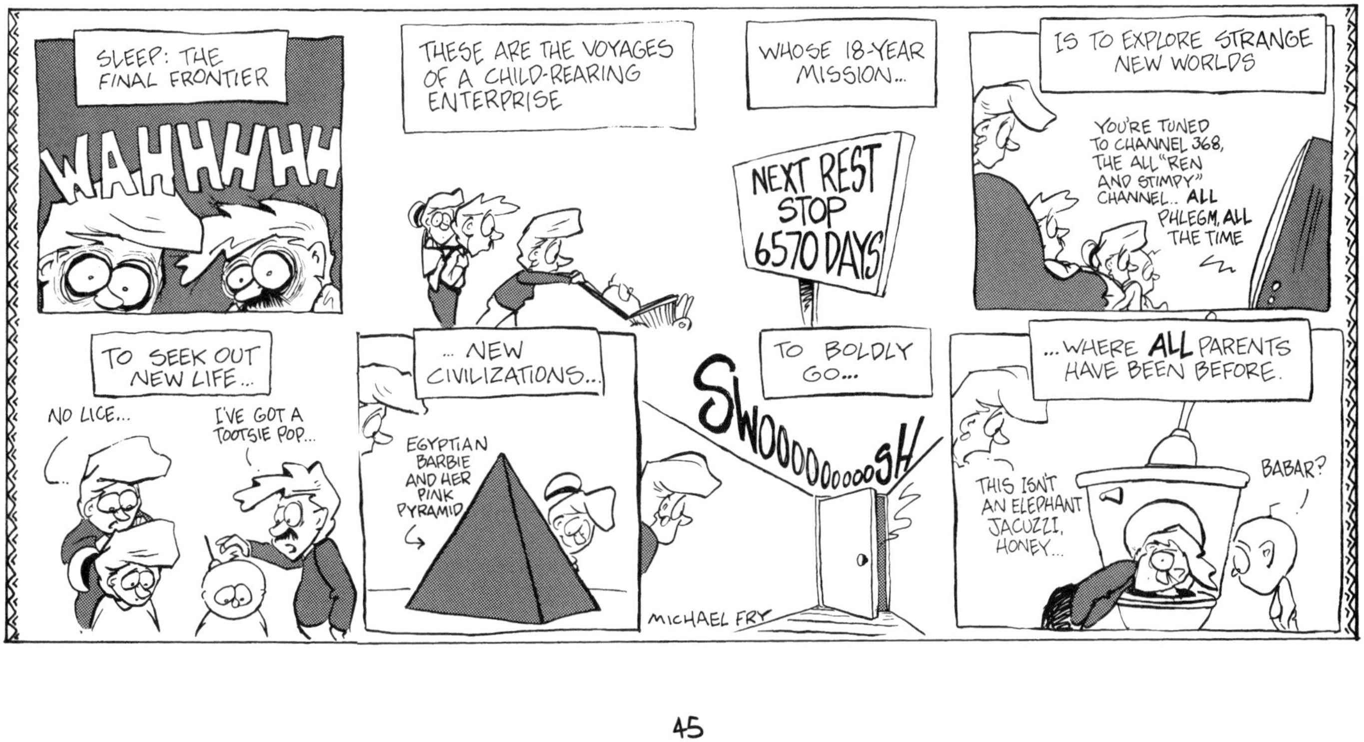
SLEEP: THE FINAL FRONTIER
WAHHHHH
THESE ARE THE VOYAGES OF A CHILD-REARING ENTERPRISE
WHOSE 18-YEAR MISSION...
NEXT REST STOP 6570 DAYS
IS TO EXPLORE STRANGE NEW WORLDS
YOU'RE TUNED TO CHANNEL 368, THE ALL "REN AND STIMPY" CHANNEL... ALL PHLEGM, ALL THE TIME
TO SEEK OUT NEW LIFE...
NO LICE...
I'VE GOT A TOOTSIE POP...
...NEW CIVILIZATIONS...
EGYPTIAN BARBIE AND HER PINK PYRAMID
TO BOLDLY GO...
SWOOOOOOOOOSH
...WHERE ALL PARENTS HAVE BEEN BEFORE.
THIS ISN'T AN ELEPHANT JACUZZI, HONEY...
BABAR?
MICHAEL FRY

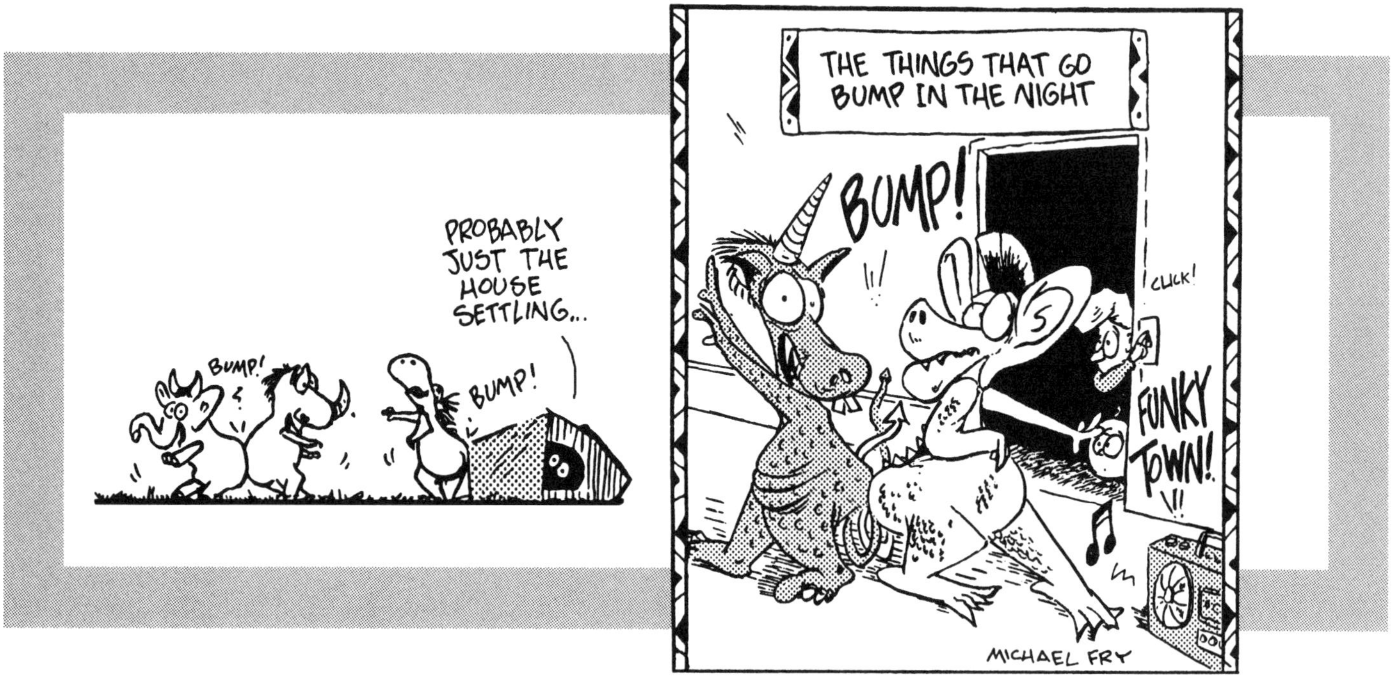
THE THINGS THAT GO BUMP IN THE NIGHT
BUMP!
CLICK!
FUNKY TOWN!
MICHAEL FRY
BUMP!
BUMP!
PROBABLY JUST THE HOUSE SETTLING...

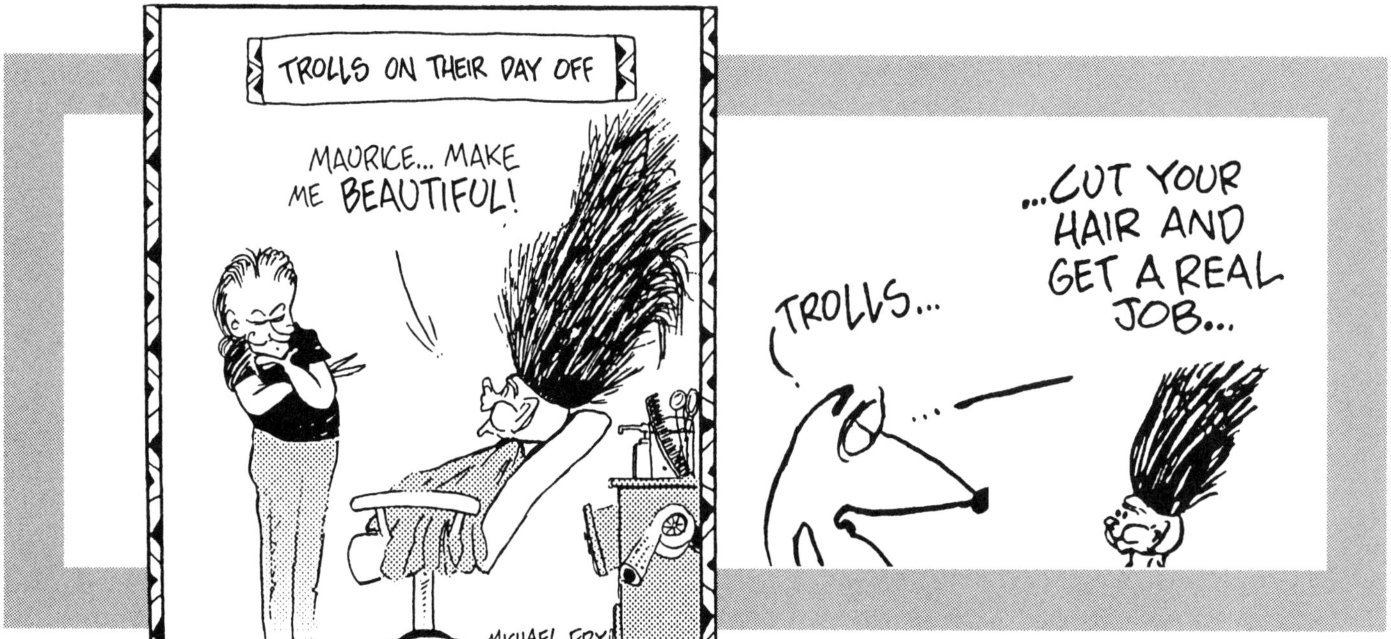
TROLLS ON THEIR DAY OFF
MAURICE... MAKE ME BEAUTIFUL!
MICHAEL FRY
TROLLS...
...CUT YOUR HAIR AND GET A REAL JOB...

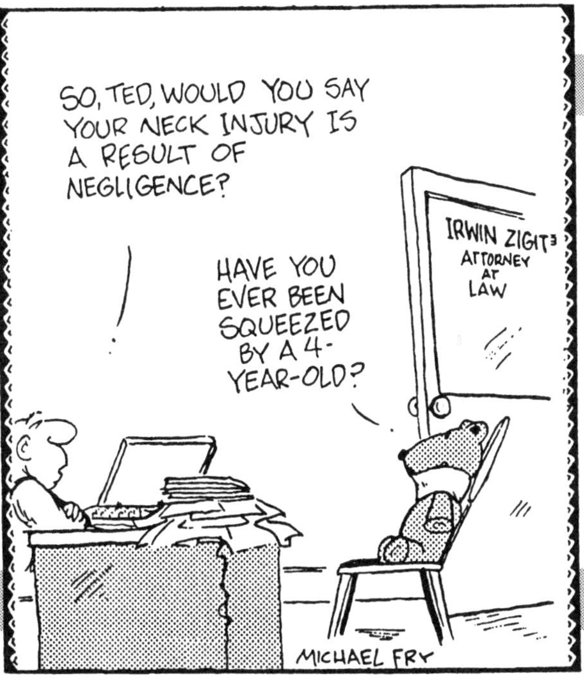
SO, TED, WOULD YOU SAY YOUR NECK INJURY IS A RESULT OF NEGLIGENCE?
HAVE YOU EVER BEEN SQUEEZED BY A 4-YEAR-OLD?
IRWIN ZIGIT3 ATTORNEY AT LAW
MICHAEL FRY

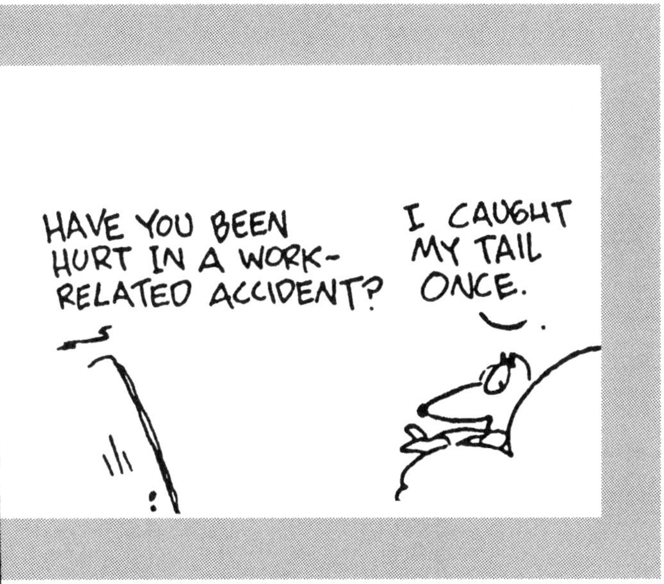
HAVE YOU BEEN HURT IN A WORK-RELATED ACCIDENT?
I CAUGHT MY TAIL ONCE.

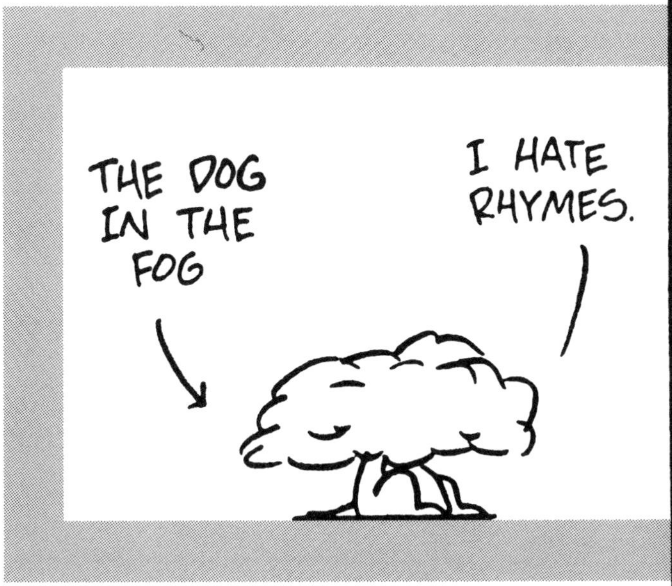
THE DOG IN THE FOG
I HATE RHYMES.

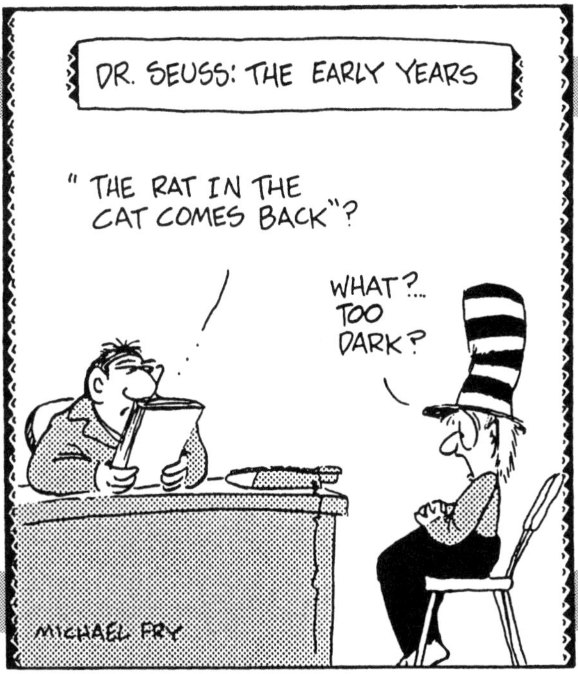
DR. SEUSS: THE EARLY YEARS
"THE RAT IN THE CAT COMES BACK"?
WHAT?... TOO DARK?
MICHAEL FRY

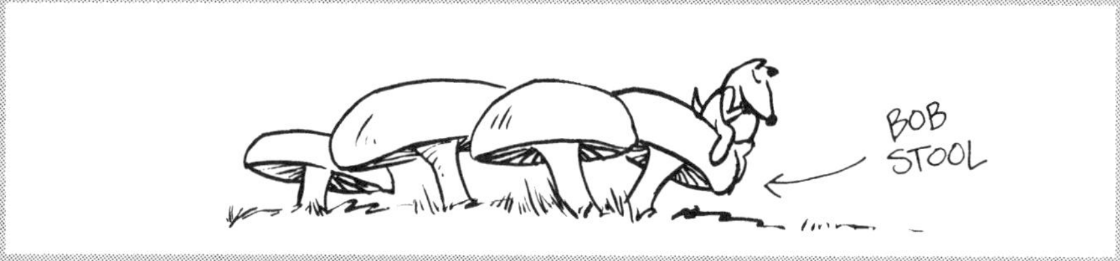
BOB STOOL

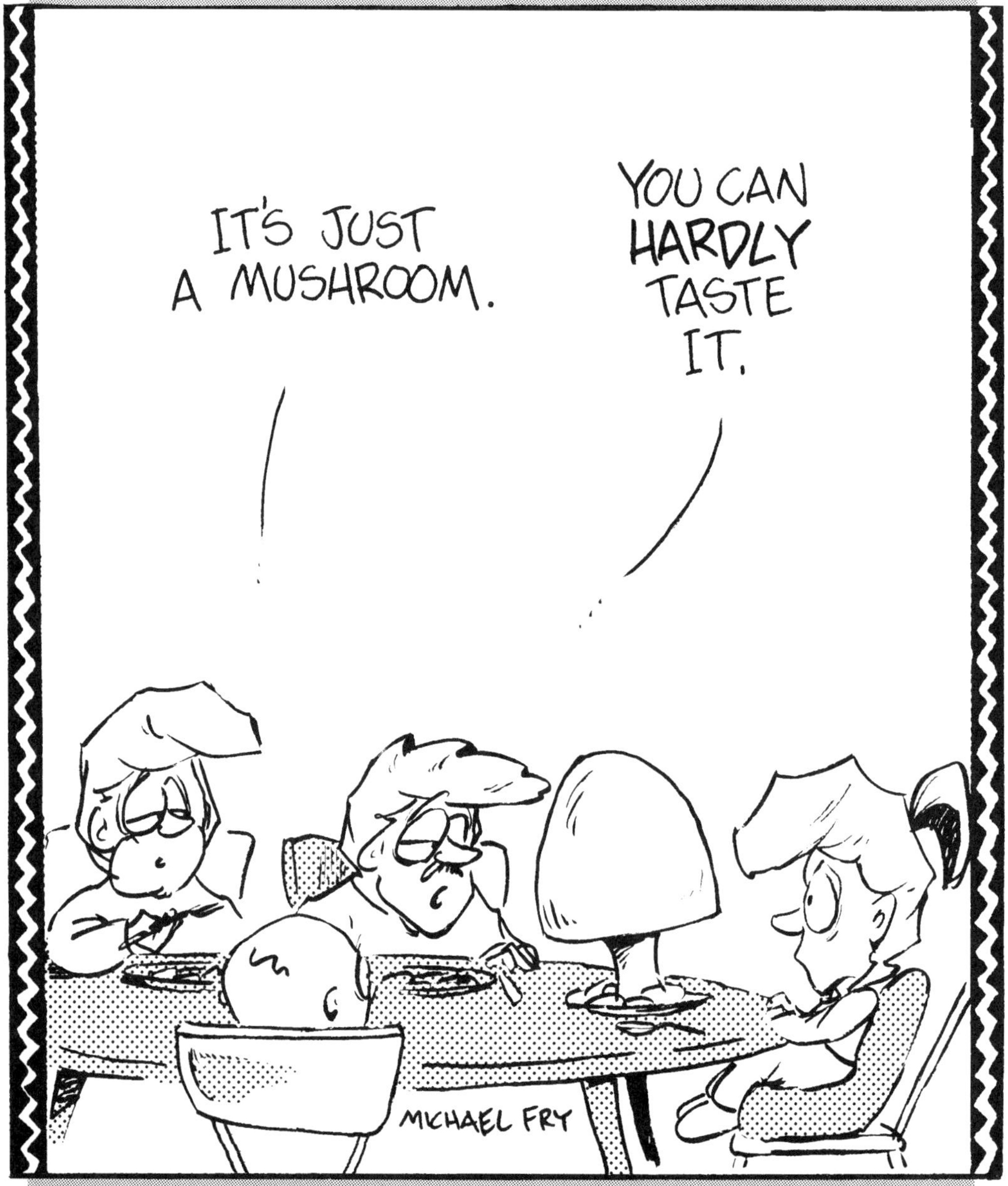
IT'S JUST A MUSHROOM.
YOU CAN HARDLY TASTE IT.
MICHAEL FRY

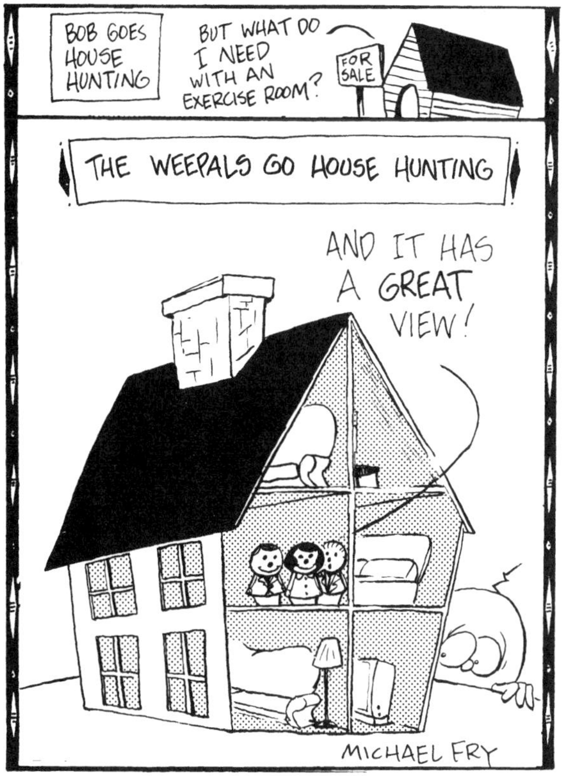
BOB GOES HOUSE HUNTING
BUT WHAT DO I NEED WITH AN EXERCISE ROOM?
FOR SALE
THE WEEPALS GO HOUSE HUNTING
AND IT HAS A GREAT VIEW!
MICHAEL FRY

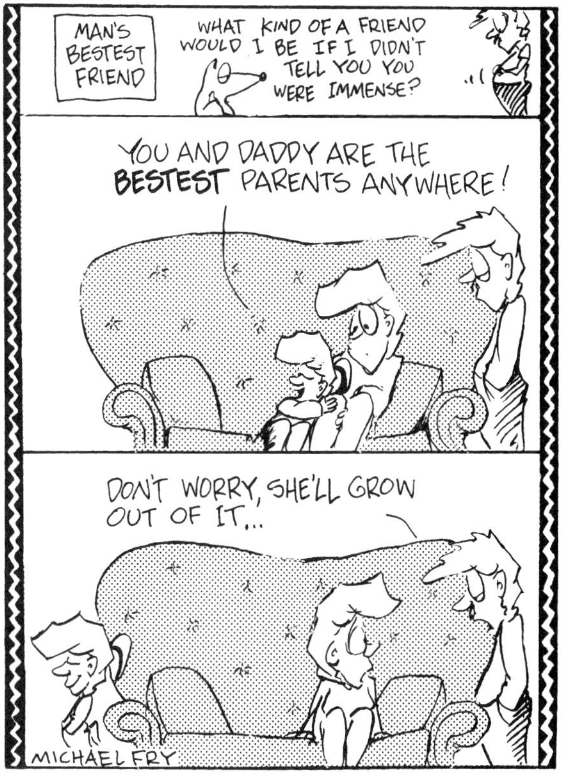
MAN'S BESTEST FRIEND
WHAT KIND OF A FRIEND WOULD I BE IF I DIDN'T TELL YOU YOU WERE IMMENSE?
YOU AND DADDY ARE THE BESTEST PARENTS ANYWHERE!
DON'T WORRY, SHE'LL GROW OUT OF IT...
MICHAEL FRY

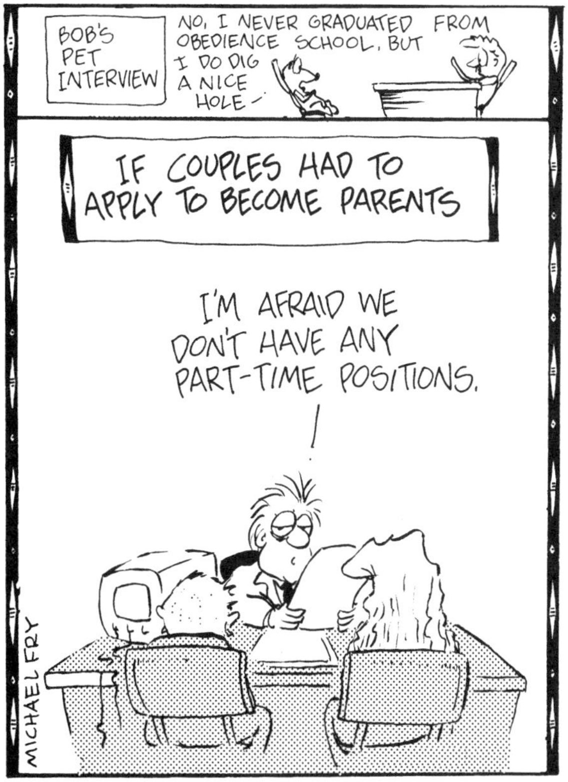
BOB'S PET INTERVIEW
NO, I NEVER GRADUATED FROM OBEDIENCE SCHOOL, BUT I DO DIG A NICE HOLE
IF COUPLES HAD TO APPLY TO BECOME PARENTS
I'M AFRAID WE DON'T HAVE ANY PART-TIME POSITIONS.
MICHAEL FRY

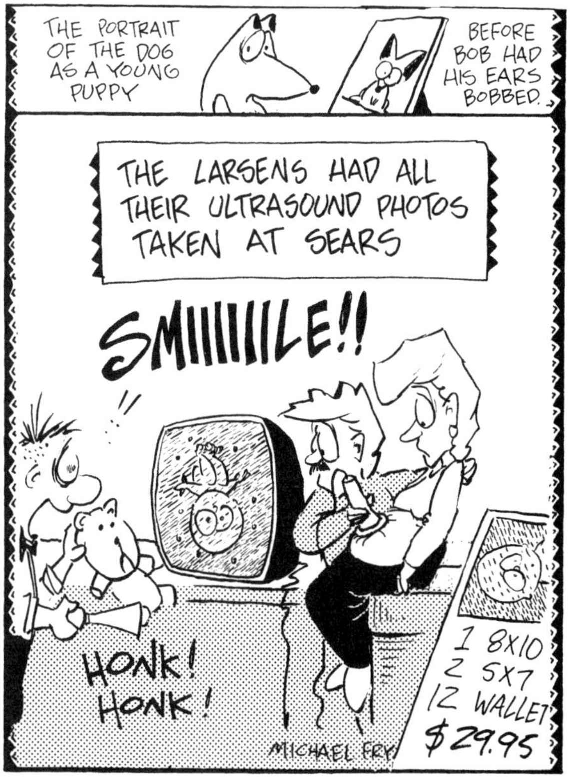
THE PORTRAIT OF THE DOG AS A YOUNG PUPPY
BEFORE BOB HAD HIS EARS BOBBED.
THE LARSENS HAD ALL THEIR ULTRASOUND PHOTOS TAKEN AT SEARS
SMIIIIIILE!!
HONK! HONK!
1 8X10
2 5X7
12 WALLET
$29.95
MICHAEL FRY

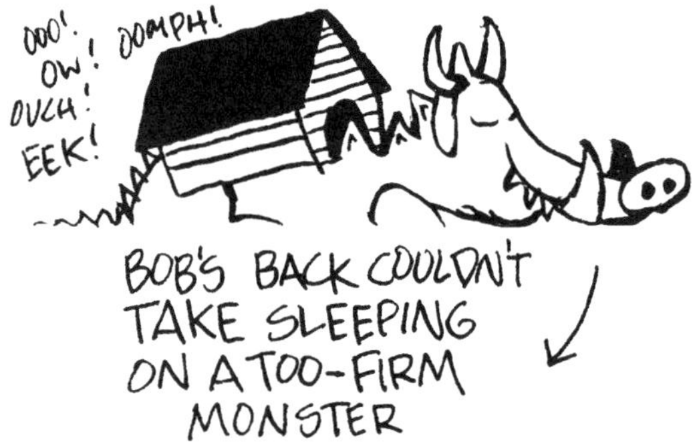
OOO! OW! OUCH! EEK!
OOMPH!
BOB'S BACK COULDN'T TAKE SLEEPING ON A TOO-FIRM MONSTER

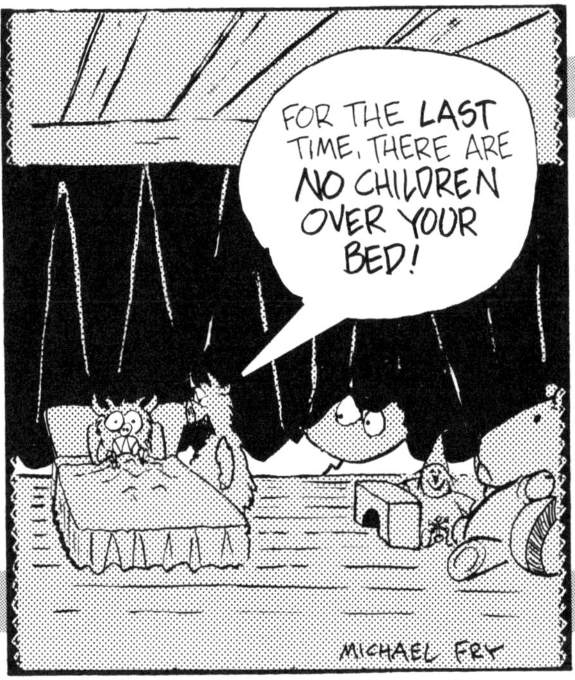
FOR THE LAST TIME, THERE ARE NO CHILDREN OVER YOUR BED!
MICHAEL FRY

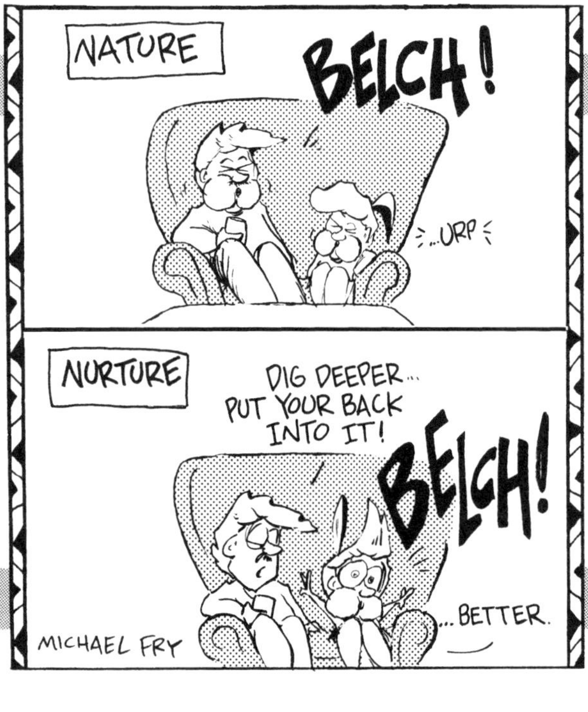
NATURE
BELCH!
...URP
NURTURE
DIG DEEPER... PUT YOUR BACK INTO IT!
BELCH!
...BETTER.
MICHAEL FRY

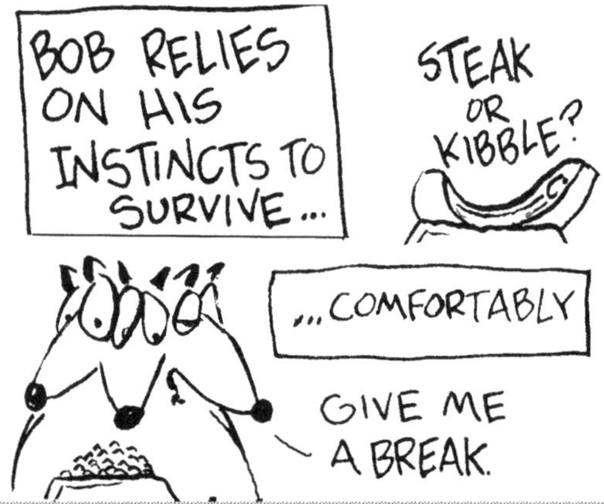
BOB RELIES ON HIS INSTINCTS TO SURVIVE...
STEAK OR KIBBLE?
...COMFORTABLY
GIVE ME A BREAK.

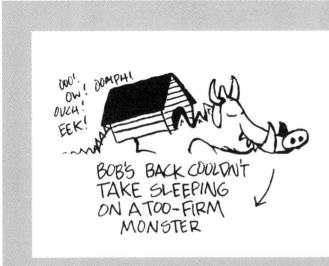

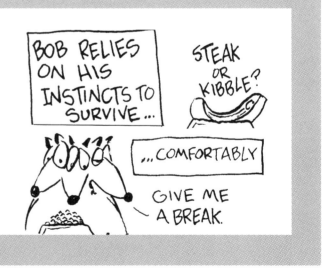

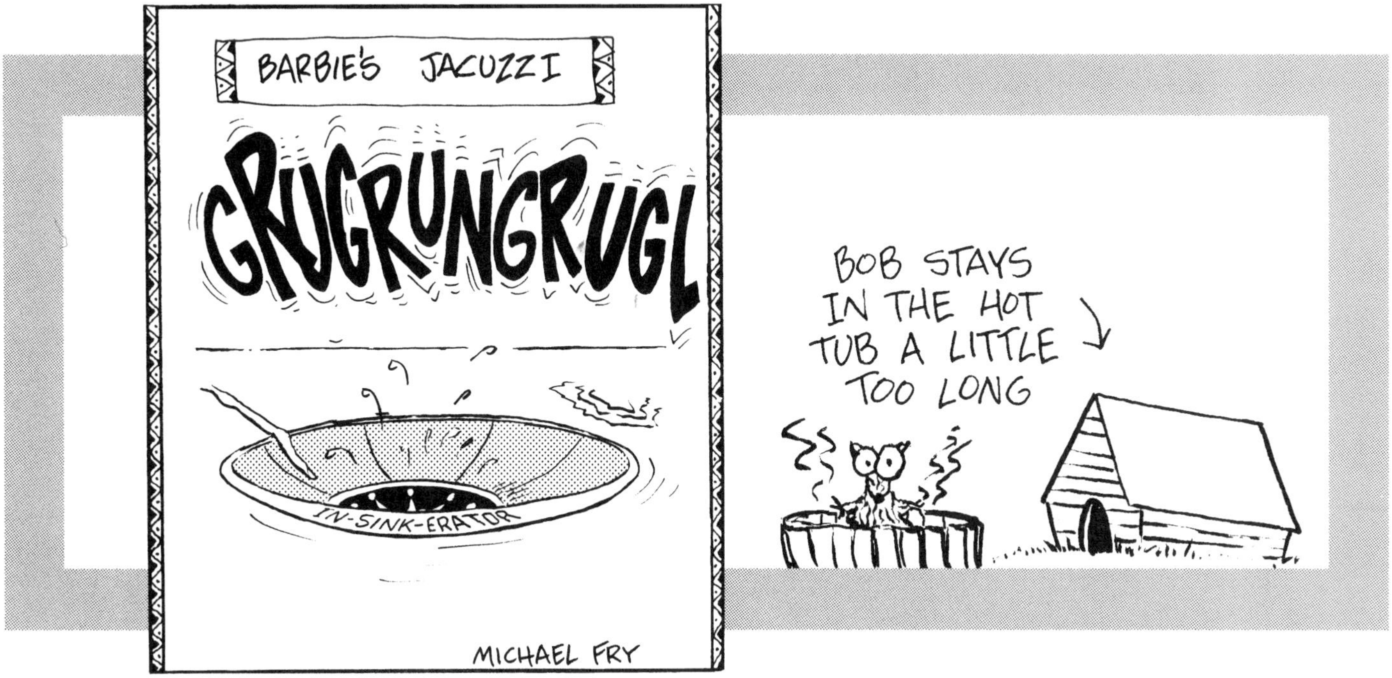
BARBIE'S JACUZZI
GRUGRUNGRUGL
IN-SINK-ERATOR
MICHAEL FRY
BOB STAYS IN THE HOT TUB A LITTLE TOO LONG

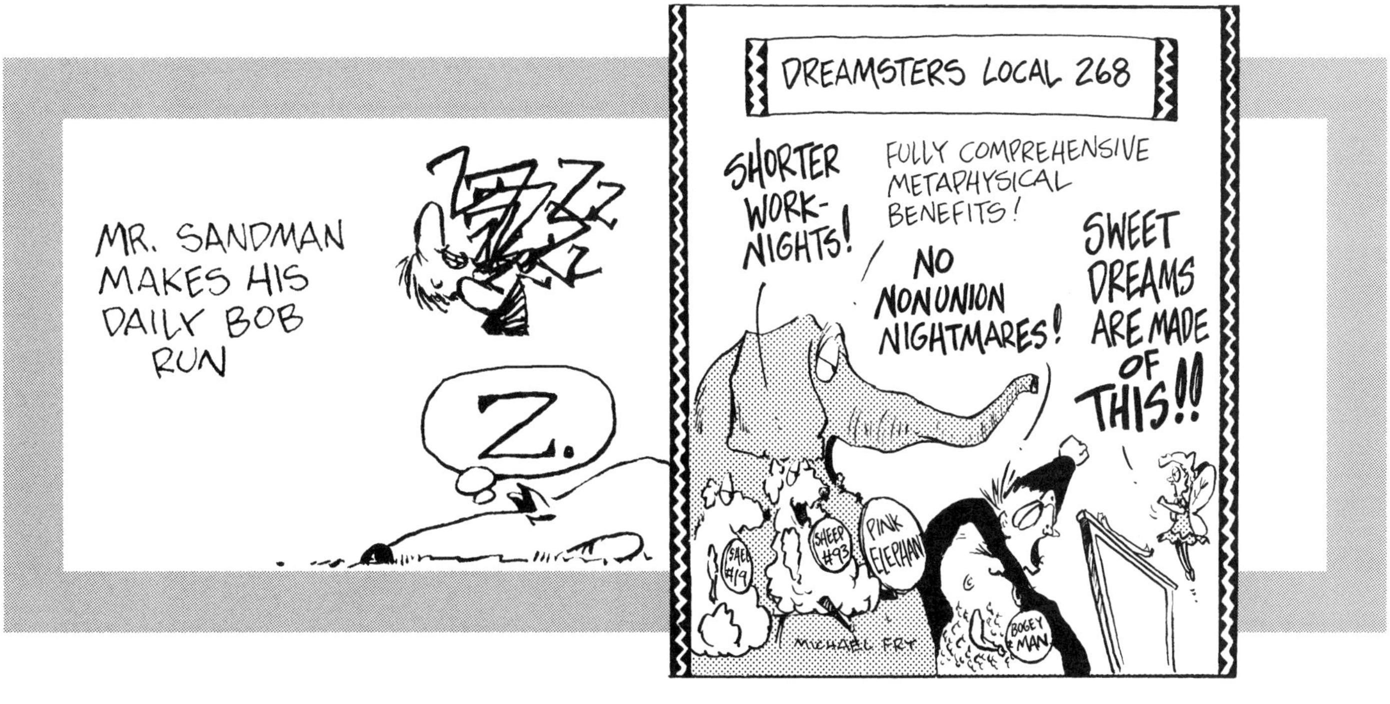
MR. SANDMAN MAKES HIS DAILY BOB RUN
Z.
DREAMSTERS LOCAL 268
SHORTER WORK-NIGHTS!
FULLY COMPREHENSIVE METAPHYSICAL BENEFITS!
NO NONUNION NIGHTMARES!
SWEET DREAMS ARE MADE OF THIS!!
SHEEP #93
PINK ELEPHANT
BOGEY MAN
MICHAEL FRY

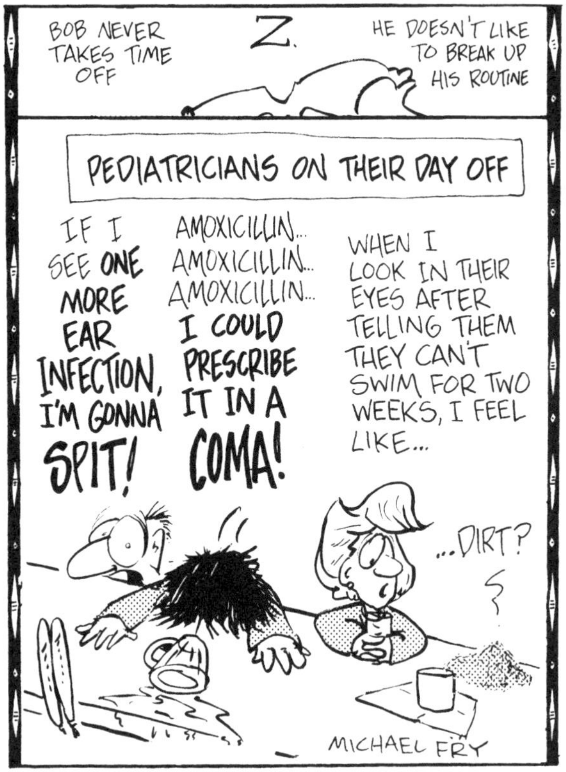
BOB NEVER TAKES TIME OFF
Z.
HE DOESN'T LIKE TO BREAK UP HIS ROUTINE
PEDIATRICIANS ON THEIR DAY OFF
IF I SEE ONE MORE EAR INFECTION, I'M GONNA SPIT!
AMOXICILLIN... AMOXICILLIN... AMOXICILLIN... I COULD PRESCRIBE IT IN A COMA!
WHEN I LOOK IN THEIR EYES AFTER TELLING THEM THEY CAN'T SWIM FOR TWO WEEKS, I FEEL LIKE...
...DIRT?
MICHAEL FRY

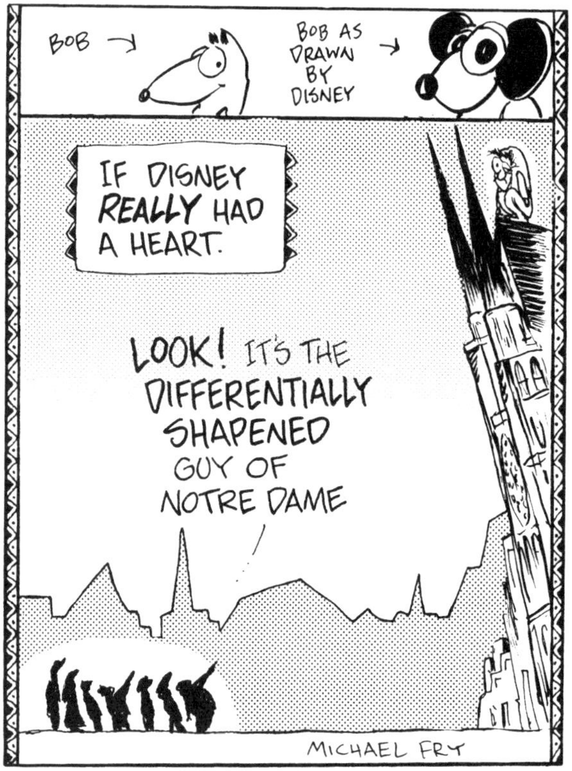
BOB
BOB AS DRAWN BY DISNEY
IF DISNEY REALLY HAD A HEART.
LOOK! IT'S THE DIFFERENTIALLY SHAPENED GUY OF NOTRE DAME
MICHAEL FRY

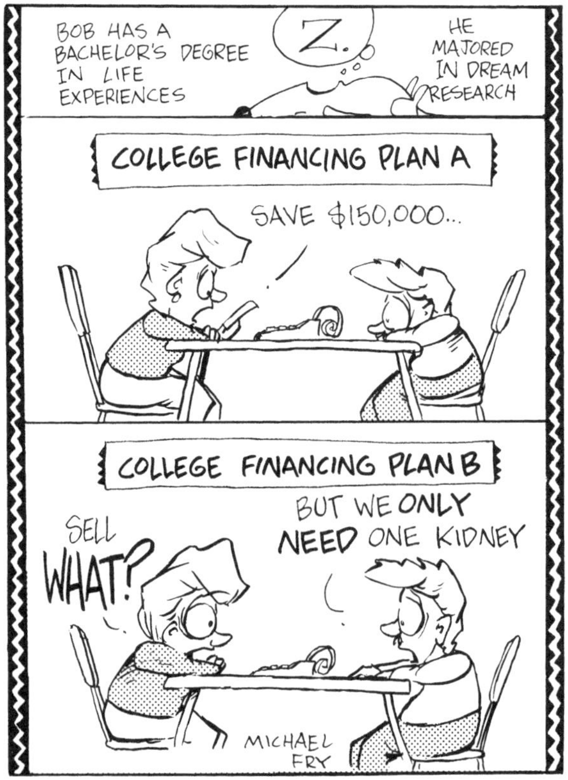
BOB HAS A BACHELOR'S DEGREE IN LIFE EXPERIENCES
Z.
HE MAJORED IN DREAM RESEARCH
COLLEGE FINANCING PLAN A
SAVE $150,000...
COLLEGE FINANCING PLAN B
SELL WHAT?
BUT WE ONLY NEED ONE KIDNEY
MICHAEL FRY

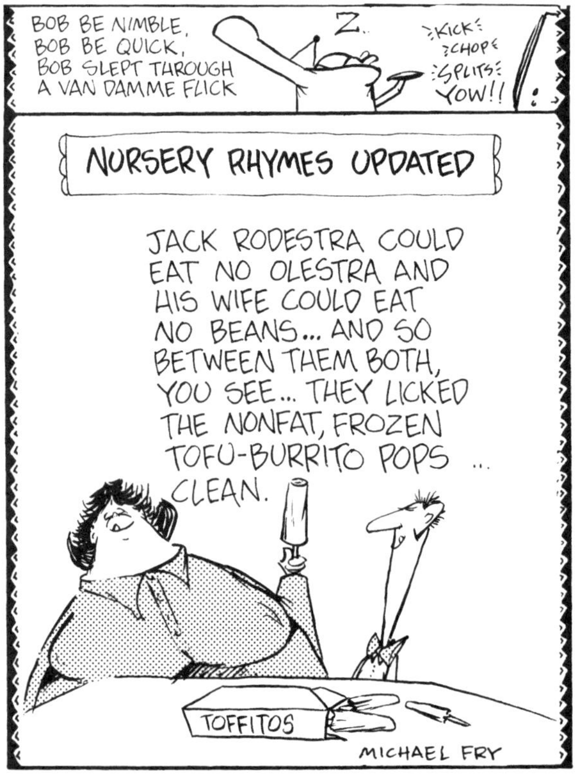
BOB BE NIMBLE, BOB BE QUICK, BOB SLEPT THROUGH A VAN DAMME FLICK
Z.
KICK
CHOP
SPLITS
YOW!!
NURSERY RHYMES UPDATED
JACK RODESTRA COULD EAT NO OLESTRA AND HIS WIFE COULD EAT NO BEANS... AND SO BETWEEN THEM BOTH, YOU SEE... THEY LICKED THE NONFAT, FROZEN TOFU-BURRITO POPS ... CLEAN.
TOFFITOS
MICHAEL FRY

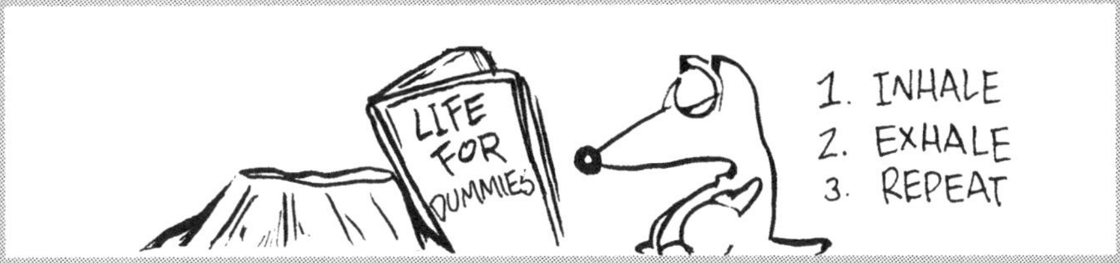
LIFE FOR DUMMIES
1. INHALE
2. EXHALE
3. REPEAT

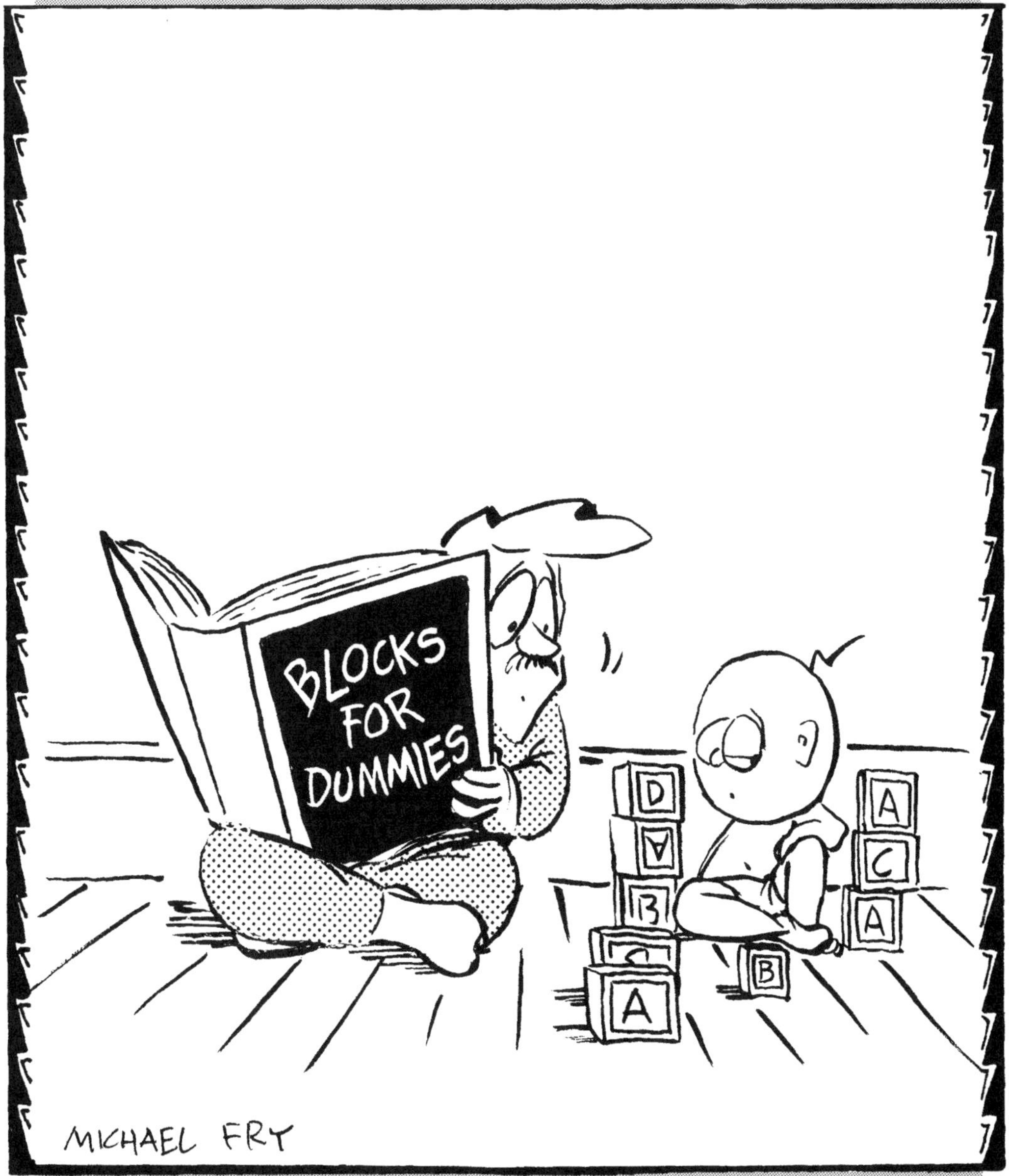
BLOCKS FOR DUMMIES
MICHAEL FRY

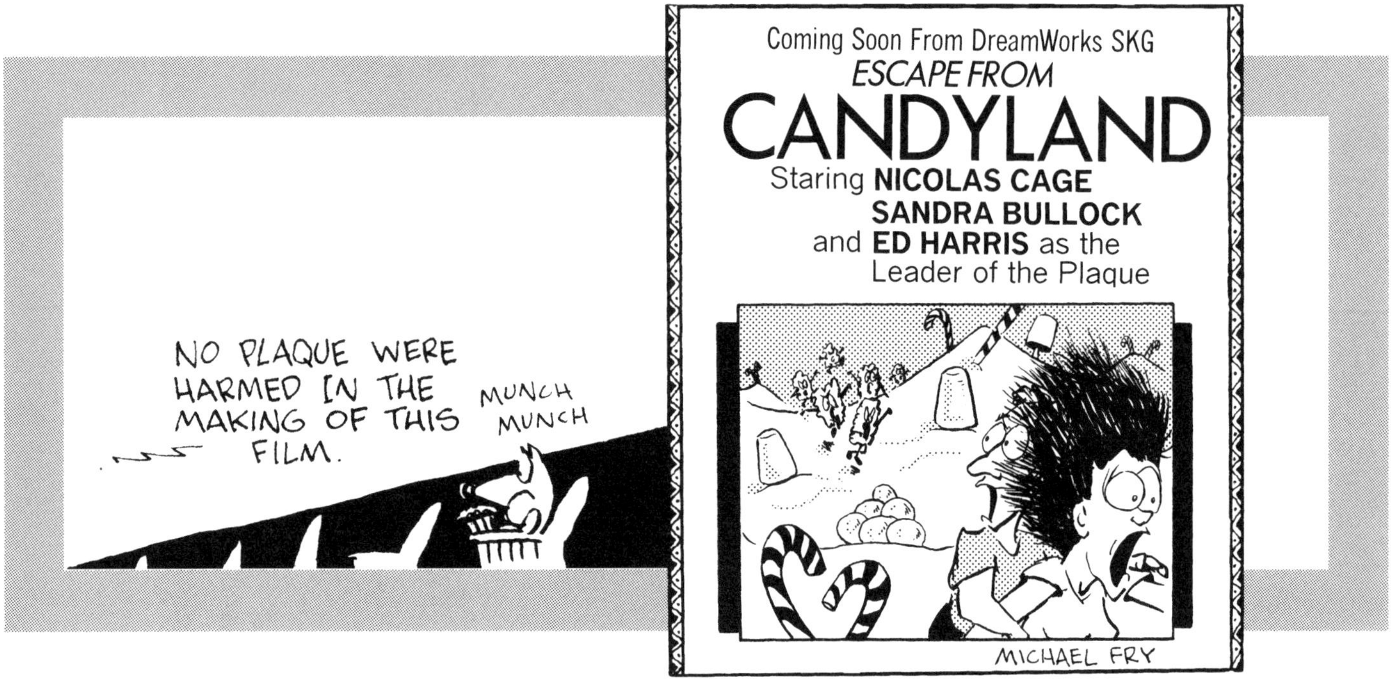

Coming Soon From DreamWorks SKG
ESCAPE FROM
CANDYLAND
Staring NICOLAS CAGE
SANDRA BULLOCK
and ED HARRIS as the
Leader of the Plaque
NO PLAQUE WERE HARMED IN THE MAKING OF THIS FILM.
MUNCH MUNCH
MICHAEL FRY

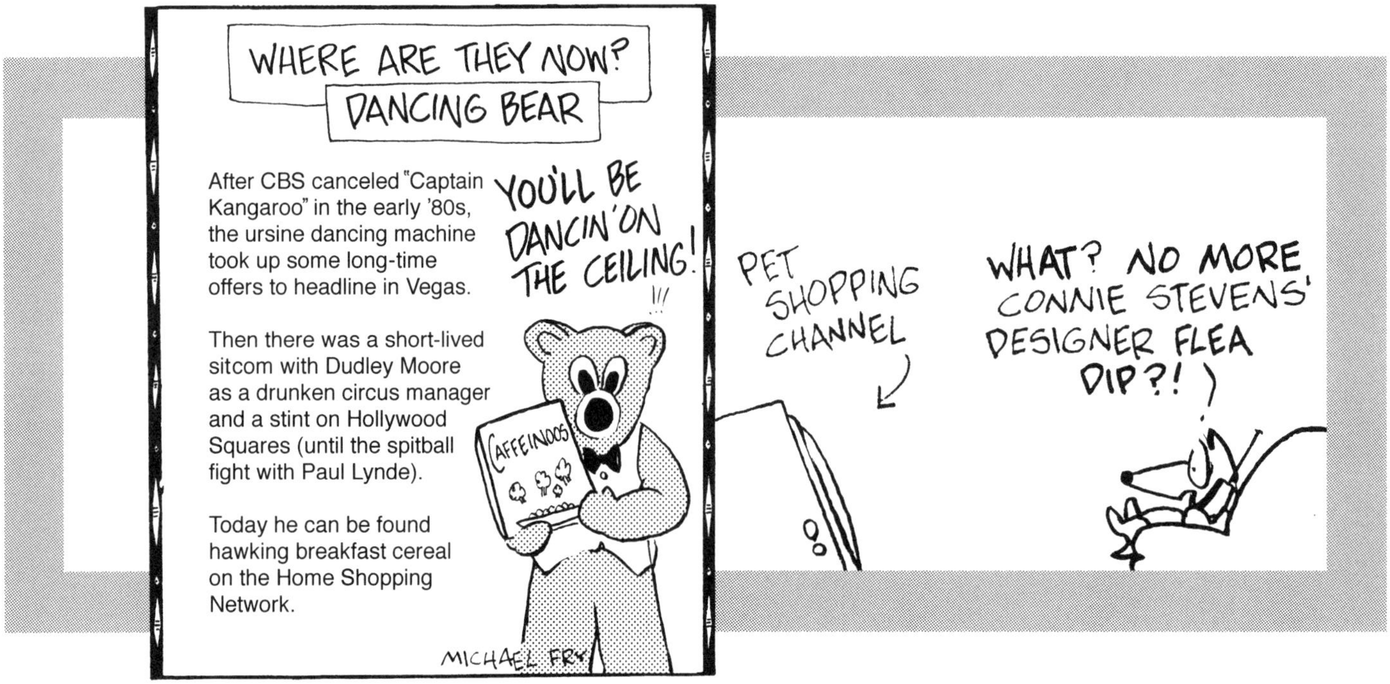

WHERE ARE THEY NOW?
DANCING BEAR
After CBS canceled "Captain Kangaroo" in the early '80s, the ursine dancing machine took up some long-time offers to headline in Vegas.
Then there was a short-lived sitcom with Dudley Moore as a drunken circus manager and a stint on Hollywood Squares (until the spitball fight with Paul Lynde).
Today he can be found hawking breakfast cereal on the Home Shopping Network.
YOU'LL BE DANCIN' ON THE CEILING!
CAFFEINOOS
MICHAEL FRY
PET SHOPPING CHANNEL
WHAT? NO MORE CONNIE STEVENS' DESIGNER FLEA DIP?!

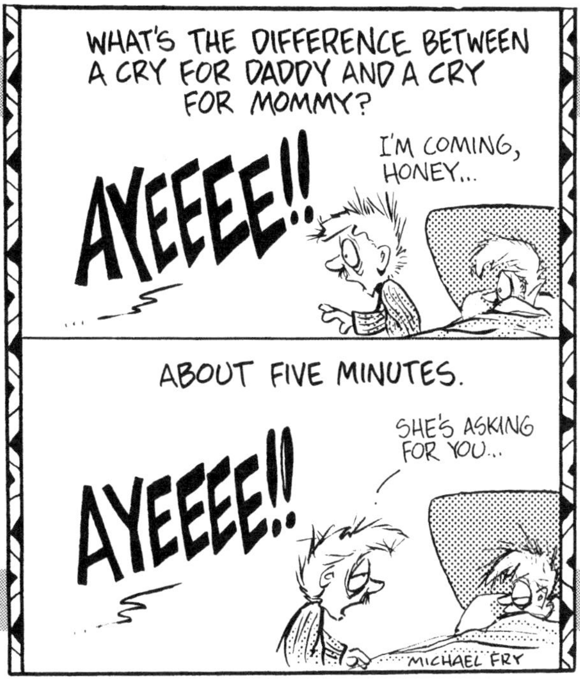
WHAT'S THE DIFFERENCE BETWEEN A CRY FOR DADDY AND A CRY FOR MOMMY?
AYEEEE!!
I'M COMING, HONEY...
ABOUT FIVE MINUTES.
AYEEEE!!
SHE'S ASKING FOR YOU...
MICHAEL FRY

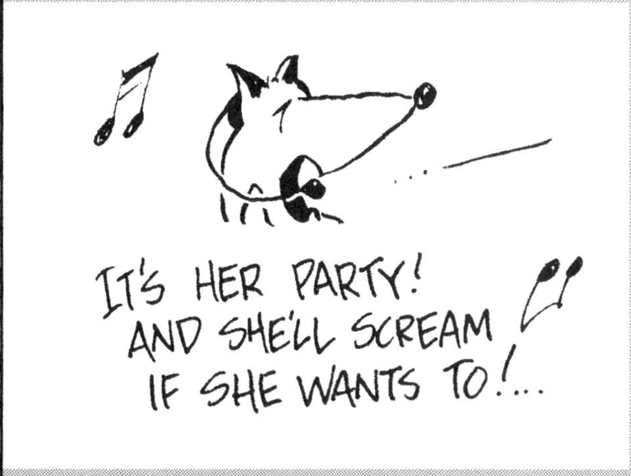
IT'S HER PARTY! AND SHE'LL SCREAM IF SHE WANTS TO!...

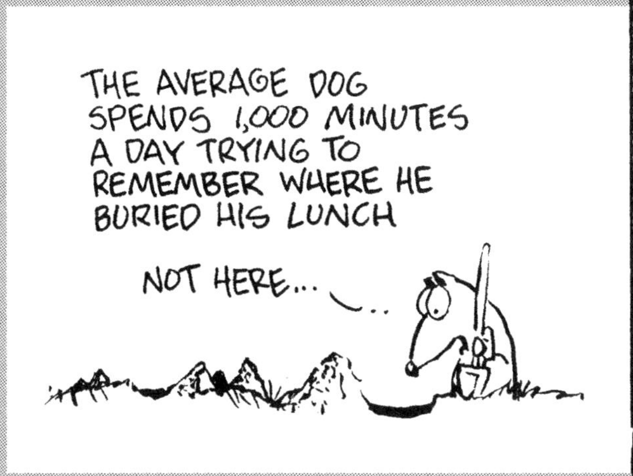
THE AVERAGE DOG SPENDS 1,000 MINUTES A DAY TRYING TO REMEMBER WHERE HE BURIED HIS LUNCH
NOT HERE...

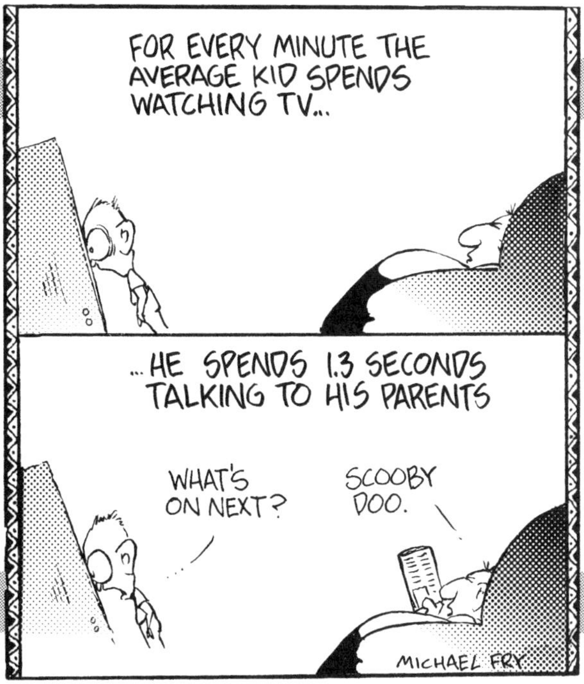
FOR EVERY MINUTE THE AVERAGE KID SPENDS WATCHING TV...
...HE SPENDS 1.3 SECONDS TALKING TO HIS PARENTS
WHAT'S ON NEXT?
SCOOBY DOO.
MICHAEL FRY

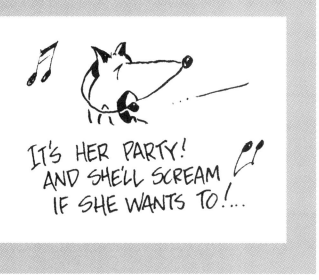

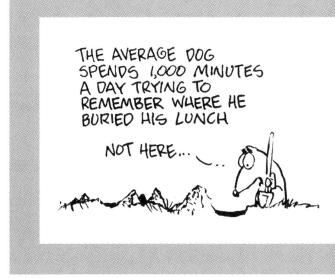

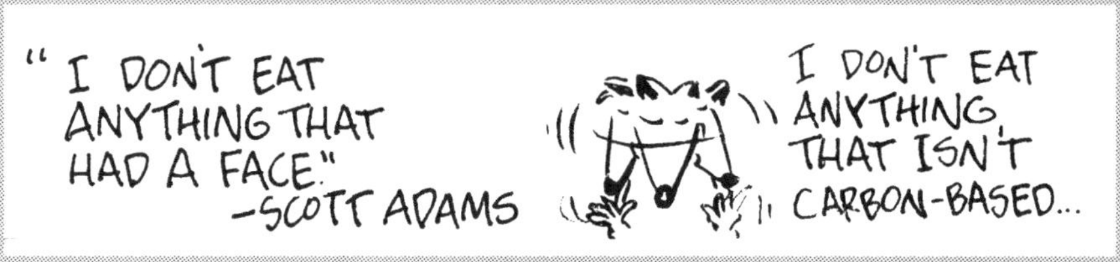
"I DON'T EAT ANYTHING THAT HAD A FACE." -SCOTT ADAMS
I DON'T EAT ANYTHING THAT ISN'T CARBON-BASED...

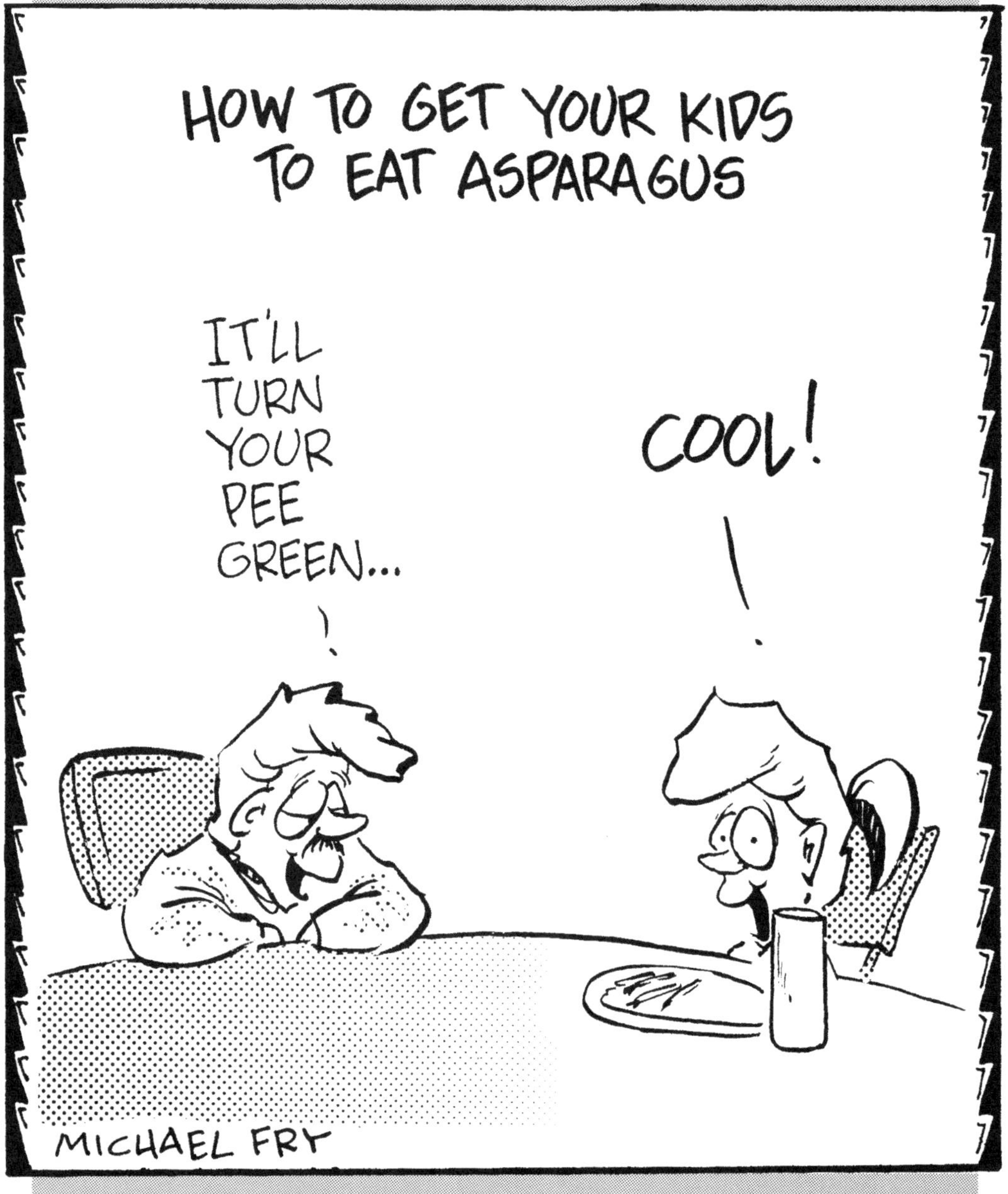
HOW TO GET YOUR KIDS TO EAT ASPARAGUS
IT'LL TURN YOUR PEE GREEN...
COOL!
MICHAEL FRY

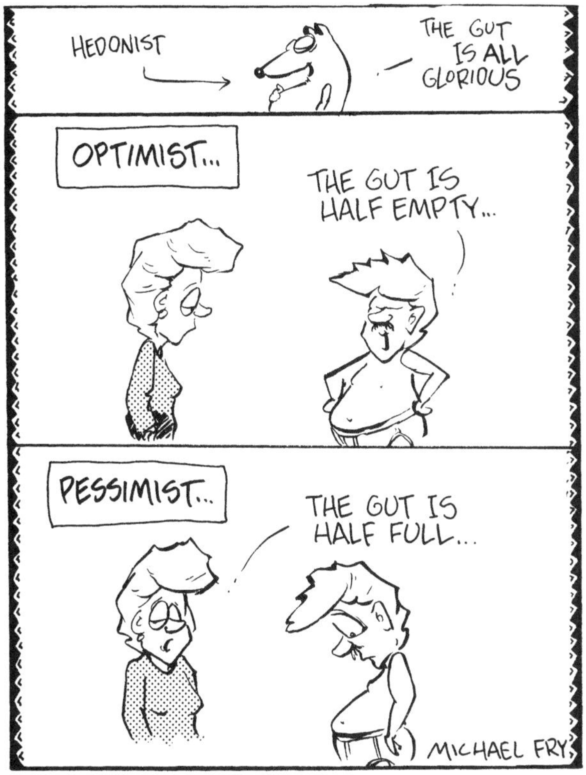
HEDONIST
THE GUT IS ALL GLORIOUS
OPTIMIST...
THE GUT IS HALF EMPTY...
PESSIMIST...
THE GUT IS HALF FULL...
MICHAEL FRY

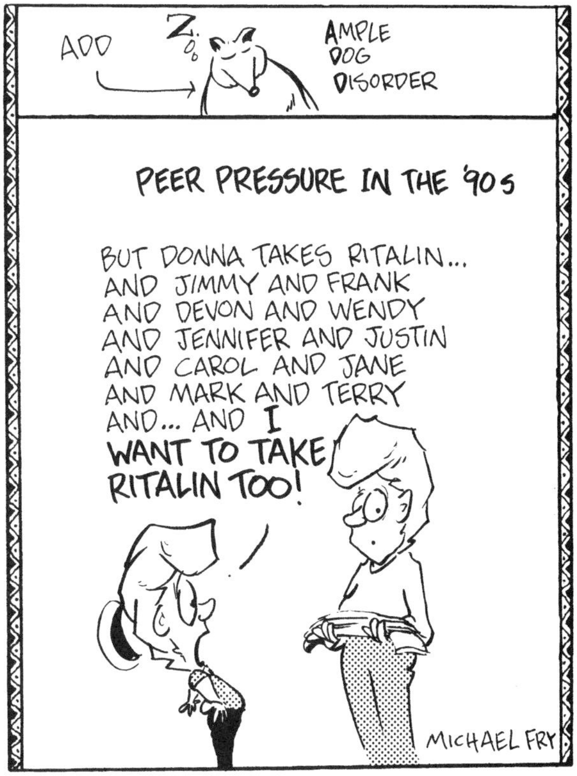
ADD
Z
AMPLE DOG DISORDER
PEER PRESSURE IN THE '90s
BUT DONNA TAKES RITALIN... AND JIMMY AND FRANK AND DEVON AND WENDY AND JENNIFER AND JUSTIN AND CAROL AND JANE AND MARK AND TERRY AND... AND I WANT TO TAKE RITALIN TOO!
MICHAEL FRY

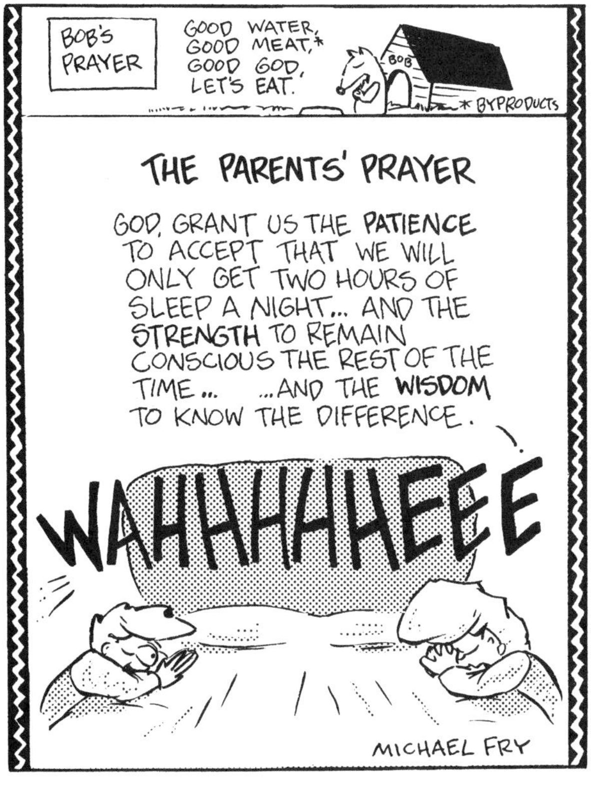
BOB'S PRAYER
GOOD WATER, GOOD MEAT,* GOOD GOD, LET'S EAT.
BOB
* BYPRODUCTS
THE PARENTS' PRAYER
GOD, GRANT US THE PATIENCE TO ACCEPT THAT WE WILL ONLY GET TWO HOURS OF SLEEP A NIGHT... AND THE STRENGTH TO REMAIN CONSCIOUS THE REST OF THE TIME... ...AND THE WISDOM TO KNOW THE DIFFERENCE.
WAHHHHHEEEE
MICHAEL FRY

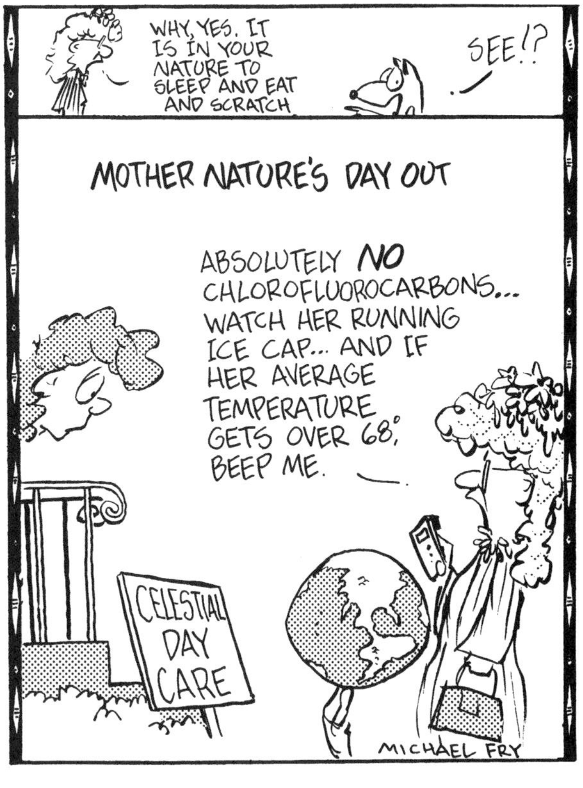
WHY, YES. IT IS IN YOUR NATURE TO SLEEP AND EAT AND SCRATCH
SEE!?
MOTHER NATURE'S DAY OUT
ABSOLUTELY NO CHLOROFLUOROCARBONS... WATCH HER RUNNING ICE CAP... AND IF HER AVERAGE TEMPERATURE GETS OVER 68°, BEEP ME.
CELESTIAL DAY CARE
MICHAEL FRY

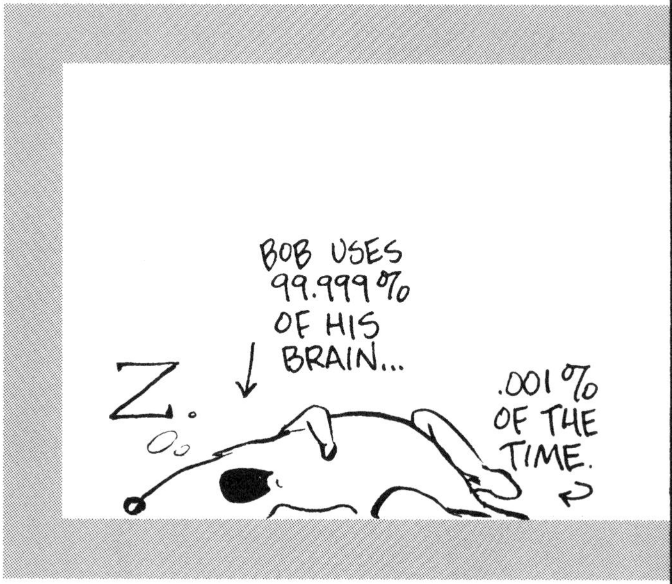
Z.
BOB USES 99.999% OF HIS BRAIN...
.001% OF THE TIME.

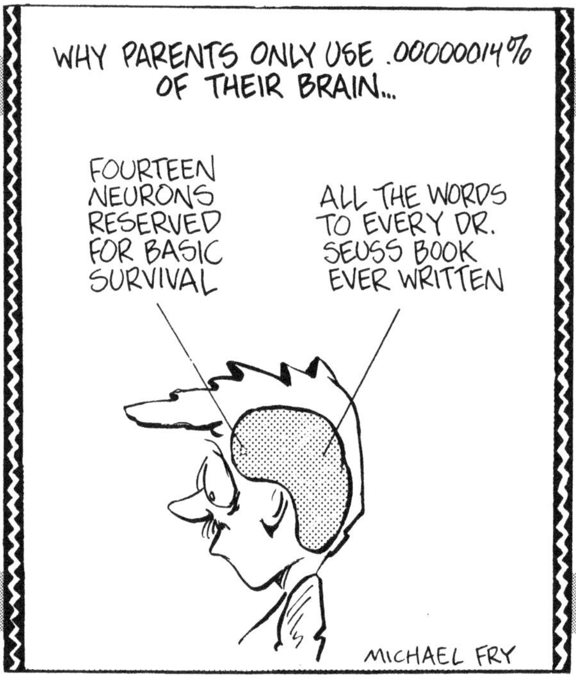
WHY PARENTS ONLY USE .00000014% OF THEIR BRAIN...
FOURTEEN NEURONS RESERVED FOR BASIC SURVIVAL
ALL THE WORDS TO EVERY DR. SEUSS BOOK EVER WRITTEN
MICHAEL FRY

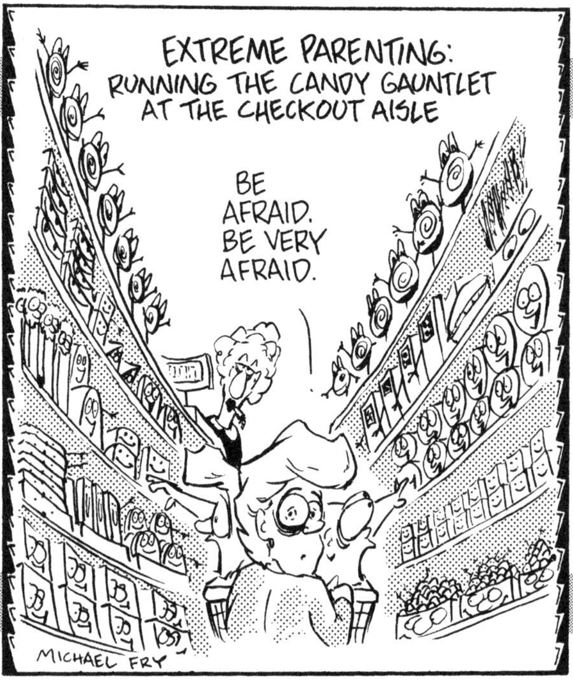
EXTREME PARENTING: RUNNING THE CANDY GAUNTLET AT THE CHECKOUT AISLE
BE AFRAID. BE VERY AFRAID.
MICHAEL FRY

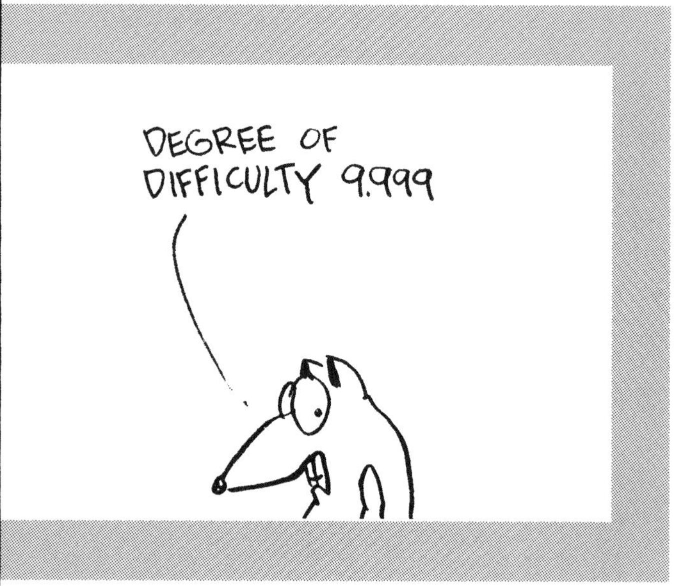
DEGREE OF DIFFICULTY 9.999

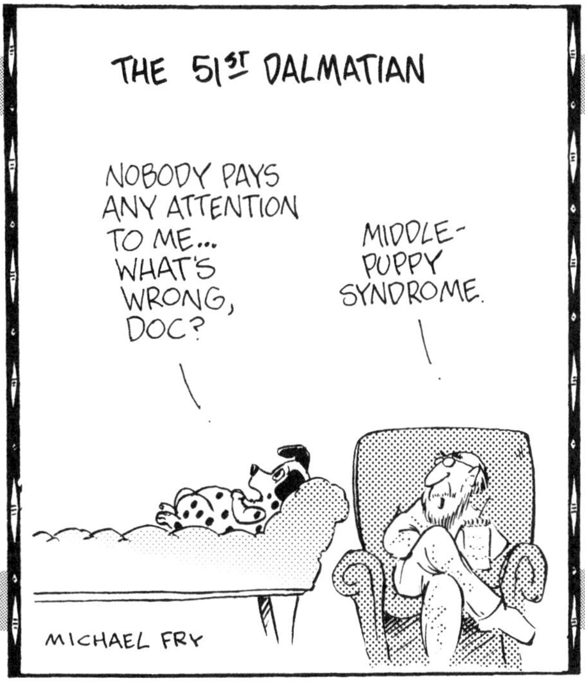
THE 51ST DALMATIAN
NOBODY PAYS ANY ATTENTION TO ME... WHAT'S WRONG, DOC?
MIDDLE-PUPPY SYNDROME.
MICHAEL FRY

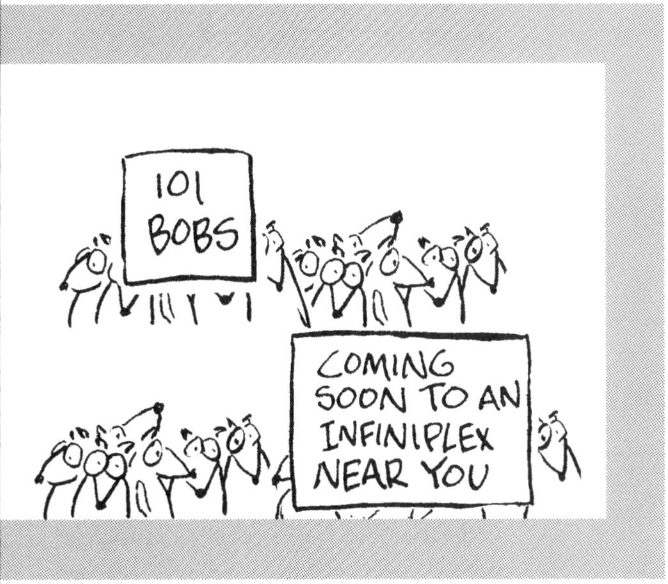
101 BOBS
COMING SOON TO AN INFINIPLEX NEAR YOU

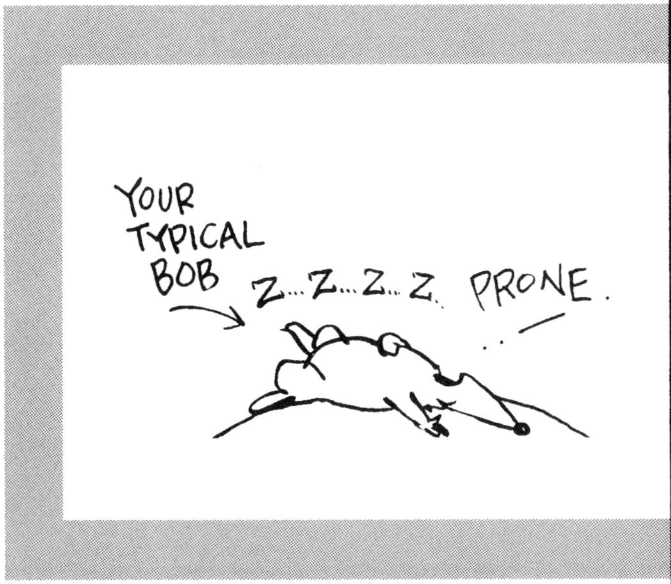
YOUR TYPICAL BOB
Z...Z...Z...Z
PRONE.

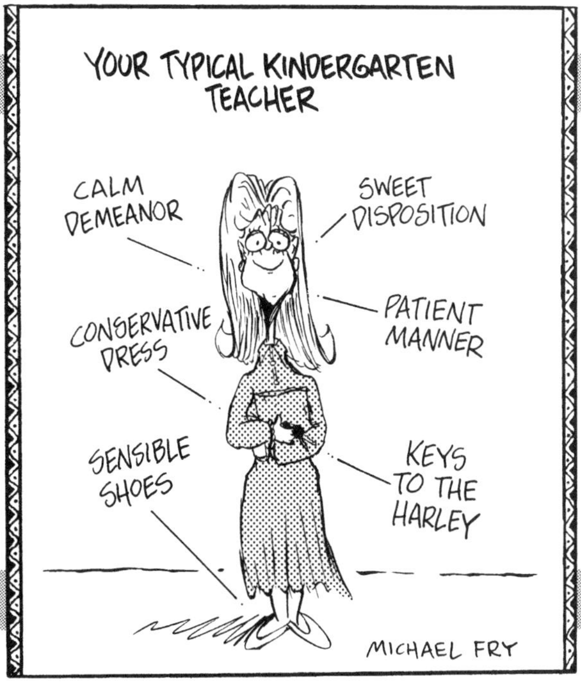
YOUR TYPICAL KINDERGARTEN TEACHER
CALM DEMEANOR
SWEET DISPOSITION
CONSERVATIVE DRESS
PATIENT MANNER
SENSIBLE SHOES
KEYS TO THE HARLEY
MICHAEL FRY

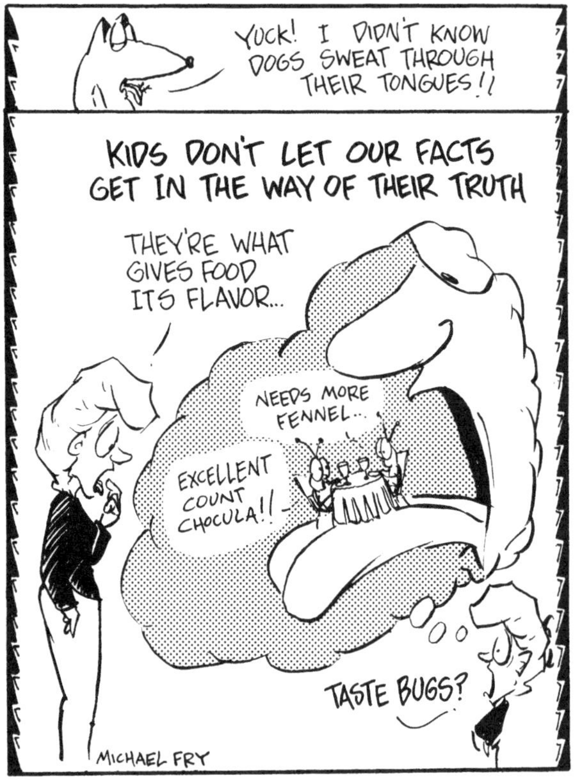
YUCK! I DIDN'T KNOW DOGS SWEAT THROUGH THEIR TONGUES!!
KIDS DON'T LET OUR FACTS GET IN THE WAY OF THEIR TRUTH
THEY'RE WHAT GIVES FOOD ITS FLAVOR...
NEEDS MORE FENNEL...
EXCELLENT COUNT CHOCULA!!
TASTE BUGS?
MICHAEL FRY

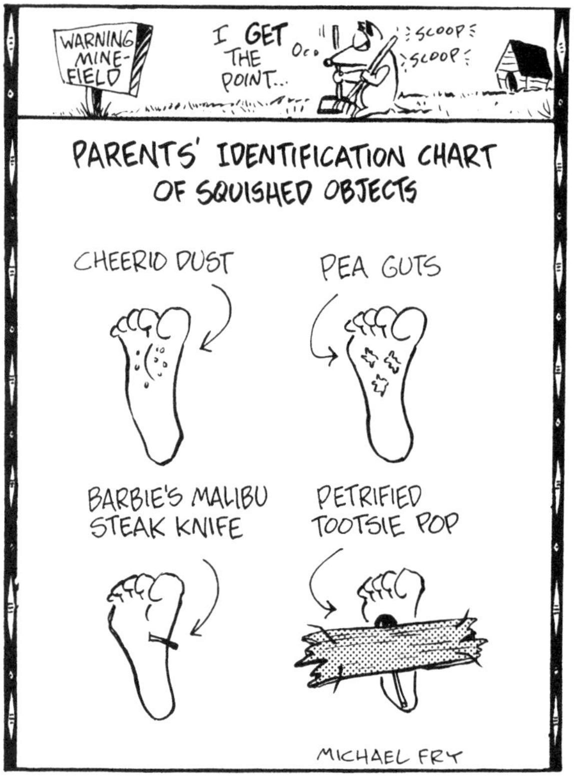
WARNING MINE-FIELD
I GET THE POINT...
SCOOP
SCOOP
PARENTS' IDENTIFICATION CHART OF SQUISHED OBJECTS
CHEERIO DUST
PEA GUTS
BARBIE'S MALIBU STEAK KNIFE
PETRIFIED TOOTSIE POP
MICHAEL FRY

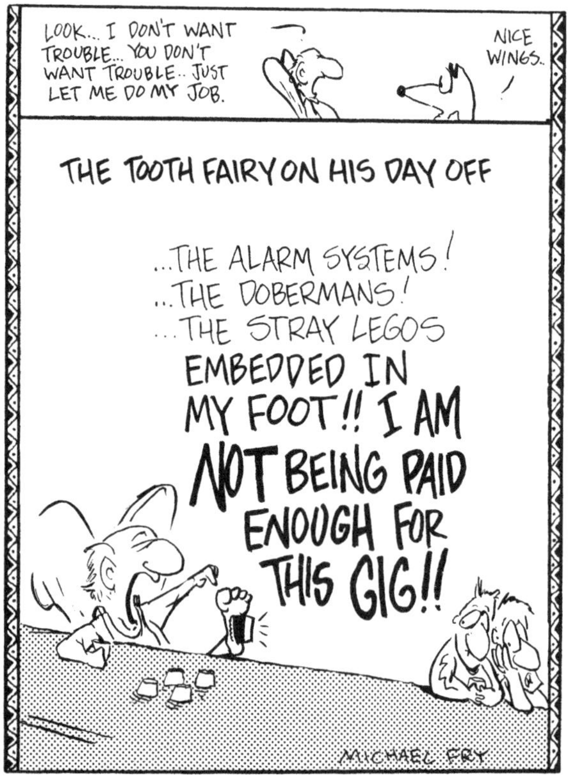
LOOK... I DON'T WANT TROUBLE... YOU DON'T WANT TROUBLE... JUST LET ME DO MY JOB.
NICE WINGS.
THE TOOTH FAIRY ON HIS DAY OFF
...THE ALARM SYSTEMS!
...THE DOBERMANS!
...THE STRAY LEGOS EMBEDDED IN MY FOOT!! I AM NOT BEING PAID ENOUGH FOR THIS GIG!!
MICHAEL FRY

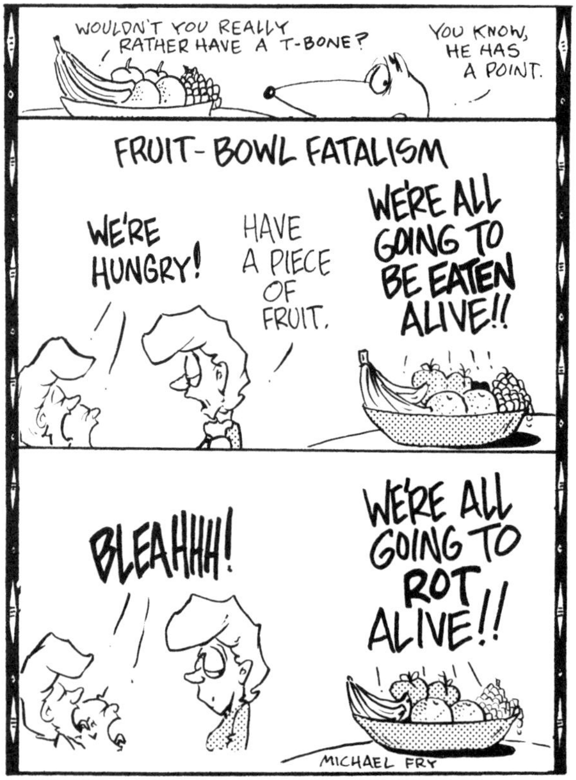
WOULDN'T YOU REALLY RATHER HAVE A T-BONE?
YOU KNOW, HE HAS A POINT.
FRUIT-BOWL FATALISM
WE'RE HUNGRY!
HAVE A PIECE OF FRUIT.
WE'RE ALL GOING TO BE EATEN ALIVE!!
BLEAHHH!
WE'RE ALL GOING TO ROT ALIVE!!
MICHAEL FRY

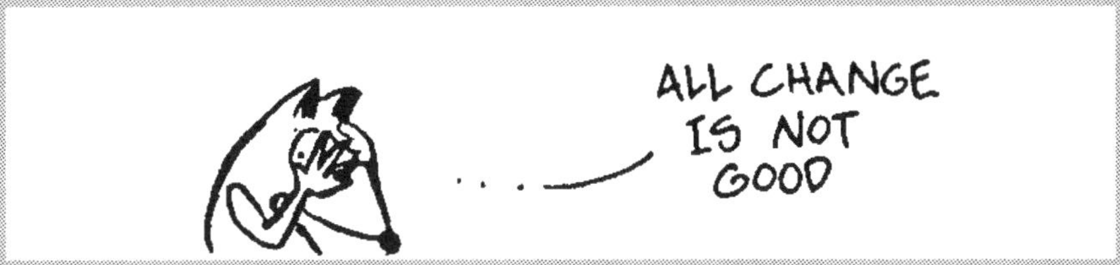
ALL CHANGE IS NOT GOOD

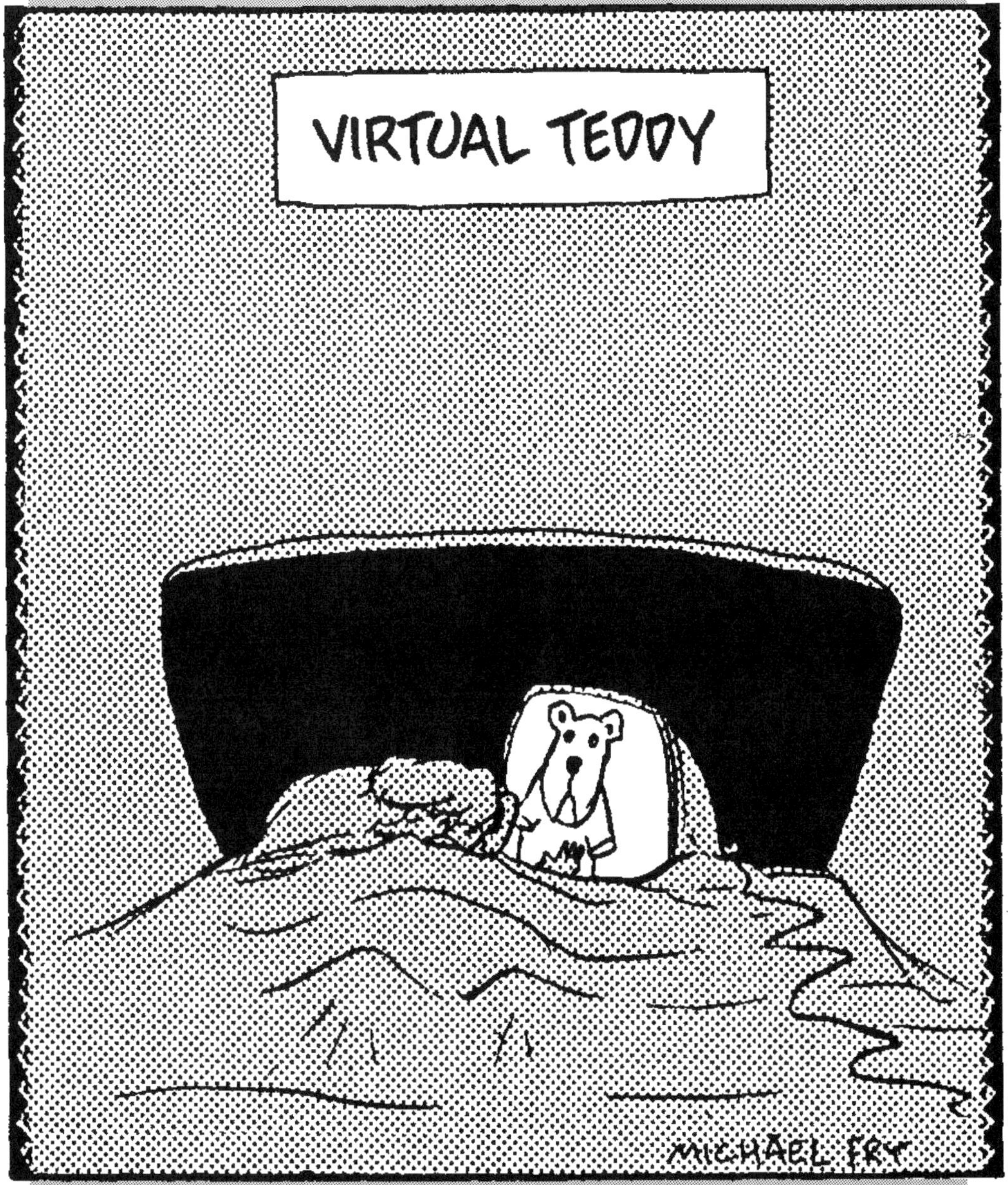
VIRTUAL TEDDY
MICHAEL FRY

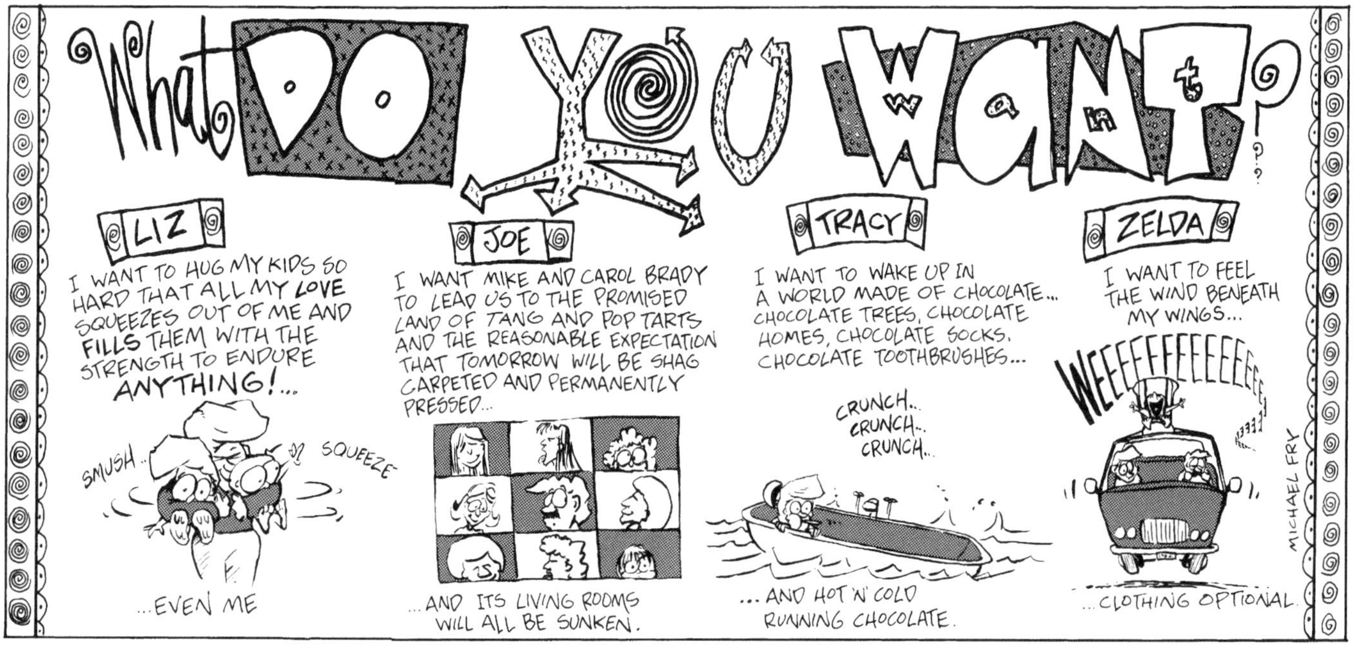
What DO YOU WANT?
LIZ
I WANT TO HUG MY KIDS SO HARD THAT ALL MY LOVE SQUEEZES OUT OF ME AND FILLS THEM WITH THE STRENGTH TO ENDURE ANYTHING!...
SMUSH..
SQUEEZE
...EVEN ME
JOE
I WANT MIKE AND CAROL BRADY TO LEAD US TO THE PROMISED LAND OF TANG AND POP TARTS AND THE REASONABLE EXPECTATION THAT TOMORROW WILL BE SHAG CARPETED AND PERMANENTLY PRESSED...
...AND ITS LIVING ROOMS WILL ALL BE SUNKEN.
TRACY
I WANT TO WAKE UP IN A WORLD MADE OF CHOCOLATE... CHOCOLATE TREES, CHOCOLATE HOMES, CHOCOLATE SOCKS, CHOCOLATE TOOTHBRUSHES...
CRUNCH.. CRUNCH.. CRUNCH..
...AND HOT 'N' COLD RUNNING CHOCOLATE.
ZELDA
I WANT TO FEEL THE WIND BENEATH MY WINGS...
WEEEEEEEEEEEEEEE
...CLOTHING OPTIONAL.
MICHAEL FRY

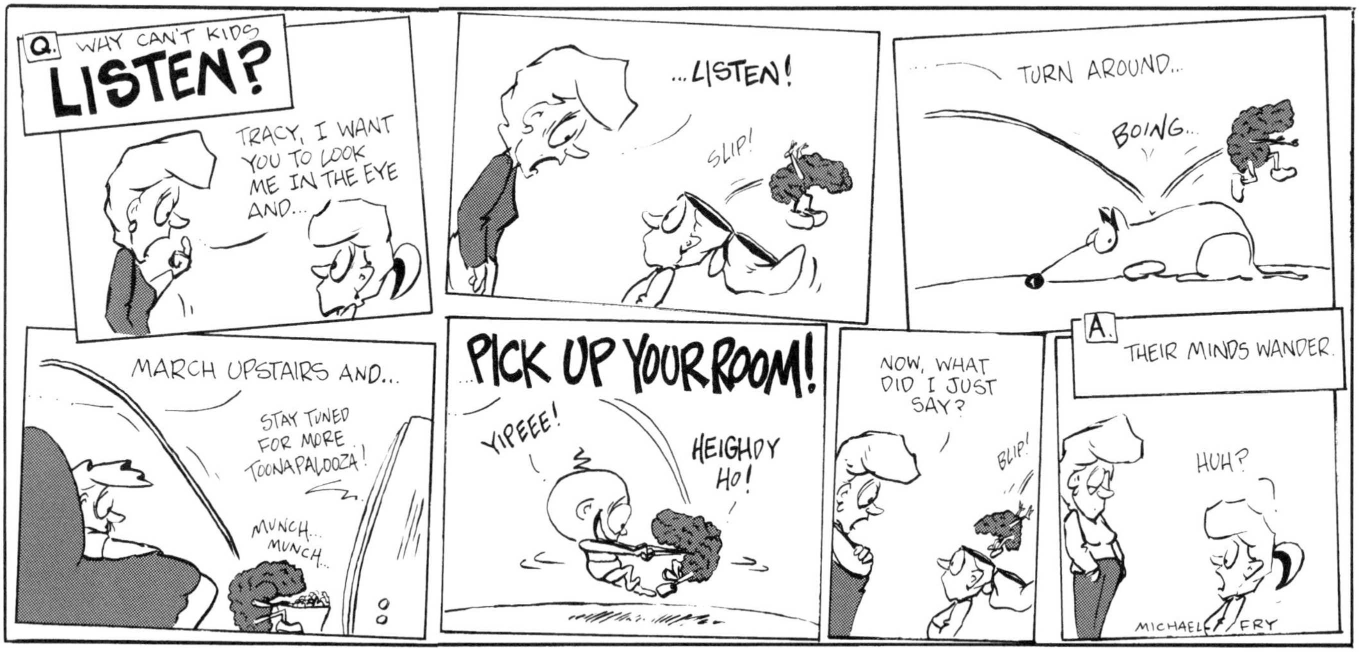
Q. WHY CAN'T KIDS LISTEN?
TRACY, I WANT YOU TO LOOK ME IN THE EYE AND...
...LISTEN!
SLIP!
TURN AROUND...
BOING..
MARCH UPSTAIRS AND...
STAY TUNED FOR MORE TOONAPALOOZA!
MUNCH... MUNCH...
...PICK UP YOUR ROOM!
YIPEEE!
HEIGHDY HO!
NOW, WHAT DID I JUST SAY?
BLIP!
A. THEIR MINDS WANDER.
HUH?
MICHAEL FRY

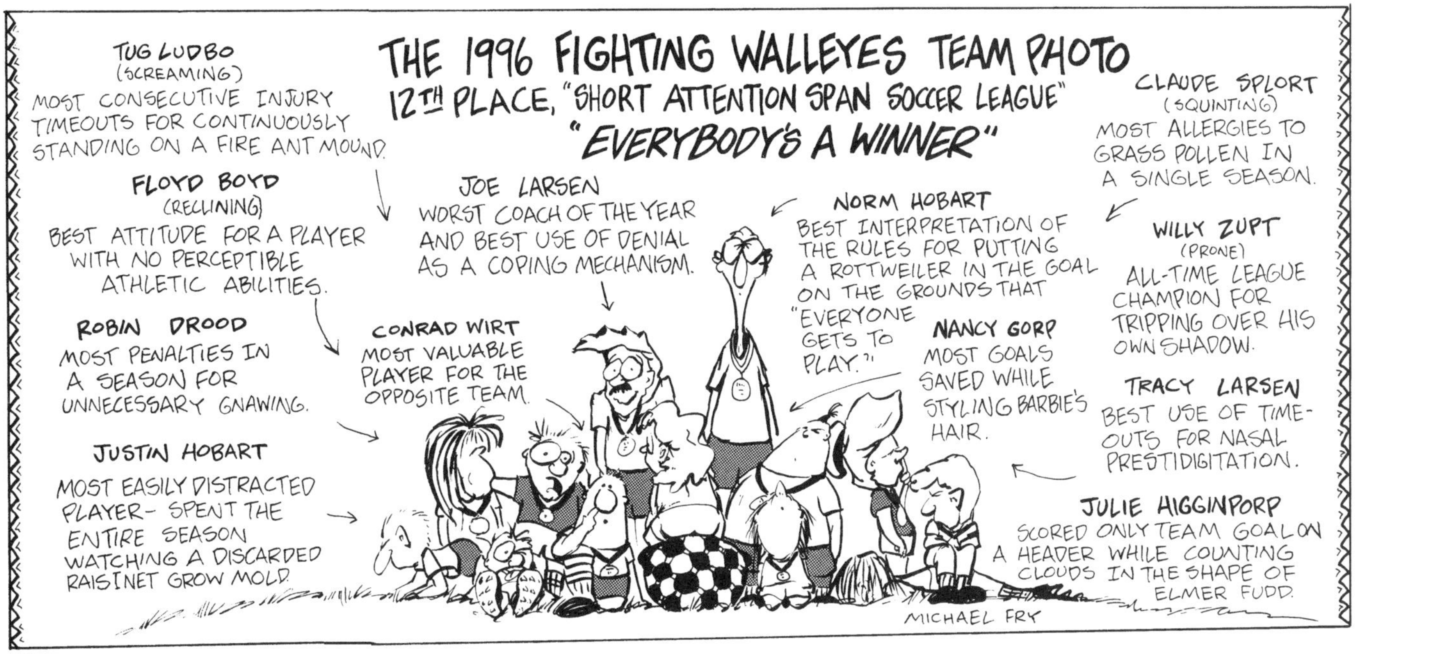
THE 1996 FIGHTING WALLEYES TEAM PHOTO
12TH PLACE, "SHORT ATTENTION SPAN SOCCER LEAGUE"
"EVERYBODY'S A WINNER"
TUG LUDBO (SCREAMING) MOST CONSECUTIVE INJURY TIMEOUTS FOR CONTINUOUSLY STANDING ON A FIRE ANT MOUND.
FLOYD BOYD (RECLINING) BEST ATTITUDE FOR A PLAYER WITH NO PERCEPTIBLE ATHLETIC ABILITIES.
ROBIN DROOD MOST PENALTIES IN A SEASON FOR UNNECESSARY GNAWING.
JUSTIN HOBART MOST EASILY DISTRACTED PLAYER- SPENT THE ENTIRE SEASON WATCHING A DISCARDED RAISINET GROW MOLD.
JOE LARSEN WORST COACH OF THE YEAR AND BEST USE OF DENIAL AS A COPING MECHANISM.
CONRAD WIRT MOST VALUABLE PLAYER FOR THE OPPOSITE TEAM.
NORM HOBART BEST INTERPRETATION OF THE RULES FOR PUTTING A ROTTWEILER IN THE GOAL ON THE GROUNDS THAT "EVERYONE GETS TO PLAY."
NANCY GORP MOST GOALS SAVED WHILE STYLING BARBIE'S HAIR.
CLAUDE SPLORT (SQUINTING) MOST ALLERGIES TO GRASS POLLEN IN A SINGLE SEASON.
WILLY ZUPT (PRONE) ALL-TIME LEAGUE CHAMPION FOR TRIPPING OVER HIS OWN SHADOW.
TRACY LARSEN BEST USE OF TIME-OUTS FOR NASAL PRESTIDIGITATION.
JULIE HIGGINPORP SCORED ONLY TEAM GOAL ON A HEADER WHILE COUNTING CLOUDS IN THE SHAPE OF ELMER FUDD.
MICHAEL FRY

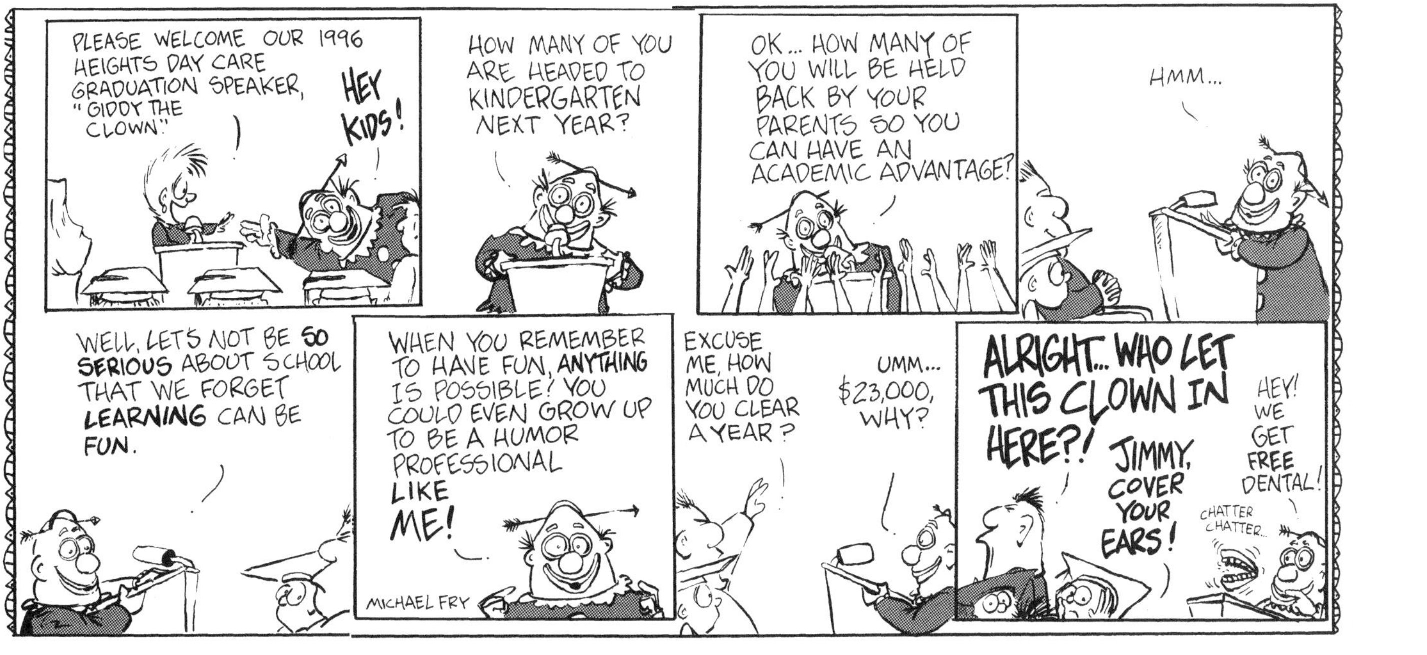
PLEASE WELCOME OUR 1996 HEIGHTS DAY CARE GRADUATION SPEAKER, "GIDDY THE CLOWN."
HEY KIDS!
HOW MANY OF YOU ARE HEADED TO KINDERGARTEN NEXT YEAR?
OK... HOW MANY OF YOU WILL BE HELD BACK BY YOUR PARENTS SO YOU CAN HAVE AN ACADEMIC ADVANTAGE?
HMM...
WELL, LET'S NOT BE SO SERIOUS ABOUT SCHOOL THAT WE FORGET LEARNING CAN BE FUN.
WHEN YOU REMEMBER TO HAVE FUN, ANYTHING IS POSSIBLE! YOU COULD EVEN GROW UP TO BE A HUMOR PROFESSIONAL LIKE ME!
MICHAEL FRY
EXCUSE ME, HOW MUCH DO YOU CLEAR A YEAR?
UMM... $23,000, WHY?
ALRIGHT... WHO LET THIS CLOWN IN HERE?!
JIMMY, COVER YOUR EARS!
HEY! WE GET FREE DENTAL!
CHATTER CHATTER...

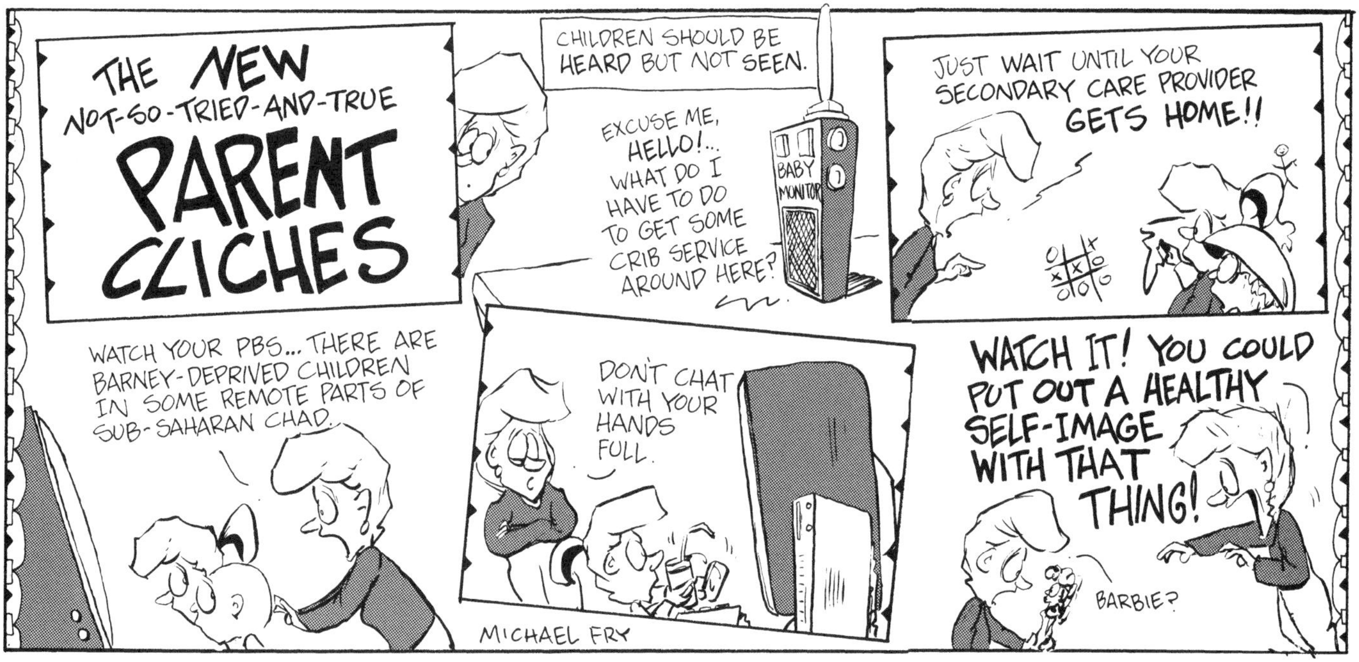
THE NEW NOT-SO-TRIED-AND-TRUE PARENT CLICHES
CHILDREN SHOULD BE HEARD BUT NOT SEEN.
EXCUSE ME, HELLO!... WHAT DO I HAVE TO DO TO GET SOME CRIB SERVICE AROUND HERE?
BABY MONITOR
JUST WAIT UNTIL YOUR SECONDARY CARE PROVIDER GETS HOME!!
WATCH YOUR PBS... THERE ARE BARNEY-DEPRIVED CHILDREN IN SOME REMOTE PARTS OF SUB-SAHARAN CHAD.
DON'T CHAT WITH YOUR HANDS FULL.
WATCH IT! YOU COULD PUT OUT A HEALTHY SELF-IMAGE WITH THAT THING!
BARBIE?
MICHAEL FRY

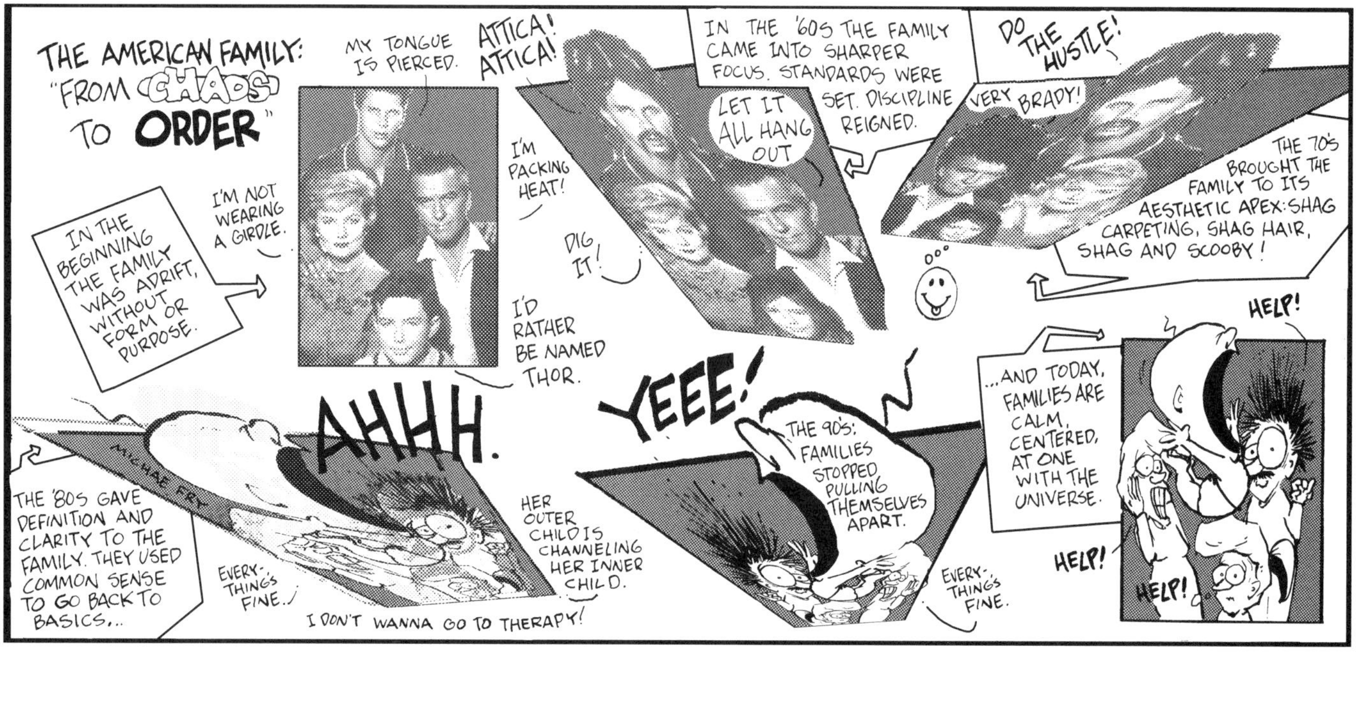
THE AMERICAN FAMILY: "FROM CHAOS TO ORDER"
IN THE BEGINNING THE FAMILY WAS ADRIFT, WITHOUT FORM OR PURPOSE.
I'M NOT WEARING A GIRDLE.
MY TONGUE IS PIERCED.
I'M PACKING HEAT!
DIG IT!
I'D RATHER BE NAMED THOR.
ATTICA! ATTICA!
LET IT ALL HANG OUT
IN THE '60S THE FAMILY CAME INTO SHARPER FOCUS. STANDARDS WERE SET. DISCIPLINE REIGNED.
DO THE HUSTLE!
VERY BRADY!
THE 70'S BROUGHT THE FAMILY TO ITS AESTHETIC APEX: SHAG CARPETING, SHAG HAIR, SHAG AND SCOOBY!
AHHH.
THE '80S GAVE DEFINITION AND CLARITY TO THE FAMILY. THEY USED COMMON SENSE TO GO BACK TO BASICS...
EVERY-THING'S FINE.
I DON'T WANNA GO TO THERAPY!
HER OUTER CHILD IS CHANNELING HER INNER CHILD.
YEEE!
THE 90'S: FAMILIES STOPPED PULLING THEMSELVES APART.
EVERY-THING'S FINE.
...AND TODAY, FAMILIES ARE CALM, CENTERED, AT ONE WITH THE UNIVERSE.
HELP!
HELP!
HELP!
MICHAEL FRY

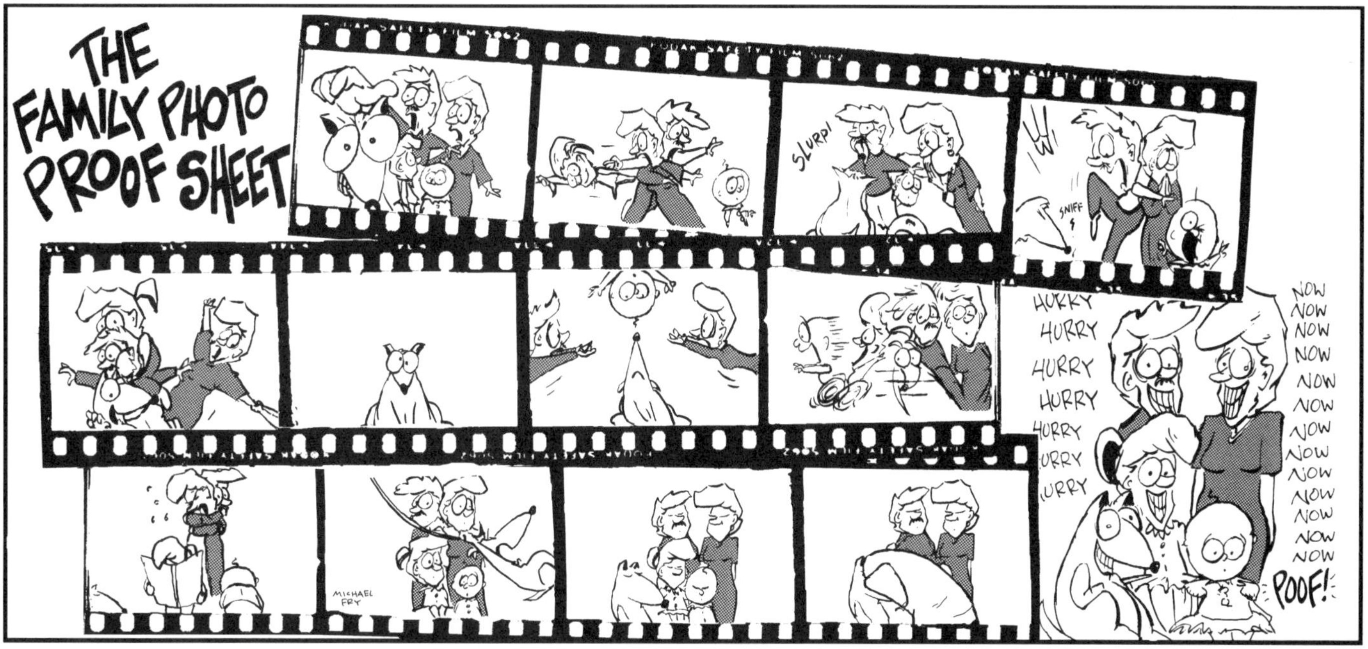
THE FAMILY PHOTO PROOF SHEET
SLURP!
SNIFF
HURRY HURRY HURRY HURRY HURRY HURRY HURRY
NOW NOW NOW NOW NOW NOW NOW NOW NOW NOW NOW NOW NOW
POOF!
MICHAEL FRY

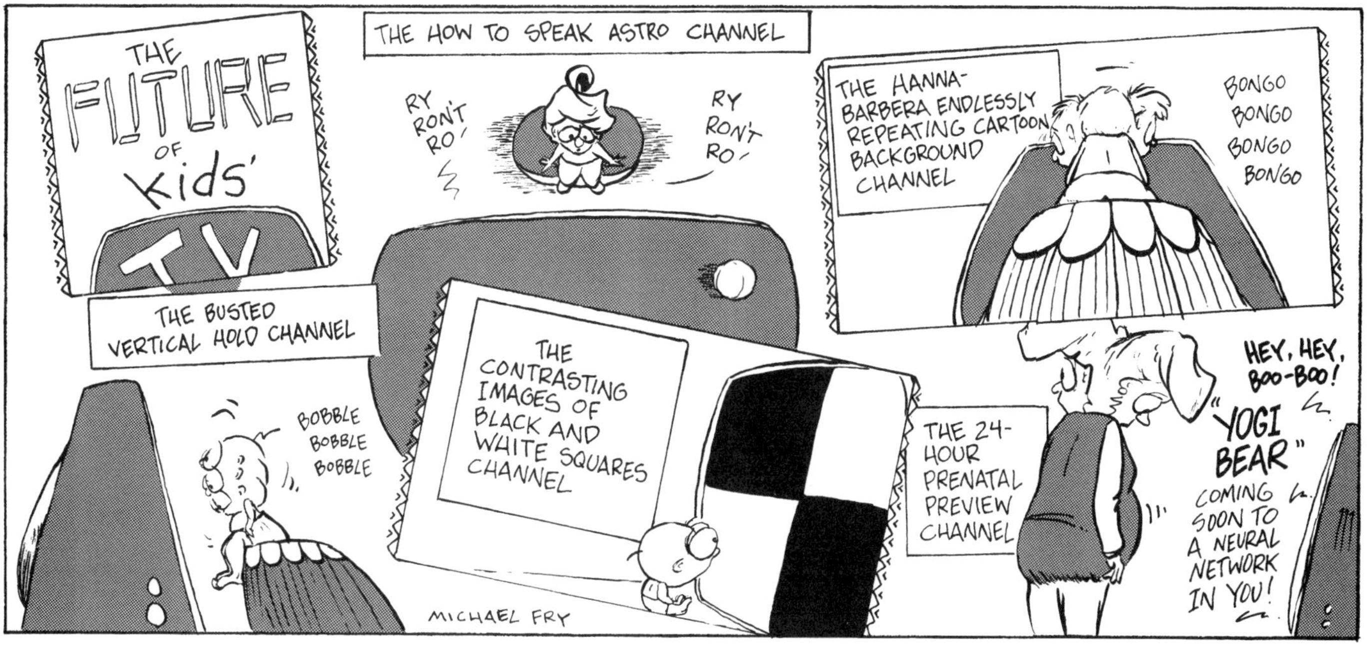
THE FUTURE OF Kids' TV
THE HOW TO SPEAK ASTRO CHANNEL
RY RON'T RO'
RY RON'T RO'
THE HANNA-BARBERA ENDLESSLY REPEATING CARTOON BACKGROUND CHANNEL
BONGO BONGO BONGO BONGO
THE BUSTED VERTICAL HOLD CHANNEL
BOBBLE BOBBLE BOBBLE
THE CONTRASTING IMAGES OF BLACK AND WHITE SQUARES CHANNEL
THE 24-HOUR PRENATAL PREVIEW CHANNEL
HEY, HEY, BOO-BOO!
"YOGI BEAR" COMING SOON TO A NEURAL NETWORK IN YOU!
MICHAEL FRY

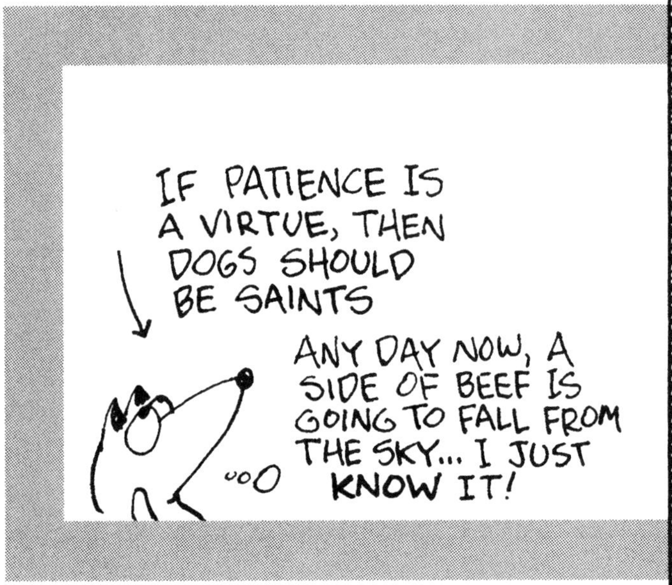
IF PATIENCE IS A VIRTUE, THEN DOGS SHOULD BE SAINTS
ANY DAY NOW, A SIDE OF BEEF IS GOING TO FALL FROM THE SKY... I JUST KNOW IT!

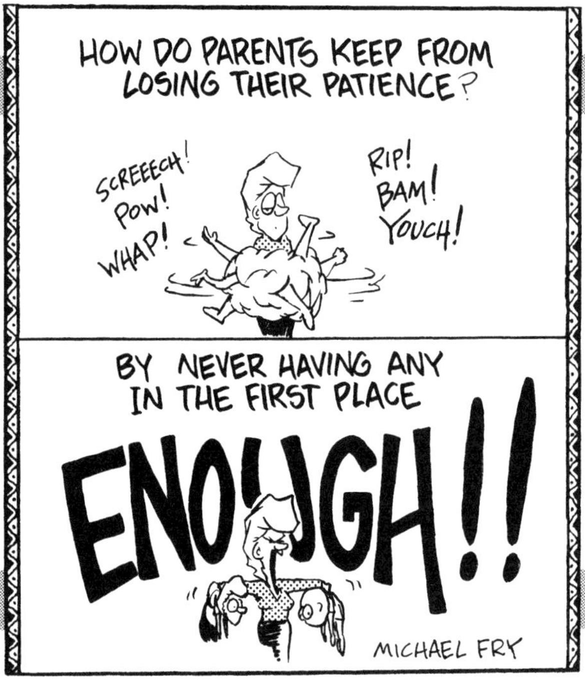
HOW DO PARENTS KEEP FROM LOSING THEIR PATIENCE?
SCREEECH! POW! WHAP!
RIP! BAM! YOUCH!
BY NEVER HAVING ANY IN THE FIRST PLACE
ENOUGH!!
MICHAEL FRY

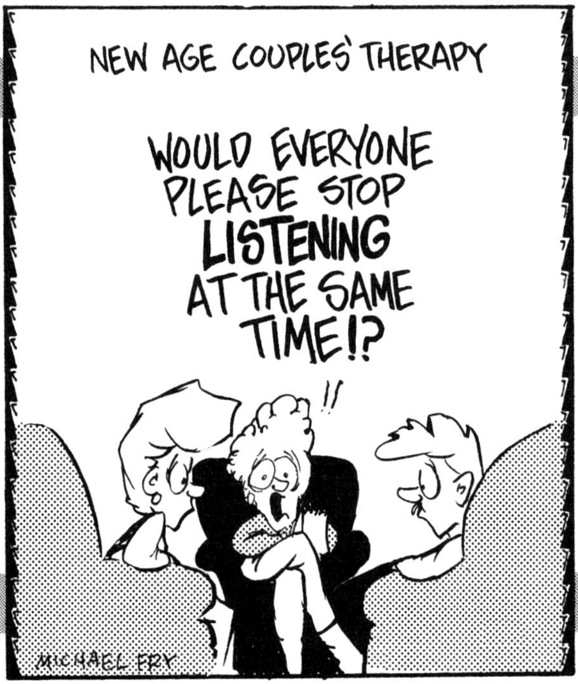
NEW AGE COUPLES' THERAPY
WOULD EVERYONE PLEASE STOP LISTENING AT THE SAME TIME!?
MICHAEL FRY

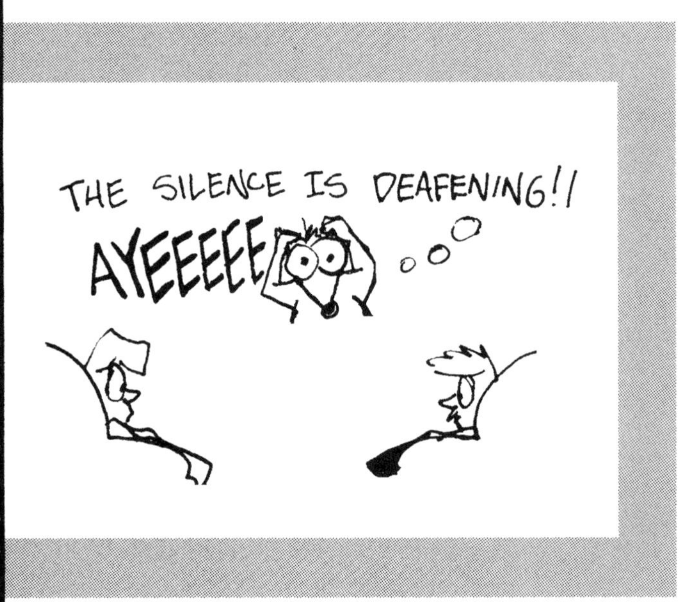
THE SILENCE IS DEAFENING!!
AYEEEEE

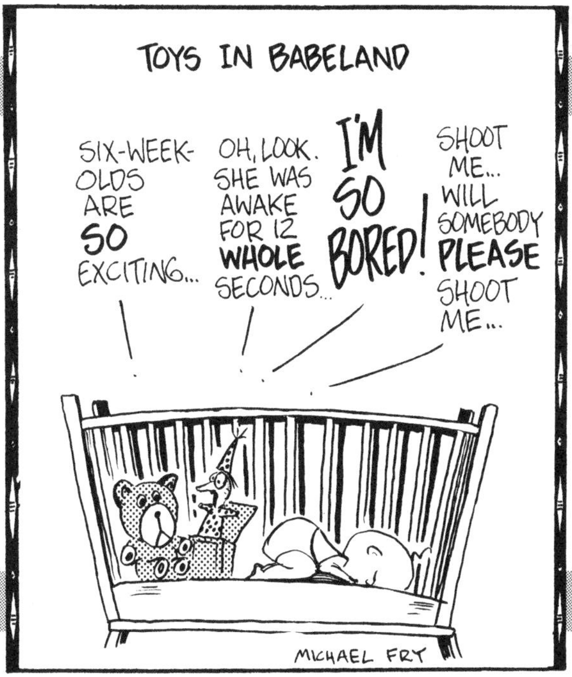
TOYS IN BABELAND
SIX-WEEK-OLDS ARE SO EXCITING...
OH, LOOK. SHE WAS AWAKE FOR 12 WHOLE SECONDS...
I'M SO BORED!
SHOOT ME... WILL SOMEBODY PLEASE SHOOT ME...
MICHAEL FRY

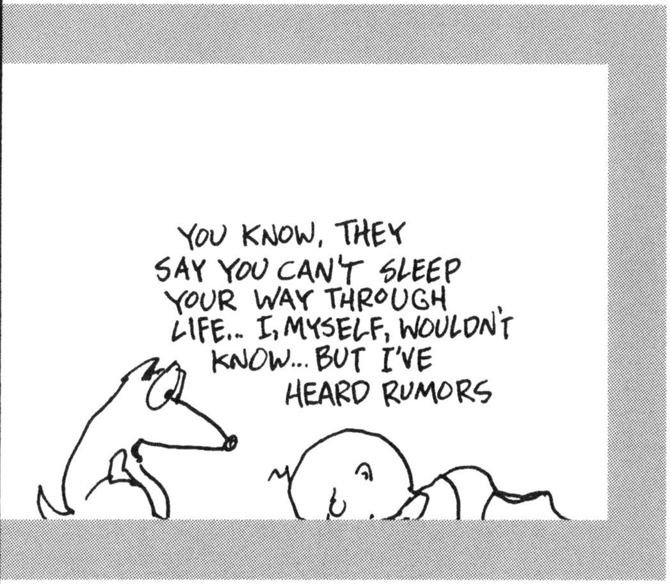
YOU KNOW, THEY SAY YOU CAN'T SLEEP YOUR WAY THROUGH LIFE... I, MYSELF, WOULDN'T KNOW... BUT I'VE HEARD RUMORS

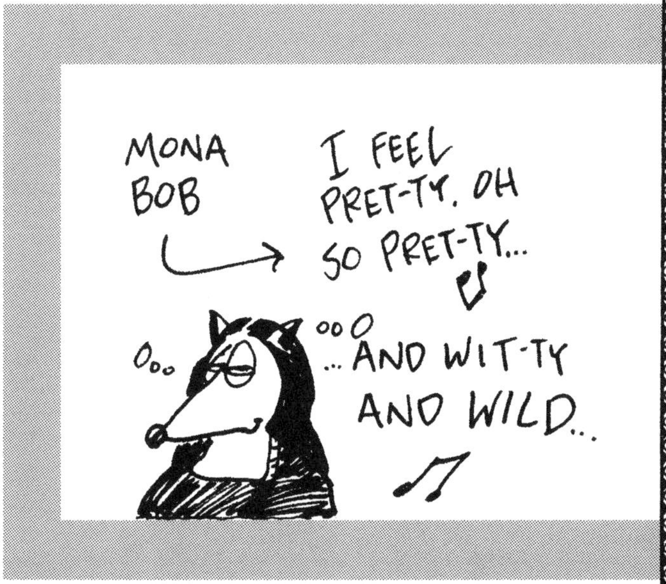
MONA BOB
I FEEL PRET-TY, OH SO PRET-TY...
...AND WIT-TY AND WILD...

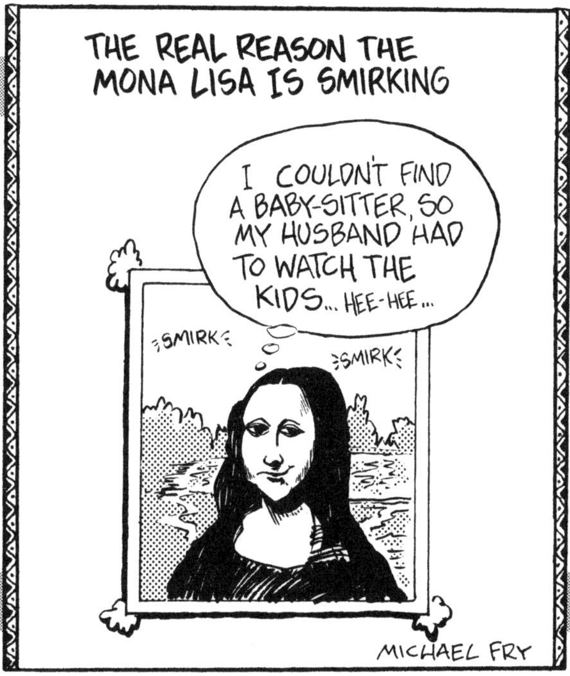
THE REAL REASON THE MONA LISA IS SMIRKING
I COULDN'T FIND A BABY-SITTER, SO MY HUSBAND HAD TO WATCH THE KIDS... HEE-HEE...
SMIRK
SMIRK
MICHAEL FRY

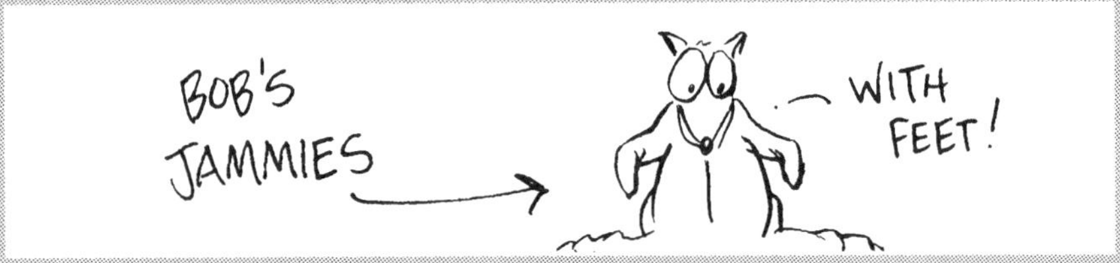
BOB'S JAMMIES
WITH FEET!

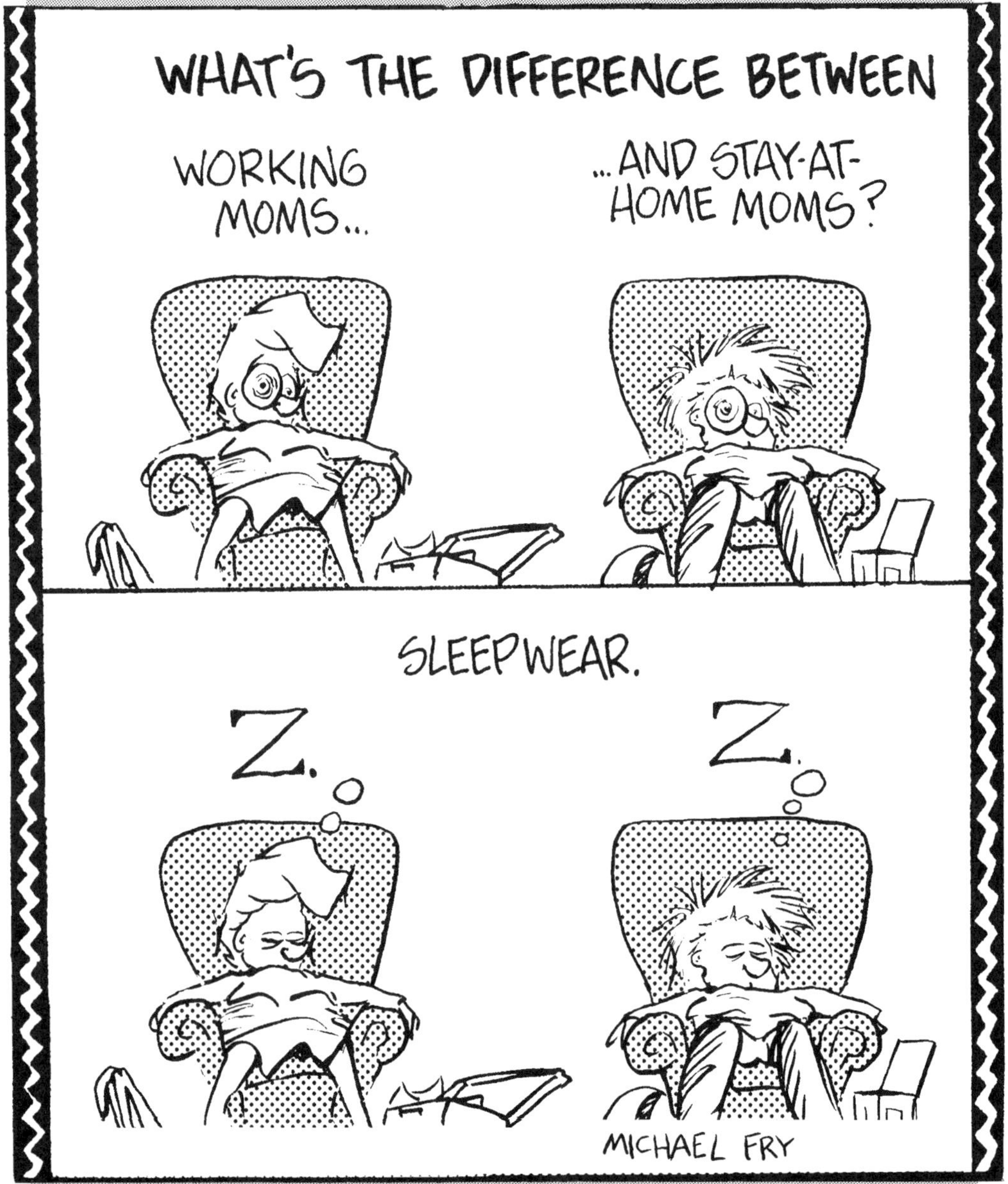
WHAT'S THE DIFFERENCE BETWEEN
WORKING MOMS...
...AND STAY-AT-HOME MOMS?
SLEEPWEAR.
Z.
Z.
MICHAEL FRY

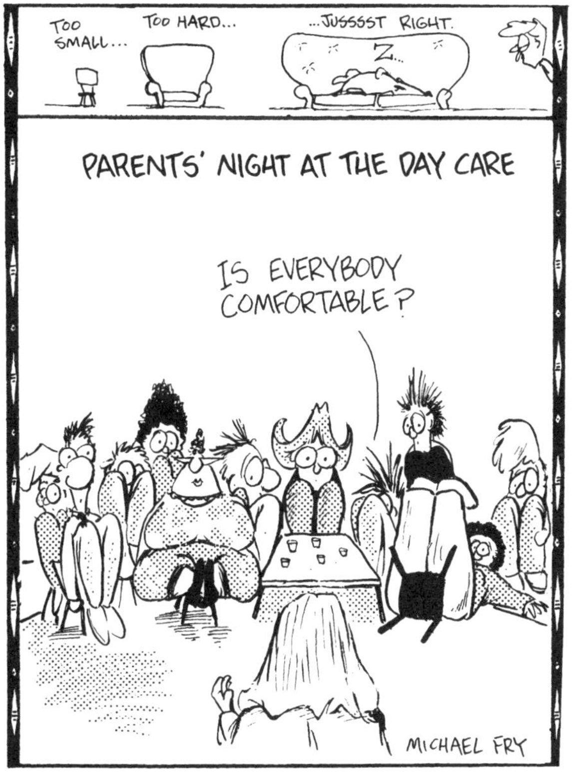
TOO SMALL...
TOO HARD...
...JUSSSST RIGHT.
Z...
PARENTS' NIGHT AT THE DAY CARE
IS EVERYBODY COMFORTABLE?
MICHAEL FRY

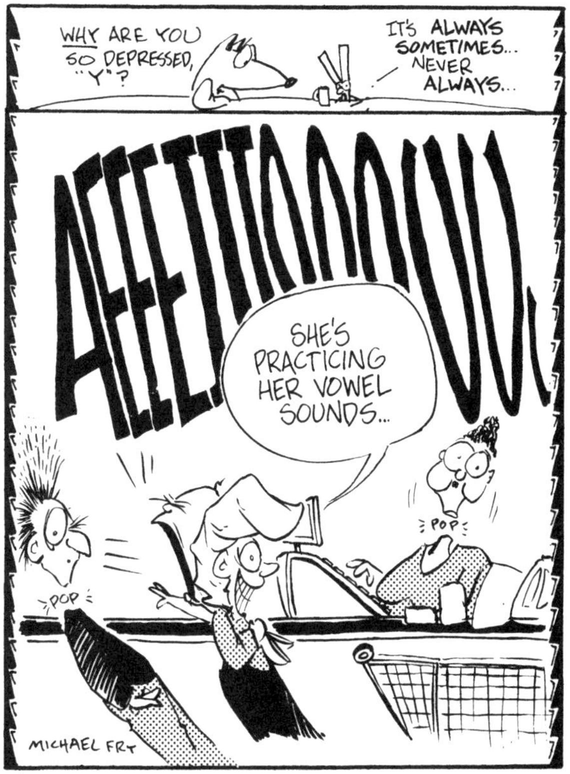
WHY ARE YOU SO DEPRESSED, "Y"?
IT'S ALWAYS SOMETIMES... NEVER ALWAYS...
AEEIIIOOOUU
SHE'S PRACTICING HER VOWEL SOUNDS...
POP
POP
MICHAEL FRY

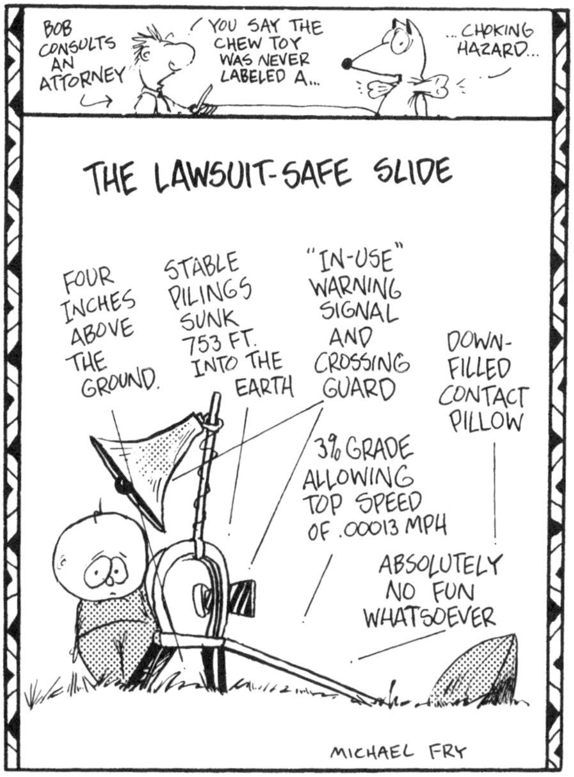
BOB CONSULTS AN ATTORNEY
YOU SAY THE CHEW TOY WAS NEVER LABELED A...
...CHOKING HAZARD...
THE LAWSUIT-SAFE SLIDE
FOUR INCHES ABOVE THE GROUND.
STABLE PILINGS SUNK 753 FT. INTO THE EARTH
"IN-USE" WARNING SIGNAL AND CROSSING GUARD
DOWN-FILLED CONTACT PILLOW
3% GRADE ALLOWING TOP SPEED OF .00013 MPH
ABSOLUTELY NO FUN WHATSOEVER
MICHAEL FRY

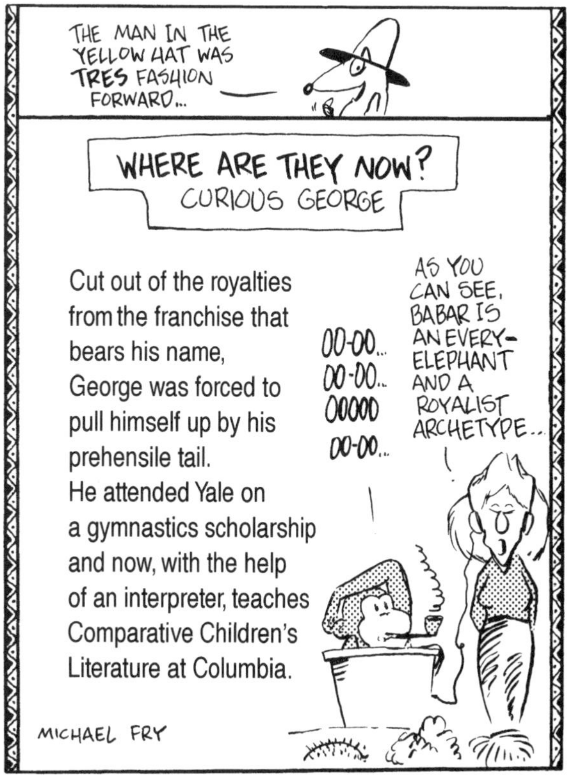
THE MAN IN THE YELLOW HAT WAS TRES FASHION FORWARD...
WHERE ARE THEY NOW?
CURIOUS GEORGE
Cut out of the royalties from the franchise that bears his name, George was forced to pull himself up by his prehensile tail. He attended Yale on a gymnastics scholarship and now, with the help of an interpreter, teaches Comparative Children's Literature at Columbia.
OO-OO... OO-OO... OOOOO OO-OO...
AS YOU CAN SEE, BABAR IS AN EVERY-ELEPHANT AND A ROYALIST ARCHETYPE...
MICHAEL FRY

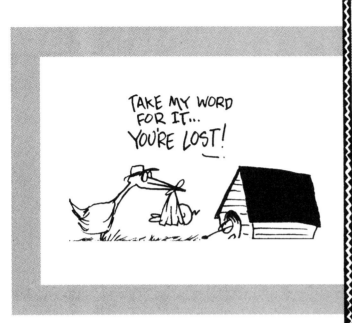

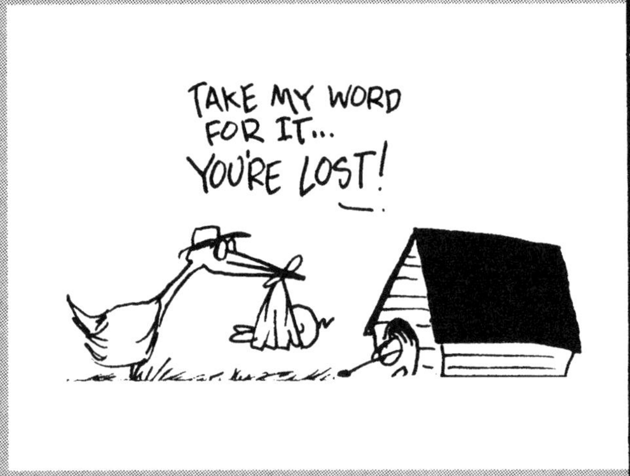
TAKE MY WORD FOR IT... YOU'RE LOST!

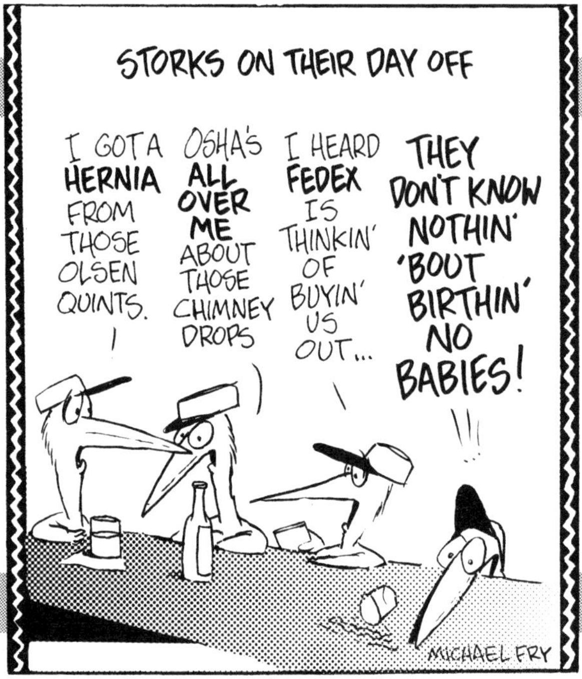
STORKS ON THEIR DAY OFF
I GOT A **HERNIA** FROM THOSE OLSEN QUINTS.
OSHA'S **ALL OVER ME** ABOUT THOSE CHIMNEY DROPS
I HEARD **FEDEX** IS THINKIN' OF BUYIN' US OUT...
THEY DON'T KNOW NOTHIN' 'BOUT BIRTHIN' NO BABIES!
MICHAEL FRY

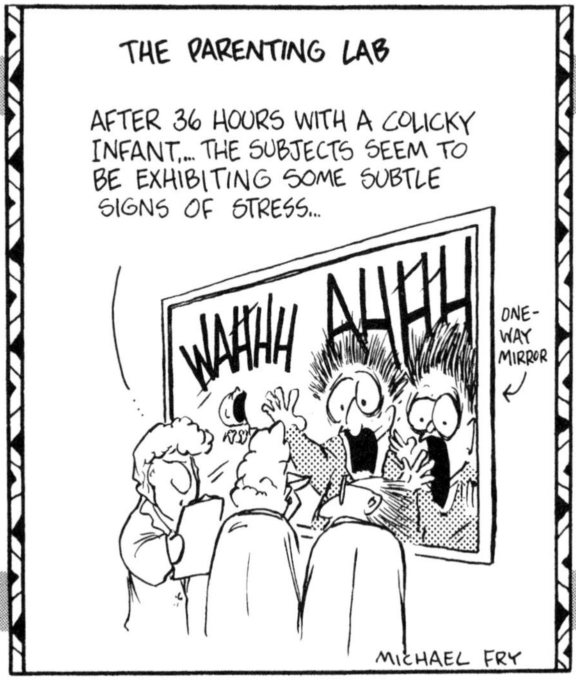
THE PARENTING LAB
AFTER 36 HOURS WITH A COLICKY INFANT... THE SUBJECTS SEEM TO BE EXHIBITING SOME SUBTLE SIGNS OF STRESS...
WAHHH
AHHH
ONE-WAY MIRROR
MICHAEL FRY

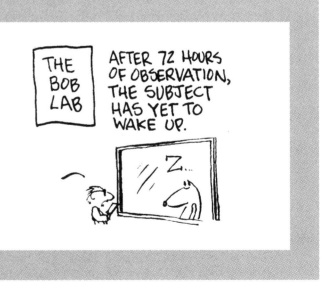

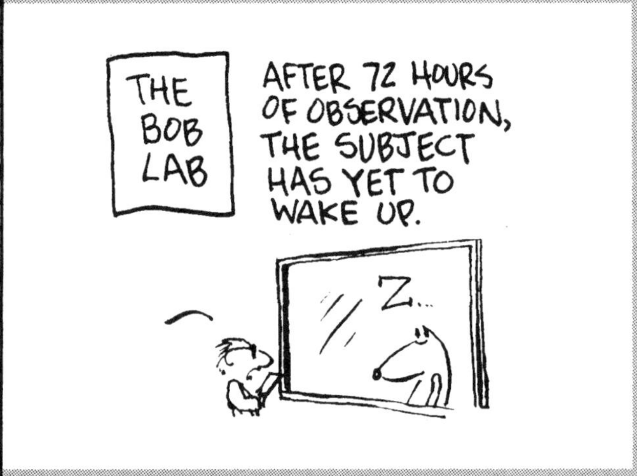
THE BOB LAB
AFTER 72 HOURS OF OBSERVATION, THE SUBJECT HAS YET TO WAKE UP.
Z...

KIDS' MOTIVATIONAL SPEAKING

I DIDN'T GET A BARBIE'S MY-SIZE MALIBU BEACH HOUSE BY **WISHING** FOR IT... I WHINED **MY BUTT OFF FOR IT!**

WHEN LIFE GIVES YOU LEMONS... **WHINE**

LIFE IS 1% INSPIRATION AND 99% **WHINING**

MICHAEL FRY

BOB THE DOG: VEGETATIONAL SPEAKING →

FETCH **ONCE** AND THERE'LL BE **NO** END TO IT! RESIST TO THE CORE OF YOUR BEING!

BOB'S BED

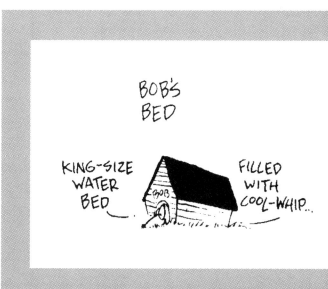

KING-SIZE WATER BED —

FILLED WITH COOL-WHIP...

THE FAMILY BED

FANTASY

REALITY

MICHAEL FRY

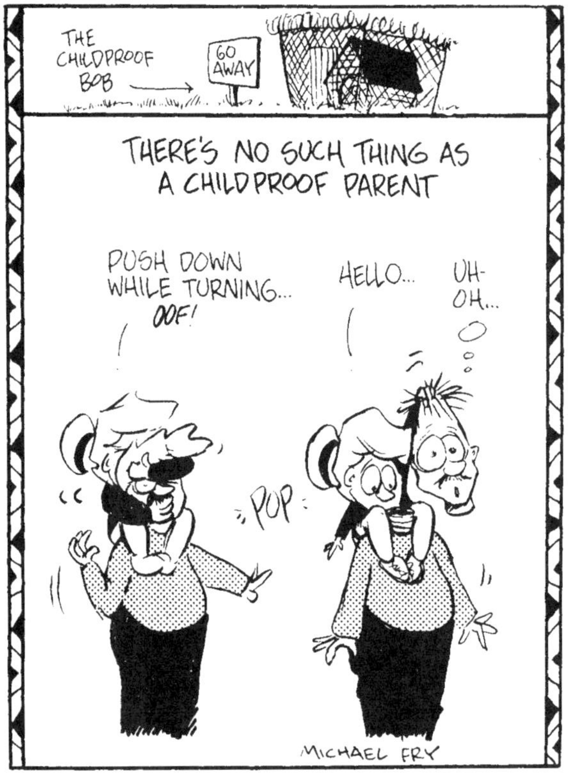
THE CHILDPROOF BOB
GO AWAY
THERE'S NO SUCH THING AS A CHILDPROOF PARENT
PUSH DOWN WHILE TURNING... OOF!
POP
HELLO...
UH-OH...
MICHAEL FRY

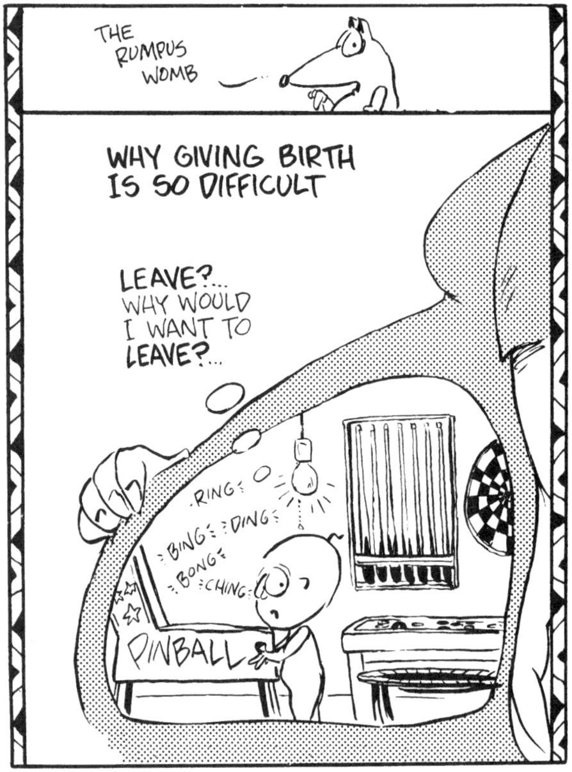
THE RUMPUS WOMB
WHY GIVING BIRTH IS SO DIFFICULT
LEAVE?... WHY WOULD I WANT TO LEAVE?...
RING
DING
BING
BONG
CHING
PINBALL

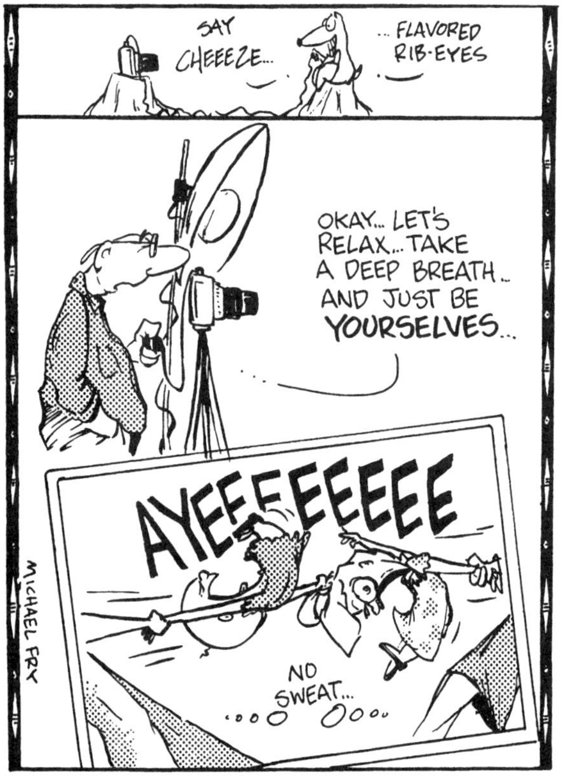
SAY CHEEEZE...
...FLAVORED RIB-EYES
OKAY... LET'S RELAX... TAKE A DEEP BREATH... AND JUST BE YOURSELVES...
AYEEEEEEEE
NO SWEAT...
MICHAEL FRY

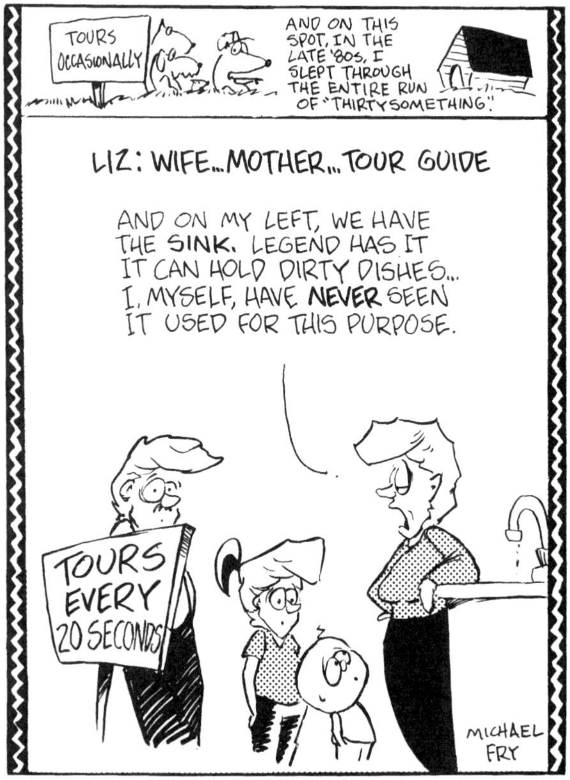
TOURS OCCASIONALLY
AND ON THIS SPOT, IN THE LATE '80s, I SLEPT THROUGH THE ENTIRE RUN OF "THIRTYSOMETHING."
LIZ: WIFE...MOTHER...TOUR GUIDE
AND ON MY LEFT, WE HAVE THE SINK. LEGEND HAS IT IT CAN HOLD DIRTY DISHES... I, MYSELF, HAVE NEVER SEEN IT USED FOR THIS PURPOSE.
TOURS EVERY 20 SECONDS
MICHAEL FRY

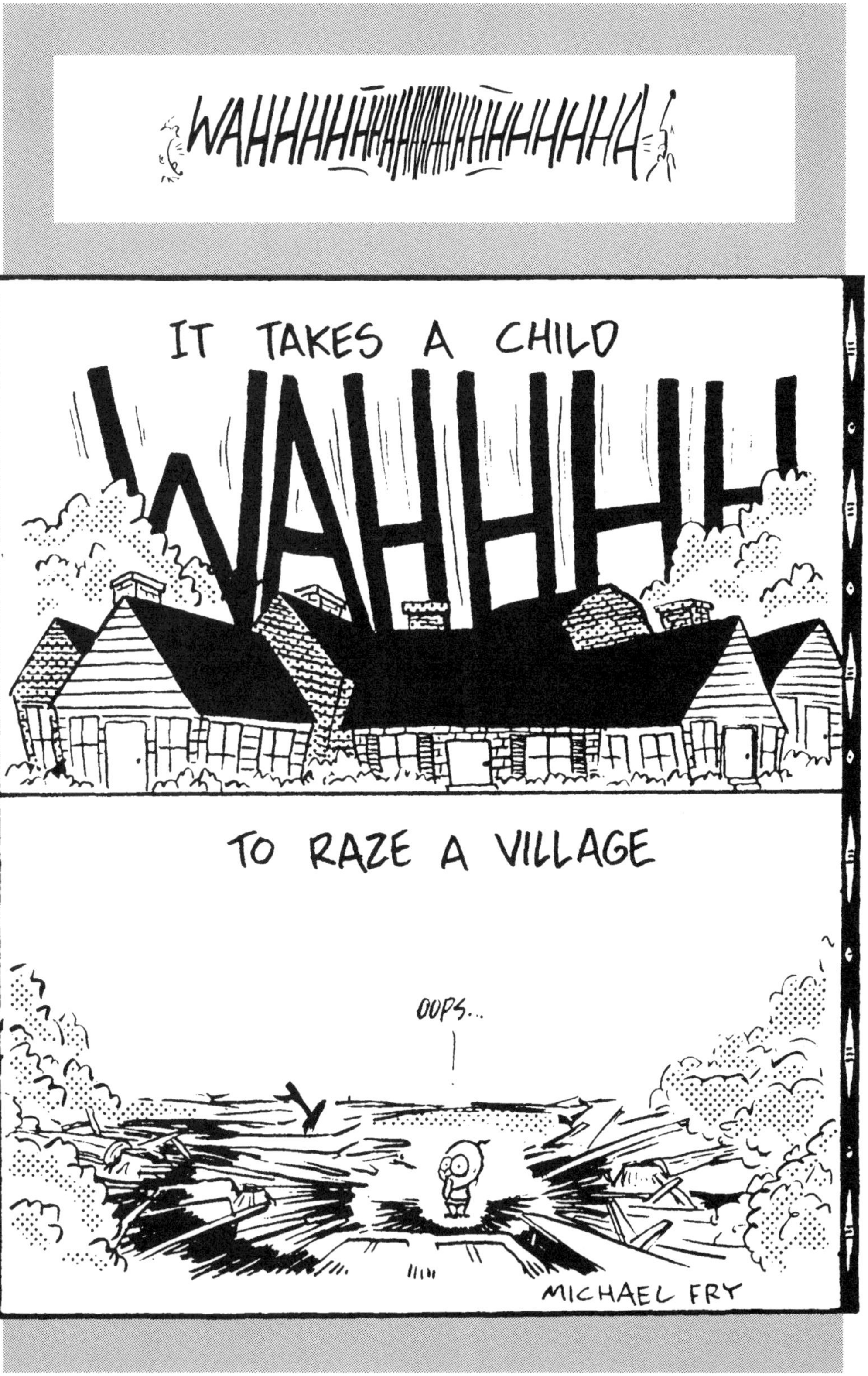
WAHHHHHHHHHHHHHHHHHHHHHA
IT TAKES A CHILD
WAHHHH
TO RAZE A VILLAGE
OOPS...
MICHAEL FRY

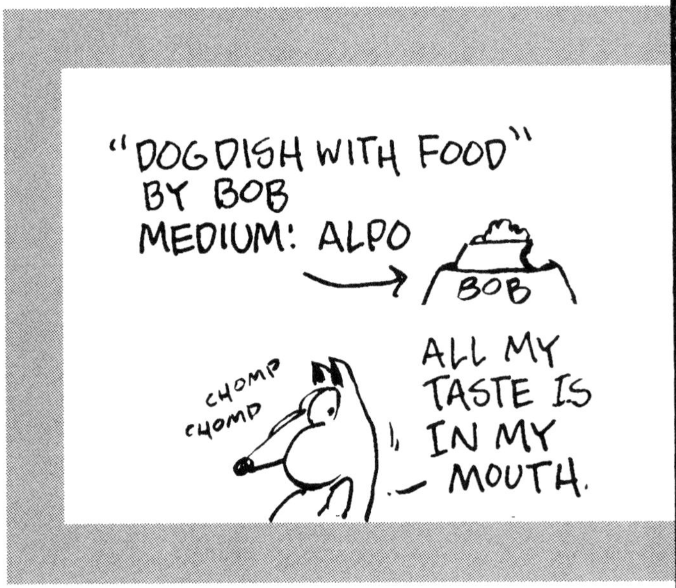
"DOG DISH WITH FOOD"
BY BOB
MEDIUM: ALPO
BOB
CHOMP
CHOMP
ALL MY TASTE IS IN MY MOUTH.

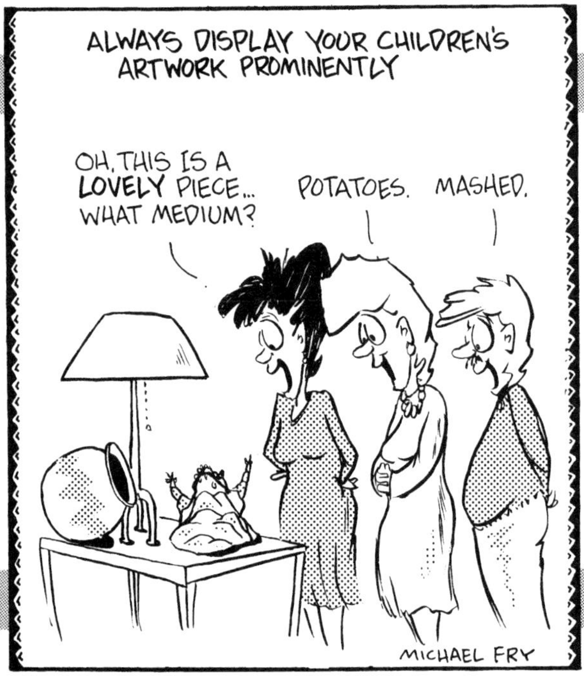
ALWAYS DISPLAY YOUR CHILDREN'S ARTWORK PROMINENTLY
OH, THIS IS A LOVELY PIECE... WHAT MEDIUM?
POTATOES.
MASHED.
MICHAEL FRY

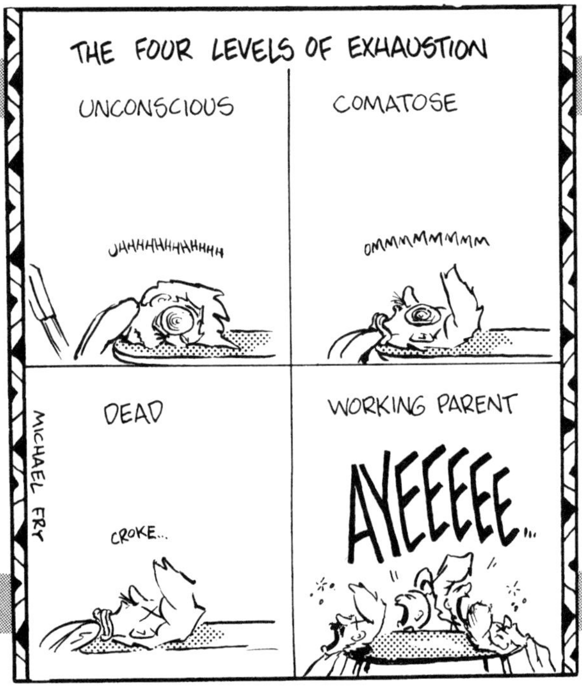
THE FOUR LEVELS OF EXHAUSTION
UNCONSCIOUS
UHHHHHHHHHHHH
COMATOSE
OMMMMMMMM
DEAD
CROKE...
WORKING PARENT
AYEEEEE...
MICHAEL FRY

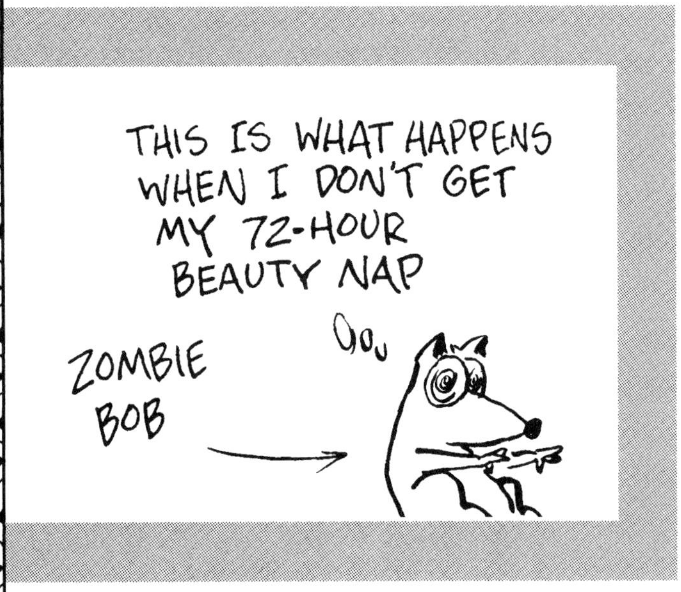
THIS IS WHAT HAPPENS WHEN I DON'T GET MY 72-HOUR BEAUTY NAP
ZOMBIE BOB

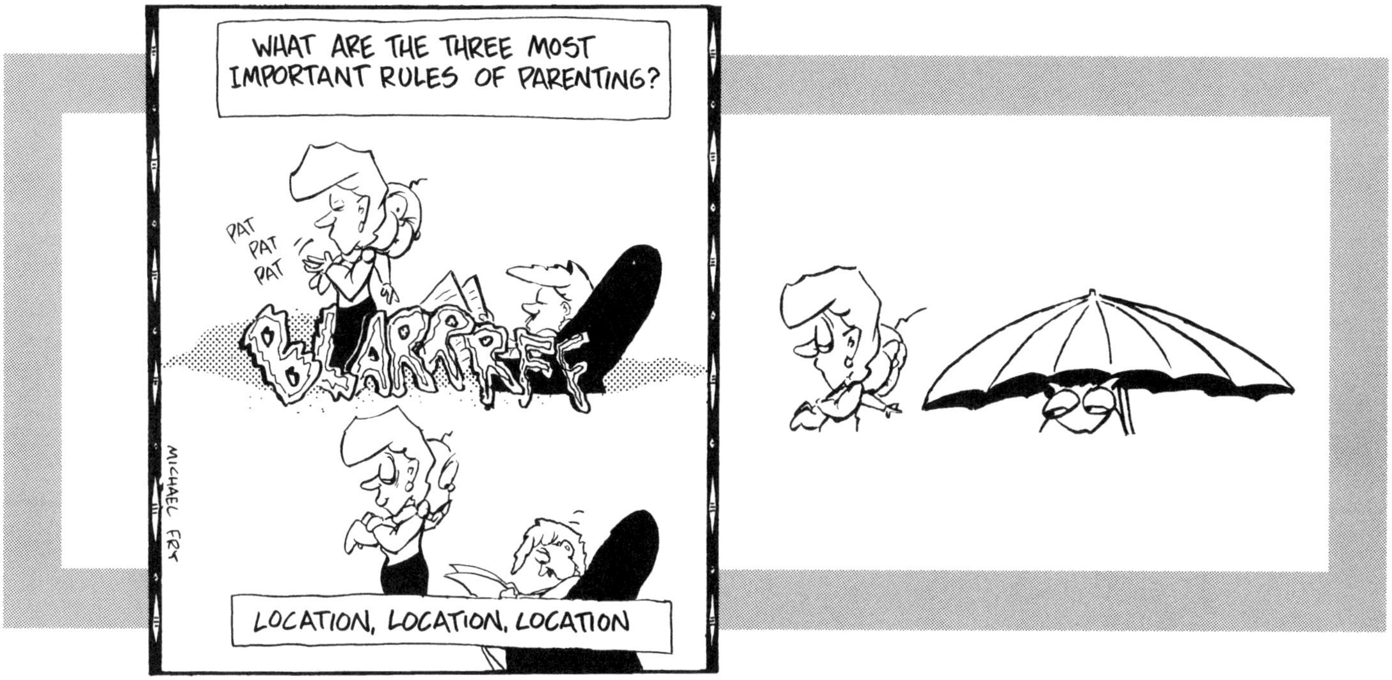
WHAT ARE THE THREE MOST IMPORTANT RULES OF PARENTING?
PAT PAT PAT
MICHAEL FRY
LOCATION, LOCATION, LOCATION

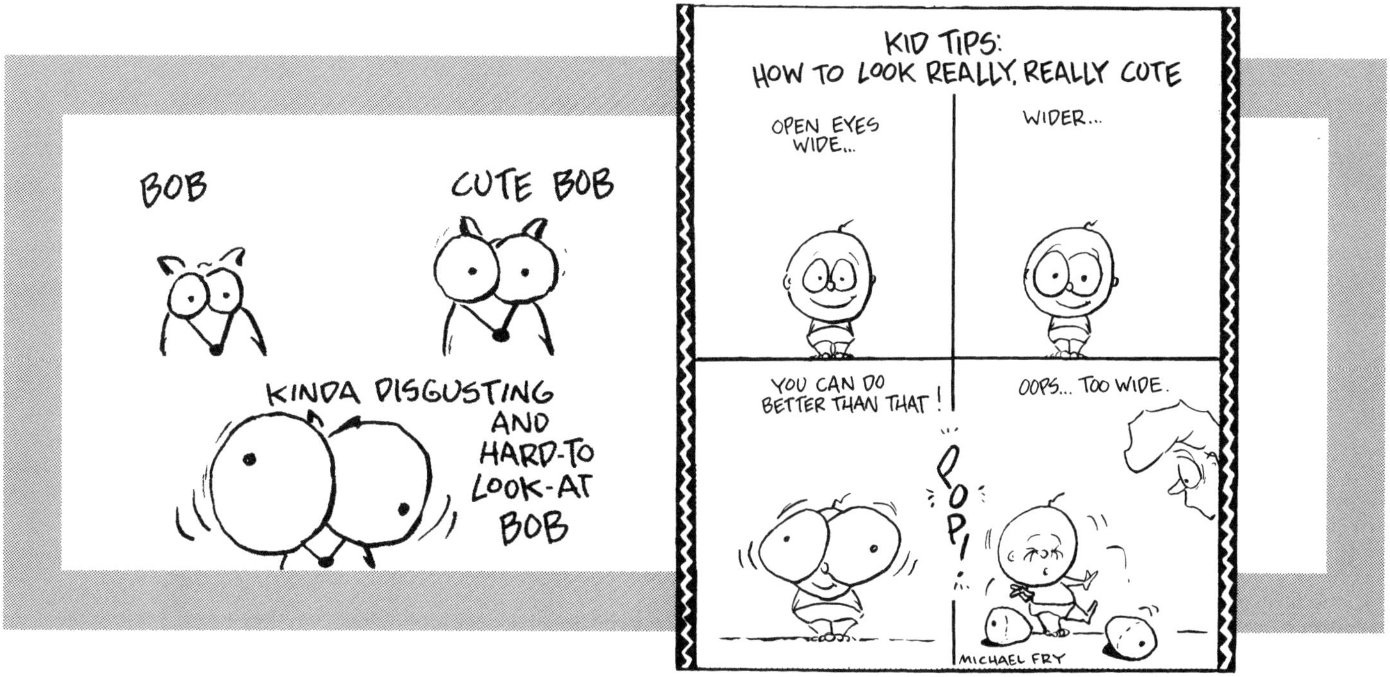
BOB
CUTE BOB
KINDA DISGUSTING AND HARD-TO LOOK-AT BOB
KID TIPS: HOW TO LOOK REALLY, REALLY CUTE
OPEN EYES WIDE...
WIDER...
YOU CAN DO BETTER THAN THAT!
POP!
OOPS... TOO WIDE.
MICHAEL FRY

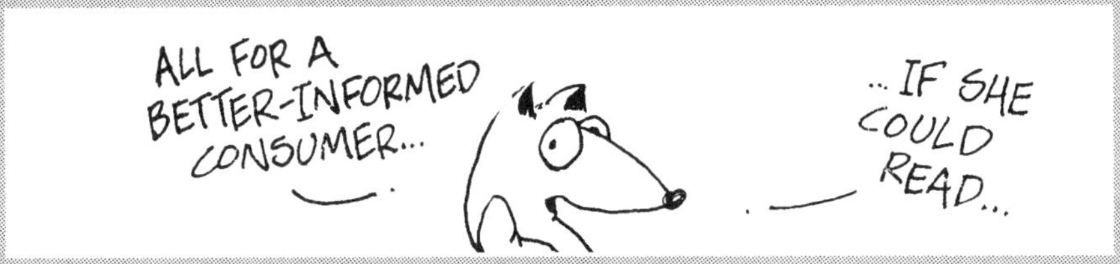
ALL FOR A BETTER-INFORMED CONSUMER...
...IF SHE COULD READ...

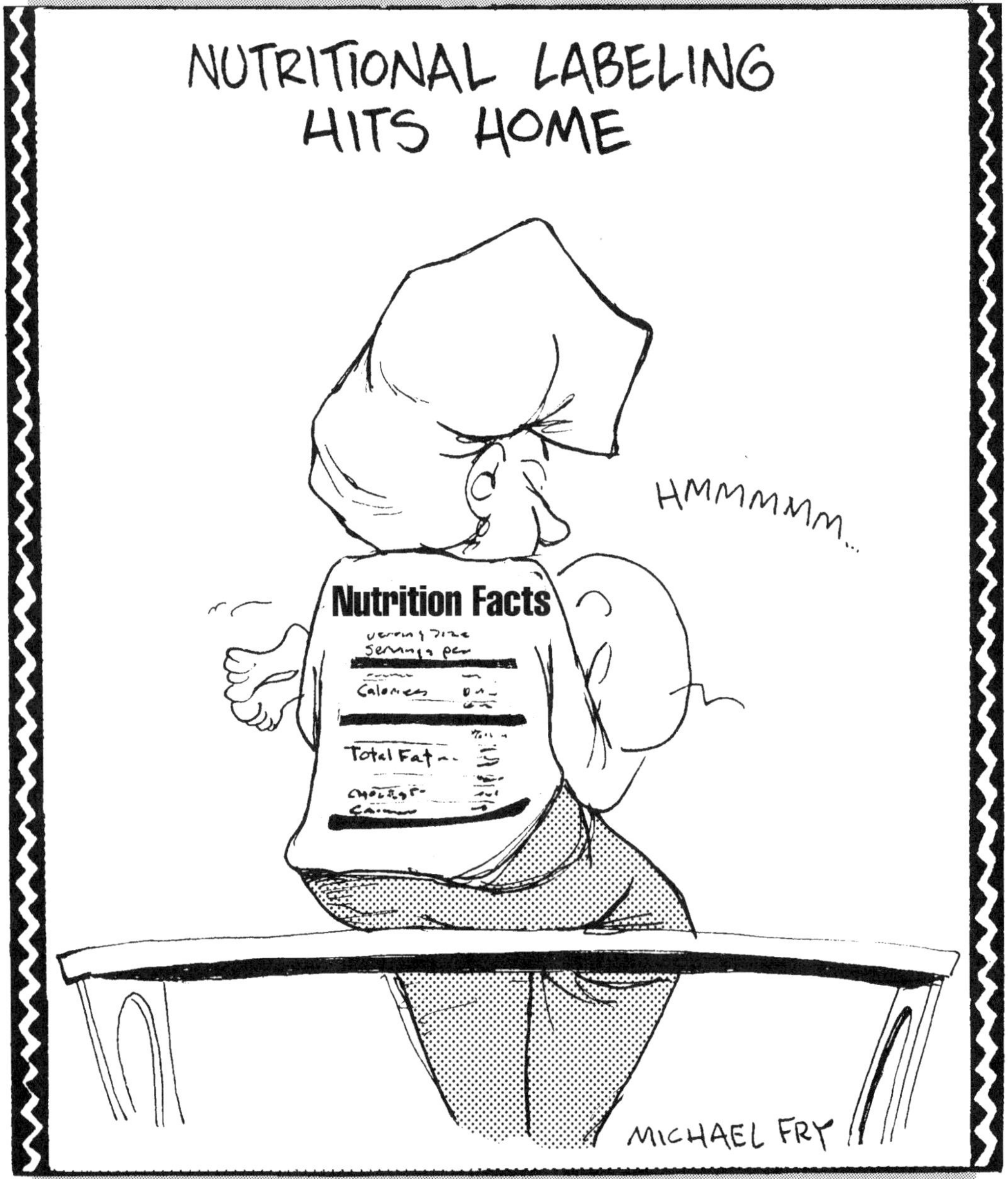
NUTRITIONAL LABELING HITS HOME
HMMMMM...
Nutrition Facts
Calories
Total Fat
MICHAEL FRY

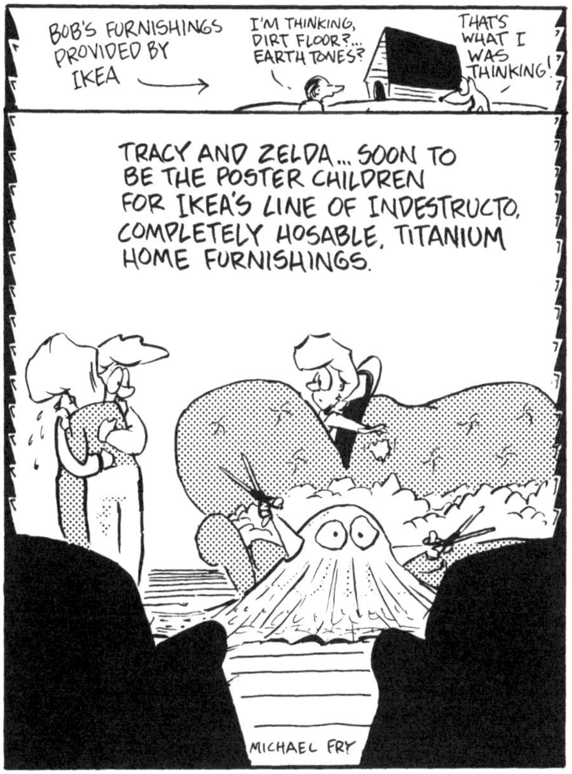
BOB'S FURNISHINGS PROVIDED BY IKEA
I'M THINKING, DIRT FLOOR?... EARTH TONES?
THAT'S WHAT I WAS THINKING!
TRACY AND ZELDA... SOON TO BE THE POSTER CHILDREN FOR IKEA'S LINE OF INDESTRUCTO, COMPLETELY HOSABLE, TITANIUM HOME FURNISHINGS.
MICHAEL FRY

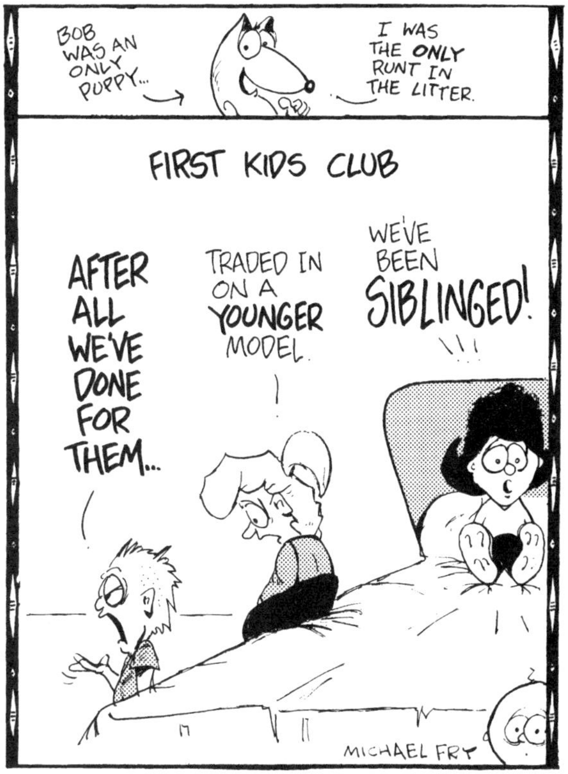
BOB WAS AN ONLY PUPPY...
I WAS THE ONLY RUNT IN THE LITTER.
FIRST KIDS CLUB
AFTER ALL WE'VE DONE FOR THEM...
TRADED IN ON A YOUNGER MODEL.
WE'VE BEEN SIBLINGED!
MICHAEL FRY

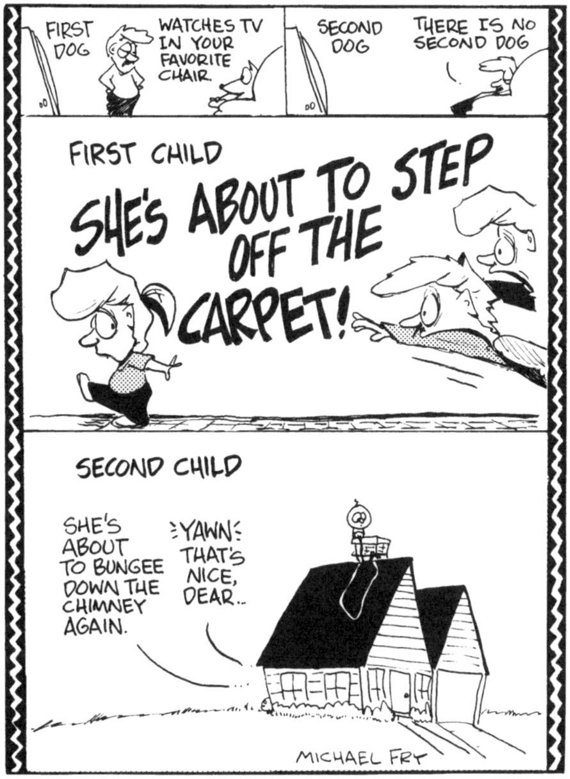
FIRST DOG
WATCHES TV IN YOUR FAVORITE CHAIR
SECOND DOG
THERE IS NO SECOND DOG
FIRST CHILD
SHE'S ABOUT TO STEP OFF THE CARPET!
SECOND CHILD
SHE'S ABOUT TO BUNGEE DOWN THE CHIMNEY AGAIN.
YAWN THAT'S NICE, DEAR..
MICHAEL FRY

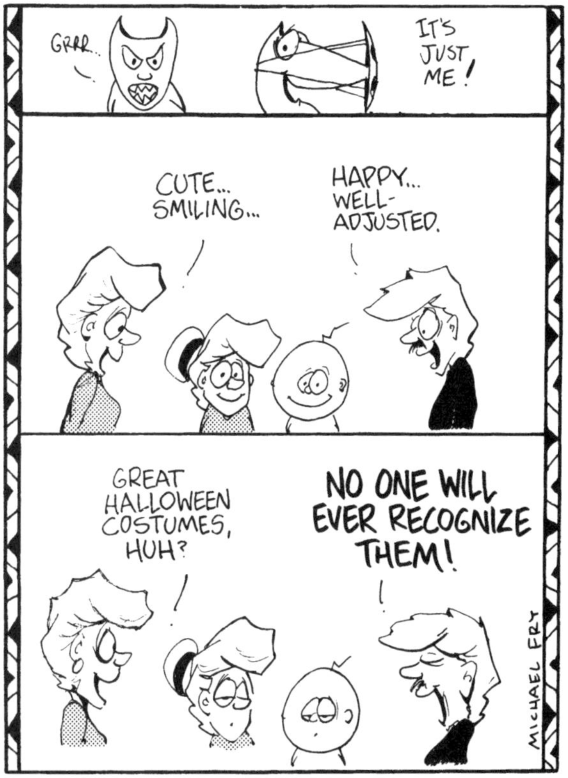
GRRR..
IT'S JUST ME!
CUTE... SMILING...
HAPPY... WELL-ADJUSTED.
GREAT HALLOWEEN COSTUMES, HUH?
NO ONE WILL EVER RECOGNIZE THEM!
MICHAEL FRY

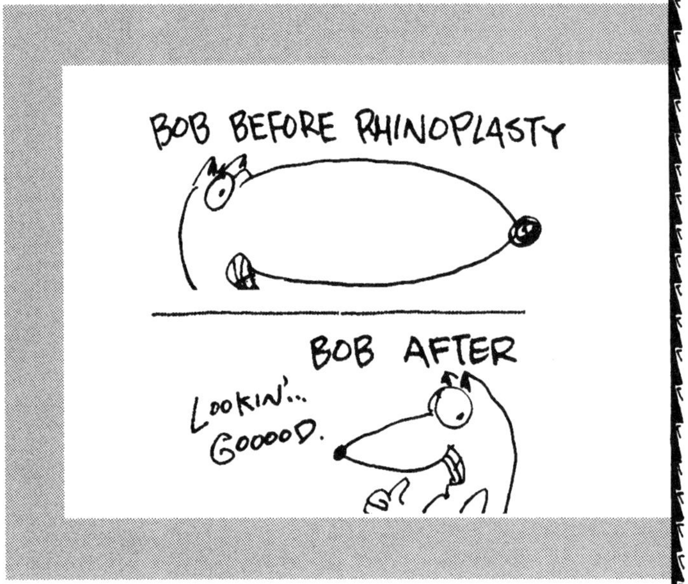
BOB BEFORE RHINOPLASTY
BOB AFTER
LOOKIN'... GOOOOD.

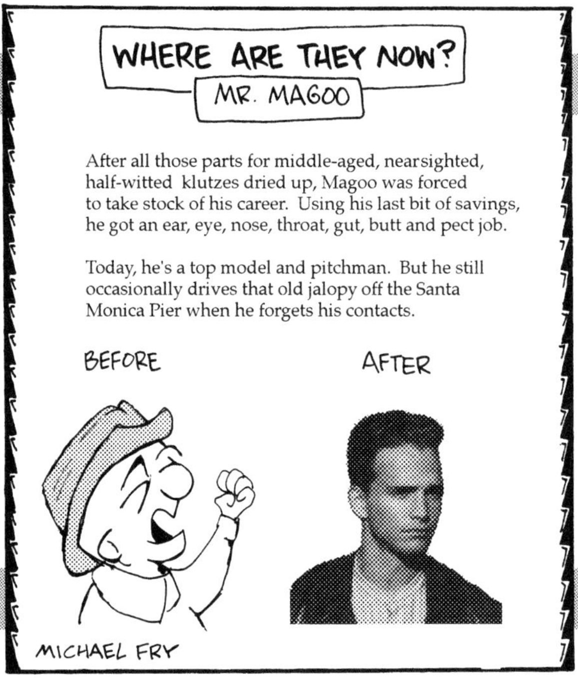
WHERE ARE THEY NOW?
MR. MAGOO
After all those parts for middle-aged, nearsighted, half-witted klutzes dried up, Magoo was forced to take stock of his career. Using his last bit of savings, he got an ear, eye, nose, throat, gut, butt and pect job.
Today, he's a top model and pitchman. But he still occasionally drives that old jalopy off the Santa Monica Pier when he forgets his contacts.
BEFORE
AFTER
MICHAEL FRY

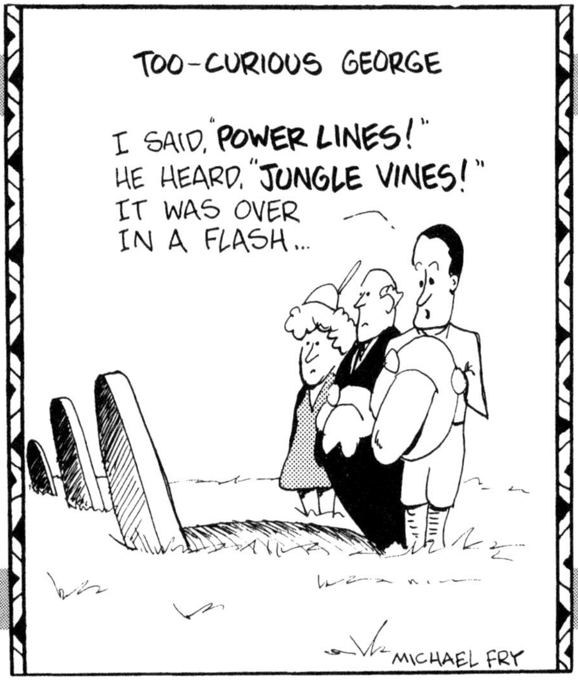
TOO-CURIOUS GEORGE
I SAID, "POWER LINES!" HE HEARD, "JUNGLE VINES!" IT WAS OVER IN A FLASH...
MICHAEL FRY

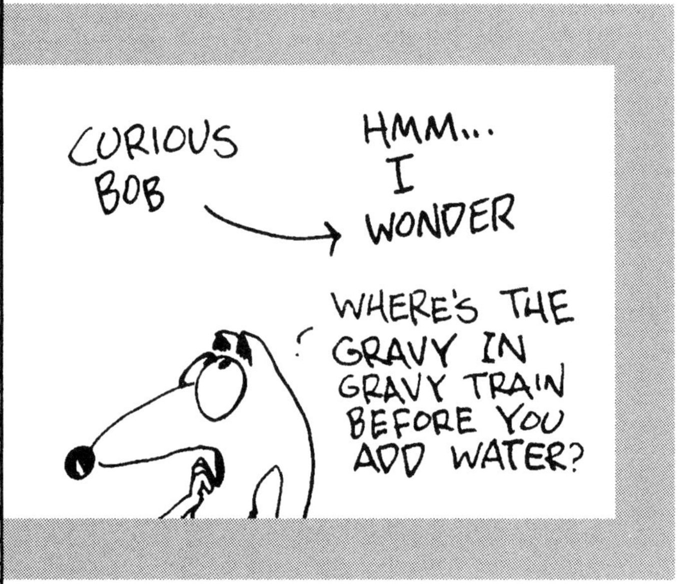
CURIOUS BOB
HMM... I WONDER
WHERE'S THE GRAVY IN GRAVY TRAIN BEFORE YOU ADD WATER?

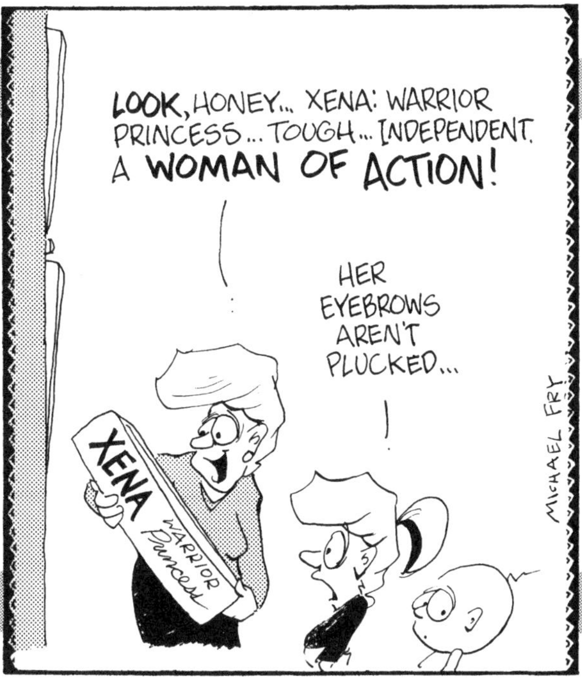
LOOK, HONEY... XENA: WARRIOR PRINCESS... TOUGH... INDEPENDENT. A WOMAN OF ACTION!
HER EYEBROWS AREN'T PLUCKED...
XENA
XENA WARRIOR Princess
MICHAEL FRY

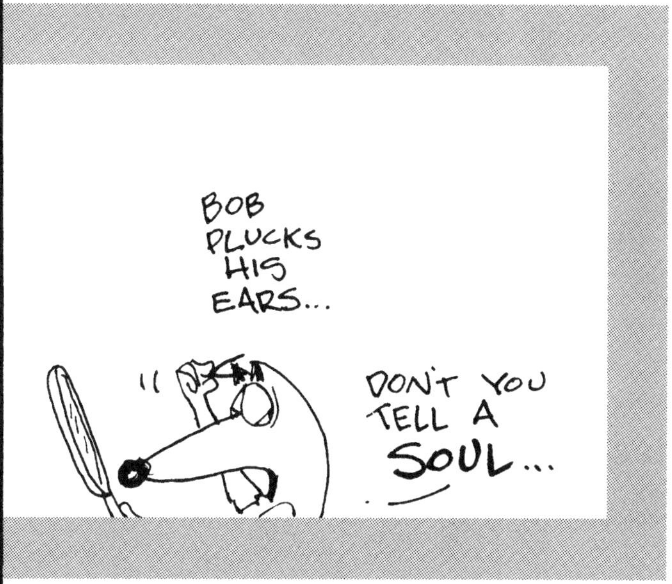
BOB PLUCKS HIS EARS...
DON'T YOU TELL A SOUL...

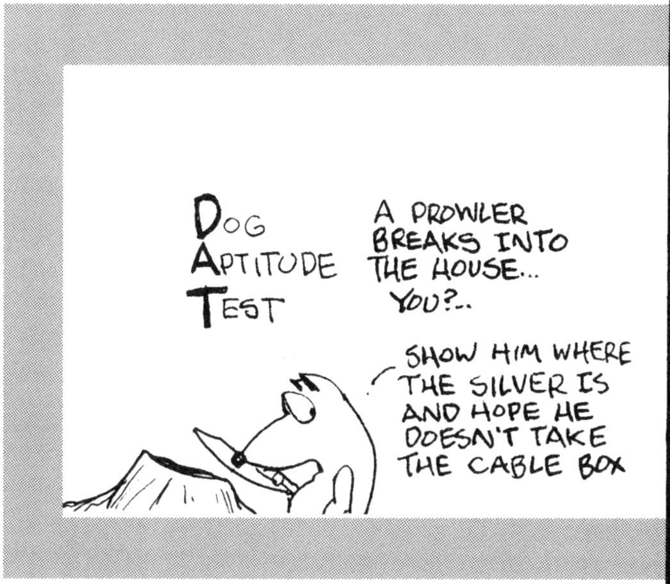
DOG APTITUDE TEST
A PROWLER BREAKS INTO THE HOUSE... YOU?..
SHOW HIM WHERE THE SILVER IS AND HOPE HE DOESN'T TAKE THE CABLE BOX

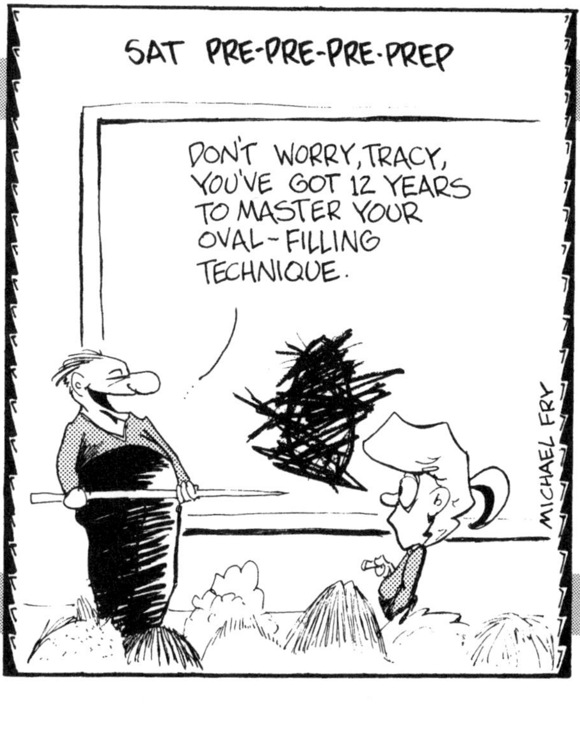
SAT PRE-PRE-PRE-PREP
DON'T WORRY, TRACY, YOU'VE GOT 12 YEARS TO MASTER YOUR OVAL-FILLING TECHNIQUE.
MICHAEL FRY

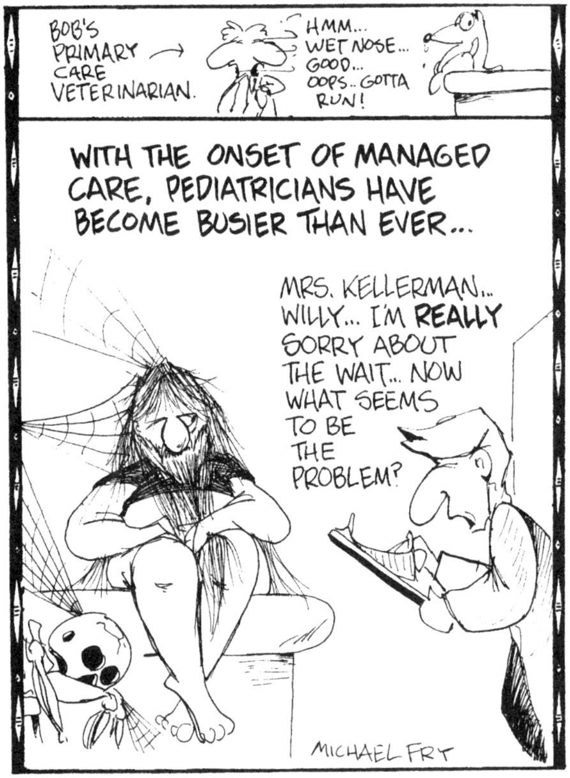
BOB'S PRIMARY CARE VETERINARIAN.
HMM... WET NOSE... GOOD... OOPS.. GOTTA RUN!
WITH THE ONSET OF MANAGED CARE, PEDIATRICIANS HAVE BECOME BUSIER THAN EVER...
MRS. KELLERMAN.. WILLY... I'M REALLY SORRY ABOUT THE WAIT... NOW WHAT SEEMS TO BE THE PROBLEM?
MICHAEL FRY

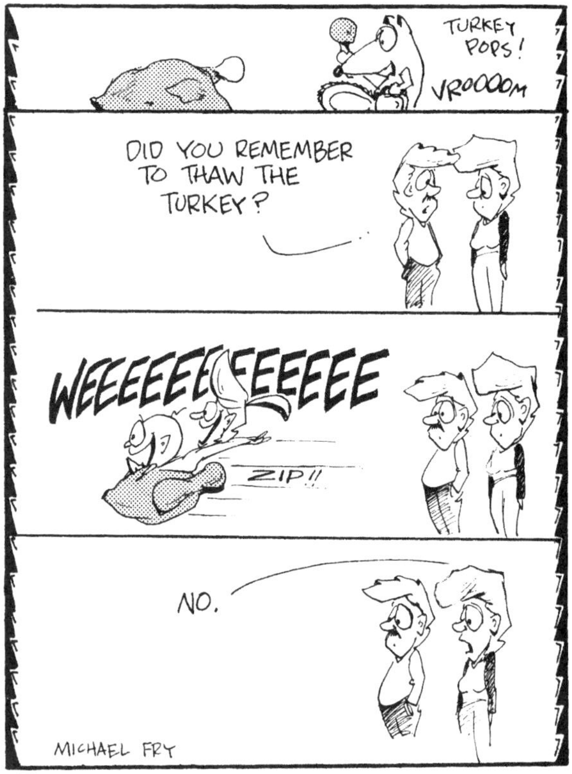
TURKEY POPS!
VROOOOM
DID YOU REMEMBER TO THAW THE TURKEY?
WEEEEEEEEEEEE
ZIP!!
NO.
MICHAEL FRY

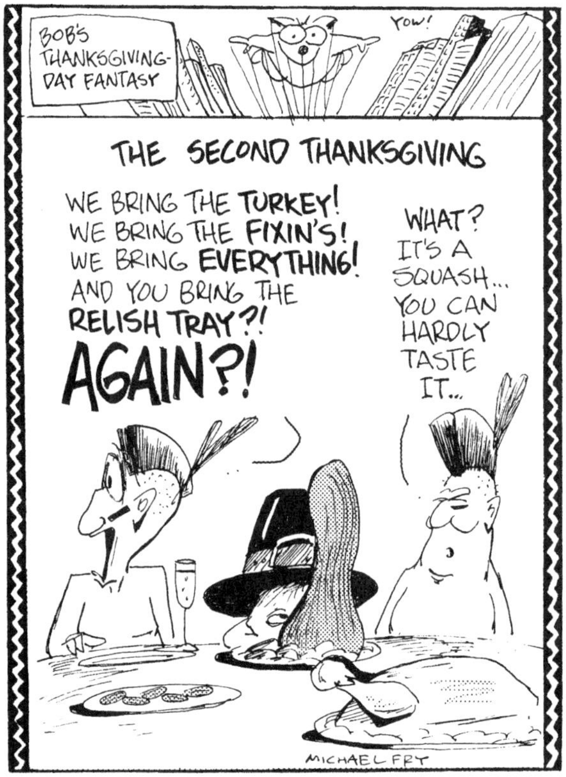
BOB'S THANKSGIVING-DAY FANTASY
YOW!
THE SECOND THANKSGIVING
WE BRING THE TURKEY! WE BRING THE FIXIN'S! WE BRING EVERYTHING! AND YOU BRING THE RELISH TRAY?! AGAIN?!
WHAT? IT'S A SQUASH... YOU CAN HARDLY TASTE IT...
MICHAEL FRY

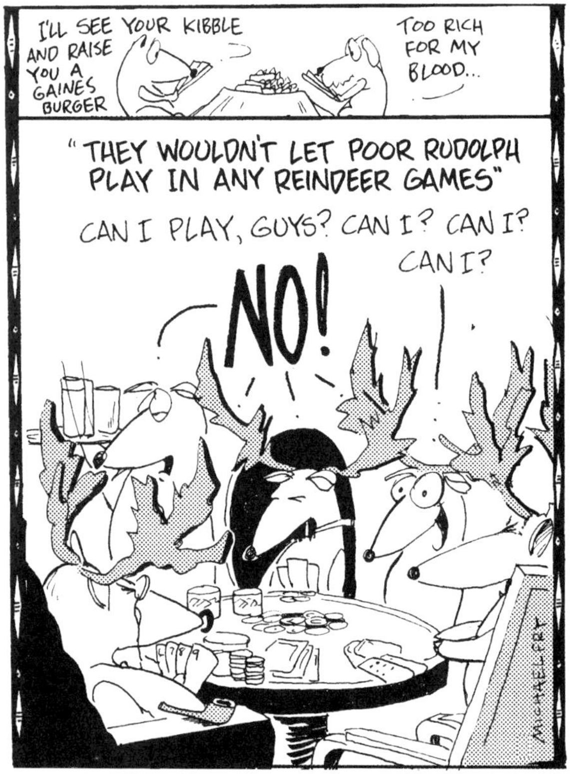
I'LL SEE YOUR KIBBLE AND RAISE YOU A GAINES BURGER
TOO RICH FOR MY BLOOD...
"THEY WOULDN'T LET POOR RUDOLPH PLAY IN ANY REINDEER GAMES"
CAN I PLAY, GUYS? CAN I? CAN I? CAN I?
NO!
MICHAEL FRY

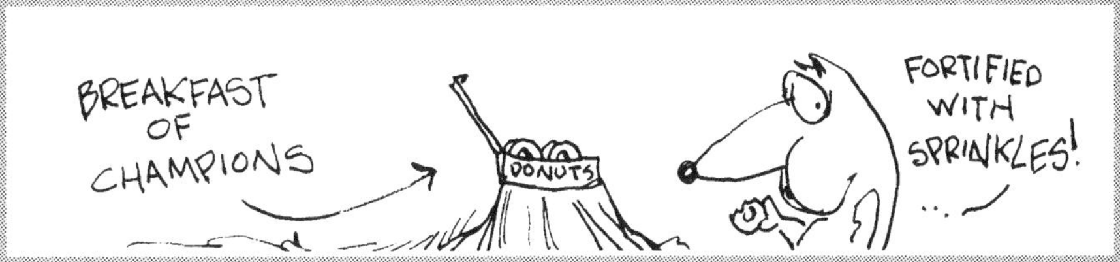
BREAKFAST OF CHAMPIONS
DONUTS
FORTIFIED WITH SPRINKLES!

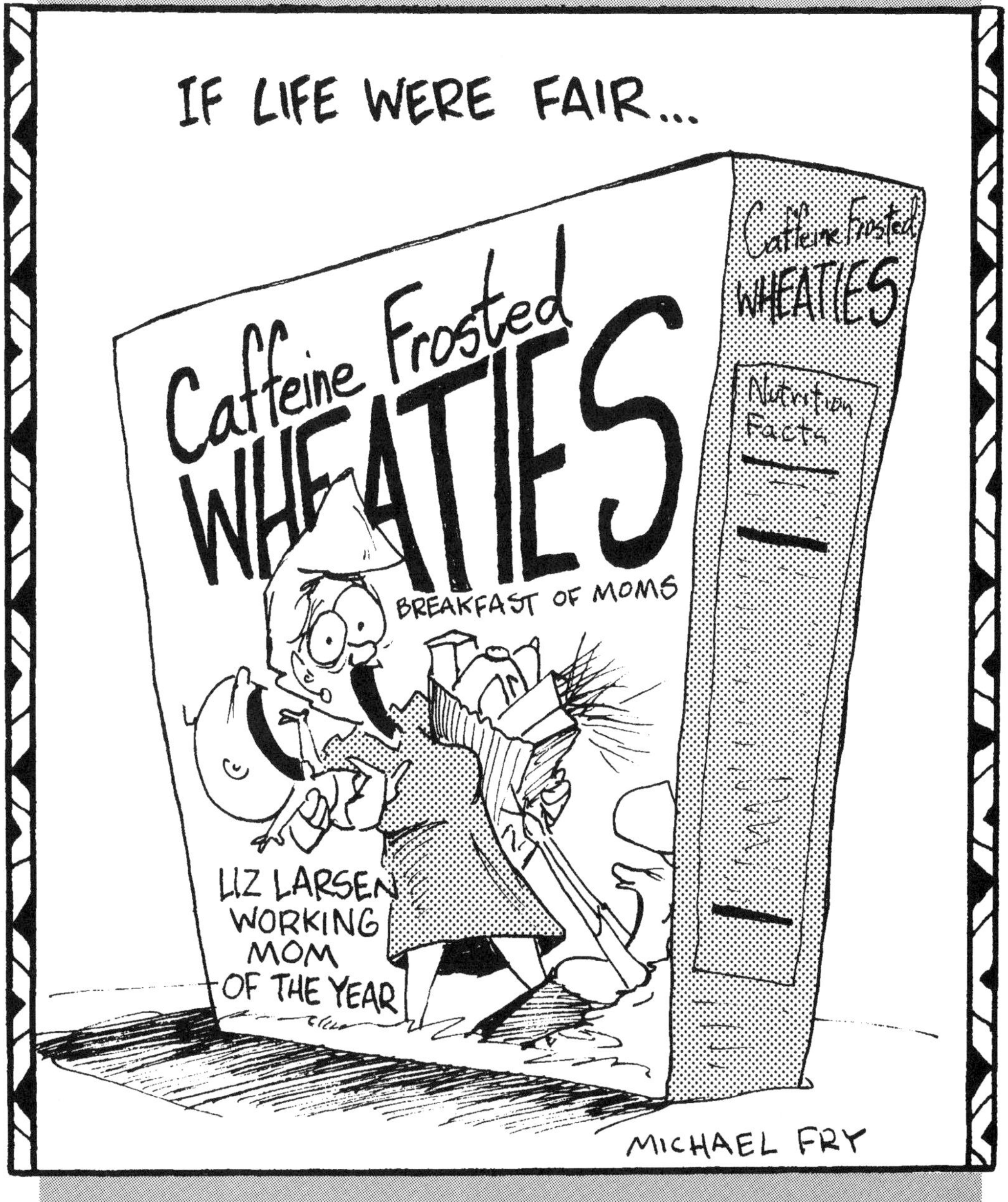
IF LIFE WERE FAIR...
Caffeine Frosted WHEATIES
BREAKFAST OF MOMS
LIZ LARSEN WORKING MOM OF THE YEAR
Caffeine Frosted WHEATIES
Nutrition Facts
MICHAEL FRY

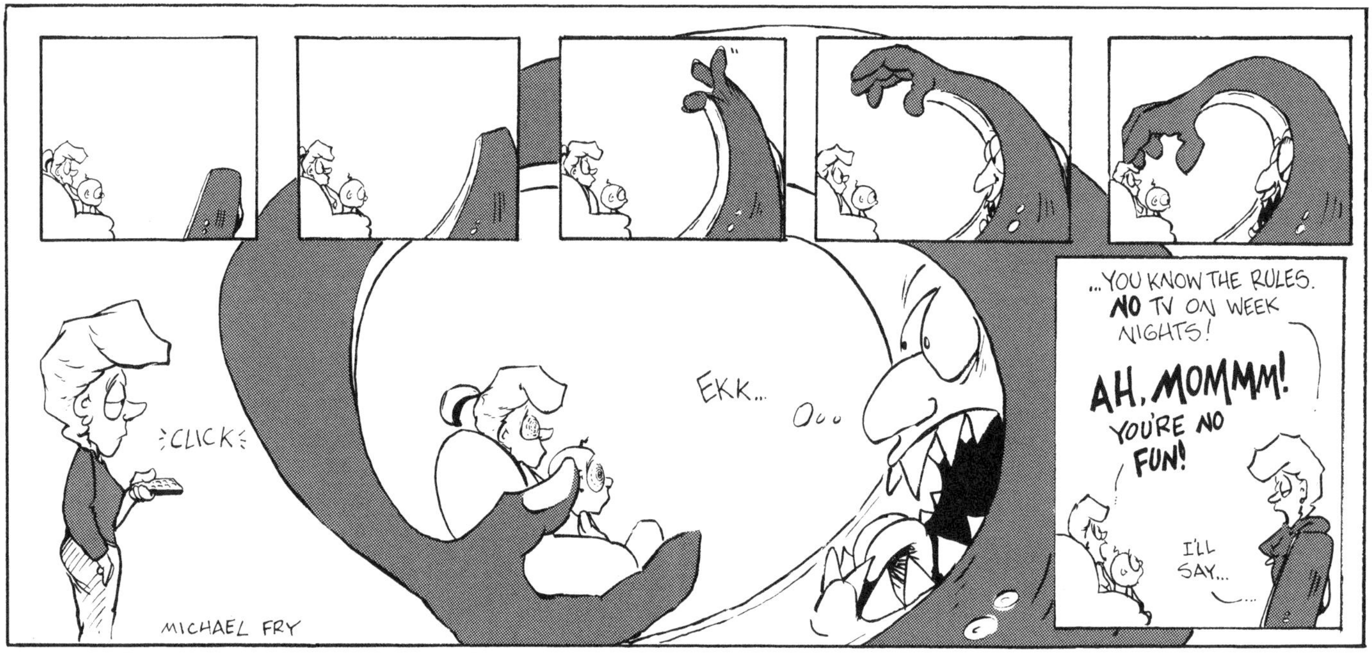
MICHAEL FRY
CLICK
EKK...
Ooo
...YOU KNOW THE RULES. NO TV ON WEEK NIGHTS!
AH, MOMMM! YOU'RE NO FUN!
I'LL SAY...

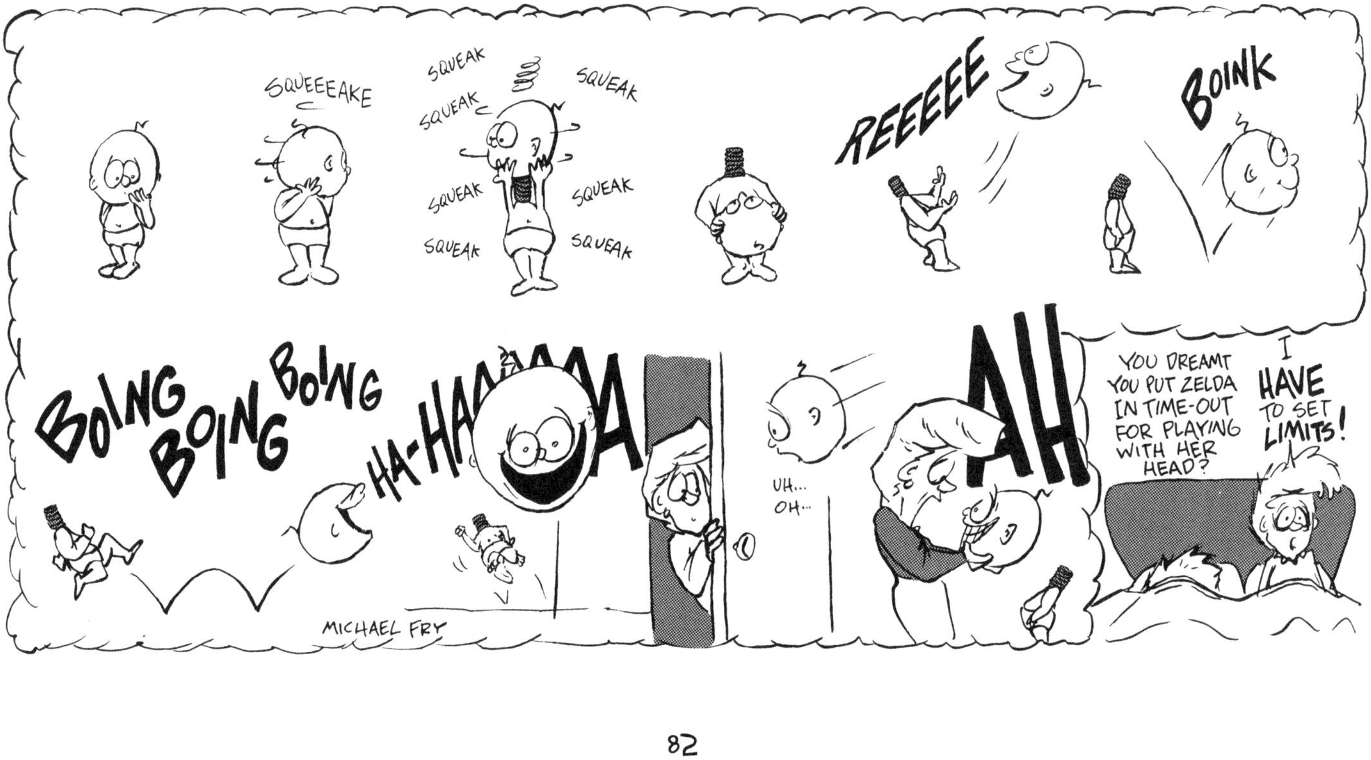
SQUEEEAKE
SQUEAK
SQUEAK
SQUEAK
SQUEAK
SQUEAK
SQUEAK
SQUEAK
REEEEE
BOINK
BOING BOING BOING
HA-HAAAAAA
UH... OH...
AH
YOU DREAMT YOU PUT ZELDA IN TIME-OUT FOR PLAYING WITH HER HEAD?
I HAVE TO SET LIMITS!
MICHAEL FRY

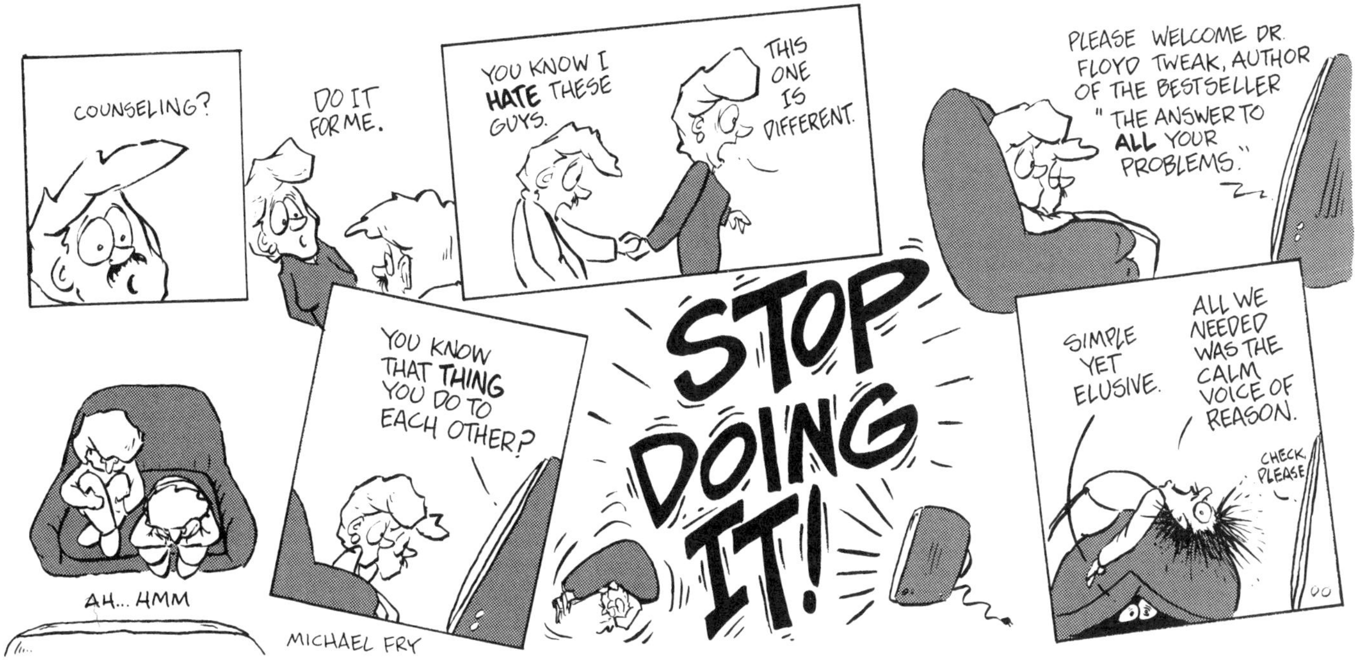
COUNSELING?
DO IT FOR ME.
YOU KNOW I HATE THESE GUYS.
THIS ONE IS DIFFERENT.
PLEASE WELCOME DR. FLOYD TWEAK, AUTHOR OF THE BESTSELLER "THE ANSWER TO ALL YOUR PROBLEMS."
AH... HMM
YOU KNOW THAT THING YOU DO TO EACH OTHER?
STOP DOING IT!
SIMPLE YET ELUSIVE.
ALL WE NEEDED WAS THE CALM VOICE OF REASON.
CHECK, PLEASE
MICHAEL FRY

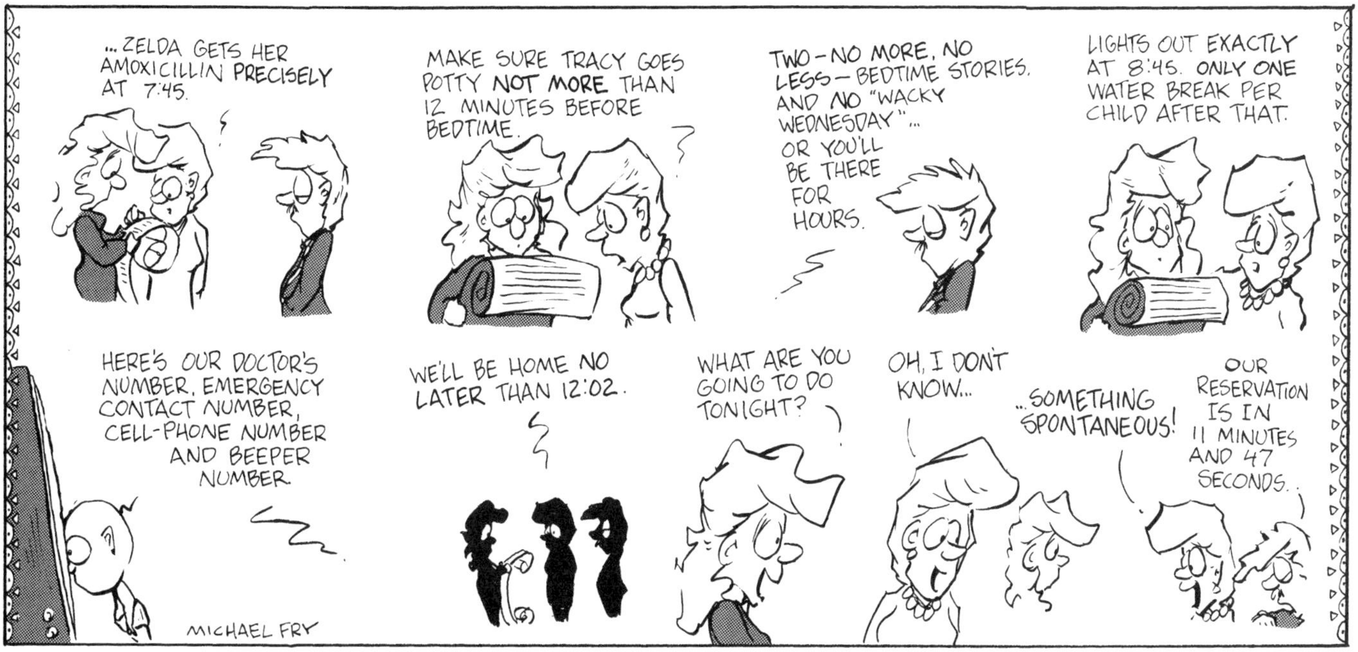
...ZELDA GETS HER AMOXICILLIN PRECISELY AT 7:45.
MAKE SURE TRACY GOES POTTY NOT MORE THAN 12 MINUTES BEFORE BEDTIME.
TWO-NO MORE, NO LESS-BEDTIME STORIES. AND NO "WACKY WEDNESDAY"...
OR YOU'LL BE THERE FOR HOURS.
LIGHTS OUT EXACTLY AT 8:45. ONLY ONE WATER BREAK PER CHILD AFTER THAT.
HERE'S OUR DOCTOR'S NUMBER, EMERGENCY CONTACT NUMBER, CELL-PHONE NUMBER AND BEEPER NUMBER.
WE'LL BE HOME NO LATER THAN 12:02.
WHAT ARE YOU GOING TO DO TONIGHT?
OH, I DON'T KNOW...
...SOMETHING SPONTANEOUS!
OUR RESERVATION IS IN 11 MINUTES AND 47 SECONDS.
MICHAEL FRY

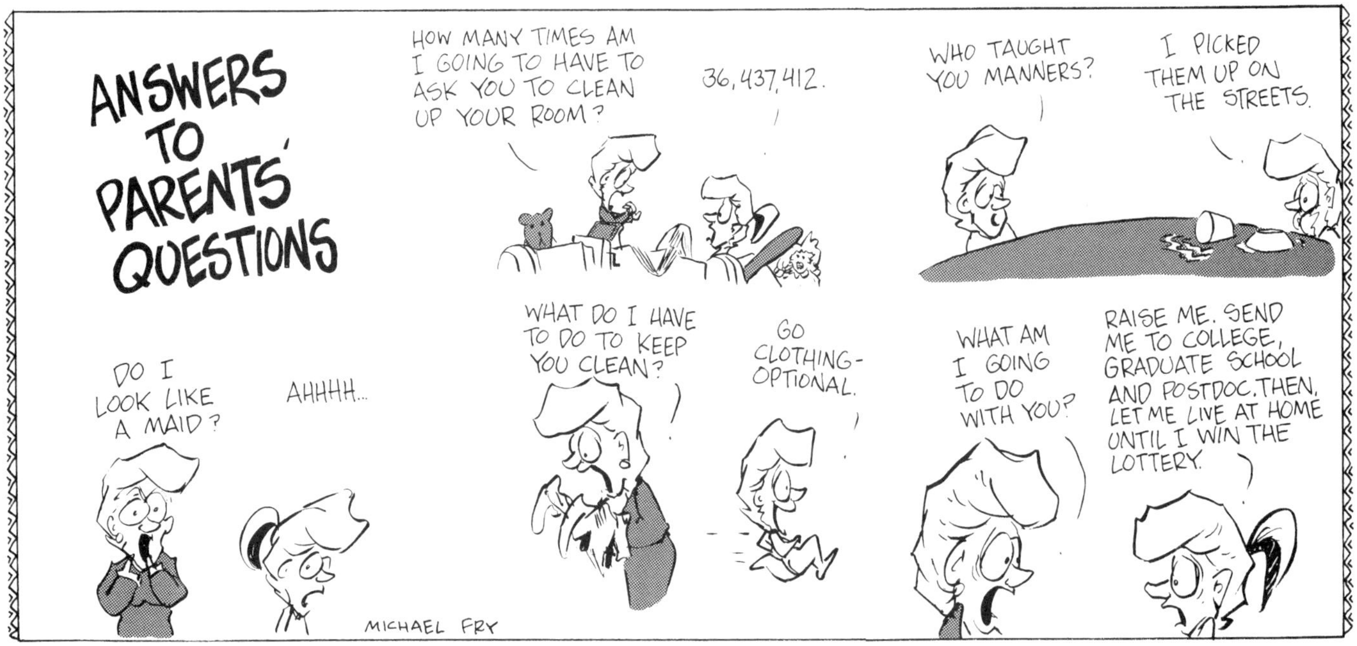
ANSWERS TO PARENTS' QUESTIONS
HOW MANY TIMES AM I GOING TO HAVE TO ASK YOU TO CLEAN UP YOUR ROOM?
36,437,412.
WHO TAUGHT YOU MANNERS?
I PICKED THEM UP ON THE STREETS.
DO I LOOK LIKE A MAID?
AHHHH...
WHAT DO I HAVE TO DO TO KEEP YOU CLEAN?
GO CLOTHING-OPTIONAL.
WHAT AM I GOING TO DO WITH YOU?
RAISE ME. SEND ME TO COLLEGE, GRADUATE SCHOOL AND POSTDOC. THEN, LET ME LIVE AT HOME UNTIL I WIN THE LOTTERY.
MICHAEL FRY

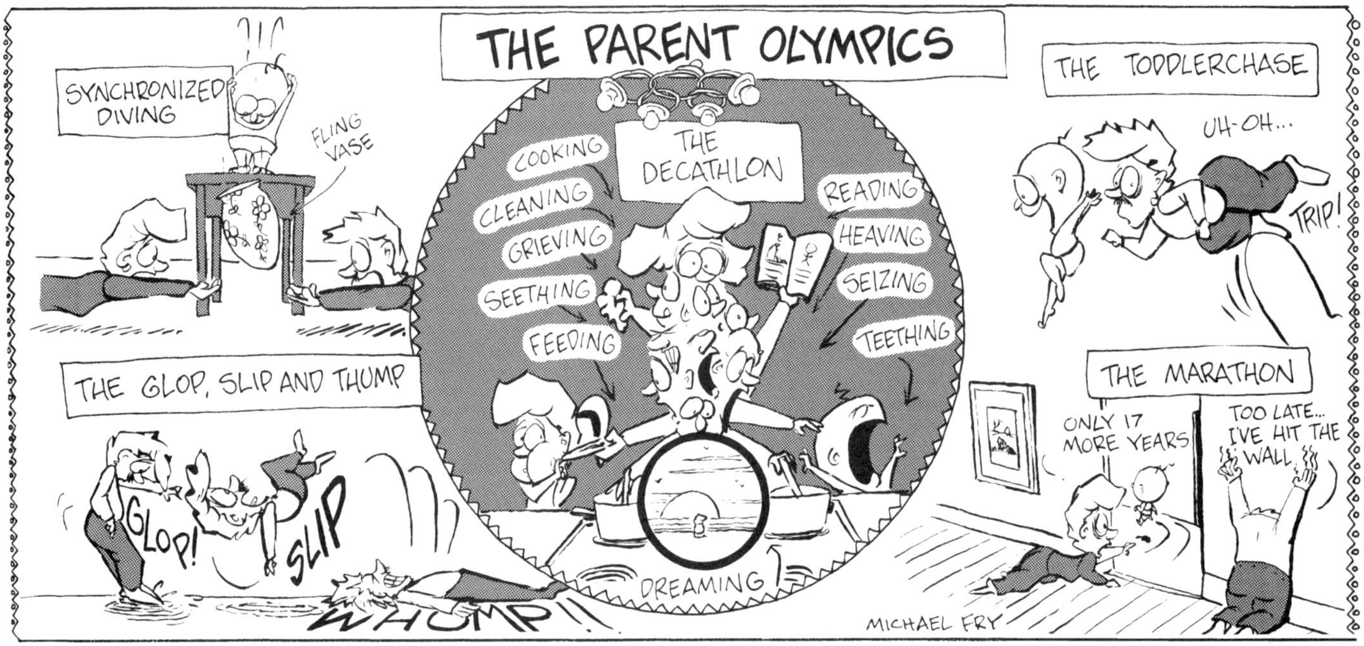
THE PARENT OLYMPICS
SYNCHRONIZED DIVING
FLING VASE
THE DECATHLON
COOKING
CLEANING
GRIEVING
SEETHING
FEEDING
READING
HEAVING
SEIZING
TEETHING
DREAMING
THE TODDLERCHASE
UH-OH...
TRIP!
THE GLOP, SLIP AND THUMP
GLOP!
SLIP
WHUMP!!
THE MARATHON
ONLY 17 MORE YEARS
TOO LATE... I'VE HIT THE WALL.
MICHAEL FRY

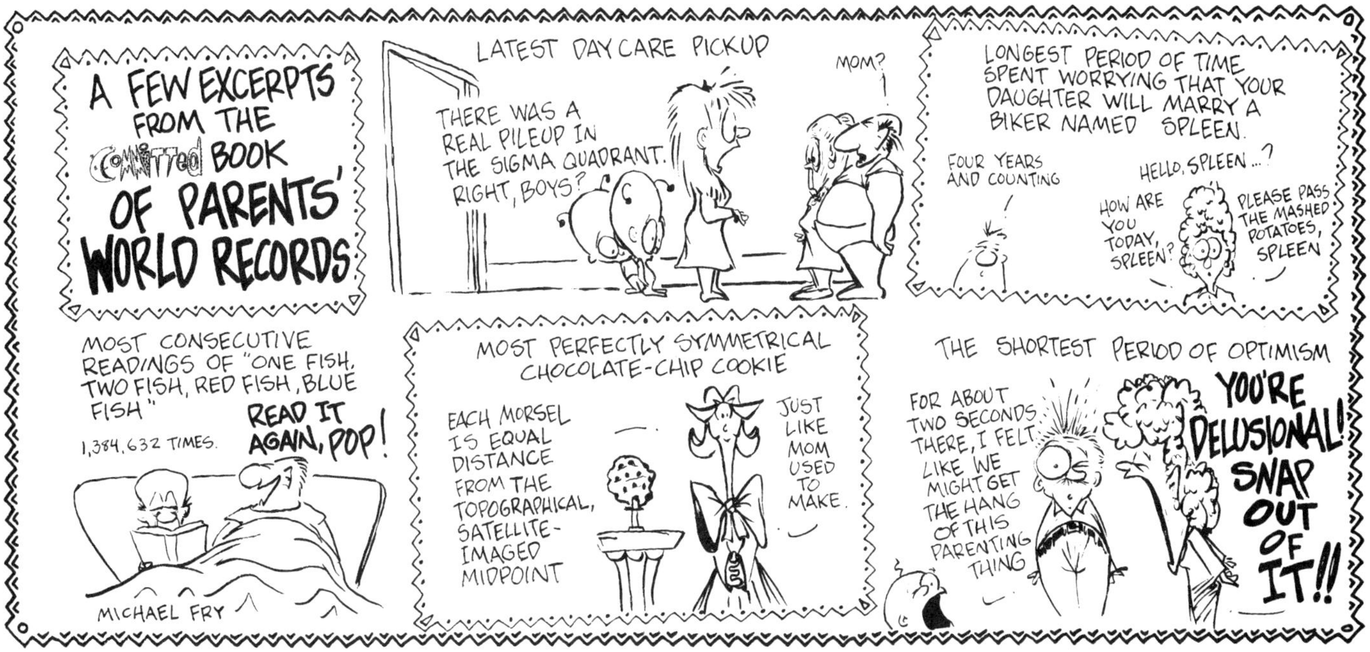
A FEW EXCERPTS FROM THE COMMITTED BOOK OF PARENTS' WORLD RECORDS
LATEST DAY CARE PICKUP
THERE WAS A REAL PILEUP IN THE SIGMA QUADRANT. RIGHT, BOYS?
MOM?
LONGEST PERIOD OF TIME SPENT WORRYING THAT YOUR DAUGHTER WILL MARRY A BIKER NAMED SPLEEN.
FOUR YEARS AND COUNTING
HELLO, SPLEEN...?
HOW ARE YOU TODAY, SPLEEN?
PLEASE PASS THE MASHED POTATOES, SPLEEN
MOST CONSECUTIVE READINGS OF "ONE FISH, TWO FISH, RED FISH, BLUE FISH"
1,384,632 TIMES.
READ IT AGAIN, POP!
MICHAEL FRY
MOST PERFECTLY SYMMETRICAL CHOCOLATE-CHIP COOKIE
EACH MORSEL IS EQUAL DISTANCE FROM THE TOPOGRAPHICAL, SATELLITE-IMAGED MIDPOINT
JUST LIKE MOM USED TO MAKE.
THE SHORTEST PERIOD OF OPTIMISM
FOR ABOUT TWO SECONDS THERE, I FELT LIKE WE MIGHT GET THE HANG OF THIS PARENTING THING
YOU'RE DELUSIONAL! SNAP OUT OF IT!!

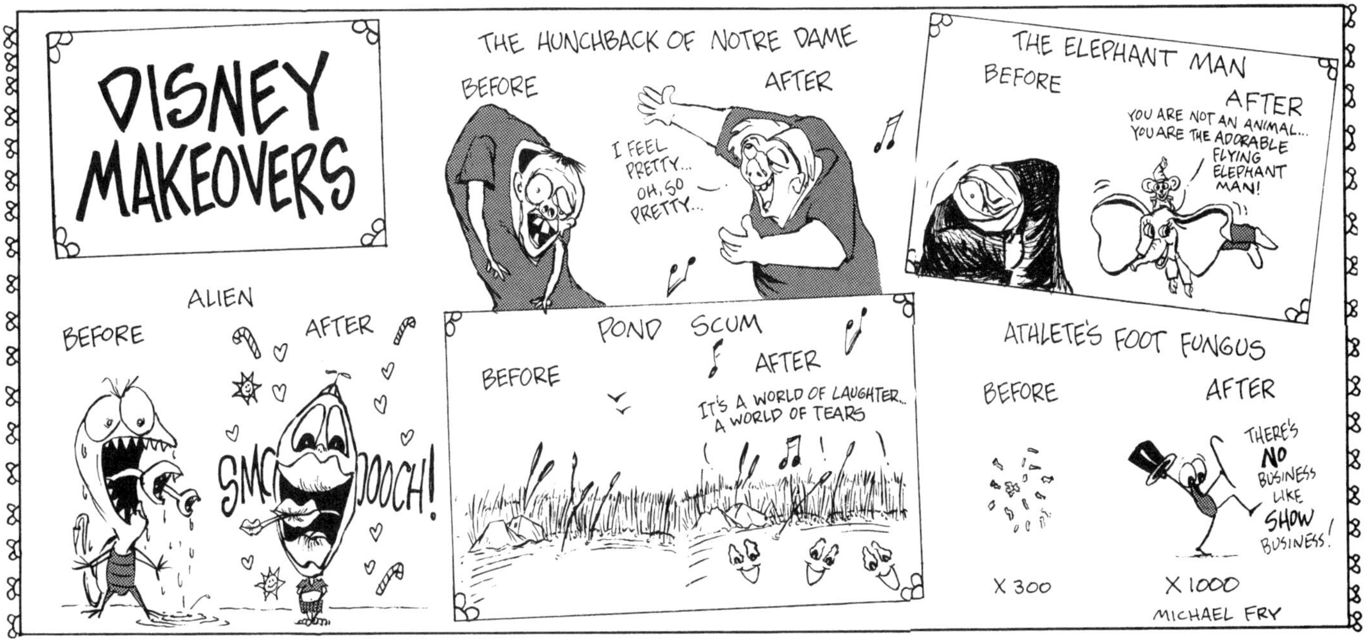
DISNEY MAKEOVERS
THE HUNCHBACK OF NOTRE DAME
BEFORE
AFTER
I FEEL PRETTY... OH, SO PRETTY...
THE ELEPHANT MAN
BEFORE
AFTER
YOU ARE NOT AN ANIMAL... YOU ARE THE ADORABLE FLYING ELEPHANT MAN!
ALIEN
BEFORE
AFTER
SMOOOOCH!
POND SCUM
BEFORE
AFTER
IT'S A WORLD OF LAUGHTER... A WORLD OF TEARS
ATHLETE'S FOOT FUNGUS
BEFORE
AFTER
THERE'S NO BUSINESS LIKE SHOW BUSINESS!
X 300
X 1000
MICHAEL FRY

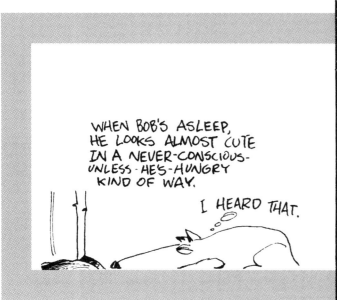

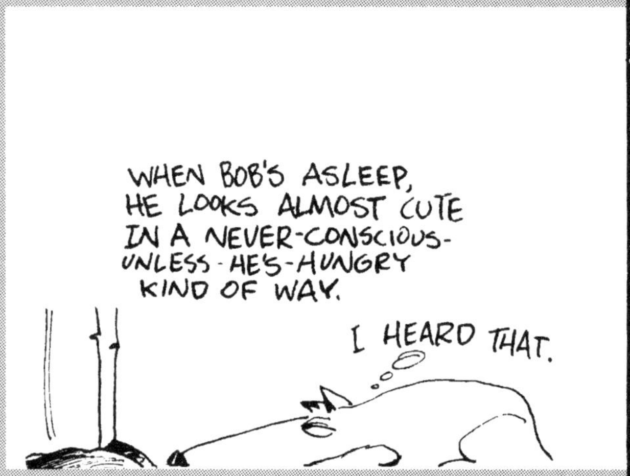
WHEN BOB'S ASLEEP, HE LOOKS ALMOST CUTE IN A NEVER-CONSCIOUS-UNLESS-HE'S-HUNGRY KIND OF WAY.
I HEARD THAT.

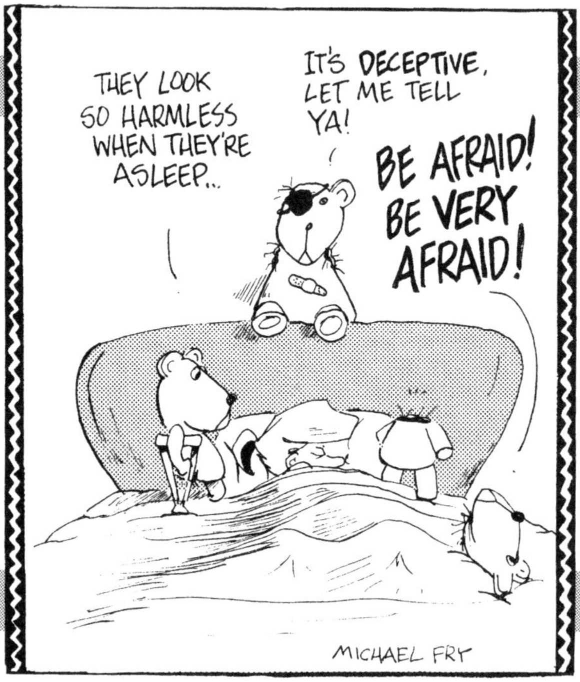
THEY LOOK SO HARMLESS WHEN THEY'RE ASLEEP...
IT'S DECEPTIVE, LET ME TELL YA!
BE AFRAID! BE VERY AFRAID!
MICHAEL FRY

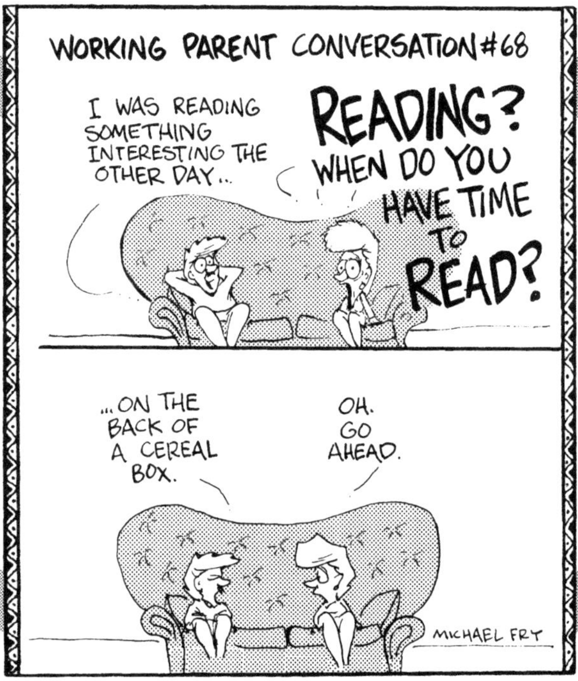
WORKING PARENT CONVERSATION #68
I WAS READING SOMETHING INTERESTING THE OTHER DAY...
READING? WHEN DO YOU HAVE TIME TO READ?
...ON THE BACK OF A CEREAL BOX.
OH. GO AHEAD.
MICHAEL FRY

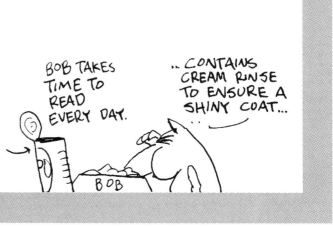

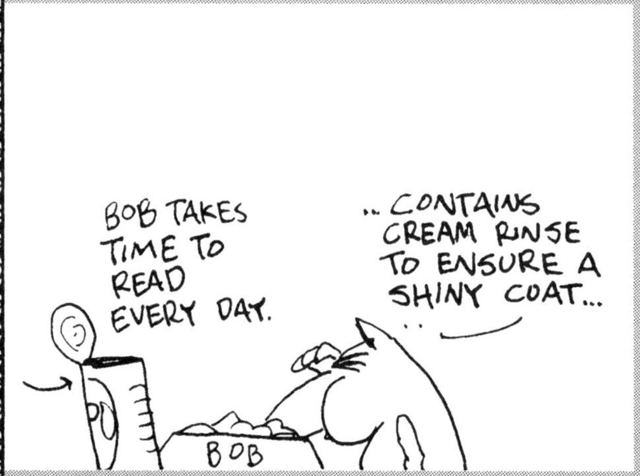
BOB TAKES TIME TO READ EVERY DAY.
...CONTAINS CREAM RINSE TO ENSURE A SHINY COAT...
BOB

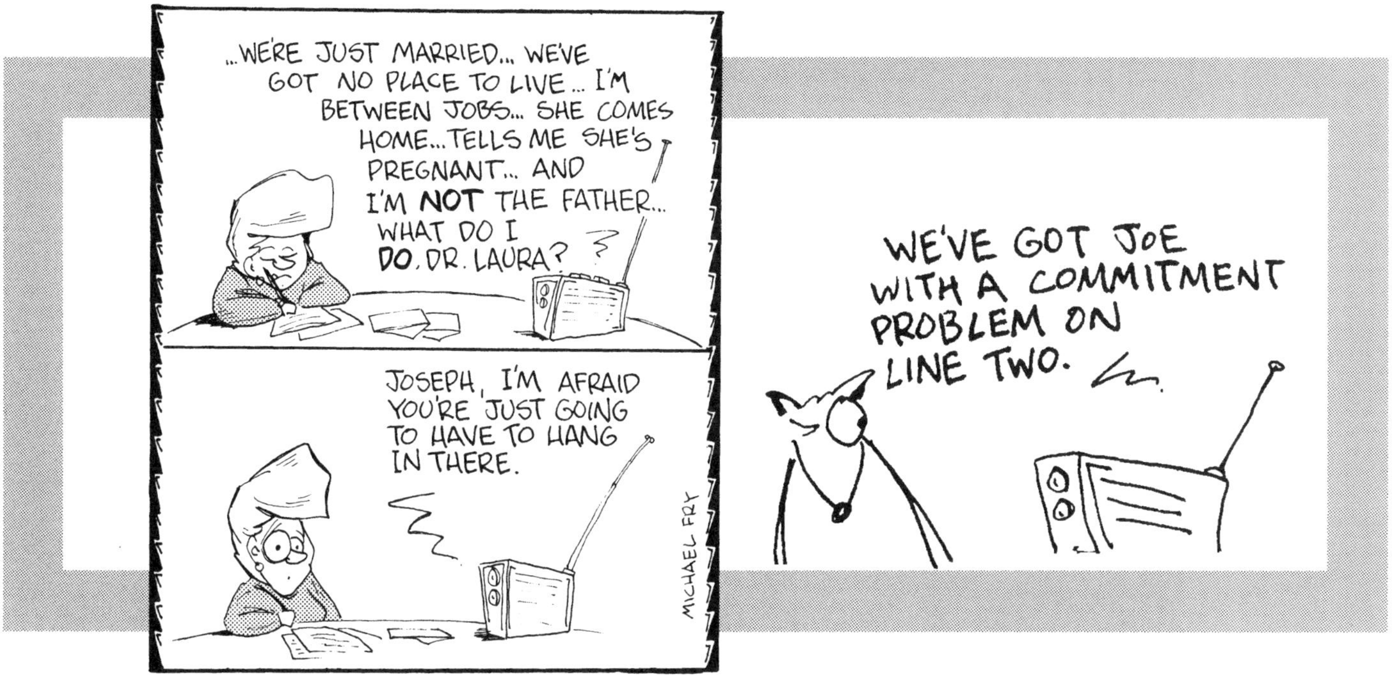
...WE'RE JUST MARRIED... WE'VE GOT NO PLACE TO LIVE... I'M BETWEEN JOBS... SHE COMES HOME... TELLS ME SHE'S PREGNANT... AND I'M NOT THE FATHER... WHAT DO I DO, DR. LAURA?
JOSEPH, I'M AFRAID YOU'RE JUST GOING TO HAVE TO HANG IN THERE.
MICHAEL FRY
WE'VE GOT JOE WITH A COMMITMENT PROBLEM ON LINE TWO.

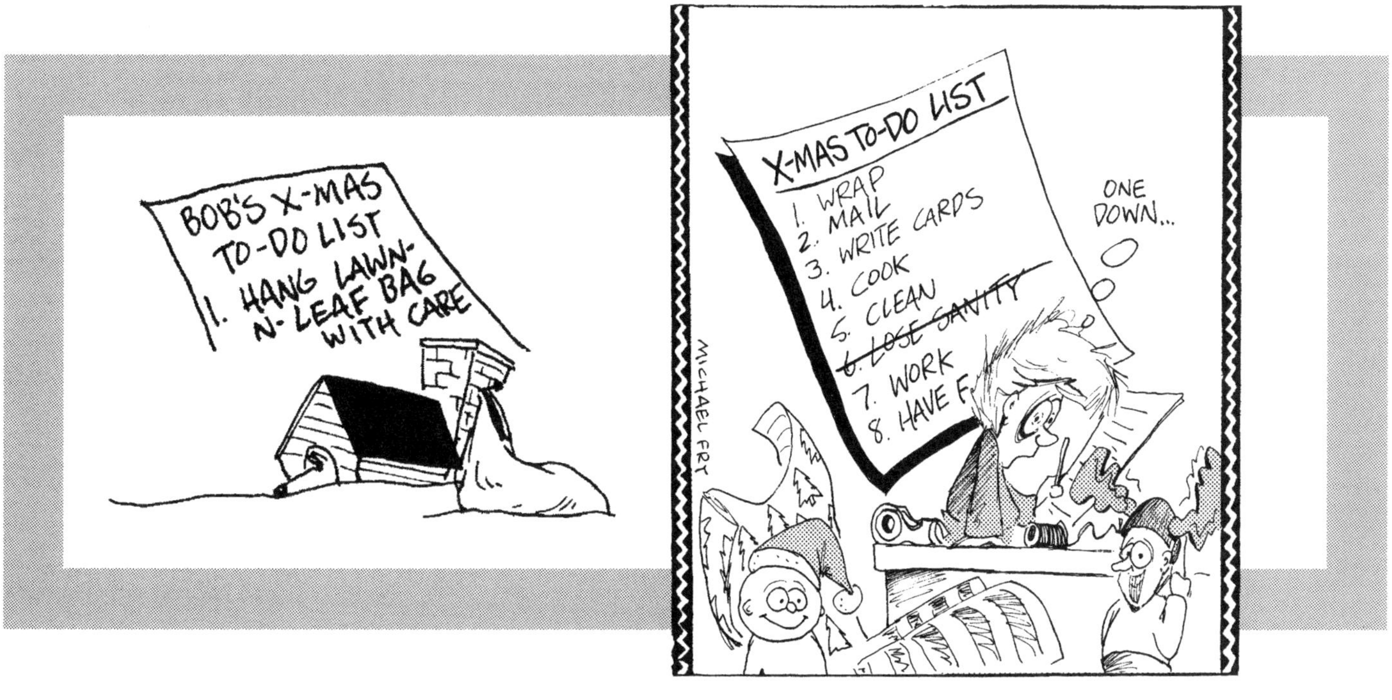
BOB'S X-MAS TO-DO LIST
1. HANG LAWN-N-LEAF BAG WITH CARE
X-MAS TO-DO LIST
1. WRAP
2. MAIL
3. WRITE CARDS
4. COOK
5. CLEAN
6. LOSE SANITY
7. WORK
8. HAVE F
ONE DOWN...
MICHAEL FRY

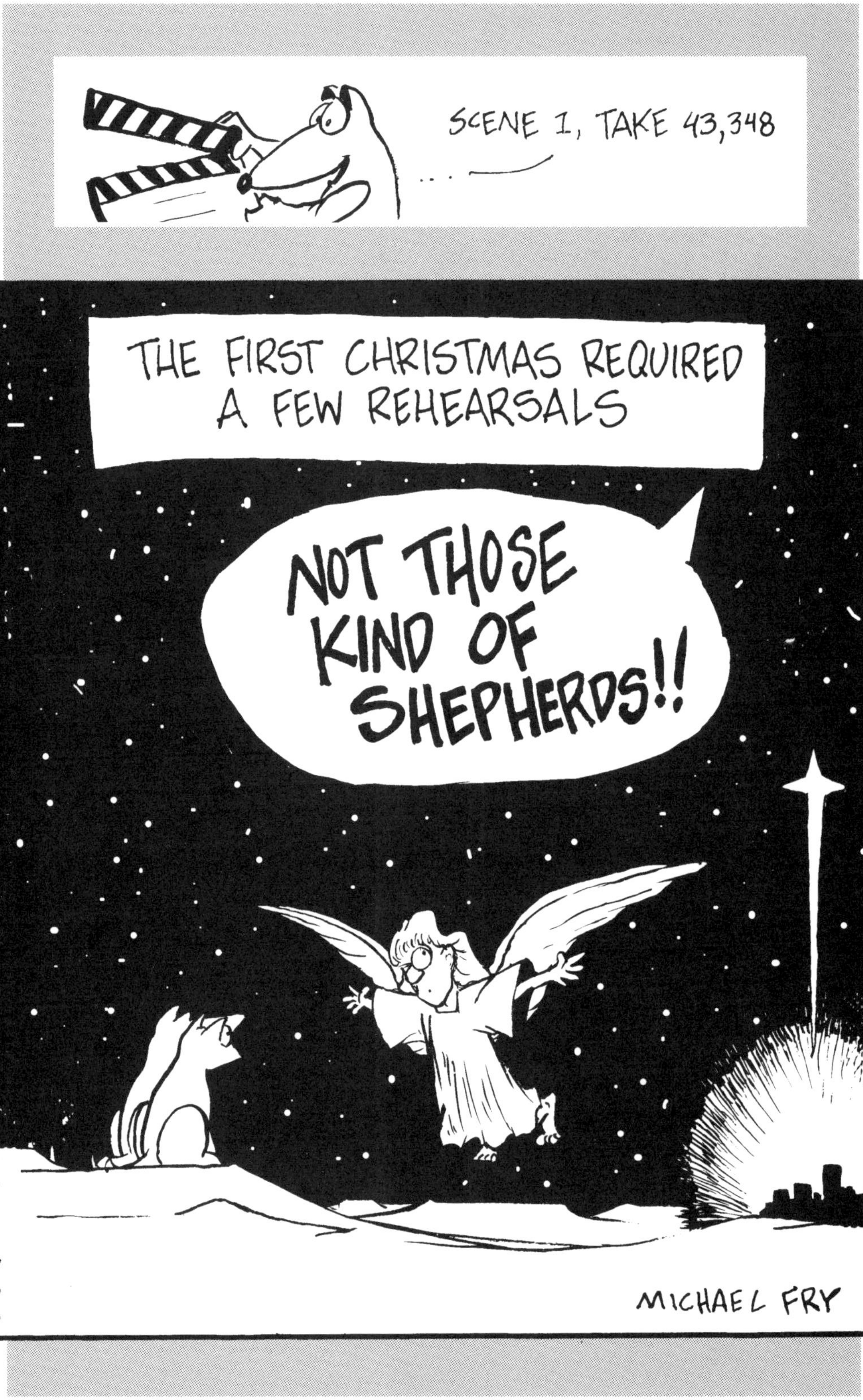
SCENE 1, TAKE 43,348
THE FIRST CHRISTMAS REQUIRED A FEW REHEARSALS
NOT THOSE KIND OF SHEPHERDS!!
MICHAEL FRY

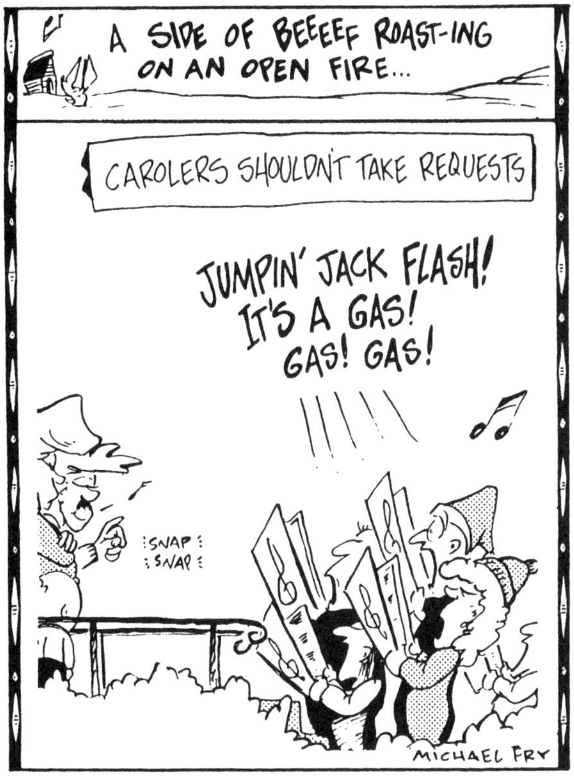
A SIDE OF BEEEEF ROAST-ING ON AN OPEN FIRE...
CAROLERS SHOULDN'T TAKE REQUESTS
JUMPIN' JACK FLASH! IT'S A GAS! GAS! GAS!
SNAP SNAP
MICHAEL FRY

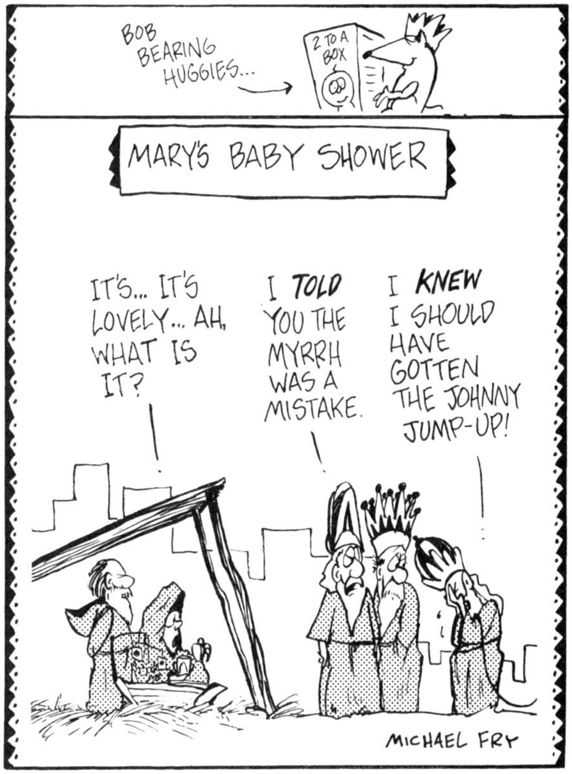
BOB BEARING HUGGIES...
2 TO A BOX
MARY'S BABY SHOWER
IT'S... IT'S LOVELY... AH, WHAT IS IT?
I TOLD YOU THE MYRRH WAS A MISTAKE.
I KNEW I SHOULD HAVE GOTTEN THE JOHNNY JUMP-UP!
MICHAEL FRY

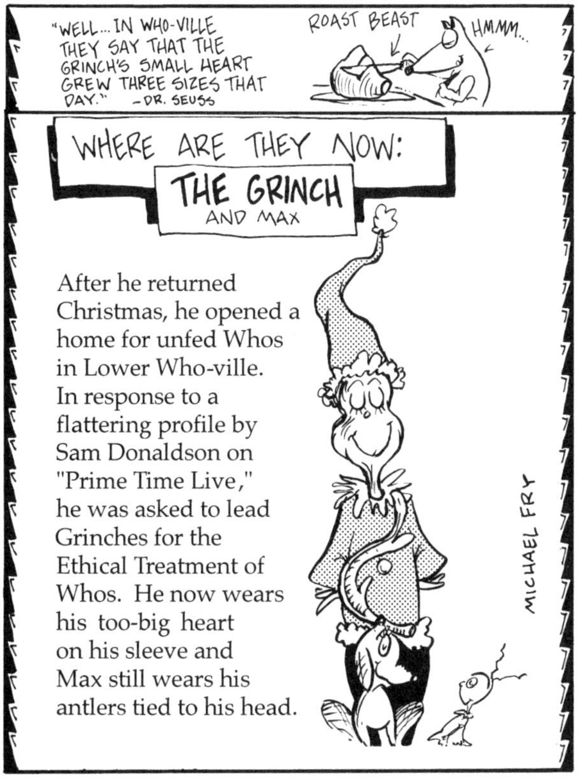
"WELL... IN WHO-VILLE THEY SAY THAT THE GRINCH'S SMALL HEART GREW THREE SIZES THAT DAY." -DR. SEUSS
ROAST BEAST
HMMM...
WHERE ARE THEY NOW:
THE GRINCH AND MAX
After he returned Christmas, he opened a home for unfed Whos in Lower Who-ville. In response to a flattering profile by Sam Donaldson on "Prime Time Live," he was asked to lead Grinches for the Ethical Treatment of Whos. He now wears his too-big heart on his sleeve and Max still wears his antlers tied to his head.
MICHAEL FRY

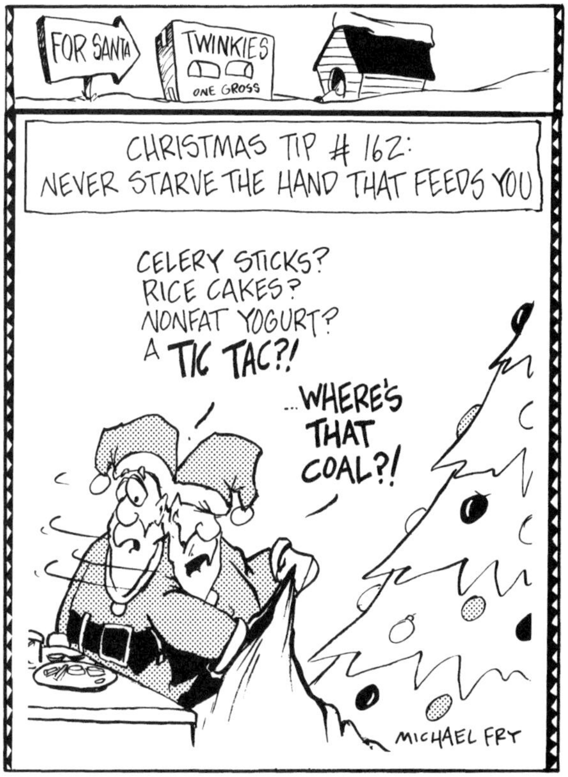
FOR SANTA
TWINKIES
ONE GROSS
CHRISTMAS TIP # 162: NEVER STARVE THE HAND THAT FEEDS YOU
CELERY STICKS? RICE CAKES? NONFAT YOGURT? A TIC TAC?!
...WHERE'S THAT COAL?!
MICHAEL FRY

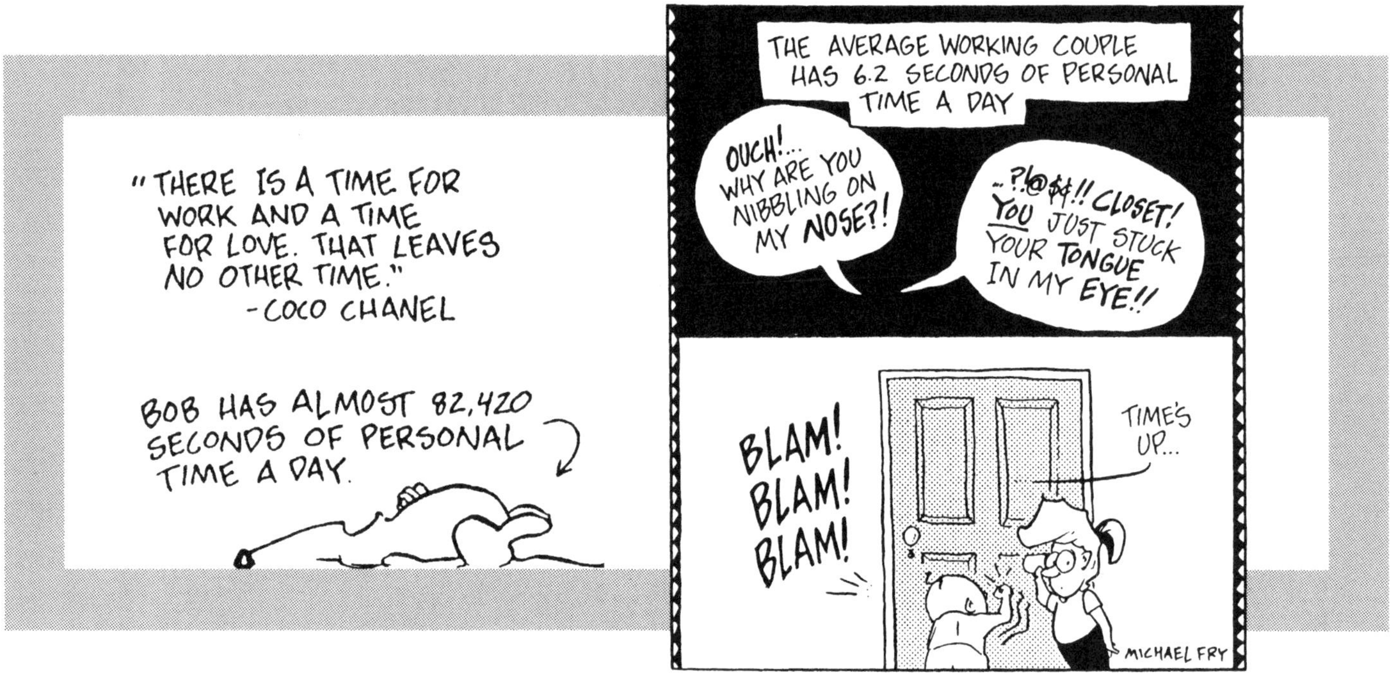
"THERE IS A TIME FOR WORK AND A TIME FOR LOVE. THAT LEAVES NO OTHER TIME."
-COCO CHANEL
BOB HAS ALMOST 82,420 SECONDS OF PERSONAL TIME A DAY.
THE AVERAGE WORKING COUPLE HAS 6.2 SECONDS OF PERSONAL TIME A DAY
OUCH!... WHY ARE YOU NIBBLING ON MY NOSE?!
..?!@$¢!! CLOSET! YOU JUST STUCK YOUR TONGUE IN MY EYE!!
BLAM! BLAM! BLAM!
TIME'S UP...
MICHAEL FRY

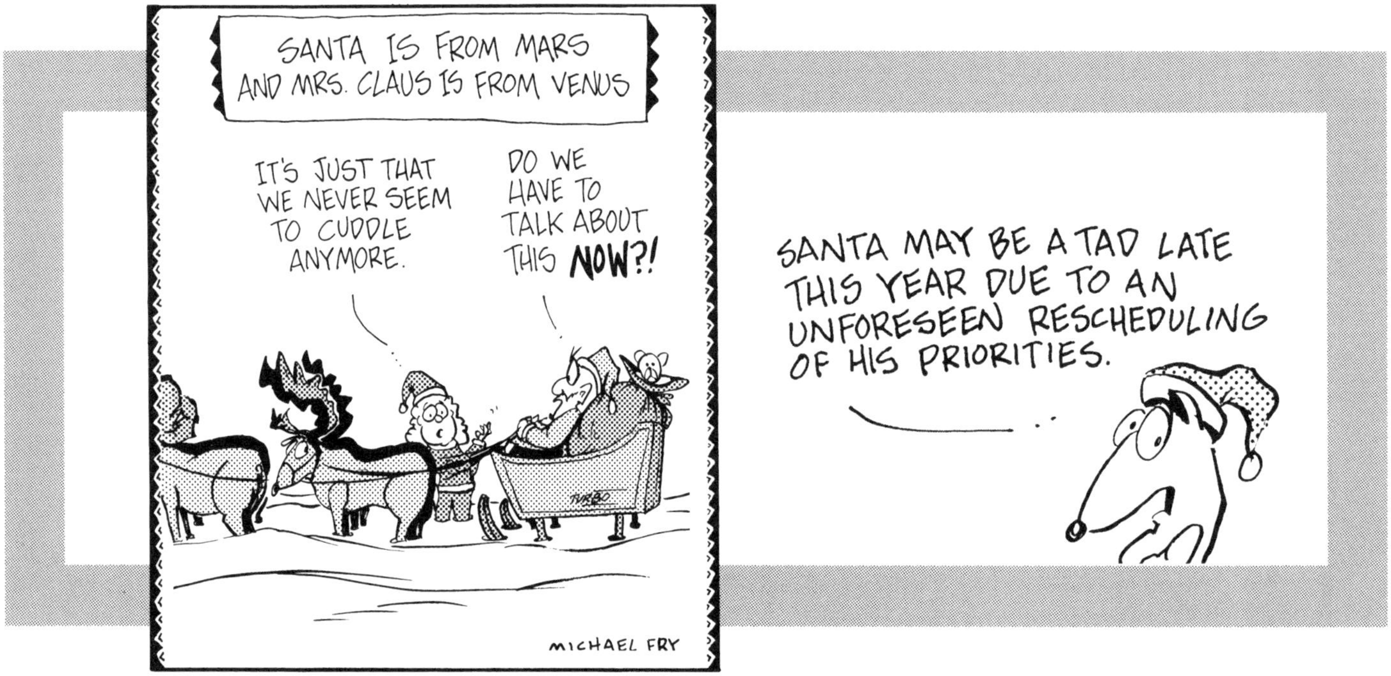
SANTA IS FROM MARS AND MRS. CLAUS IS FROM VENUS
IT'S JUST THAT WE NEVER SEEM TO CUDDLE ANYMORE.
DO WE HAVE TO TALK ABOUT THIS NOW?!
MICHAEL FRY
SANTA MAY BE A TAD LATE THIS YEAR DUE TO AN UNFORESEEN RESCHEDULING OF HIS PRIORITIES.

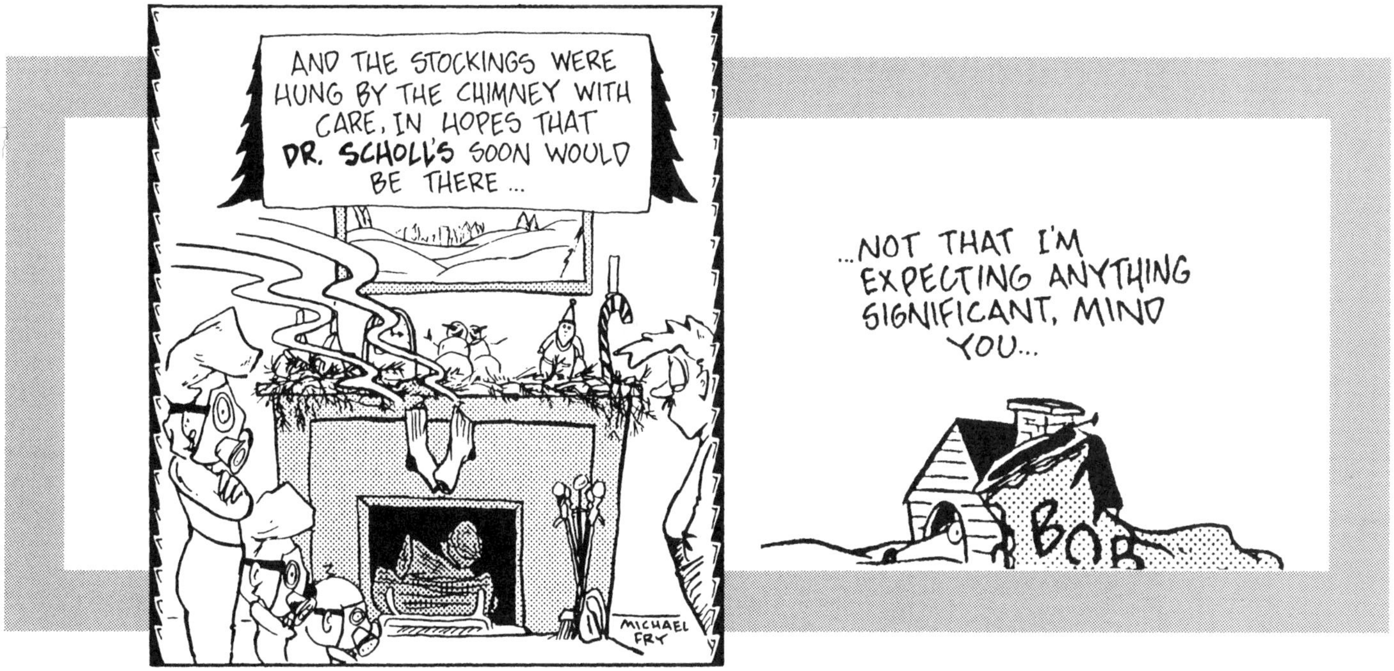
AND THE STOCKINGS WERE HUNG BY THE CHIMNEY WITH CARE, IN HOPES THAT DR. SCHOLL'S SOON WOULD BE THERE ...
MICHAEL FRY
...NOT THAT I'M EXPECTING ANYTHING SIGNIFICANT, MIND YOU...
BOB

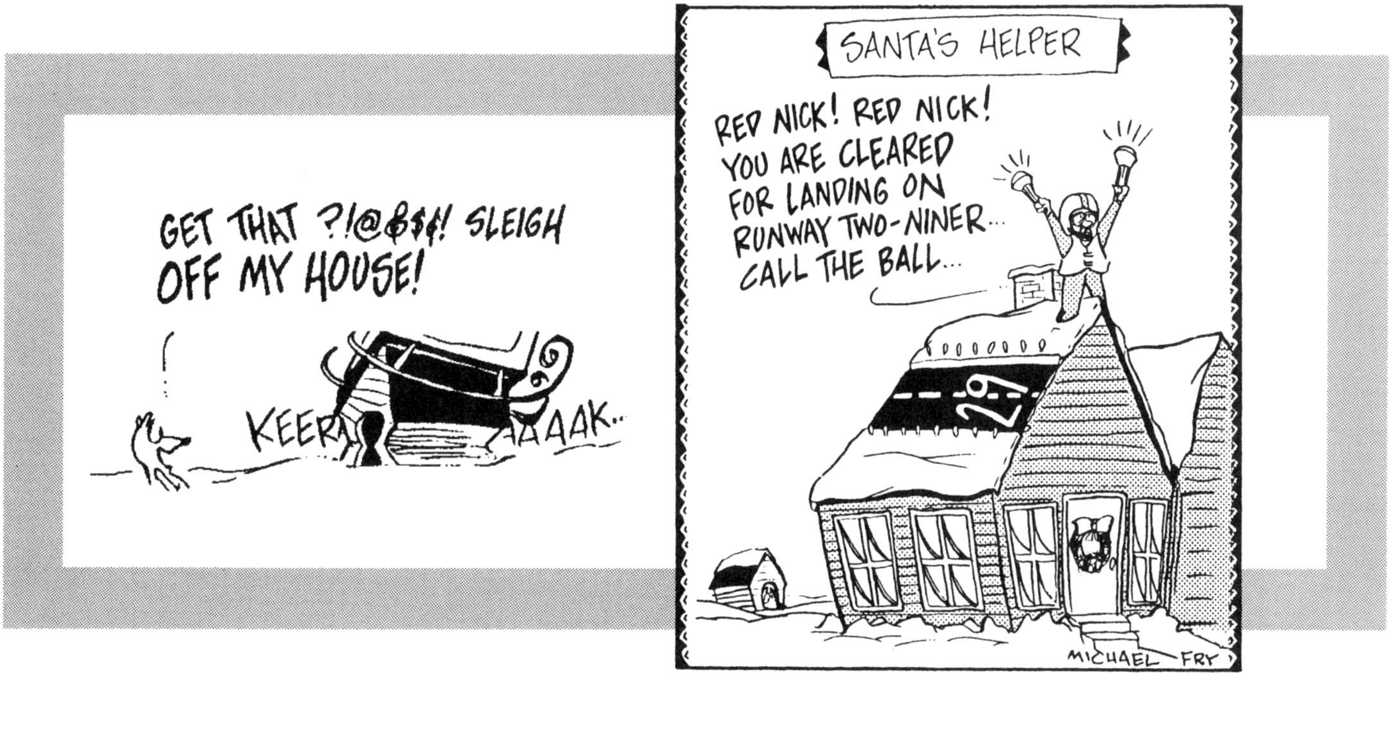
GET THAT ?!@$$¢! SLEIGH OFF MY HOUSE!
KEERAAAAK...
SANTA'S HELPER
RED NICK! RED NICK! YOU ARE CLEARED FOR LANDING ON RUNWAY TWO-NINER... CALL THE BALL...
29
MICHAEL FRY

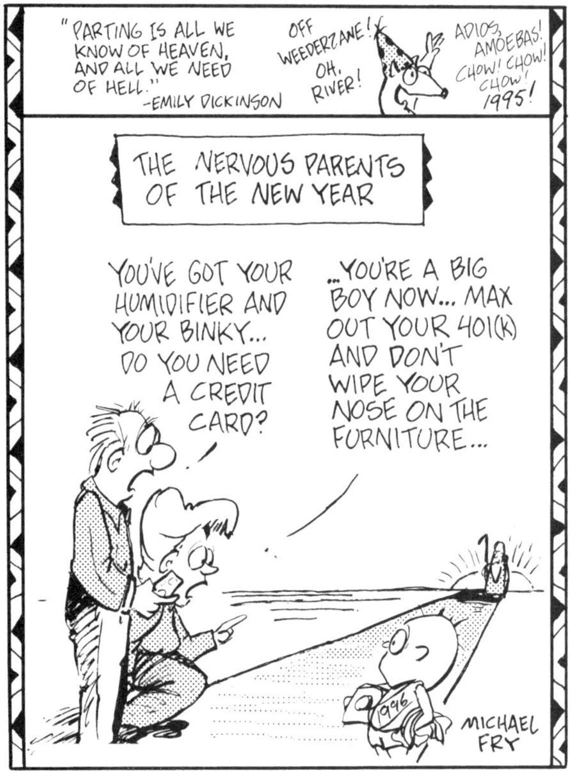
"PARTING IS ALL WE KNOW OF HEAVEN, AND ALL WE NEED OF HELL."
-EMILY DICKINSON
OFF WEEDERZANE! OH, RIVER!
ADIOS, AMOEBAS! CHOW! CHOW! CHOW! 1995!
THE NERVOUS PARENTS OF THE NEW YEAR
YOU'VE GOT YOUR HUMIDIFIER AND YOUR BINKY... DO YOU NEED A CREDIT CARD?
...YOU'RE A BIG BOY NOW... MAX OUT YOUR 401(k) AND DON'T WIPE YOUR NOSE ON THE FURNITURE...
1996
MICHAEL FRY

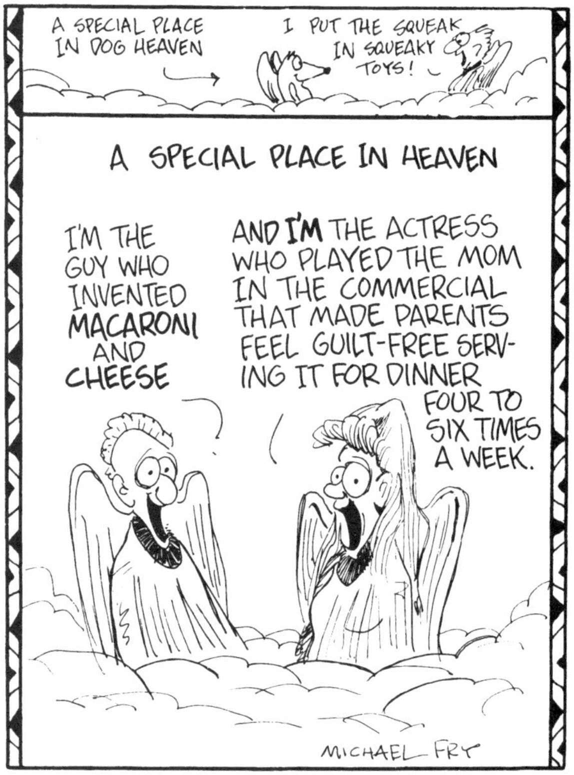
A SPECIAL PLACE IN DOG HEAVEN
I PUT THE SQUEAK IN SQUEAKY TOYS!
A SPECIAL PLACE IN HEAVEN
I'M THE GUY WHO INVENTED MACARONI AND CHEESE
AND I'M THE ACTRESS WHO PLAYED THE MOM IN THE COMMERCIAL THAT MADE PARENTS FEEL GUILT-FREE SERVING IT FOR DINNER FOUR TO SIX TIMES A WEEK.
MICHAEL FRY

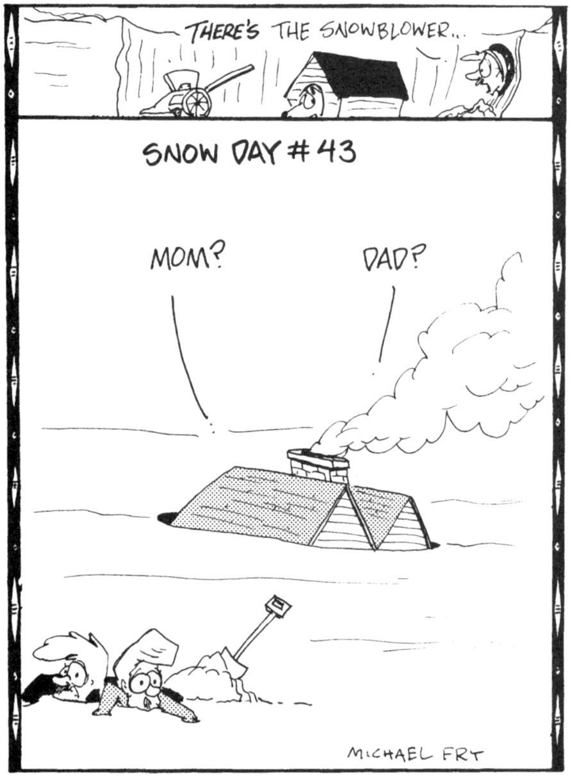
THERE'S THE SNOWBLOWER...
SNOW DAY # 43
MOM?
DAD?
MICHAEL FRY

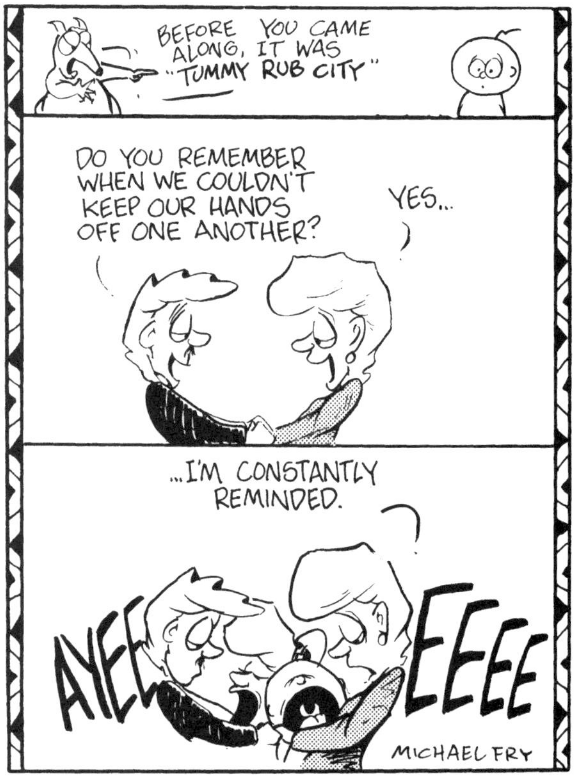
BEFORE YOU CAME ALONG, IT WAS "TUMMY RUB CITY"
DO YOU REMEMBER WHEN WE COULDN'T KEEP OUR HANDS OFF ONE ANOTHER?
YES...
...I'M CONSTANTLY REMINDED.
AYEEEEEE
MICHAEL FRY

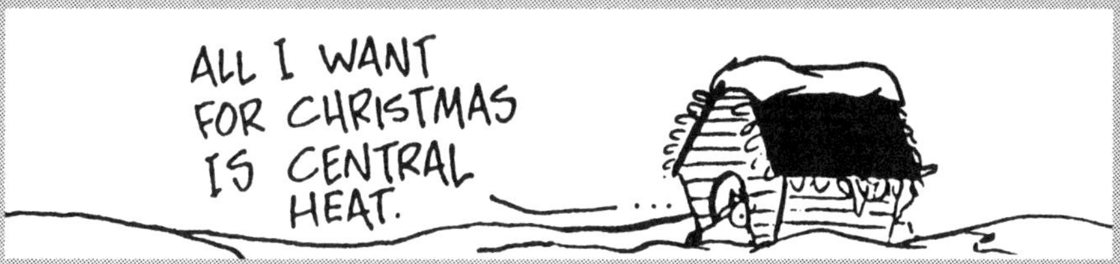
ALL I WANT FOR CHRISTMAS IS CENTRAL HEAT.

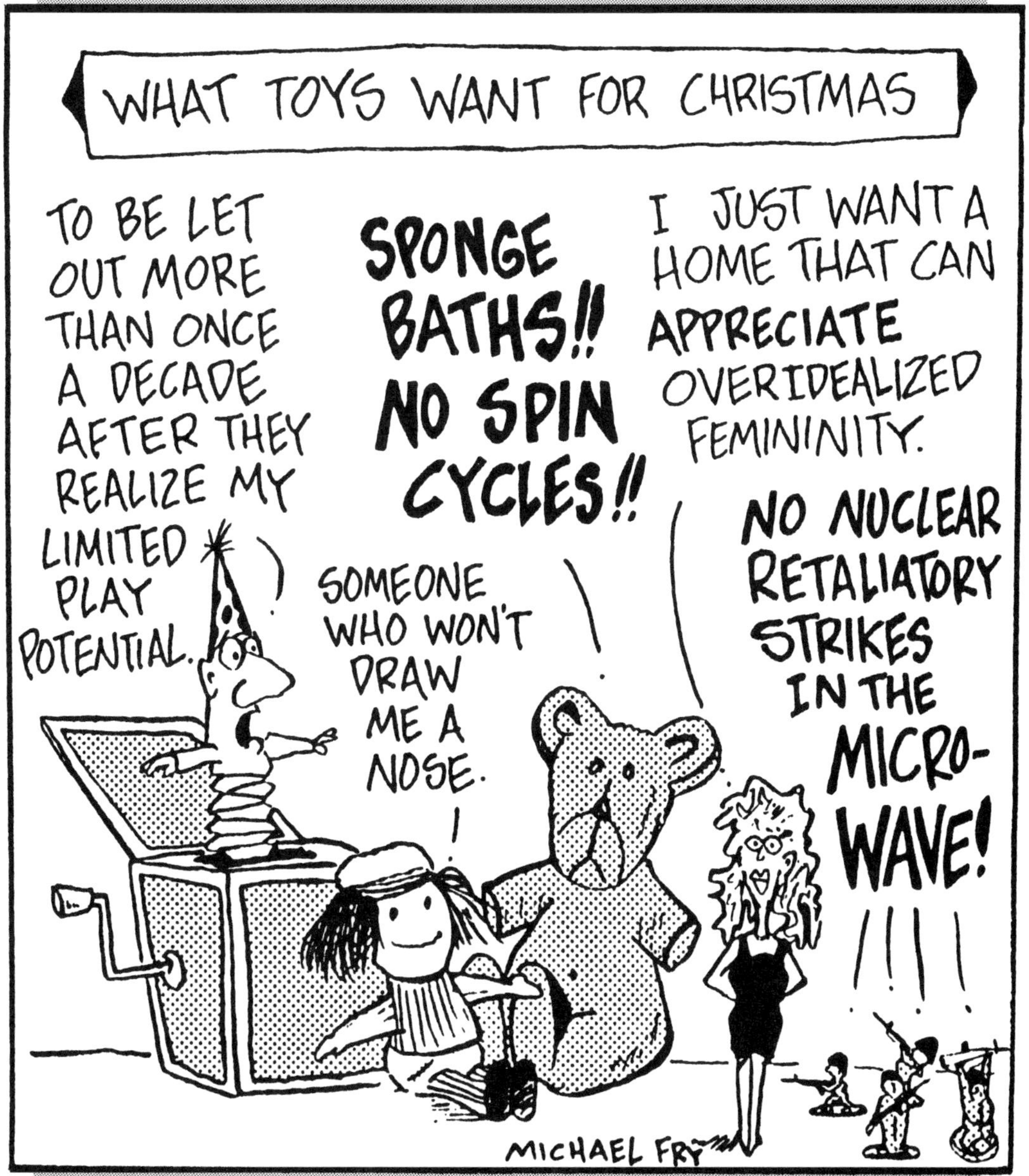
WHAT TOYS WANT FOR CHRISTMAS
TO BE LET OUT MORE THAN ONCE A DECADE AFTER THEY REALIZE MY LIMITED PLAY POTENTIAL.
SOMEONE WHO WON'T DRAW ME A NOSE.
SPONGE BATHS!! NO SPIN CYCLES!!
I JUST WANT A HOME THAT CAN APPRECIATE OVERIDEALIZED FEMININITY.
NO NUCLEAR RETALIATORY STRIKES IN THE MICRO-WAVE!
MICHAEL FRY

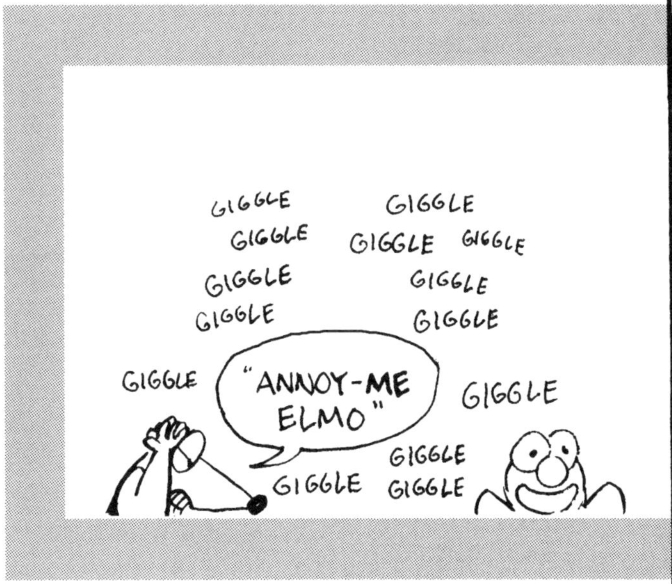
GIGGLE GIGGLE GIGGLE GIGGLE GIGGLE GIGGLE GIGGLE GIGGLE GIGGLE GIGGLE
"ANNOY-ME ELMO"
GIGGLE
GIGGLE GIGGLE GIGGLE

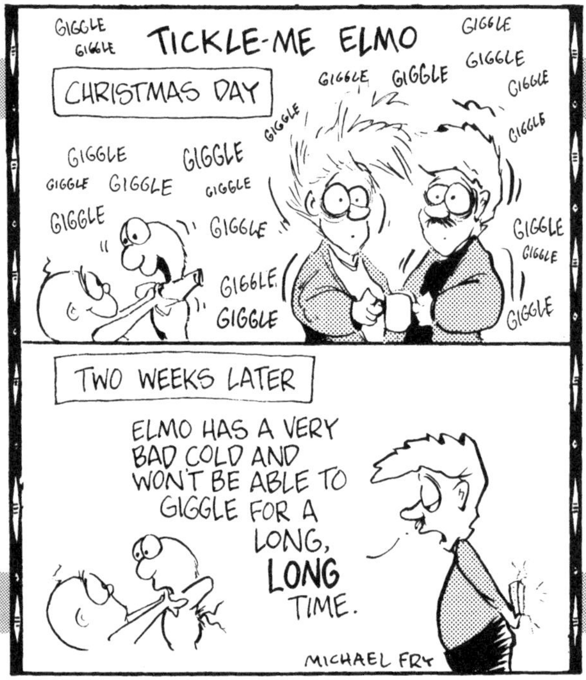
TICKLE-ME ELMO
CHRISTMAS DAY
GIGGLE GIGGLE GIGGLE GIGGLE GIGGLE GIGGLE GIGGLE GIGGLE GIGGLE GIGGLE
TWO WEEKS LATER
ELMO HAS A VERY BAD COLD AND WON'T BE ABLE TO GIGGLE FOR A LONG, LONG TIME.
MICHAEL FRY

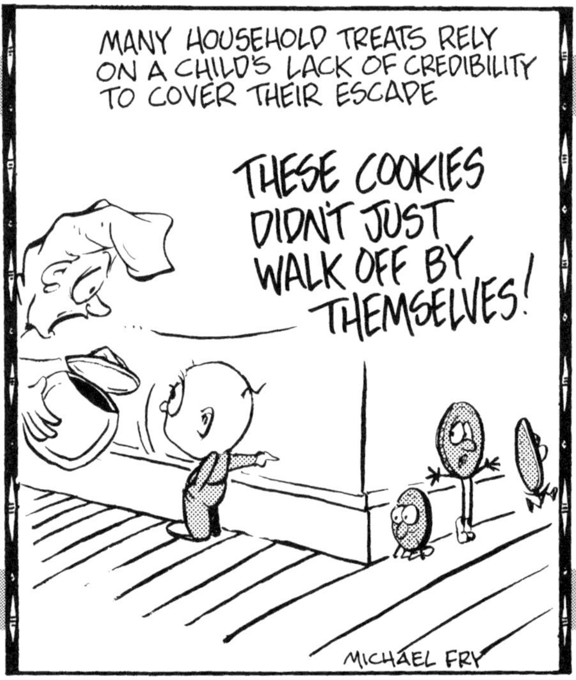
MANY HOUSEHOLD TREATS RELY ON A CHILD'S LACK OF CREDIBILITY TO COVER THEIR ESCAPE
THESE COOKIES DIDN'T JUST WALK OFF BY THEMSELVES!
MICHAEL FRY

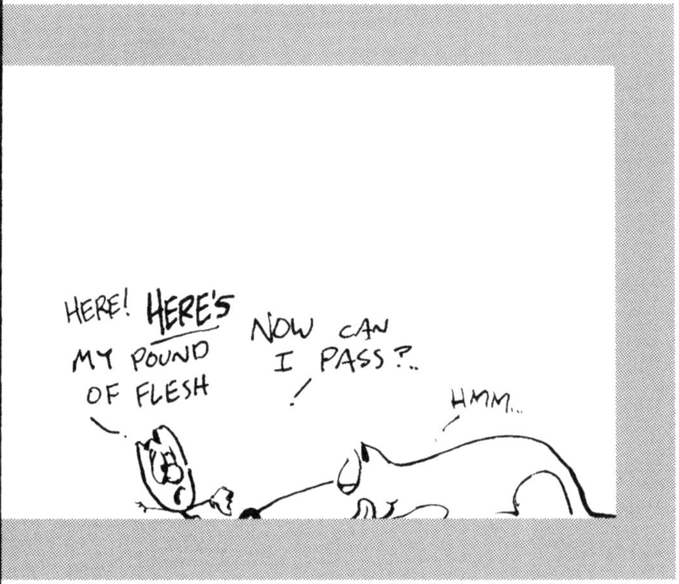
HERE! HERE'S MY POUND OF FLESH
NOW CAN I PASS?..
HMM...

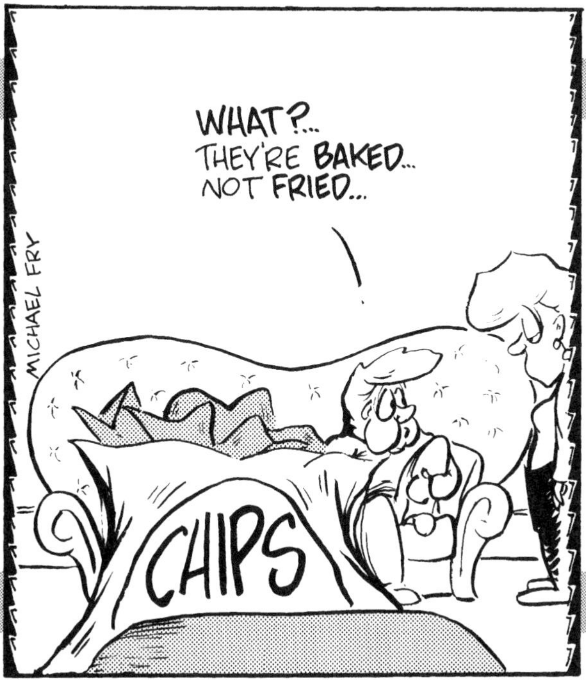
WHAT?...
THEY'RE BAKED...
NOT FRIED...
MICHAEL FRY
CHIPS

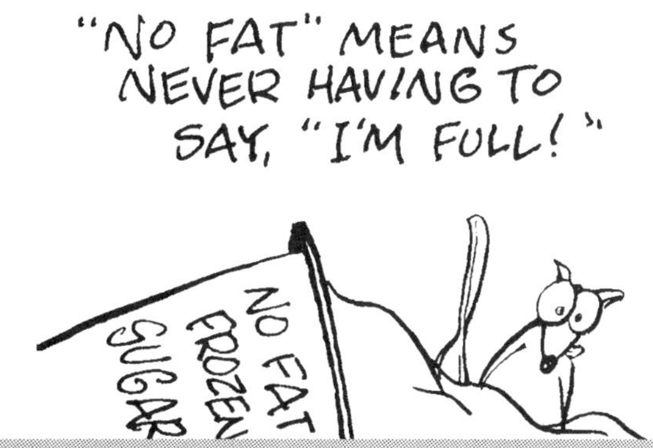
"NO FAT" MEANS NEVER HAVING TO SAY, "I'M FULL!"
NO FAT FROZEN SUGAR

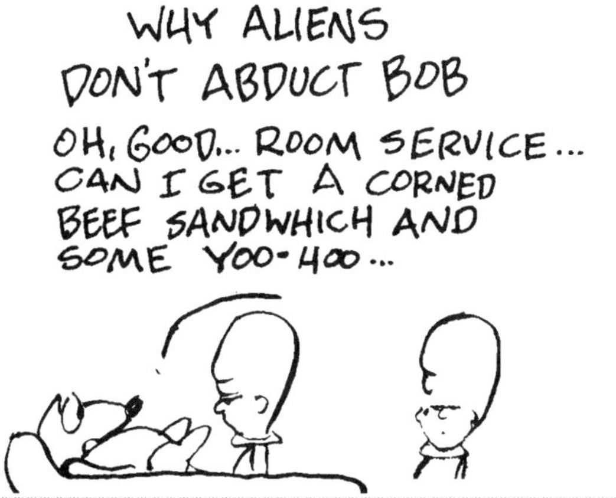
WHY ALIENS DON'T ABDUCT BOB
OH, GOOD... ROOM SERVICE... CAN I GET A CORNED BEEF SANDWHICH AND SOME YOO-HOO...

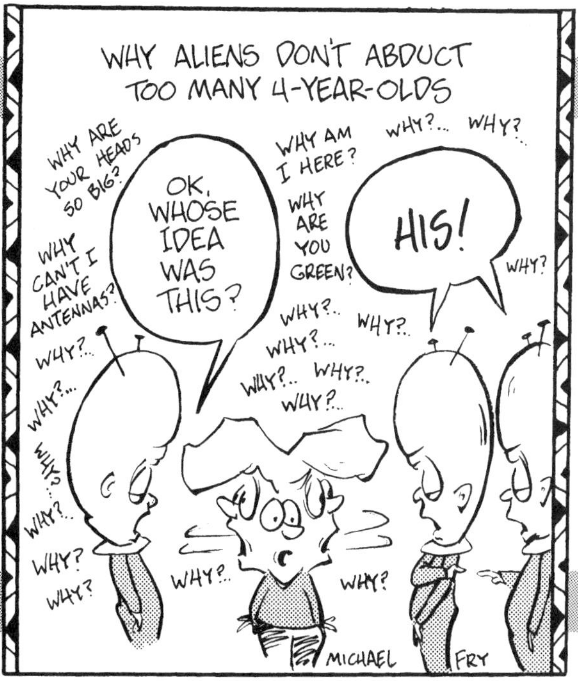
WHY ALIENS DON'T ABDUCT TOO MANY 4-YEAR-OLDS
WHY ARE YOUR HEADS SO BIG?
WHY CAN'T I HAVE ANTENNAS?
WHY AM I HERE?
WHY ARE YOU GREEN?
WHY?... WHY?...
OK, WHOSE IDEA WAS THIS?
HIS!
WHY?
WHY?... WHY?...
WHY?... WHY?... WHY?...
WHY?... WHY?... WHY?... WHY?... WHY? WHY?
WHY?... WHY?
MICHAEL FRY

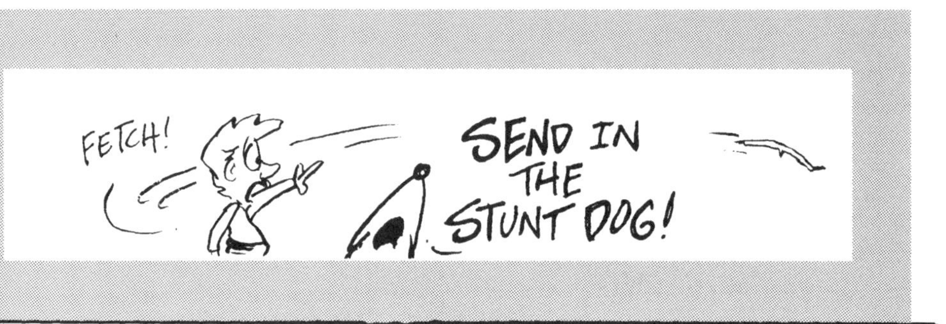
FETCH!
SEND IN THE STUNT DOG!

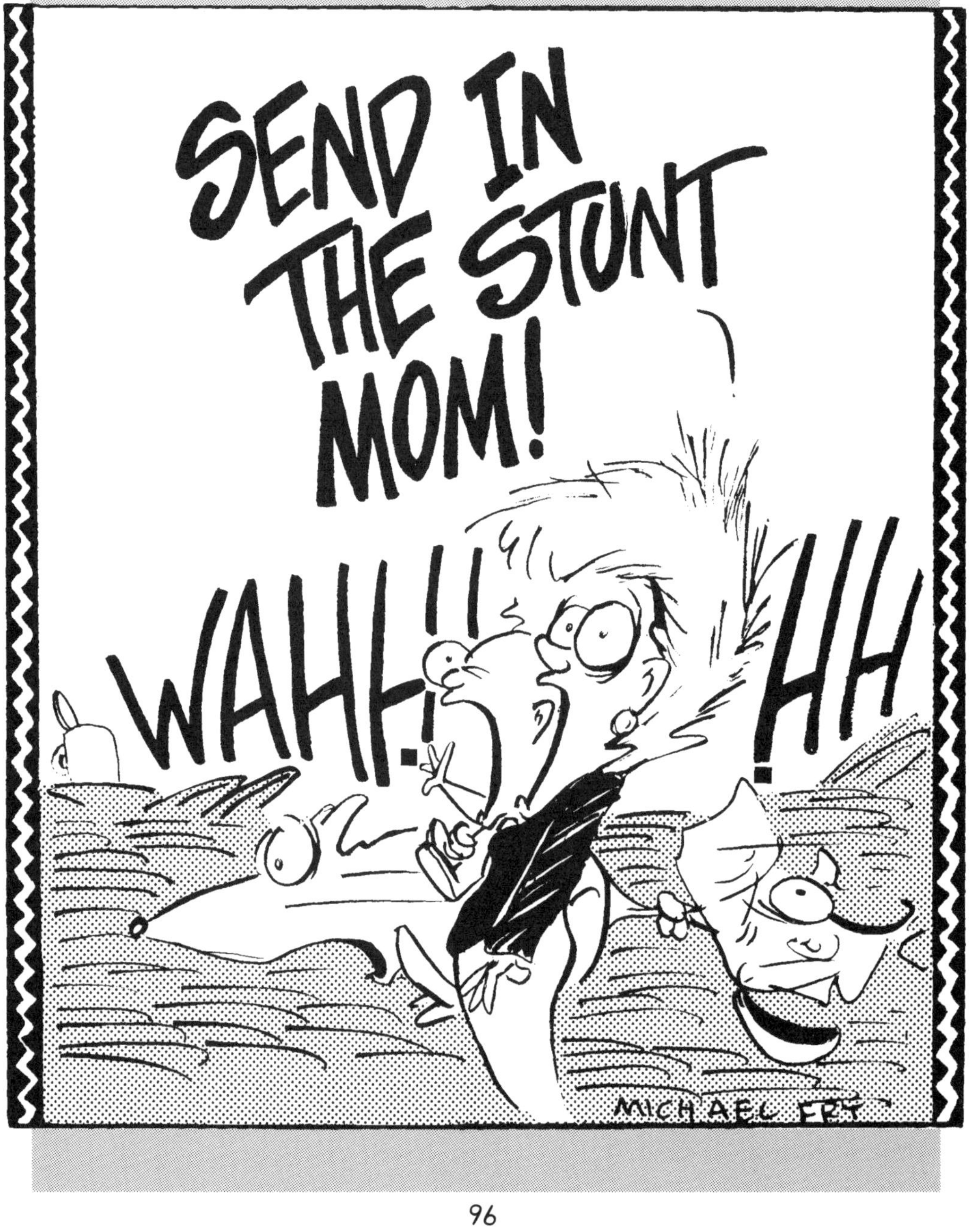
SEND IN THE STUNT MOM!
WAHH!!!HH!
MICHAEL FRY

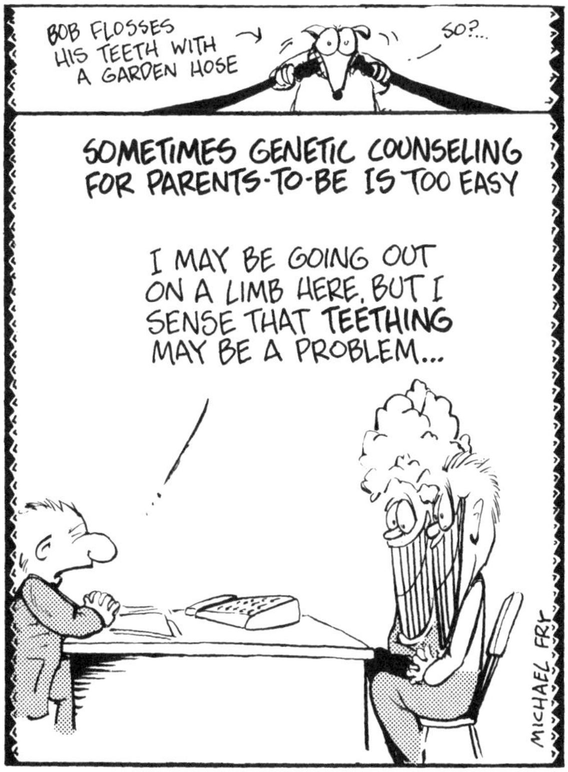
BOB FLOSSES HIS TEETH WITH A GARDEN HOSE
SO?...
SOMETIMES GENETIC COUNSELING FOR PARENTS-TO-BE IS TOO EASY
I MAY BE GOING OUT ON A LIMB HERE, BUT I SENSE THAT TEETHING MAY BE A PROBLEM...
MICHAEL FRY

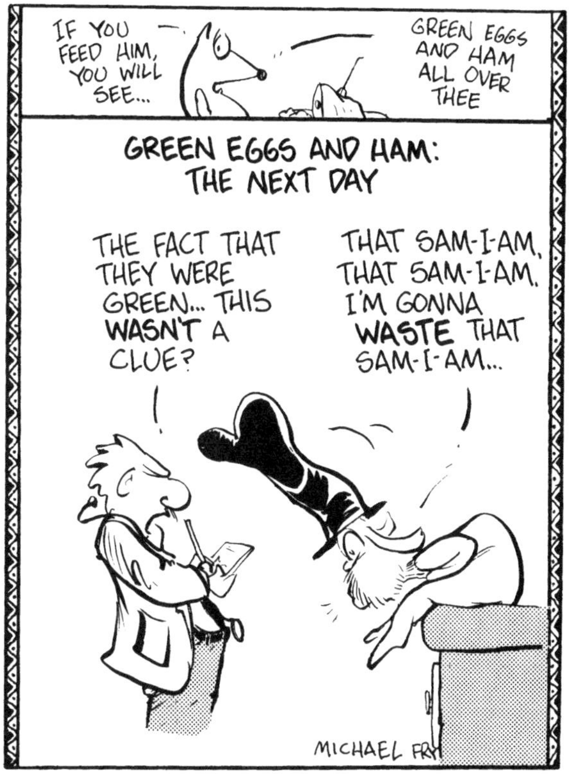
IF YOU FEED HIM, YOU WILL SEE...
GREEN EGGS AND HAM ALL OVER THEE
GREEN EGGS AND HAM: THE NEXT DAY
THE FACT THAT THEY WERE GREEN... THIS WASN'T A CLUE?
THAT SAM-I-AM, THAT SAM-I-AM, I'M GONNA WASTE THAT SAM-I-AM...
MICHAEL FRY

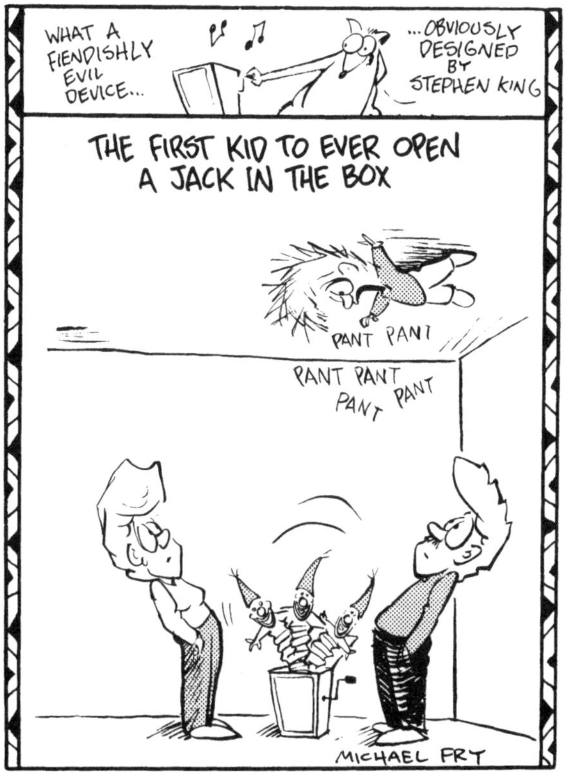
WHAT A FIENDISHLY EVIL DEVICE...
...OBVIOUSLY DESIGNED BY STEPHEN KING
THE FIRST KID TO EVER OPEN A JACK IN THE BOX
PANT PANT
PANT PANT PANT PANT
MICHAEL FRY

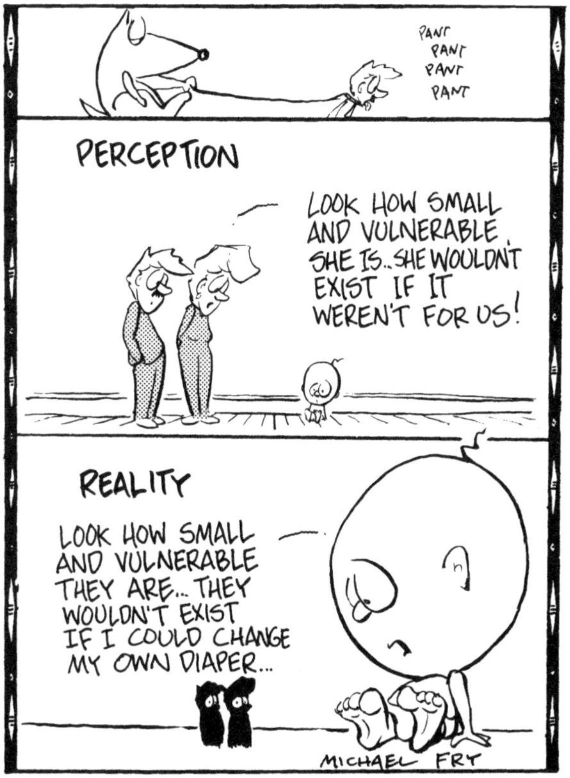
PANT PANT PANT PANT
PERCEPTION
LOOK HOW SMALL AND VULNERABLE SHE IS.. SHE WOULDN'T EXIST IF IT WEREN'T FOR US!
REALITY
LOOK HOW SMALL AND VULNERABLE THEY ARE... THEY WOULDN'T EXIST IF I COULD CHANGE MY OWN DIAPER...
MICHAEL FRY

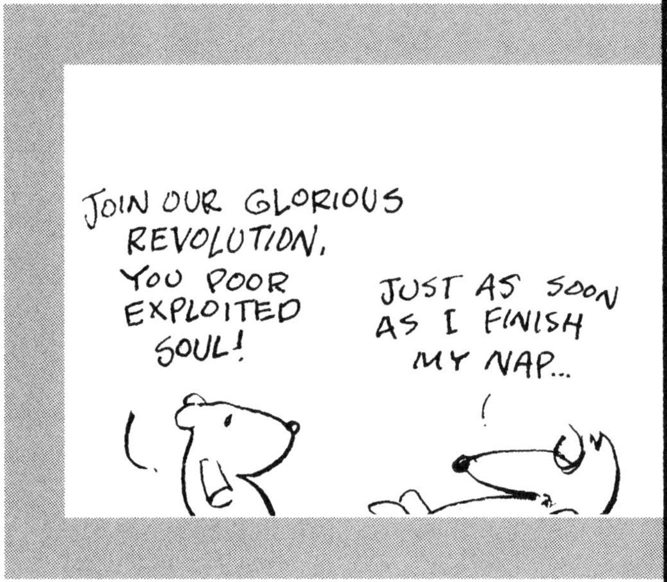
JOIN OUR GLORIOUS REVOLUTION, YOU POOR EXPLOITED SOUL!
JUST AS SOON AS I FINISH MY NAP...

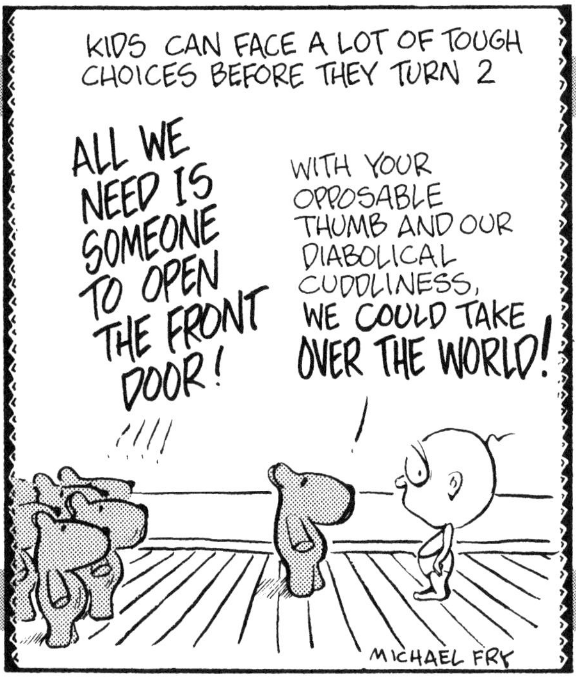
KIDS CAN FACE A LOT OF TOUGH CHOICES BEFORE THEY TURN 2
ALL WE NEED IS SOMEONE TO OPEN THE FRONT DOOR!
WITH YOUR OPPOSABLE THUMB AND OUR DIABOLICAL CUDDLINESS, WE COULD TAKE OVER THE WORLD!
MICHAEL FRY

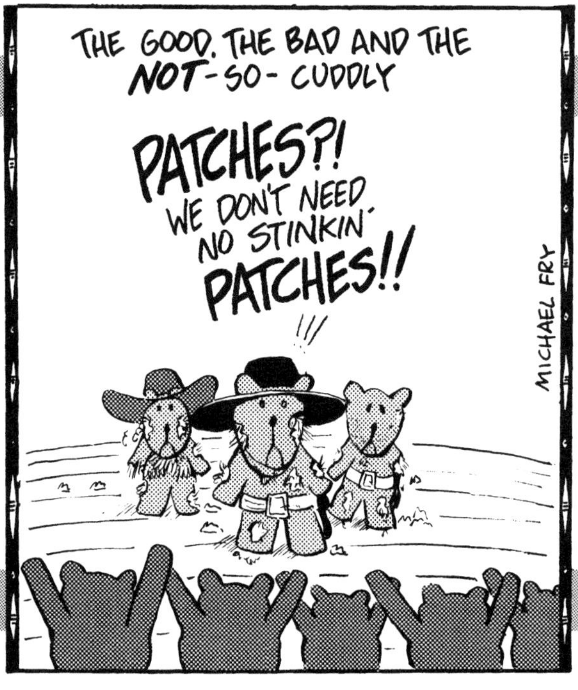
THE GOOD, THE BAD AND THE NOT-SO-CUDDLY
PATCHES?! WE DON'T NEED NO STINKIN' PATCHES!!
MICHAEL FRY

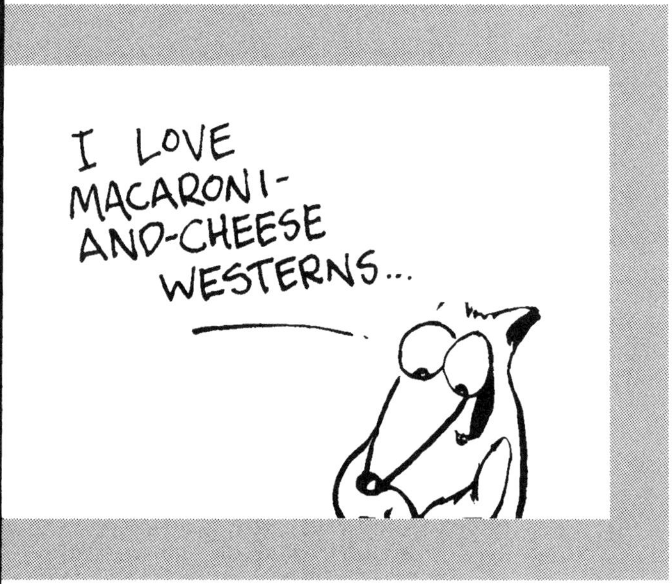
I LOVE MACARONI-AND-CHEESE WESTERNS...

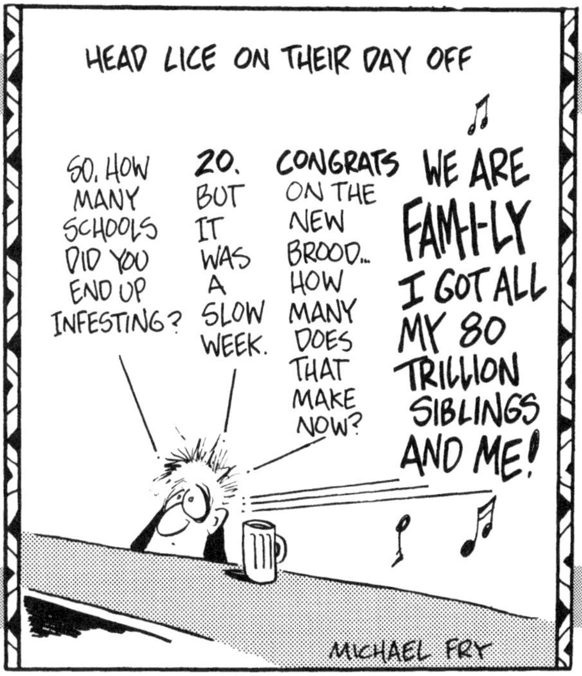
HEAD LICE ON THEIR DAY OFF
SO, HOW MANY SCHOOLS DID YOU END UP INFESTING?
20. BUT IT WAS A SLOW WEEK.
CONGRATS ON THE NEW BROOD.. HOW MANY DOES THAT MAKE NOW?
WE ARE FAM-I-LY I GOT ALL MY 80 TRILLION SIBLINGS AND ME!
MICHAEL FRY

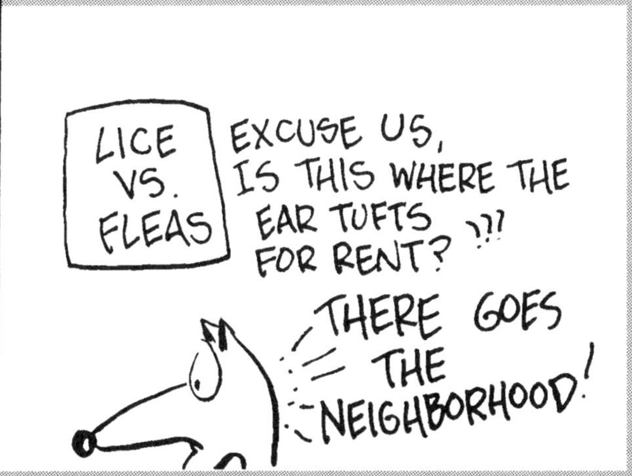
LICE VS. FLEAS
EXCUSE US, IS THIS WHERE THE EAR TUFTS FOR RENT?
THERE GOES THE NEIGHBORHOOD!

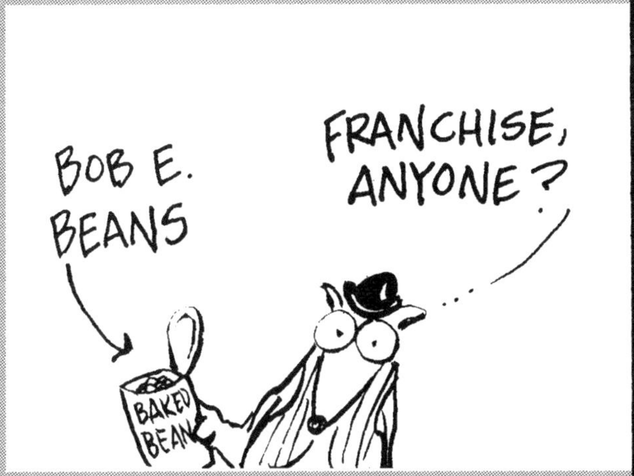
BOB E. BEANS
FRANCHISE, ANYONE?
BAKED BEAN

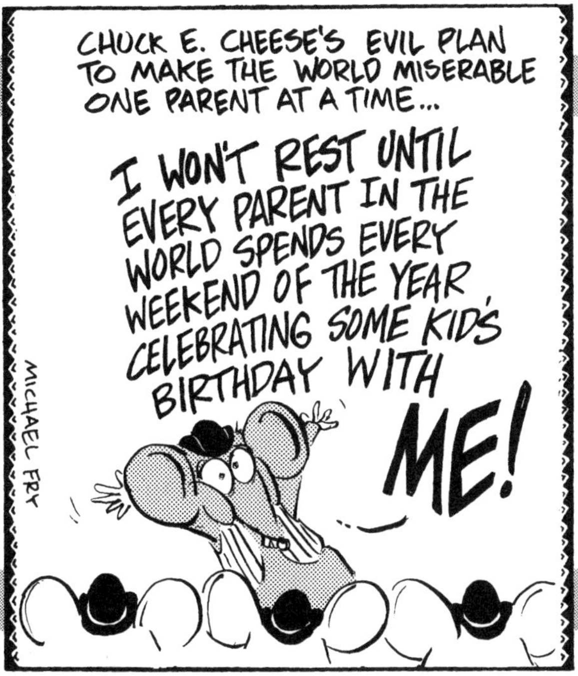
CHUCK E. CHEESE'S EVIL PLAN TO MAKE THE WORLD MISERABLE ONE PARENT AT A TIME...
I WON'T REST UNTIL EVERY PARENT IN THE WORLD SPENDS EVERY WEEKEND OF THE YEAR CELEBRATING SOME KID'S BIRTHDAY WITH ME!
MICHAEL FRY

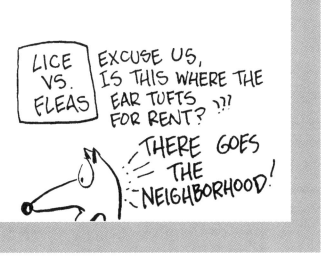

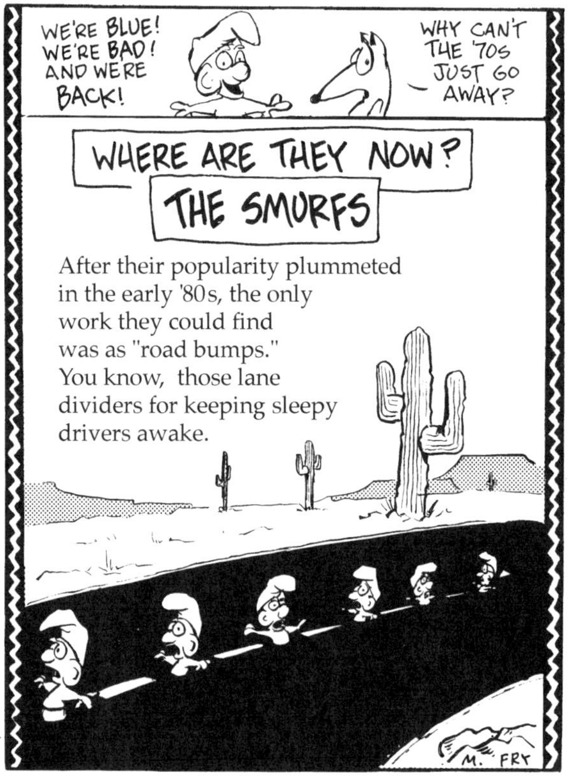

WE'RE BLUE! WE'RE BAD! AND WE'RE BACK!
WHY CAN'T THE '70s JUST GO AWAY?
WHERE ARE THEY NOW?
THE SMURFS
After their popularity plummeted in the early '80s, the only work they could find was as "road bumps." You know, those lane dividers for keeping sleepy drivers awake.
M. FRY

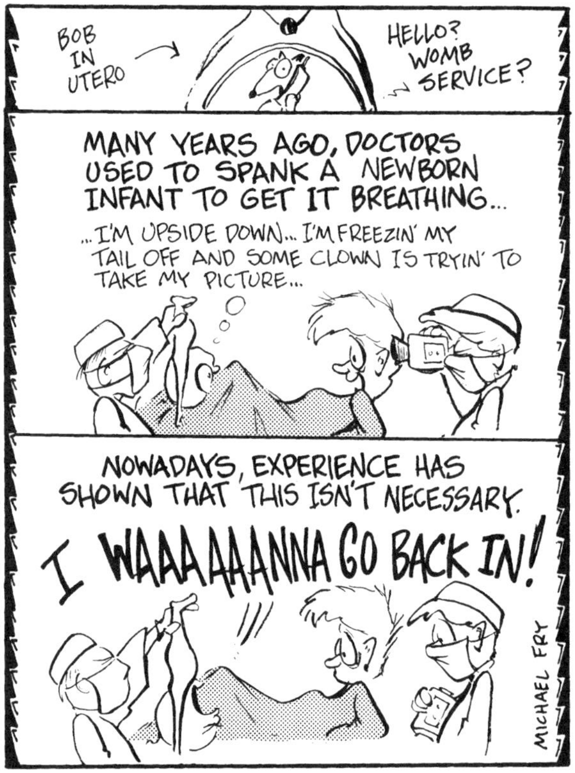

BOB IN UTERO
HELLO? WOMB SERVICE?
MANY YEARS AGO, DOCTORS USED TO SPANK A NEWBORN INFANT TO GET IT BREATHING...
...I'M UPSIDE DOWN... I'M FREEZIN' MY TAIL OFF AND SOME CLOWN IS TRYIN' TO TAKE MY PICTURE...
NOWADAYS, EXPERIENCE HAS SHOWN THAT THIS ISN'T NECESSARY.
I WAAAAAANNA GO BACK IN!
MICHAEL FRY

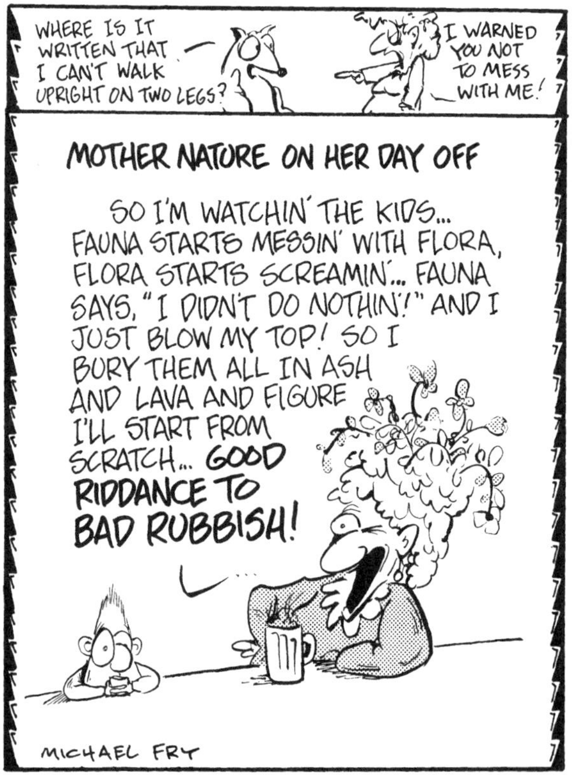

WHERE IS IT WRITTEN THAT I CAN'T WALK UPRIGHT ON TWO LEGS?
I WARNED YOU NOT TO MESS WITH ME!
MOTHER NATURE ON HER DAY OFF
SO I'M WATCHIN' THE KIDS... FAUNA STARTS MESSIN' WITH FLORA, FLORA STARTS SCREAMIN'... FAUNA SAYS, "I DIDN'T DO NOTHIN'!" AND I JUST BLOW MY TOP! SO I BURY THEM ALL IN ASH AND LAVA AND FIGURE I'LL START FROM SCRATCH... GOOD RIDDANCE TO BAD RUBBISH!
...
MICHAEL FRY

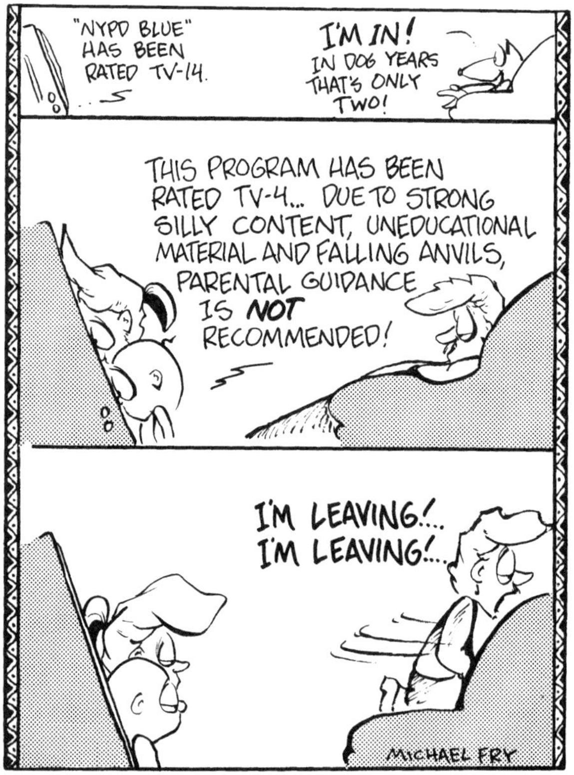

"NYPD BLUE" HAS BEEN RATED TV-14.
I'M IN! IN DOG YEARS THAT'S ONLY TWO!
THIS PROGRAM HAS BEEN RATED TV-4... DUE TO STRONG SILLY CONTENT, UNEDUCATIONAL MATERIAL AND FALLING ANVILS, PARENTAL GUIDANCE IS NOT RECOMMENDED!
I'M LEAVING!... I'M LEAVING!...
MICHAEL FRY

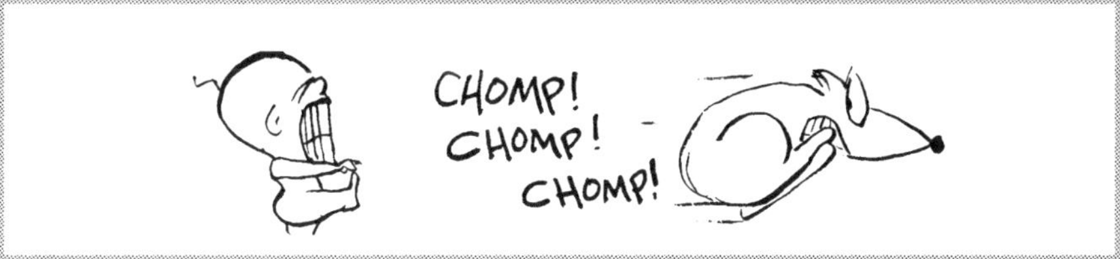
CHOMP!
CHOMP!
CHOMP!

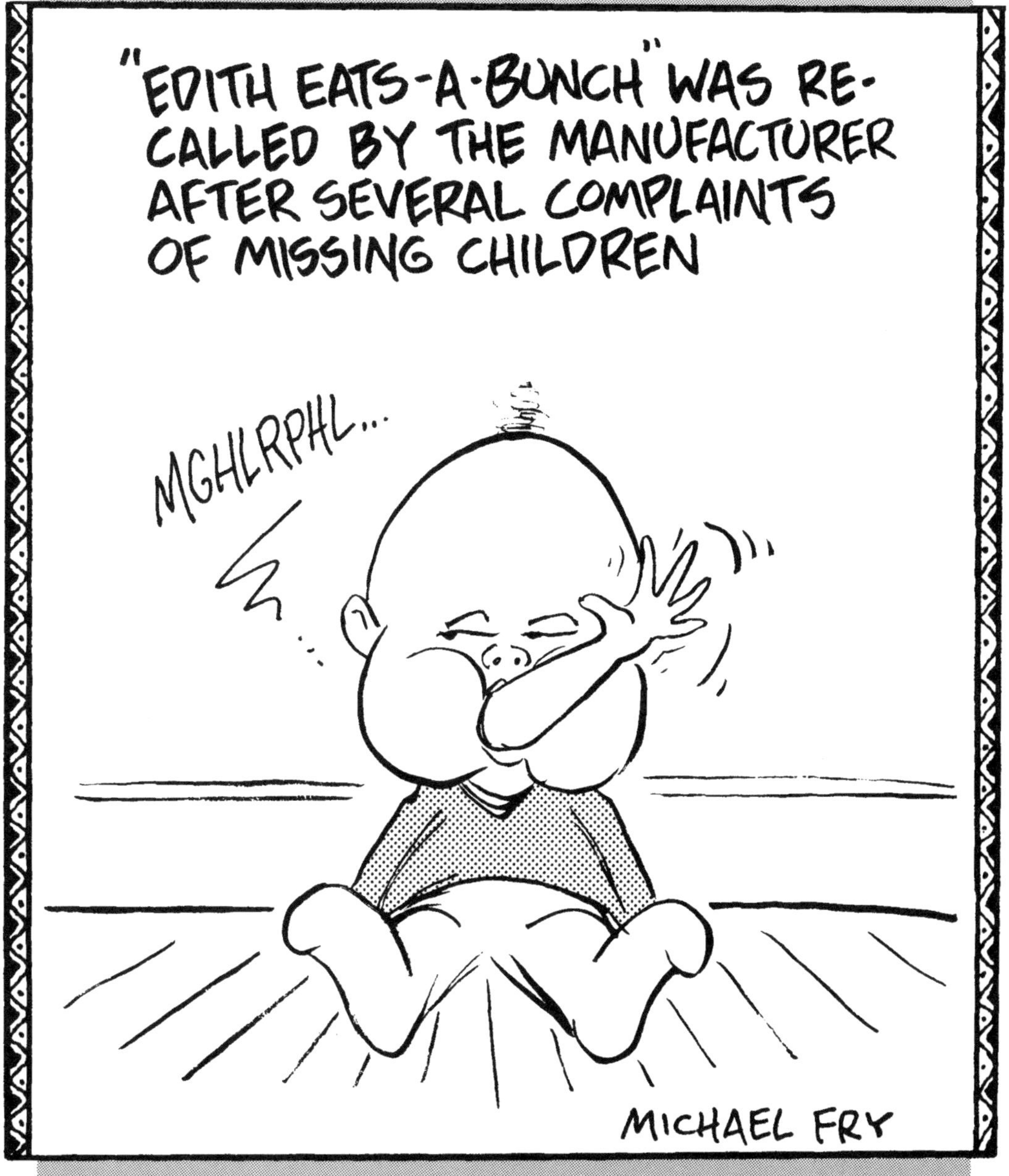
"EDITH EATS-A-BUNCH" WAS RECALLED BY THE MANUFACTURER AFTER SEVERAL COMPLAINTS OF MISSING CHILDREN
MGHLRPHL...
MICHAEL FRY

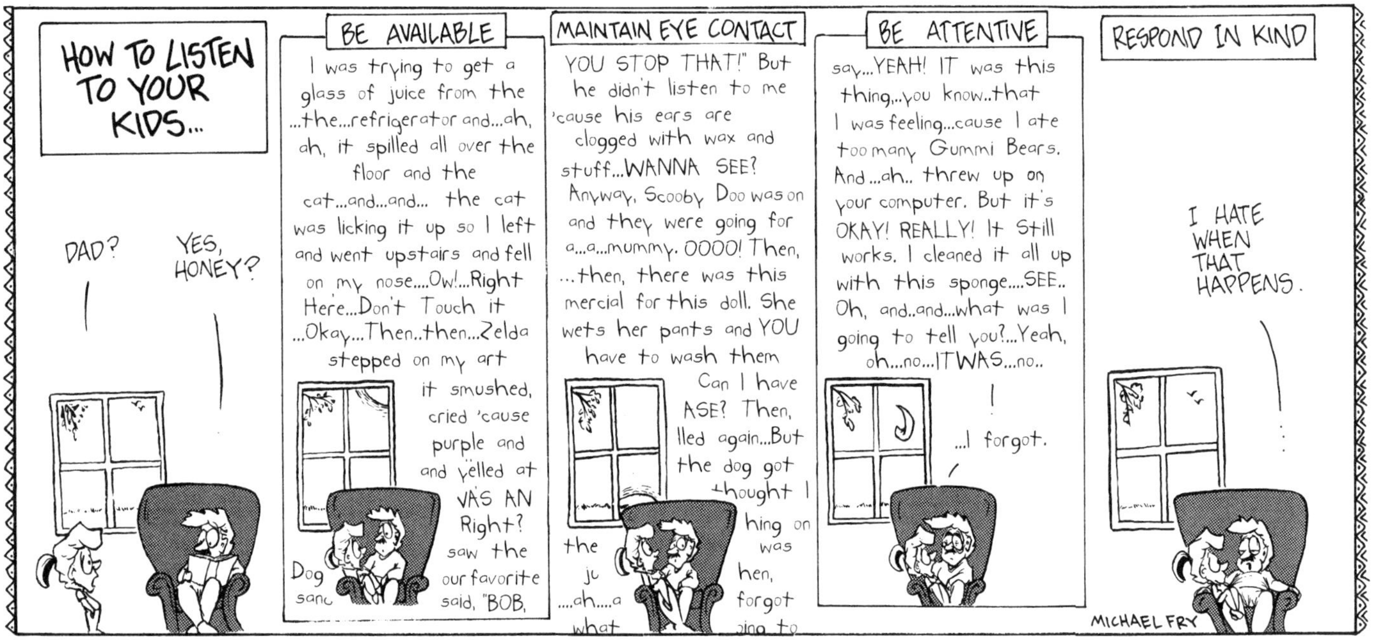
HOW TO LISTEN TO YOUR KIDS...
DAD?
YES, HONEY?
BE AVAILABLE
I was trying to get a glass of juice from the ...the...refrigerator and...ah, ah, it spilled all over the floor and the cat...and...and... the cat was licking it up so I left and went upstairs and fell on my nose....Ow!...Right Here...Don't Touch it ...Okay...Then..then...Zelda stepped on my art
it smushed, cried 'cause purple and and yelled at VAS AN Right? saw the our favorite said, "BOB,
MAINTAIN EYE CONTACT
YOU STOP THAT!" But he didn't listen to me 'cause his ears are clogged with wax and stuff...WANNA SEE? Anyway, Scooby Doo was on and they were going for a...a...mummy. OOOO! Then, ...then, there was this mercial for this doll. She wets her pants and YOU have to wash them
Can I have ASE? Then, lled again...But the dog got thought I hing on was hen, forgot
BE ATTENTIVE
say...YEAH! IT was this thing...you know..that I was feeling...cause I ate too many Gummi Bears. And...ah.. threw up on your computer. But it's OKAY! REALLY! It Still works. I cleaned it all up with this sponge....SEE.. Oh, and..and...what was I going to tell you?...Yeah, oh...no...IT WAS...no..
!
...I forgot.
RESPOND IN KIND
I HATE WHEN THAT HAPPENS.
MICHAEL FRY

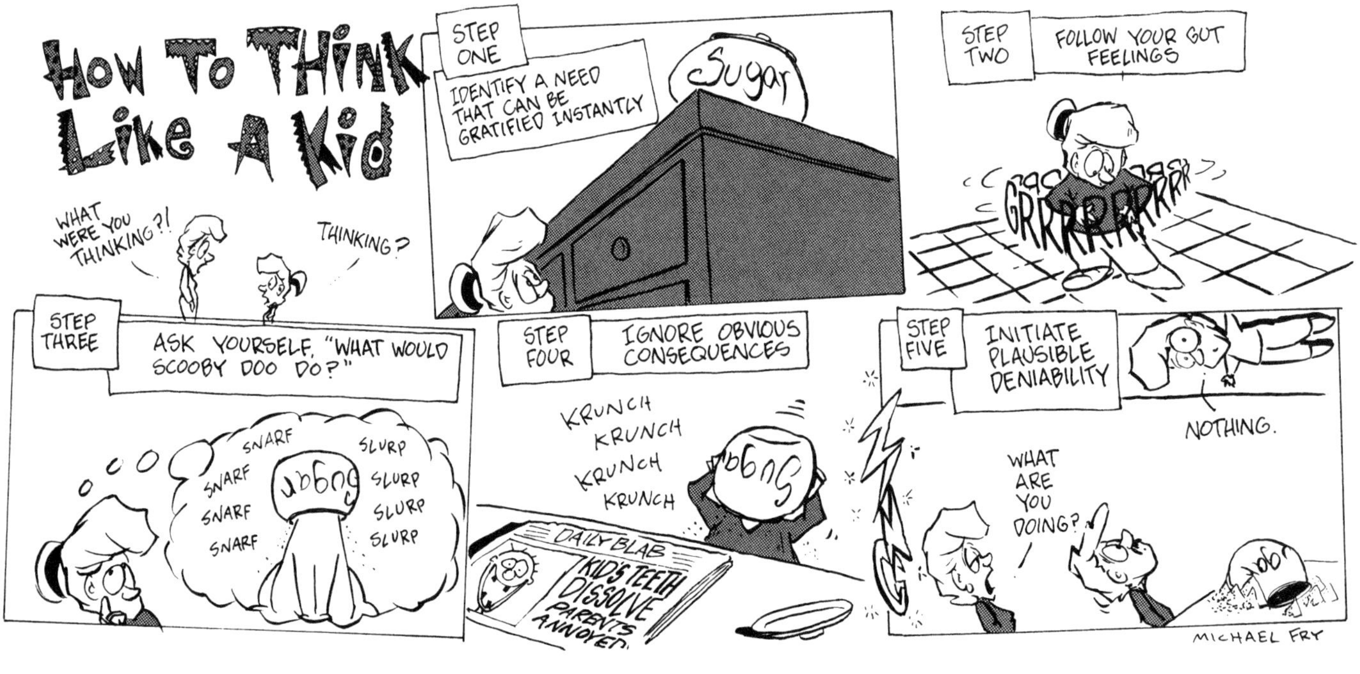
How To Think Like A Kid
WHAT WERE YOU THINKING?!
THINKING?
STEP ONE
IDENTIFY A NEED THAT CAN BE GRATIFIED INSTANTLY
Sugar
STEP TWO
FOLLOW YOUR GUT FEELINGS
GRRRRRRRRR
STEP THREE
ASK YOURSELF, "WHAT WOULD SCOOBY DOO DO?"
SNARF
SNARF
SNARF
SNARF
SLURP
SLURP
SLURP
SLURP
STEP FOUR
IGNORE OBVIOUS CONSEQUENCES
KRUNCH
KRUNCH
KRUNCH
KRUNCH
DAILY BLAB
KID'S TEETH DISSOLVE
PARENTS ANNOYED
STEP FIVE
INITIATE PLAUSIBLE DENIABILITY
WHAT ARE YOU DOING?
NOTHING.
MICHAEL FRY

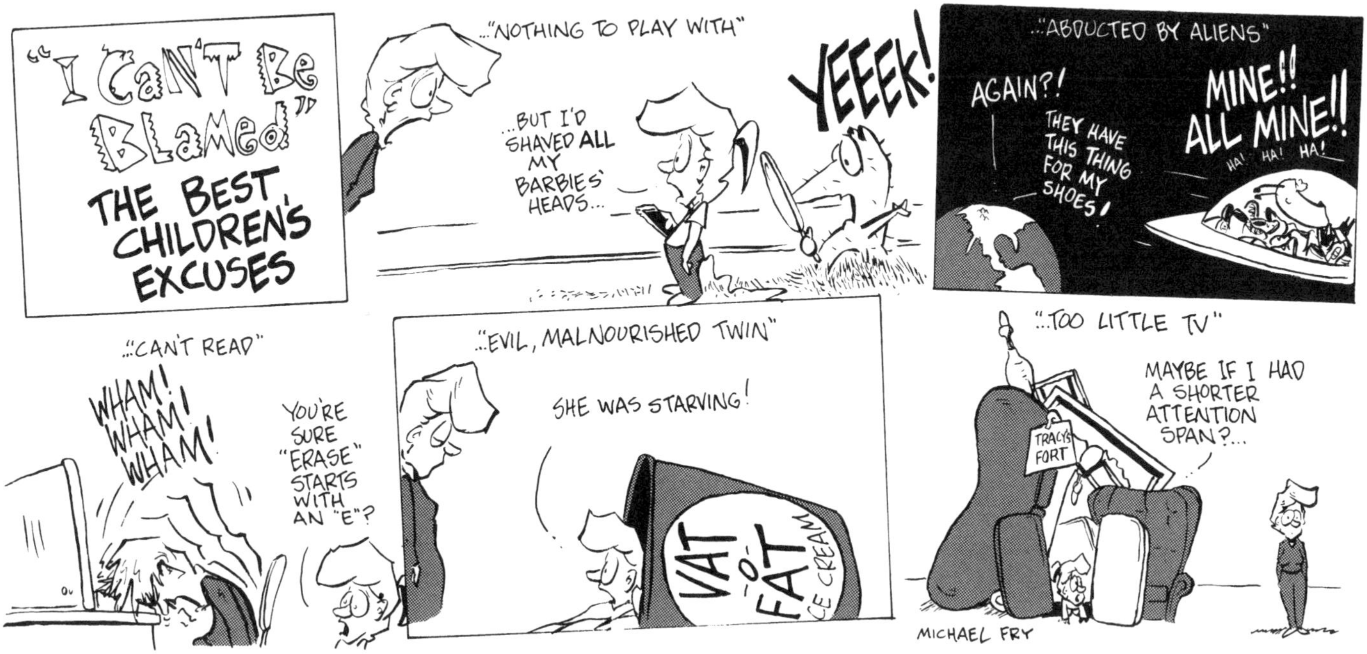
"I CAN'T BE BLAMED"
THE BEST CHILDREN'S EXCUSES
..."NOTHING TO PLAY WITH"
...BUT I'D SHAVED ALL MY BARBIES' HEADS...
YEEEK!
..."ABDUCTED BY ALIENS"
AGAIN?!
THEY HAVE THIS THING FOR MY SHOES!
MINE!! ALL MINE!!
HA! HA! HA!
..."CAN'T READ"
WHAM! WHAM! WHAM!
YOU'RE SURE "ERASE" STARTS WITH AN "E"?
..."EVIL, MALNOURISHED TWIN"
SHE WAS STARVING!
VAT-O-FAT
CE CREAM
..."TOO LITTLE TV"
TRACY'S FORT
MAYBE IF I HAD A SHORTER ATTENTION SPAN?...
MICHAEL FRY

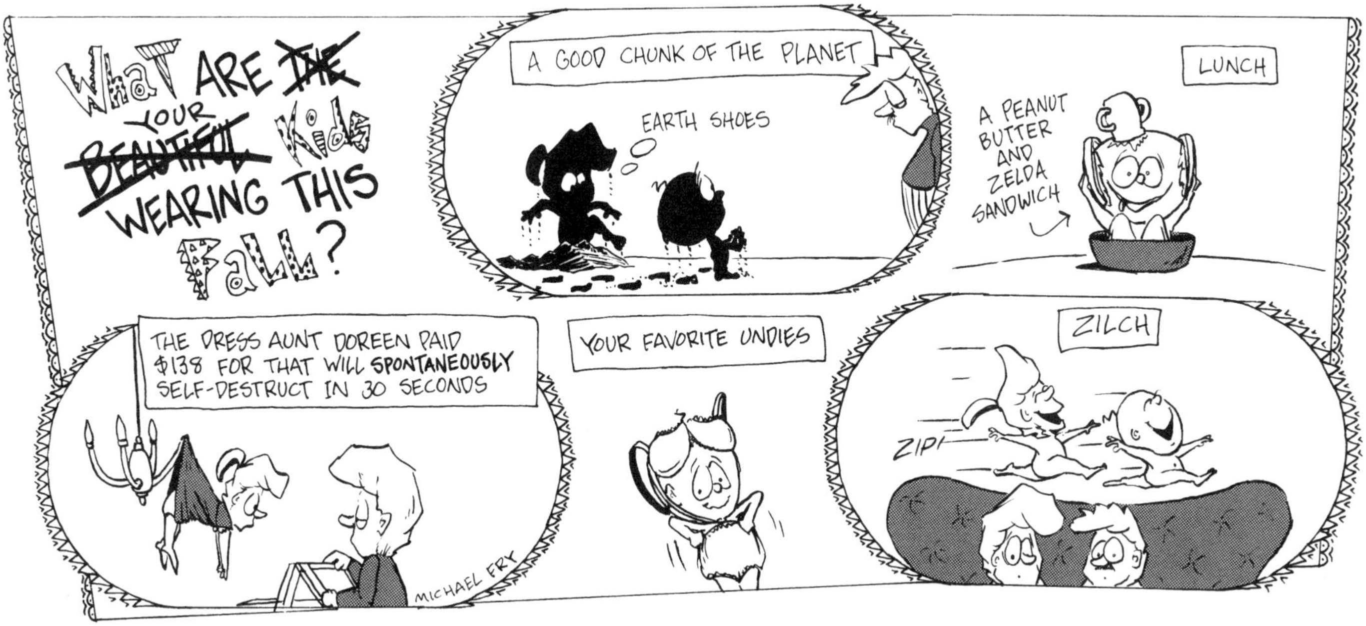
WHAT ARE ~~THE~~ YOUR ~~BEAUTIFUL~~ Kids WEARING THIS FALL?
A GOOD CHUNK OF THE PLANET
EARTH SHOES
LUNCH
A PEANUT BUTTER AND ZELDA SANDWICH
THE DRESS AUNT DOREEN PAID $138 FOR THAT WILL SPONTANEOUSLY SELF-DESTRUCT IN 30 SECONDS
YOUR FAVORITE UNDIES
ZILCH
ZIP!
MICHAEL FRY

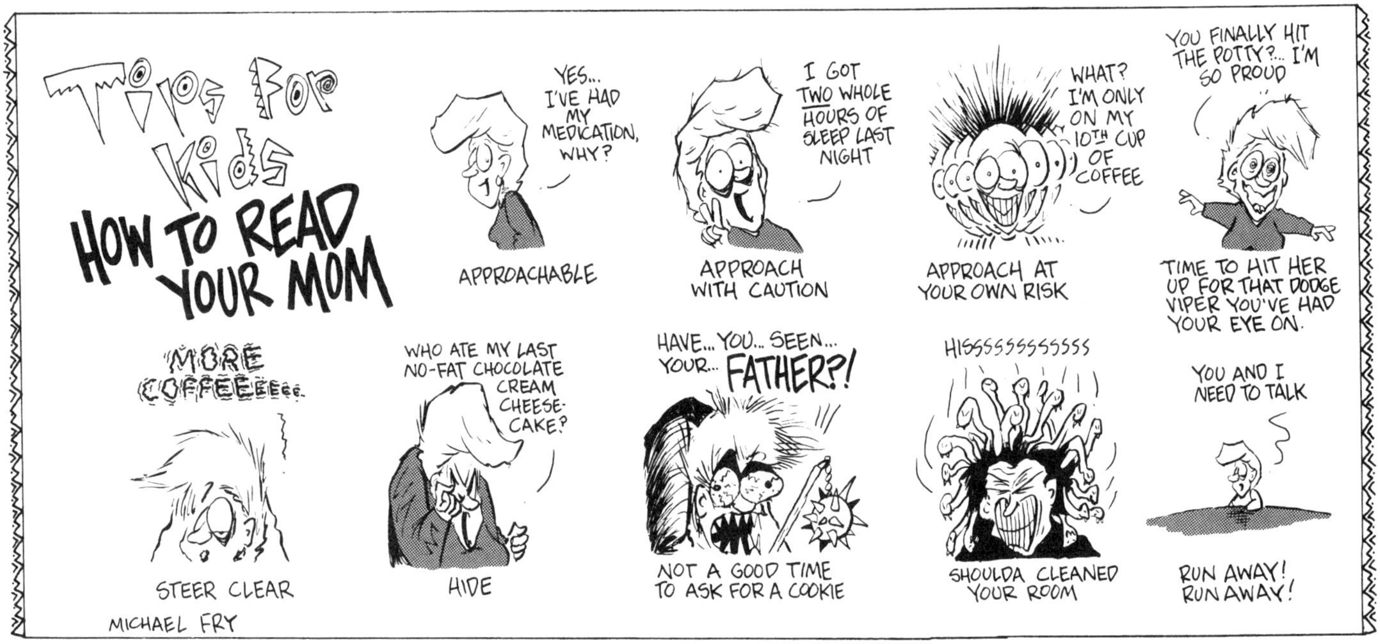

TIPS FOR KIDS
HOW TO READ YOUR MOM
YES... I'VE HAD MY MEDICATION, WHY?
APPROACHABLE
I GOT TWO WHOLE HOURS OF SLEEP LAST NIGHT
APPROACH WITH CAUTION
WHAT? I'M ONLY ON MY 10TH CUP OF COFFEE
APPROACH AT YOUR OWN RISK
YOU FINALLY HIT THE POTTY?... I'M SO PROUD
TIME TO HIT HER UP FOR THAT DODGE VIPER YOU'VE HAD YOUR EYE ON.
MORE COFFEEEEEE...
STEER CLEAR
WHO ATE MY LAST NO-FAT CHOCOLATE CREAM CHEESE-CAKE?
HIDE
HAVE... YOU... SEEN... YOUR... FATHER?!
NOT A GOOD TIME TO ASK FOR A COOKIE
HISSSSSSSSSSSS
SHOULDA CLEANED YOUR ROOM
YOU AND I NEED TO TALK
RUN AWAY! RUN AWAY!
MICHAEL FRY

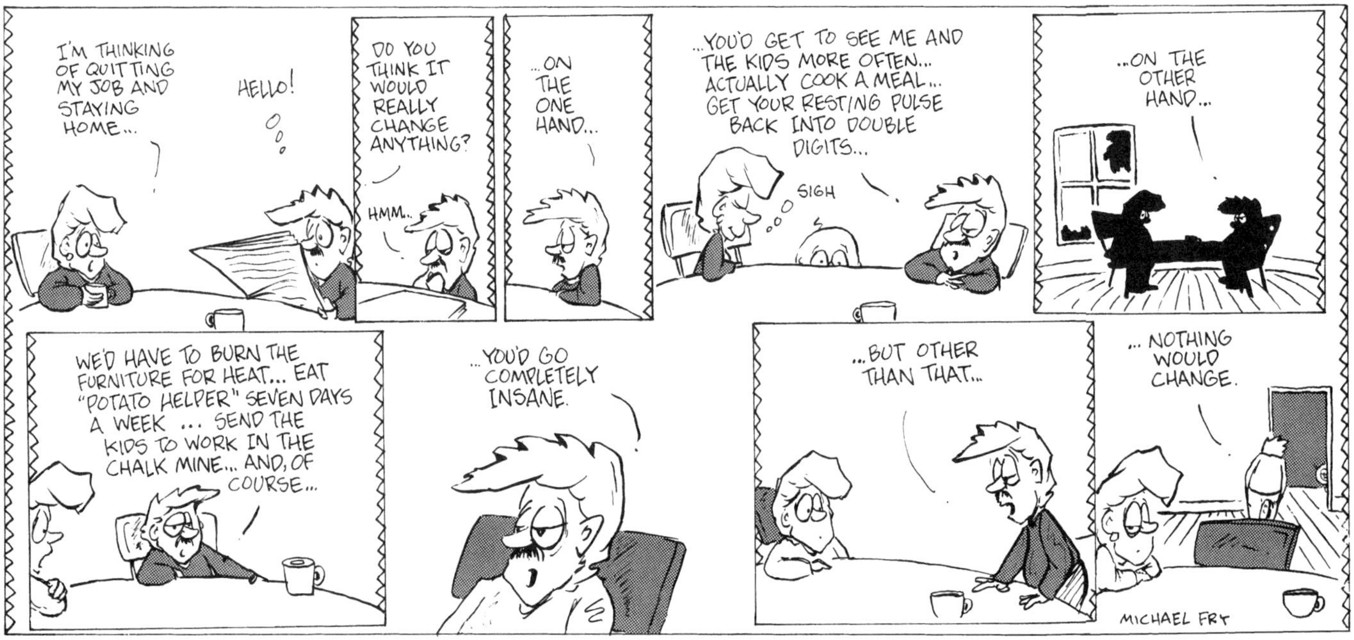

I'M THINKING OF QUITTING MY JOB AND STAYING HOME...
HELLO!
DO YOU THINK IT WOULD REALLY CHANGE ANYTHING?
HMM..
...ON THE ONE HAND...
...YOU'D GET TO SEE ME AND THE KIDS MORE OFTEN... ACTUALLY COOK A MEAL... GET YOUR RESTING PULSE BACK INTO DOUBLE DIGITS...
SIGH
...ON THE OTHER HAND...
WE'D HAVE TO BURN THE FURNITURE FOR HEAT... EAT "POTATO HELPER" SEVEN DAYS A WEEK ... SEND THE KIDS TO WORK IN THE CHALK MINE... AND, OF COURSE...
...YOU'D GO COMPLETELY INSANE.
...BUT OTHER THAN THAT...
... NOTHING WOULD CHANGE.
MICHAEL FRY

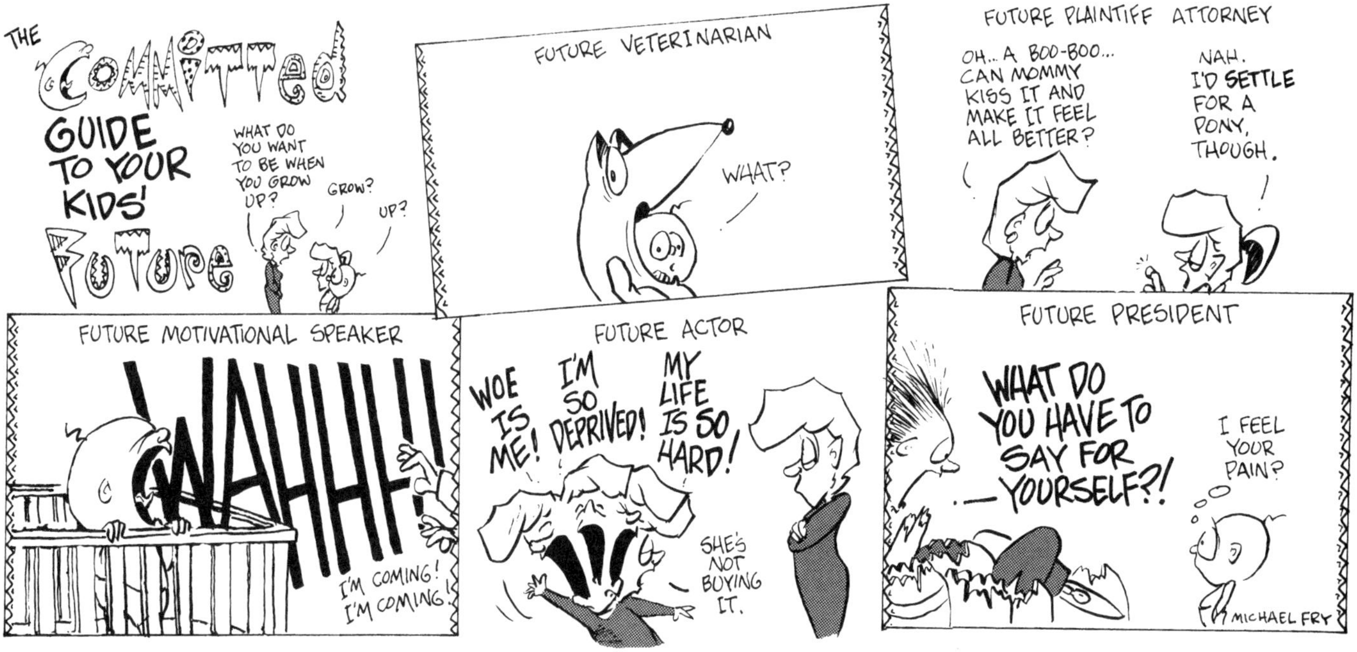
THE COMMITTED GUIDE TO YOUR KIDS' FUTURE
WHAT DO YOU WANT TO BE WHEN YOU GROW UP?
GROW?
UP?
FUTURE VETERINARIAN
WHAT?
FUTURE PLAINTIFF ATTORNEY
OH... A BOO-BOO... CAN MOMMY KISS IT AND MAKE IT FEEL ALL BETTER?
NAH. I'D SETTLE FOR A PONY, THOUGH.
FUTURE MOTIVATIONAL SPEAKER
WAHHH!
I'M COMING! I'M COMING!
FUTURE ACTOR
WOE IS ME!
I'M SO DEPRIVED!
MY LIFE IS SO HARD!
SHE'S NOT BUYING IT.
FUTURE PRESIDENT
WHAT DO YOU HAVE TO SAY FOR YOURSELF?!
I FEEL YOUR PAIN?
MICHAEL FRY

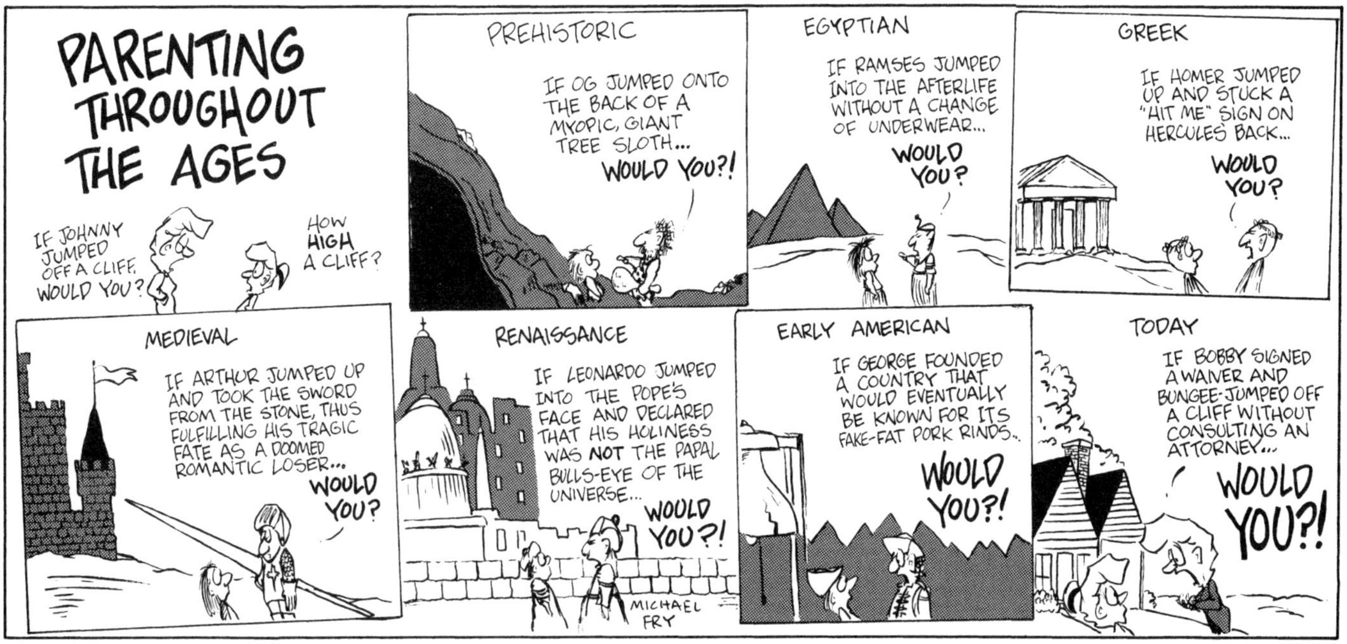
PARENTING THROUGHOUT THE AGES
IF JOHNNY JUMPED OFF A CLIFF, WOULD YOU?
HOW HIGH A CLIFF?
PREHISTORIC
IF OG JUMPED ONTO THE BACK OF A MYOPIC, GIANT TREE SLOTH... WOULD YOU?!
EGYPTIAN
IF RAMSES JUMPED INTO THE AFTERLIFE WITHOUT A CHANGE OF UNDERWEAR... WOULD YOU?
GREEK
IF HOMER JUMPED UP AND STUCK A "HIT ME" SIGN ON HERCULES' BACK... WOULD YOU?
MEDIEVAL
IF ARTHUR JUMPED UP AND TOOK THE SWORD FROM THE STONE, THUS FULFILLING HIS TRAGIC FATE AS A DOOMED ROMANTIC LOSER... WOULD YOU?
RENAISSANCE
IF LEONARDO JUMPED INTO THE POPE'S FACE AND DECLARED THAT HIS HOLINESS WAS NOT THE PAPAL BULLS-EYE OF THE UNIVERSE... WOULD YOU?!
MICHAEL FRY
EARLY AMERICAN
IF GEORGE FOUNDED A COUNTRY THAT WOULD EVENTUALLY BE KNOWN FOR ITS FAKE-FAT PORK RINDS... WOULD YOU?!
TODAY
IF BOBBY SIGNED A WAIVER AND BUNGEE-JUMPED OFF A CLIFF WITHOUT CONSULTING AN ATTORNEY... WOULD YOU?!

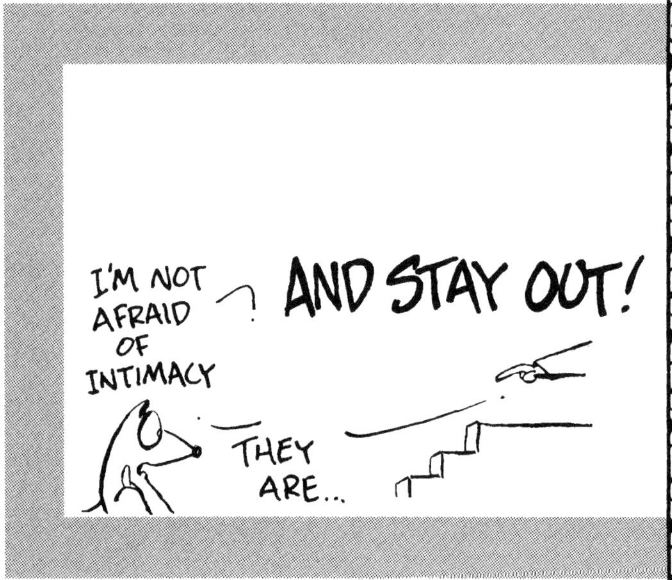
I'M NOT AFRAID OF INTIMACY
THEY ARE...
AND STAY OUT!

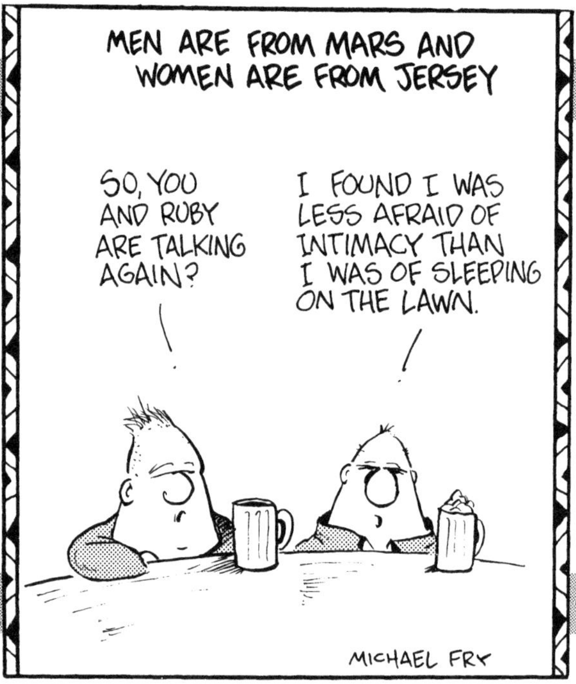
MEN ARE FROM MARS AND WOMEN ARE FROM JERSEY
SO, YOU AND RUBY ARE TALKING AGAIN?
I FOUND I WAS LESS AFRAID OF INTIMACY THAN I WAS OF SLEEPING ON THE LAWN.
MICHAEL FRY

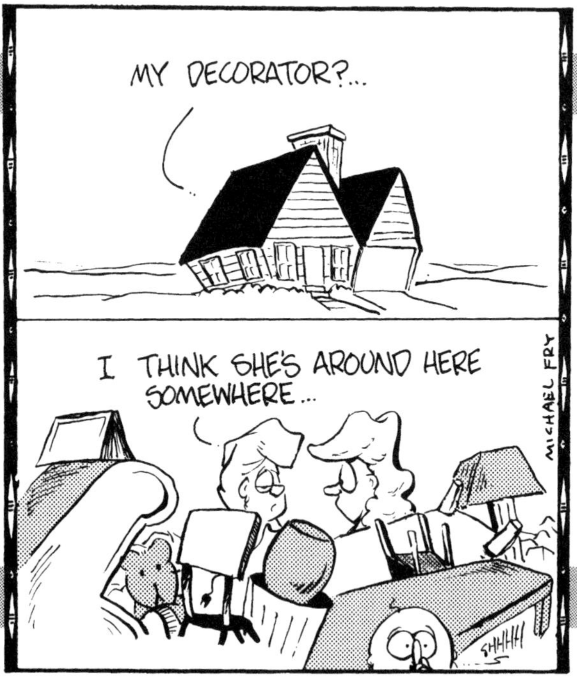
MY DECORATOR?...
I THINK SHE'S AROUND HERE SOMEWHERE...
MICHAEL FRY

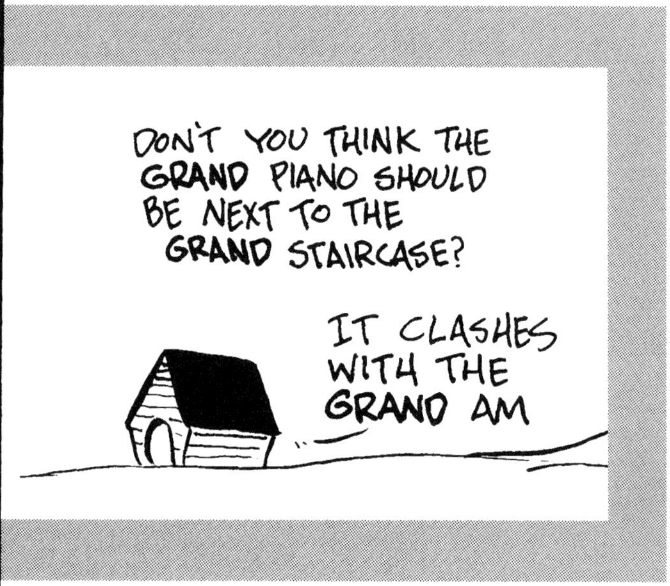
DON'T YOU THINK THE GRAND PIANO SHOULD BE NEXT TO THE GRAND STAIRCASE?
IT CLASHES WITH THE GRAND AM

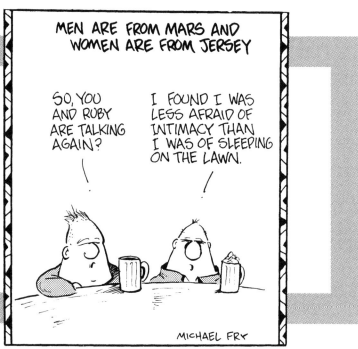

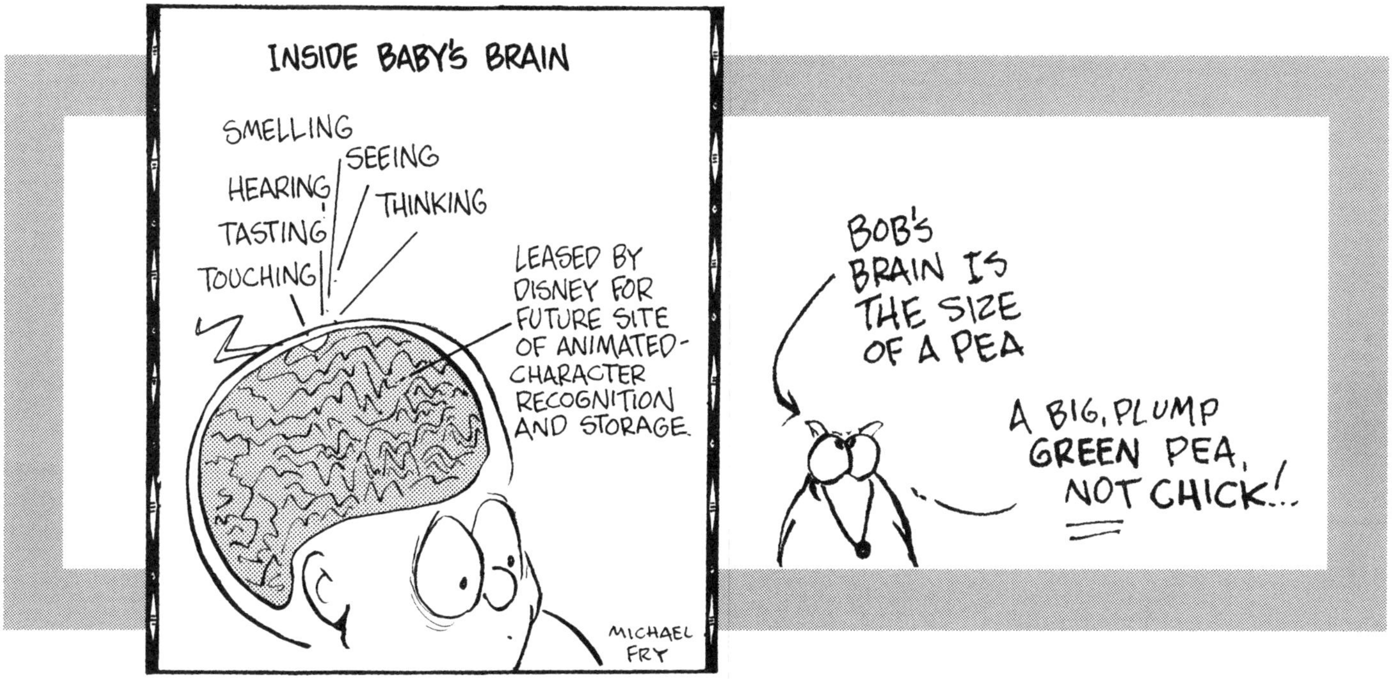
INSIDE BABY'S BRAIN
SMELLING
SEEING
HEARING
THINKING
TASTING
TOUCHING
LEASED BY DISNEY FOR FUTURE SITE OF ANIMATED-CHARACTER RECOGNITION AND STORAGE.
MICHAEL FRY
BOB'S BRAIN IS THE SIZE OF A PEA
A BIG, PLUMP GREEN PEA, NOT CHICK!..

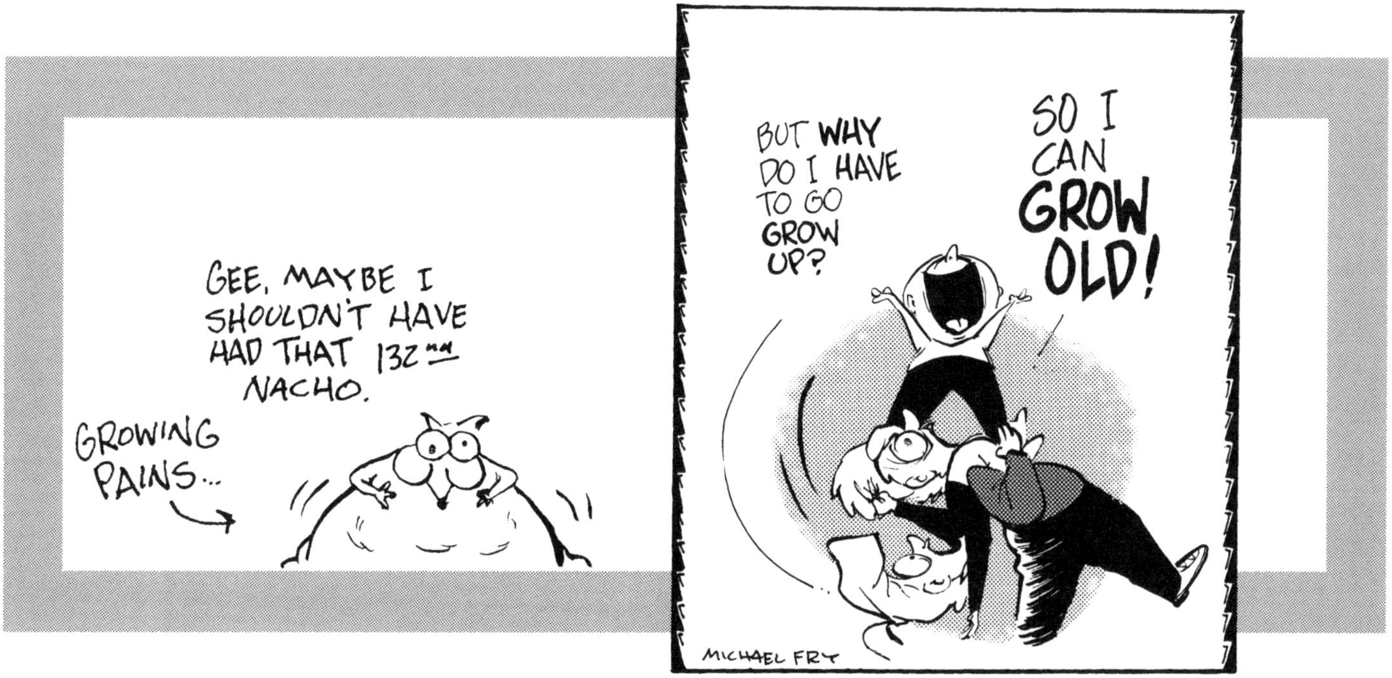
GEE, MAYBE I SHOULDN'T HAVE HAD THAT 132ND NACHO.
GROWING PAINS...
BUT WHY DO I HAVE TO GO GROW UP?
SO I CAN GROW OLD!
MICHAEL FRY

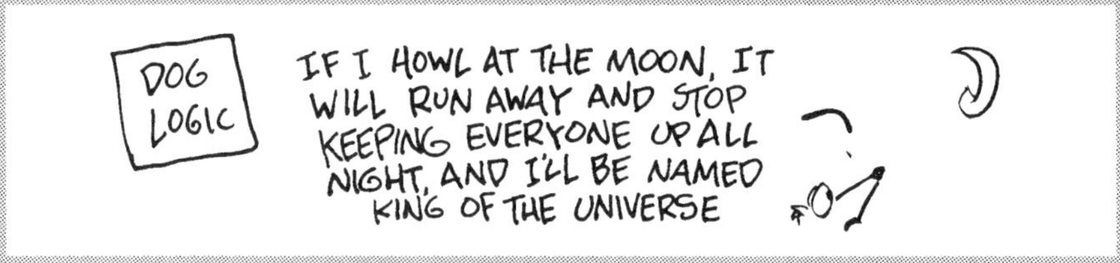
DOG LOGIC
IF I HOWL AT THE MOON, IT WILL RUN AWAY AND STOP KEEPING EVERYONE UP ALL NIGHT, AND I'LL BE NAMED KING OF THE UNIVERSE

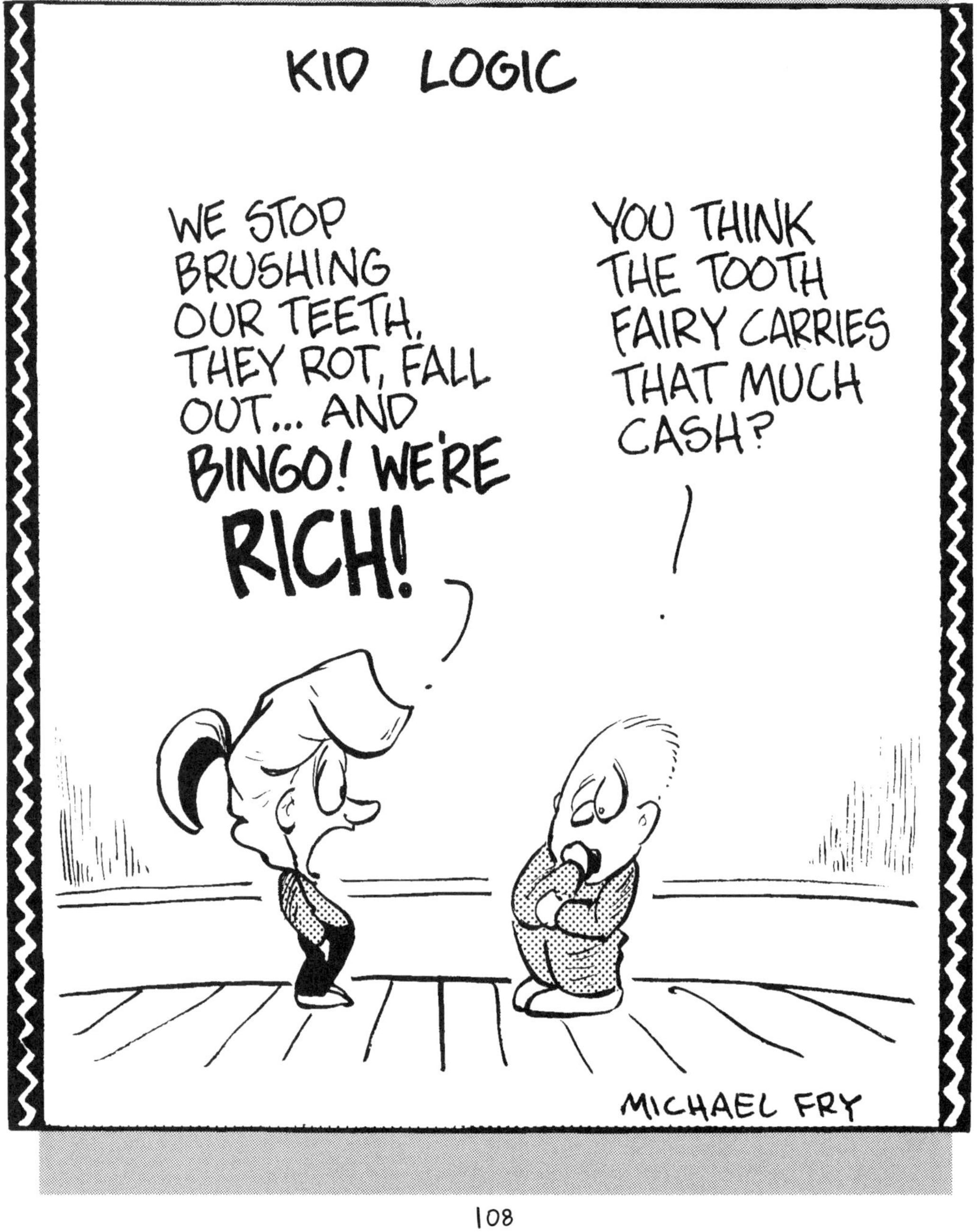
KID LOGIC
WE STOP BRUSHING OUR TEETH, THEY ROT, FALL OUT... AND BINGO! WE'RE RICH!
YOU THINK THE TOOTH FAIRY CARRIES THAT MUCH CASH?
MICHAEL FRY

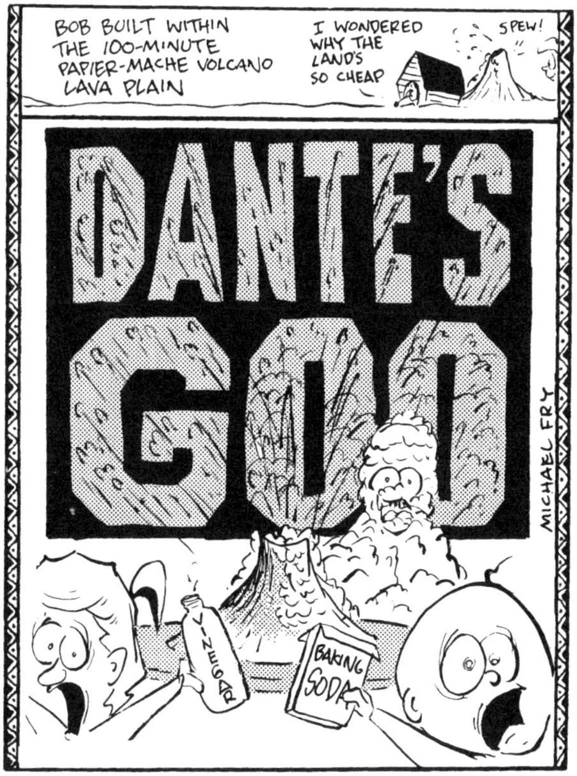
BOB BUILT WITHIN THE 100-MINUTE PAPIER-MACHE VOLCANO LAVA PLAIN
I WONDERED WHY THE LAND'S SO CHEAP
SPEW!
DANTE'S GOO
MICHAEL FRY
VINEGAR
BAKING SODA

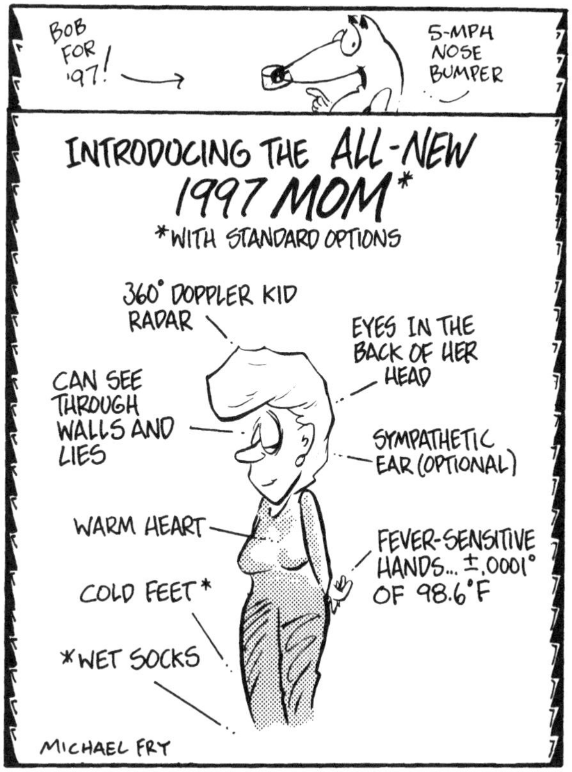
BOB FOR '97!
5-MPH NOSE BUMPER
INTRODUCING THE ALL-NEW 1997 MOM*
*WITH STANDARD OPTIONS
360° DOPPLER KID RADAR
EYES IN THE BACK OF HER HEAD
CAN SEE THROUGH WALLS AND LIES
SYMPATHETIC EAR (OPTIONAL)
WARM HEART
FEVER-SENSITIVE HANDS... ±.0001° OF 98.6°F
COLD FEET*
*WET SOCKS
MICHAEL FRY

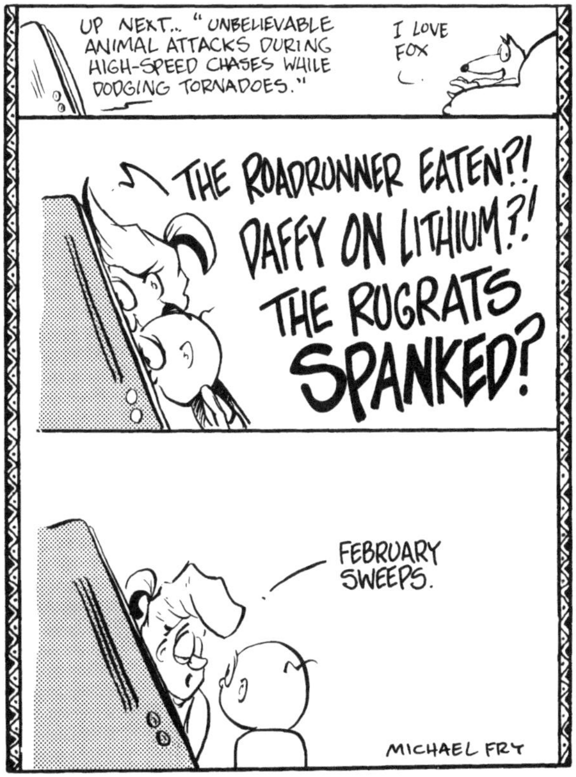
UP NEXT... "UNBELIEVABLE ANIMAL ATTACKS DURING HIGH-SPEED CHASES WHILE DODGING TORNADOES."
I LOVE FOX
THE ROADRUNNER EATEN?! DAFFY ON LITHIUM?! THE RUGRATS SPANKED?
FEBRUARY SWEEPS.
MICHAEL FRY

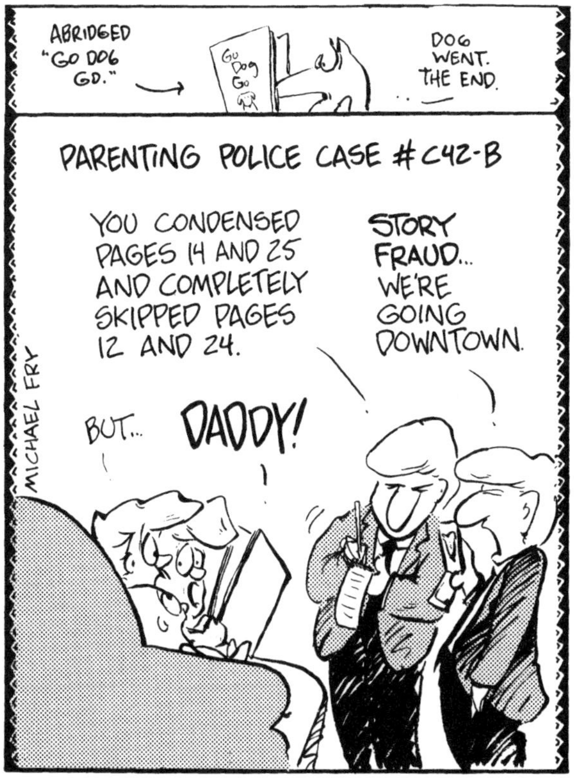
ABRIDGED "GO DOG GO."
GO Dog Go
DOG WENT. THE END.
PARENTING POLICE CASE #C42-B
YOU CONDENSED PAGES 14 AND 25 AND COMPLETELY SKIPPED PAGES 12 AND 24.
STORY FRAUD... WE'RE GOING DOWNTOWN.
BUT...
DADDY!
MICHAEL FRY

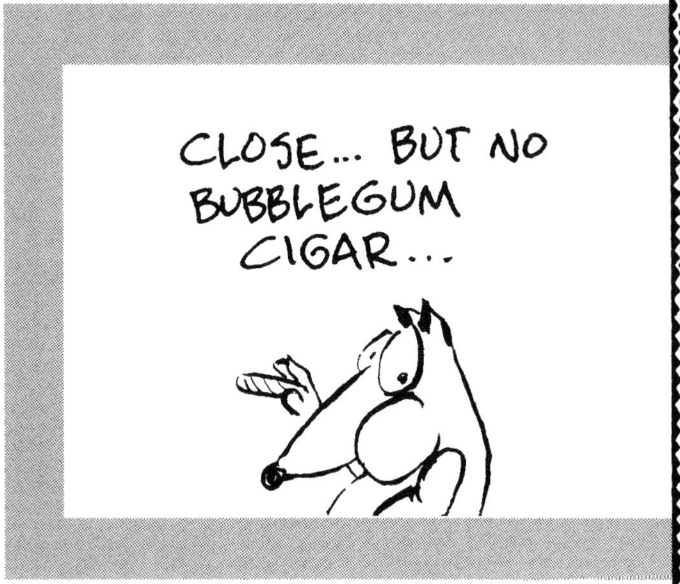
CLOSE... BUT NO BUBBLEGUM CIGAR...

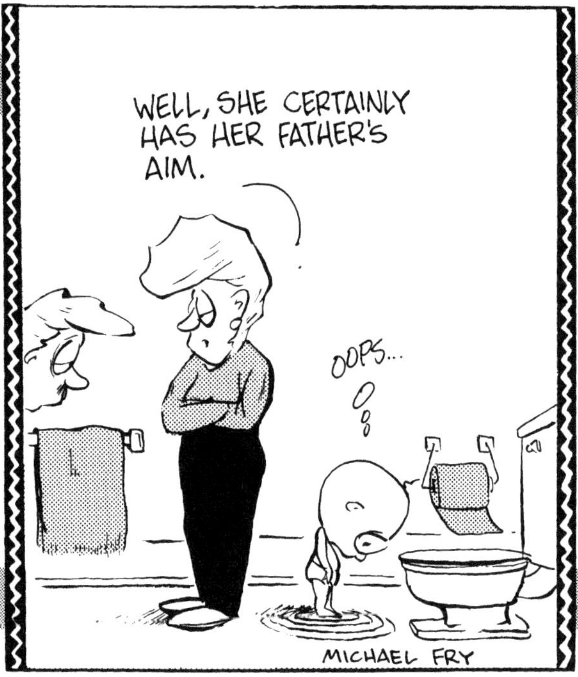
WELL, SHE CERTAINLY HAS HER FATHER'S AIM.
OOPS...
MICHAEL FRY

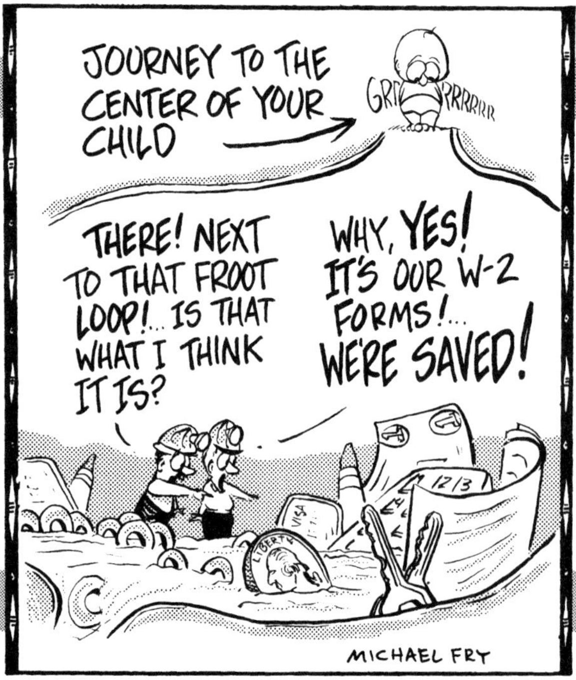
JOURNEY TO THE CENTER OF YOUR CHILD
GRRRRRRRR
THERE! NEXT TO THAT FROOT LOOP!... IS THAT WHAT I THINK IT IS?
WHY, YES! IT'S OUR W-2 FORMS!... WE'RE SAVED!
MICHAEL FRY

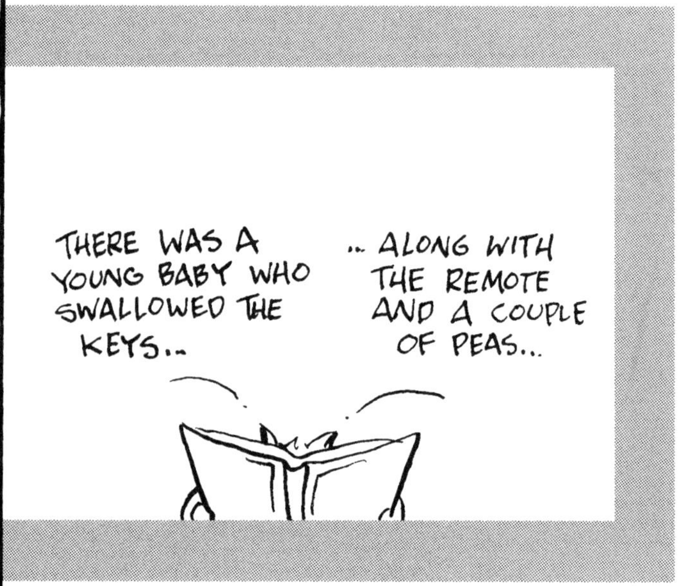
THERE WAS A YOUNG BABY WHO SWALLOWED THE KEYS...
... ALONG WITH THE REMOTE AND A COUPLE OF PEAS...

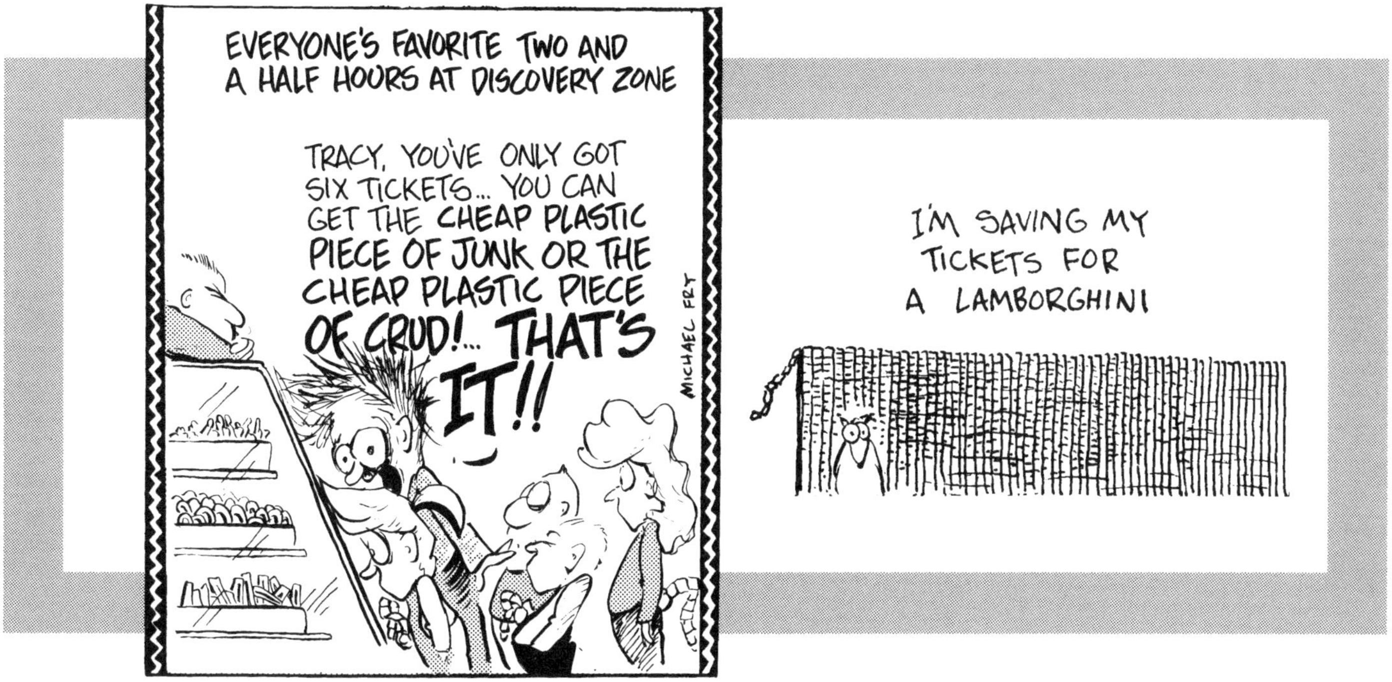
EVERYONE'S FAVORITE TWO AND A HALF HOURS AT DISCOVERY ZONE
TRACY, YOU'VE ONLY GOT SIX TICKETS... YOU CAN GET THE CHEAP PLASTIC PIECE OF JUNK OR THE CHEAP PLASTIC PIECE OF CRUD!... THAT'S IT!!
MICHAEL FRY
I'M SAVING MY TICKETS FOR A LAMBORGHINI

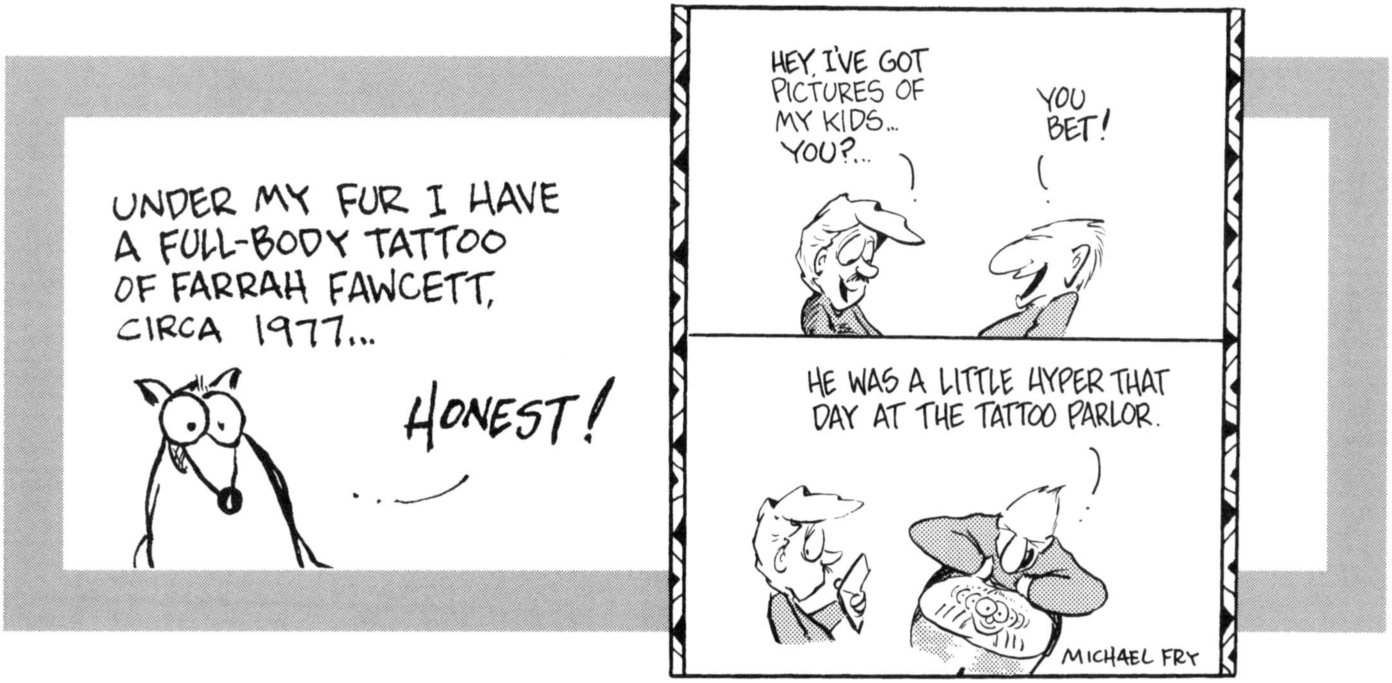
UNDER MY FUR I HAVE A FULL-BODY TATTOO OF FARRAH FAWCETT, CIRCA 1977...
HONEST!
HEY, I'VE GOT PICTURES OF MY KIDS... YOU?...
YOU BET!
HE WAS A LITTLE HYPER THAT DAY AT THE TATTOO PARLOR.
MICHAEL FRY

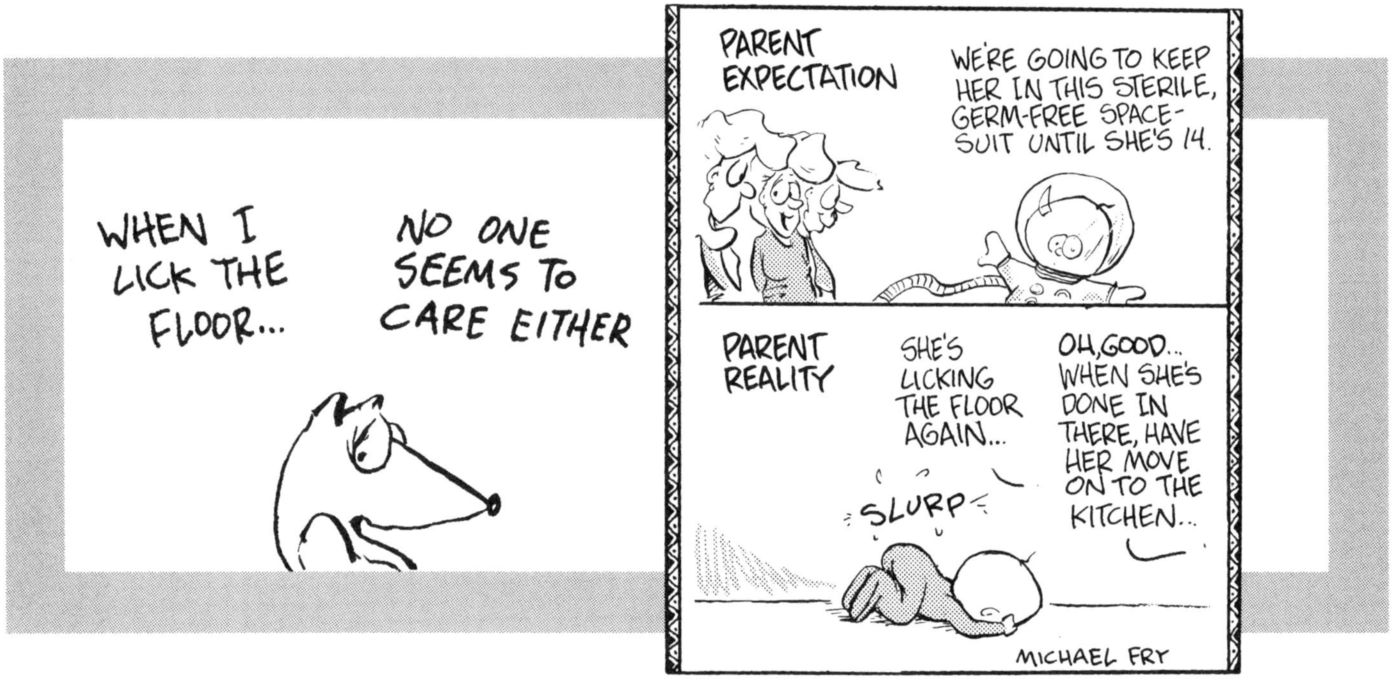
PARENT EXPECTATION
WE'RE GOING TO KEEP HER IN THIS STERILE, GERM-FREE SPACE-SUIT UNTIL SHE'S 14.
PARENT REALITY
SHE'S LICKING THE FLOOR AGAIN...
SLURP
OH, GOOD... WHEN SHE'S DONE IN THERE, HAVE HER MOVE ON TO THE KITCHEN...
MICHAEL FRY
WHEN I LICK THE FLOOR...
NO ONE SEEMS TO CARE EITHER

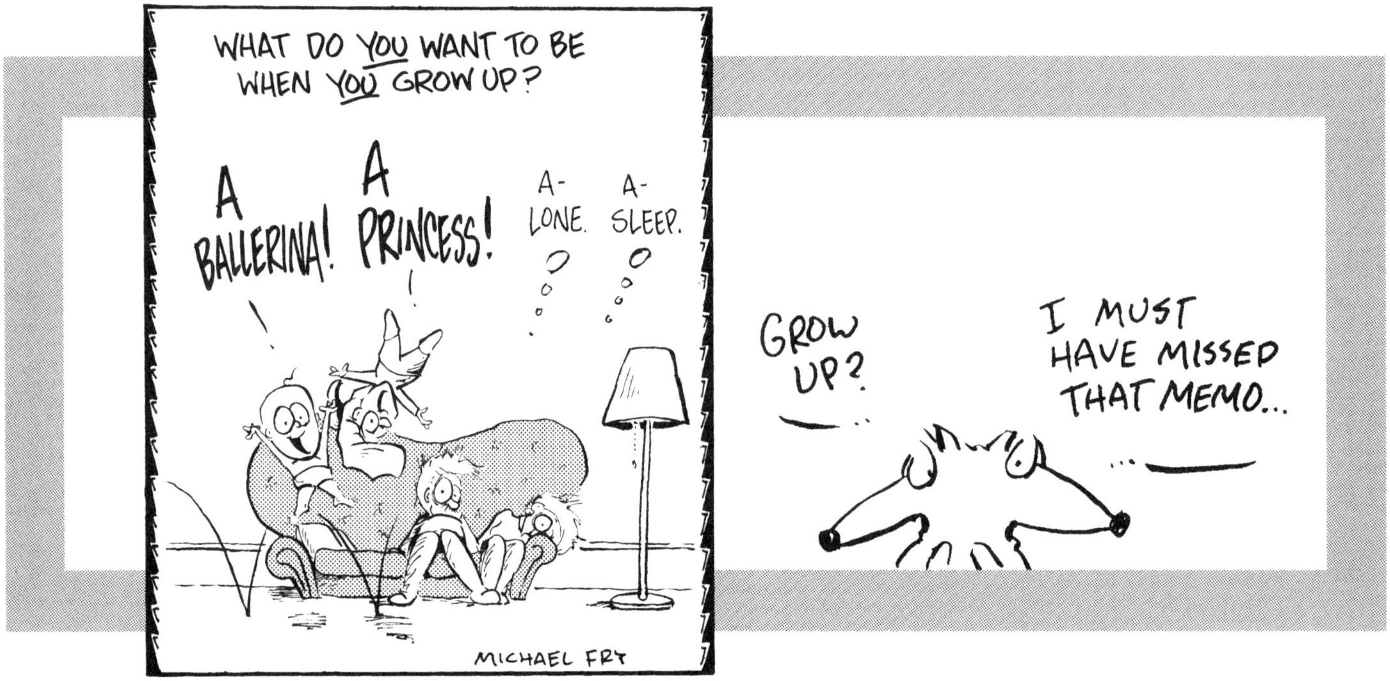
WHAT DO YOU WANT TO BE WHEN YOU GROW UP?
A BALLERINA!
A PRINCESS!
A-LONE.
A-SLEEP.
MICHAEL FRY
GROW UP?
I MUST HAVE MISSED THAT MEMO...

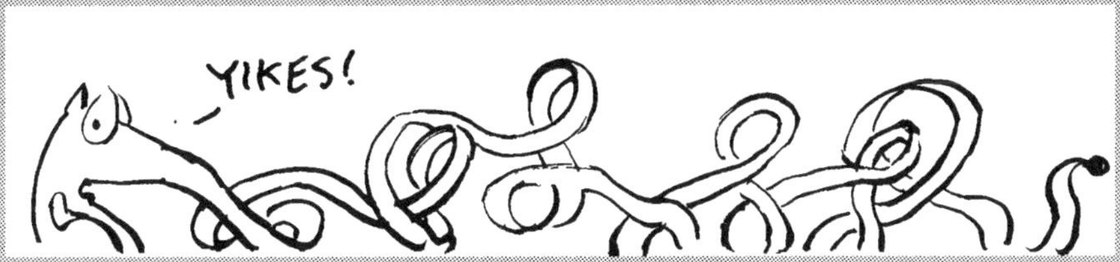
YIKES!

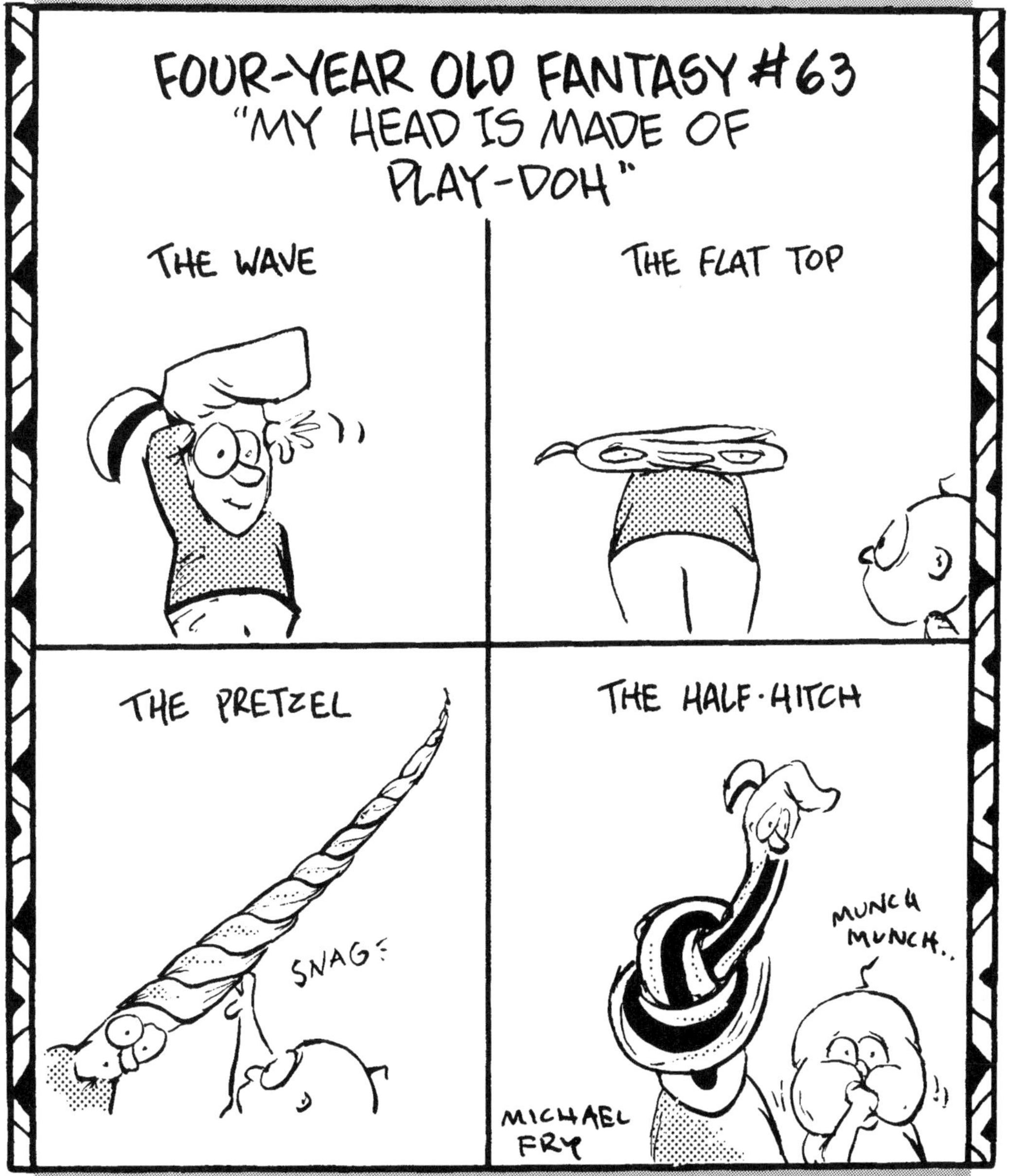
FOUR-YEAR OLD FANTASY #63
"MY HEAD IS MADE OF PLAY-DOH"
THE WAVE
THE FLAT TOP
THE PRETZEL
SNAG!
THE HALF-HITCH
MUNCH MUNCH..
MICHAEL FRY

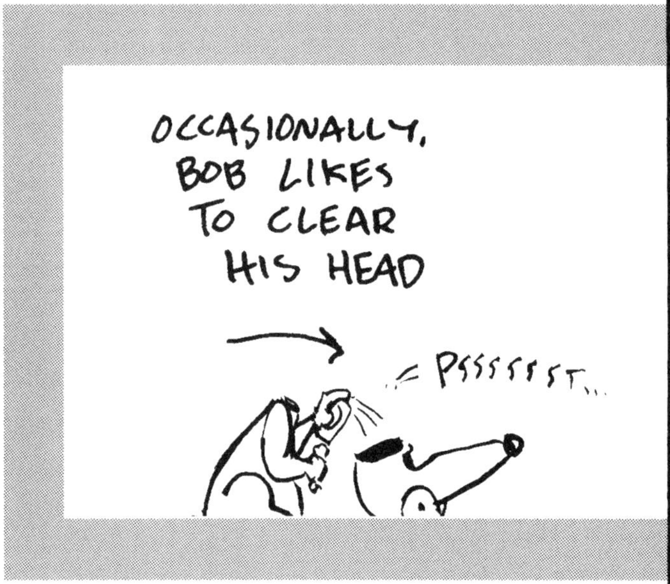
OCCASIONALLY, BOB LIKES TO CLEAR HIS HEAD
PSSSSSST...

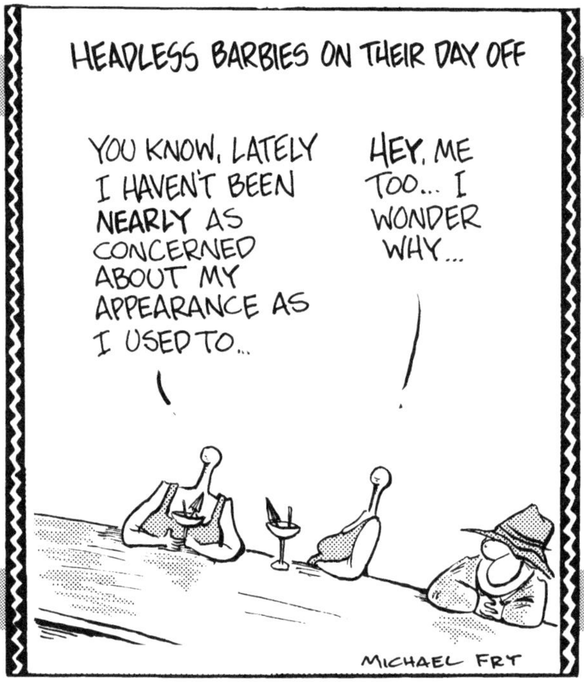
HEADLESS BARBIES ON THEIR DAY OFF
YOU KNOW, LATELY I HAVEN'T BEEN NEARLY AS CONCERNED ABOUT MY APPEARANCE AS I USED TO...
HEY, ME TOO... I WONDER WHY...
MICHAEL FRY

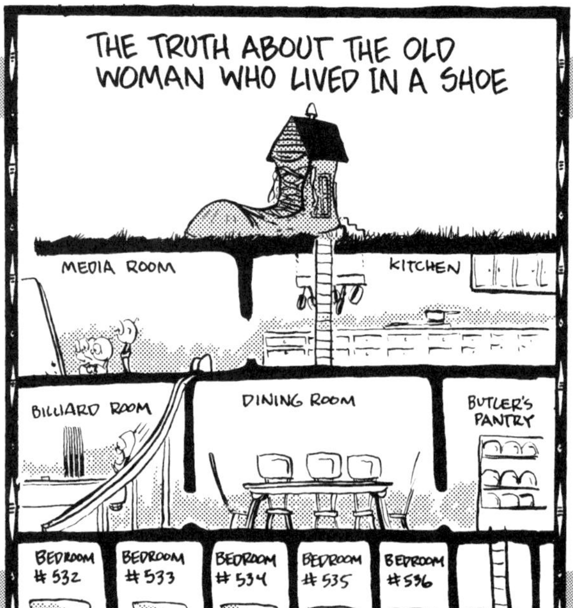
THE TRUTH ABOUT THE OLD WOMAN WHO LIVED IN A SHOE
MEDIA ROOM
KITCHEN
BILLIARD ROOM
DINING ROOM
BUTLER'S PANTRY
BEDROOM #532
BEDROOM #533
BEDROOM #534
BEDROOM #535
BEDROOM #536
MICHAEL FRY

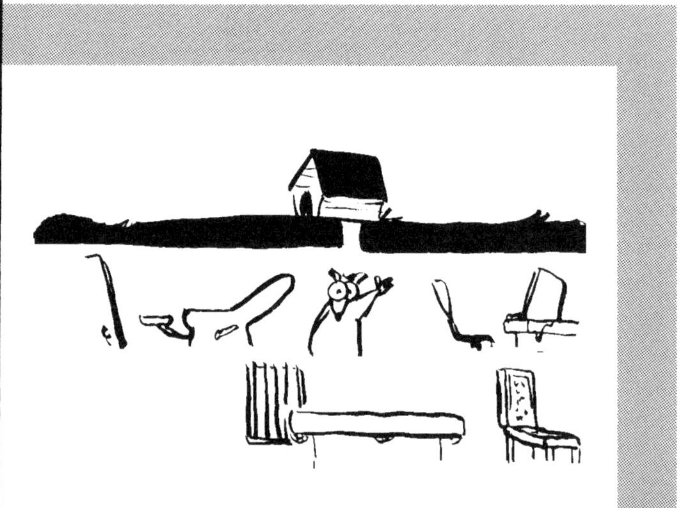

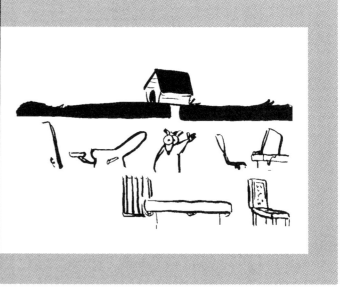

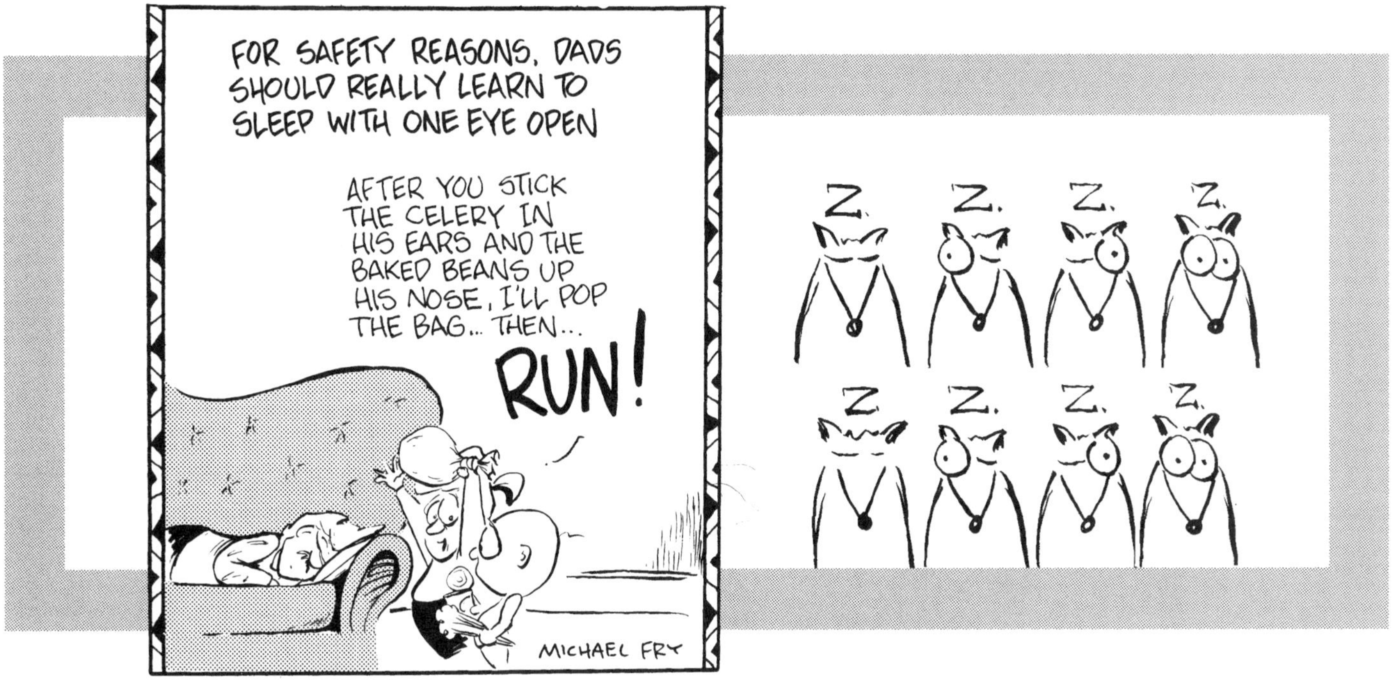
FOR SAFETY REASONS, DADS SHOULD REALLY LEARN TO SLEEP WITH ONE EYE OPEN
AFTER YOU STICK THE CELERY IN HIS EARS AND THE BAKED BEANS UP HIS NOSE, I'LL POP THE BAG... THEN...
RUN!
MICHAEL FRY
Z.
Z.
Z.
Z.
Z.
Z.
Z.
Z.

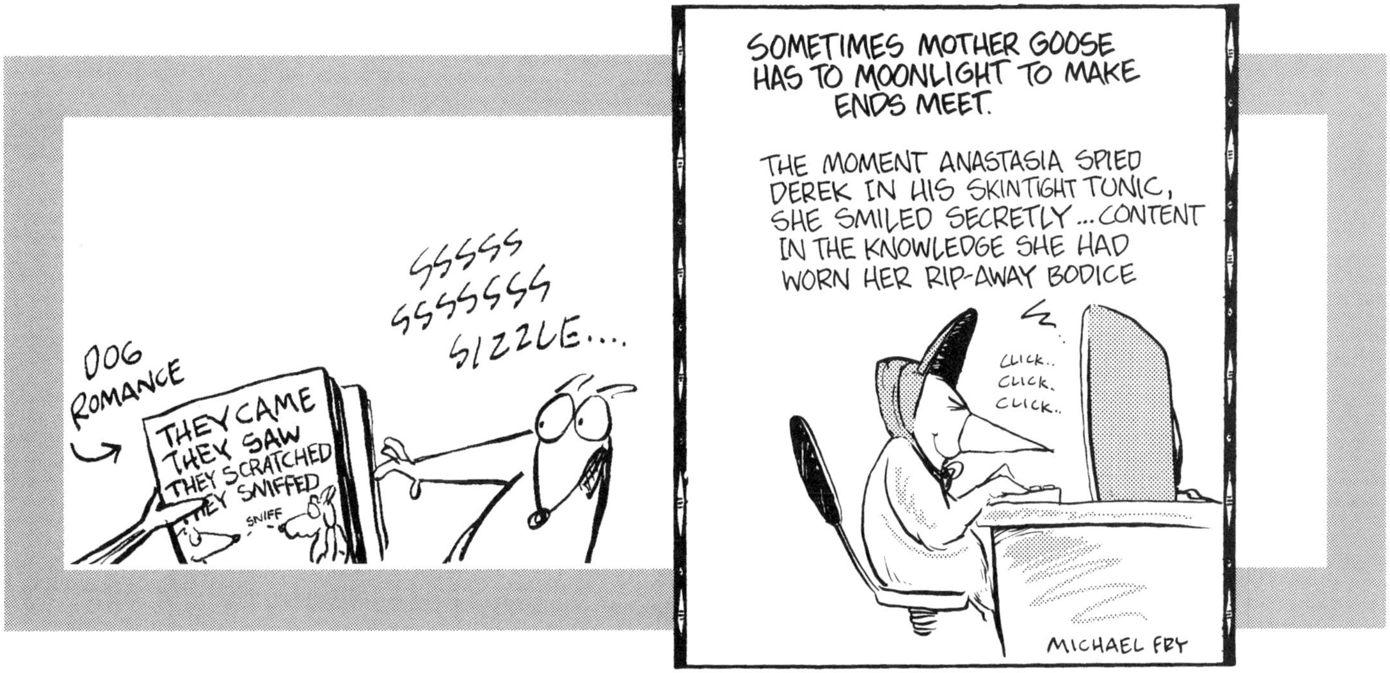
SSSSS SSSSSSS SIZZLE....
DOG ROMANCE
THEY CAME
THEY SAW
THEY SCRATCHED
HEY SNIFFED
SNIFF
SOMETIMES MOTHER GOOSE HAS TO MOONLIGHT TO MAKE ENDS MEET.
THE MOMENT ANASTASIA SPIED DEREK IN HIS SKINTIGHT TUNIC, SHE SMILED SECRETLY ...CONTENT IN THE KNOWLEDGE SHE HAD WORN HER RIP-AWAY BODICE
CLICK.. CLICK. CLICK..
MICHAEL FRY

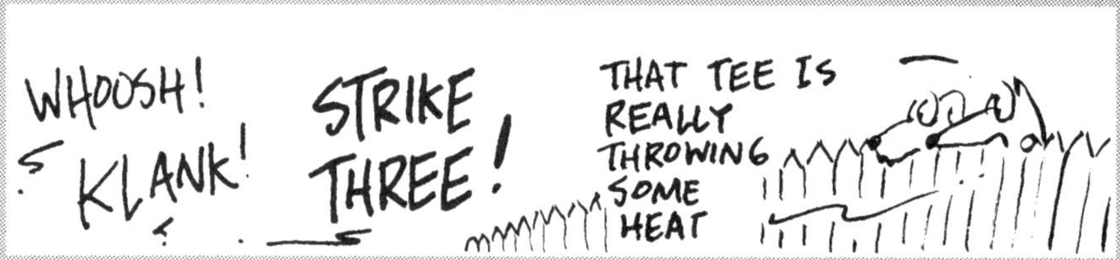
WHOOSH!
KLANK!
STRIKE THREE!
THAT TEE IS REALLY THROWING SOME HEAT

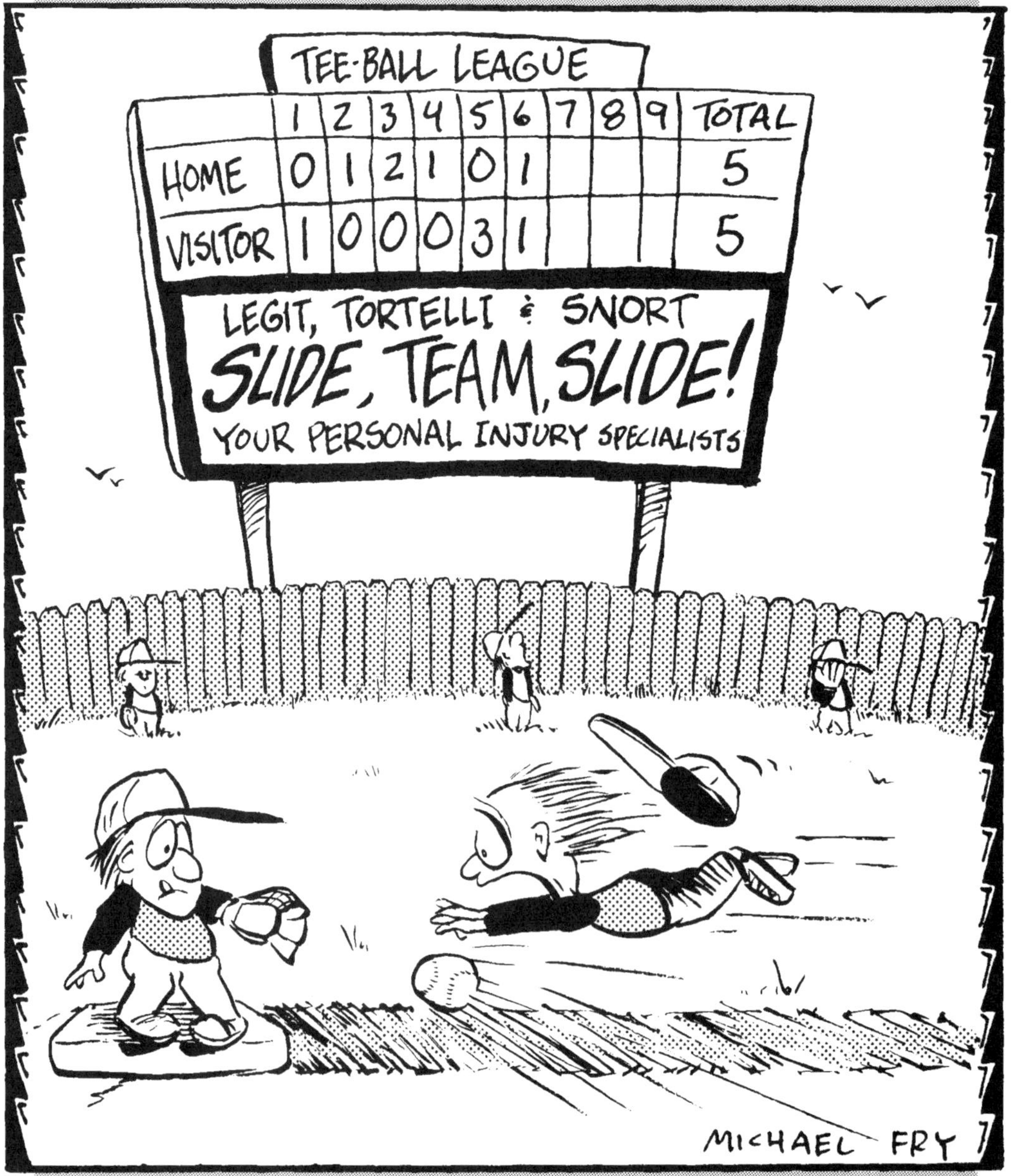
TEE-BALL LEAGUE
1 2 3 4 5 6 7 8 9 TOTAL
HOME 0 1 2 1 0 1 5
VISITOR 1 0 0 0 3 1 5
LEGIT, TORTELLI & SNORT
SLIDE, TEAM, SLIDE!
YOUR PERSONAL INJURY SPECIALISTS
MICHAEL FRY

MARTHA STEWART: THE EARLY-EARLY YEARS

AS YOU CAN SEE ... WE CAN CREATE A LOVELY DECORATIVE GARLAND USING ONLY THE STUFFING FROM THIS HAND-GUTTED TEDDY...

MICHAEL FRY

BOB SUBSCRIBES TO "MARTHA STEWART CANINE LIVING"

SOMETHING TELLS ME THE GINGHAM -N- GOLD LEAF TIE-BACKS CLASH WITH THE RANDOMLY SHED DOG HAIR...

I HEARD SOMEWHERE WE'RE SUPPOSED TO CHEW ON IT

AN OLD DRIED-UP PIG'S EAR?! WHY ON EARTH WOULD WE WANT TO DO THAT?!

WHEN YOU'RE A PARENT, EVERY DAY IS A NEW DAY OF DISCOVERY

I THINK IT'S FOR SLEEPING... BUT I'M NOT SURE... IT'S BEEN SO LONG...

I'VE HEARD TALES... BUT IT ALL COULD JUST BE A VICIOUS RUMOR...

MICHAEL FRY

BOB IS OFTEN FORCED TO MAKE SOME TOUGH SCHEDULING CHOICES...

JACUZZI OR SAUNA?... DECISIONS... DECISIONS...

AREN'T THEY SUPPOSED TO BE IN SCHOOL?

SCHOOL?

T-BALL SCHEDULE

BALLET SCHEDULE

PIANO SCHEDULE

CHOIR SCHEDULE

SOCCER SCHEDULE

SWIMMING SCHEDULE

CHESS SCHEDULE

MICHAEL FRY

TEE-BALL TRAUMA

ALL I SAID WAS "KEEP YOUR EYE ON THE BALL."

NURSE, I NEED A LITTLE SUCTION HERE!

MGHM PHGR...

MICHAEL FRY

BOB CATCHES A FOUL BALL →

I LOST IT IN THE SUN

IT'S A NIGHT GAME.

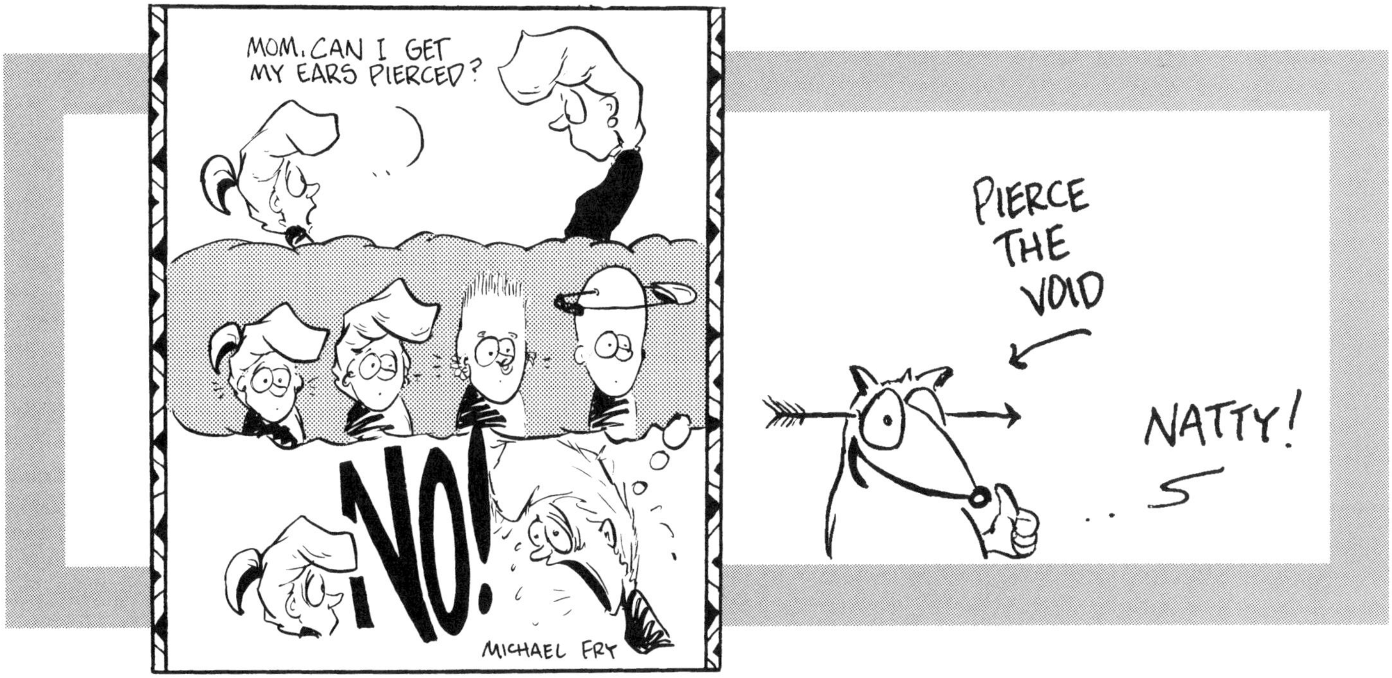
MOM, CAN I GET MY EARS PIERCED?
NO!
MICHAEL FRY
PIERCE THE VOID
NATTY!

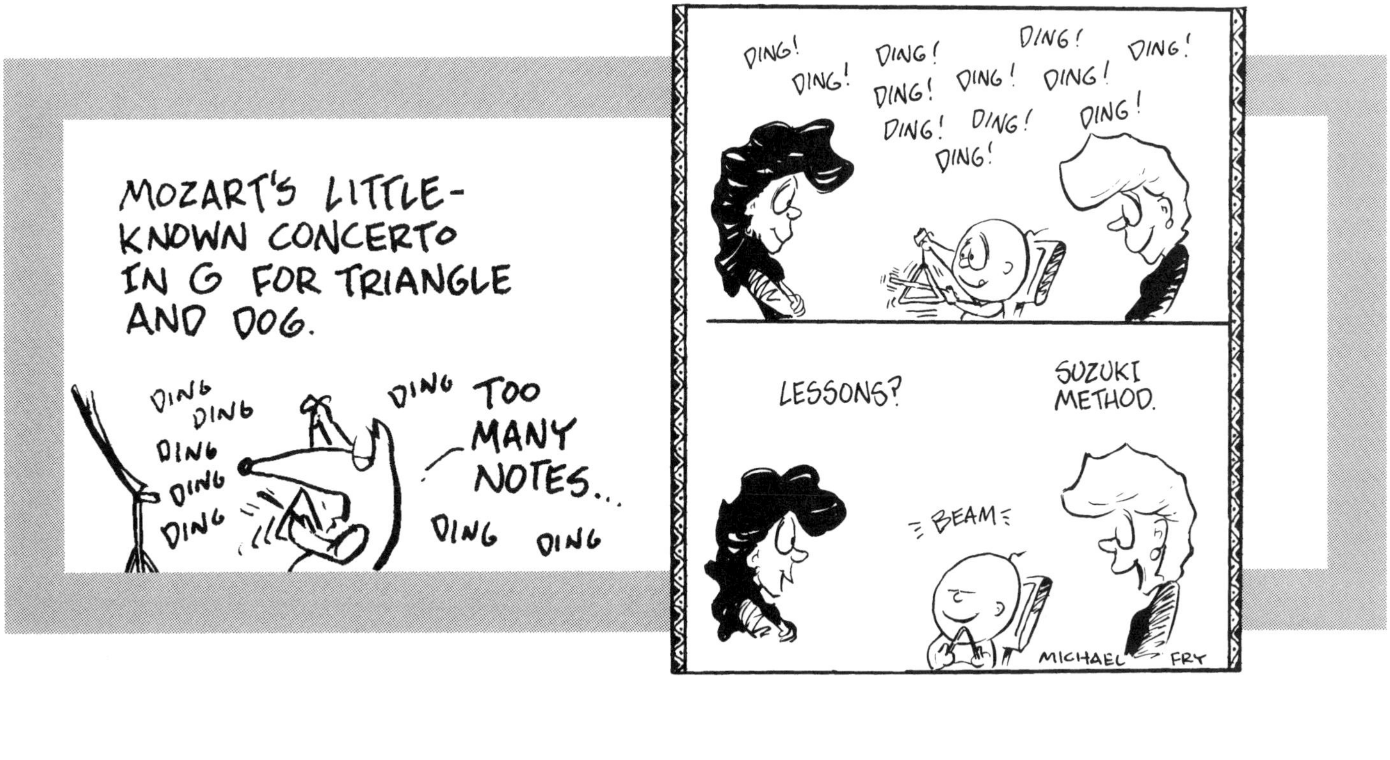
MOZART'S LITTLE-KNOWN CONCERTO IN G FOR TRIANGLE AND DOG.
TOO MANY NOTES...
LESSONS?
SUZUKI METHOD.
BEAM
MICHAEL FRY

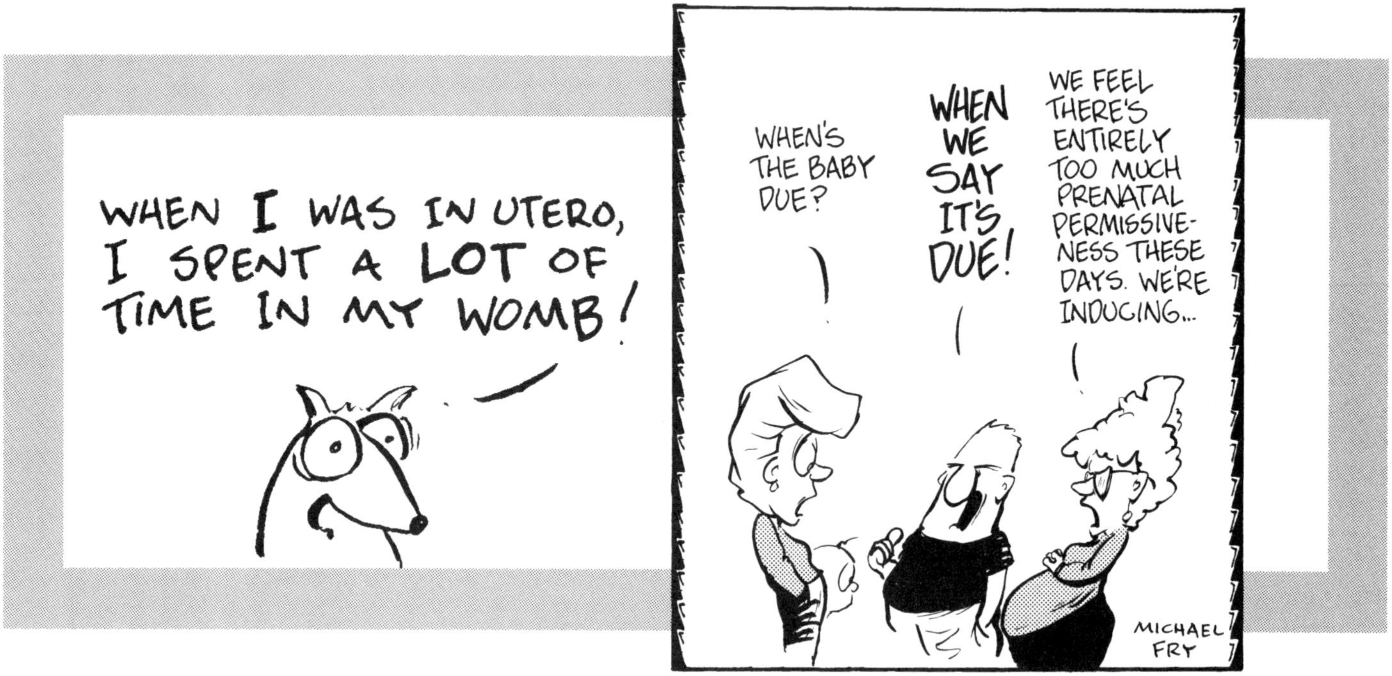
WHEN I WAS IN UTERO, I SPENT A LOT OF TIME IN MY WOMB!
WHEN'S THE BABY DUE?
WHEN WE SAY IT'S DUE!
WE FEEL THERE'S ENTIRELY TOO MUCH PRENATAL PERMISSIVE-NESS THESE DAYS. WE'RE INDUCING...
MICHAEL FRY

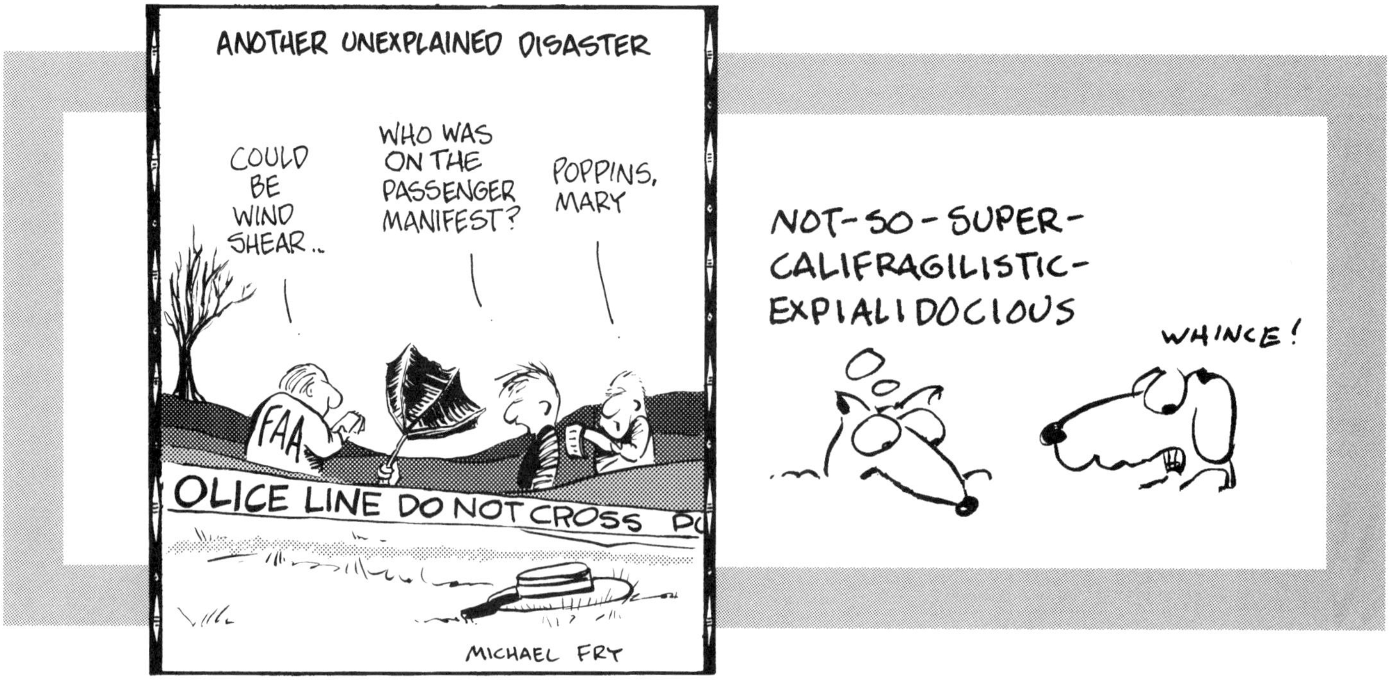
ANOTHER UNEXPLAINED DISASTER
COULD BE WIND SHEAR..
WHO WAS ON THE PASSENGER MANIFEST?
POPPINS, MARY
FAA
OLICE LINE DO NOT CROSS
MICHAEL FRY
NOT-SO-SUPER-CALIFRAGILISTIC-EXPIALIDOCIOUS
WHINCE!

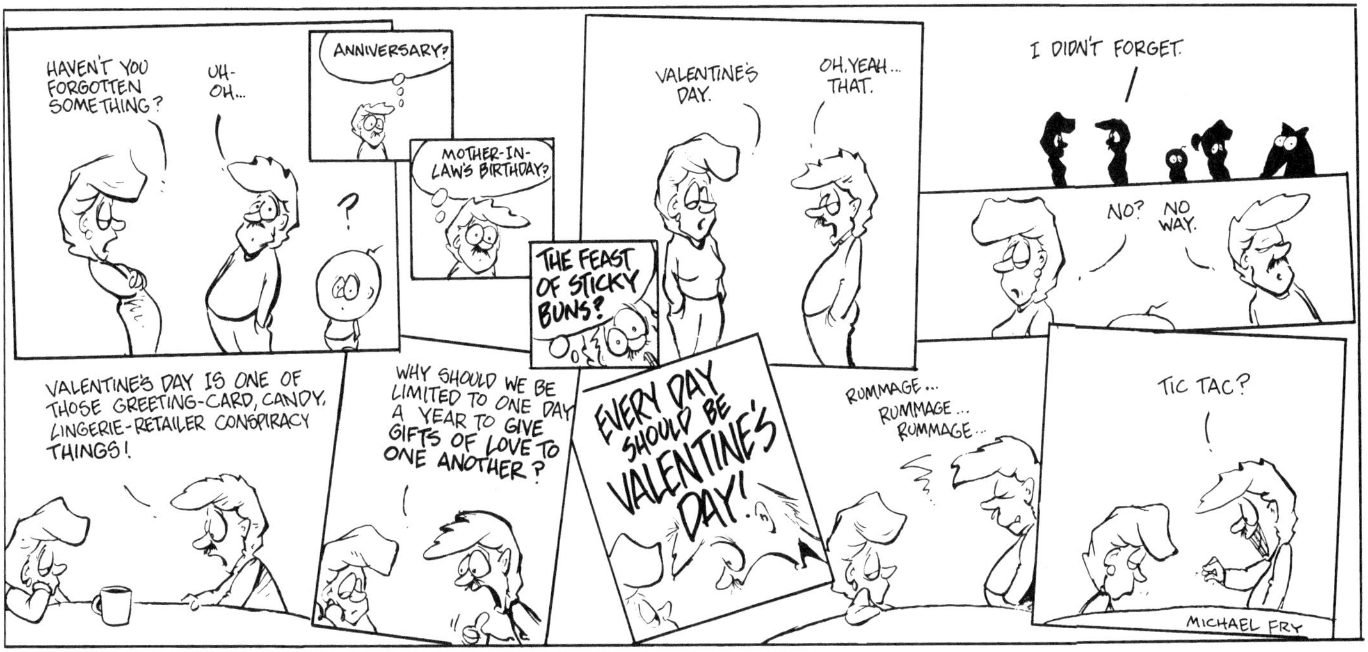

HAVEN'T YOU FORGOTTEN SOMETHING?
UH-OH...
?
ANNIVERSARY?
MOTHER-IN-LAW'S BIRTHDAY?
THE FEAST OF STICKY BUNS?
VALENTINE'S DAY.
OH, YEAH... THAT.
I DIDN'T FORGET.
NO?
NO WAY.
VALENTINE'S DAY IS ONE OF THOSE GREETING-CARD, CANDY, LINGERIE-RETAILER CONSPIRACY THINGS!
WHY SHOULD WE BE LIMITED TO ONE DAY A YEAR TO GIVE GIFTS OF LOVE TO ONE ANOTHER?
EVERY DAY SHOULD BE VALENTINE'S DAY!
RUMMAGE... RUMMAGE... RUMMAGE...
TIC TAC?
MICHAEL FRY

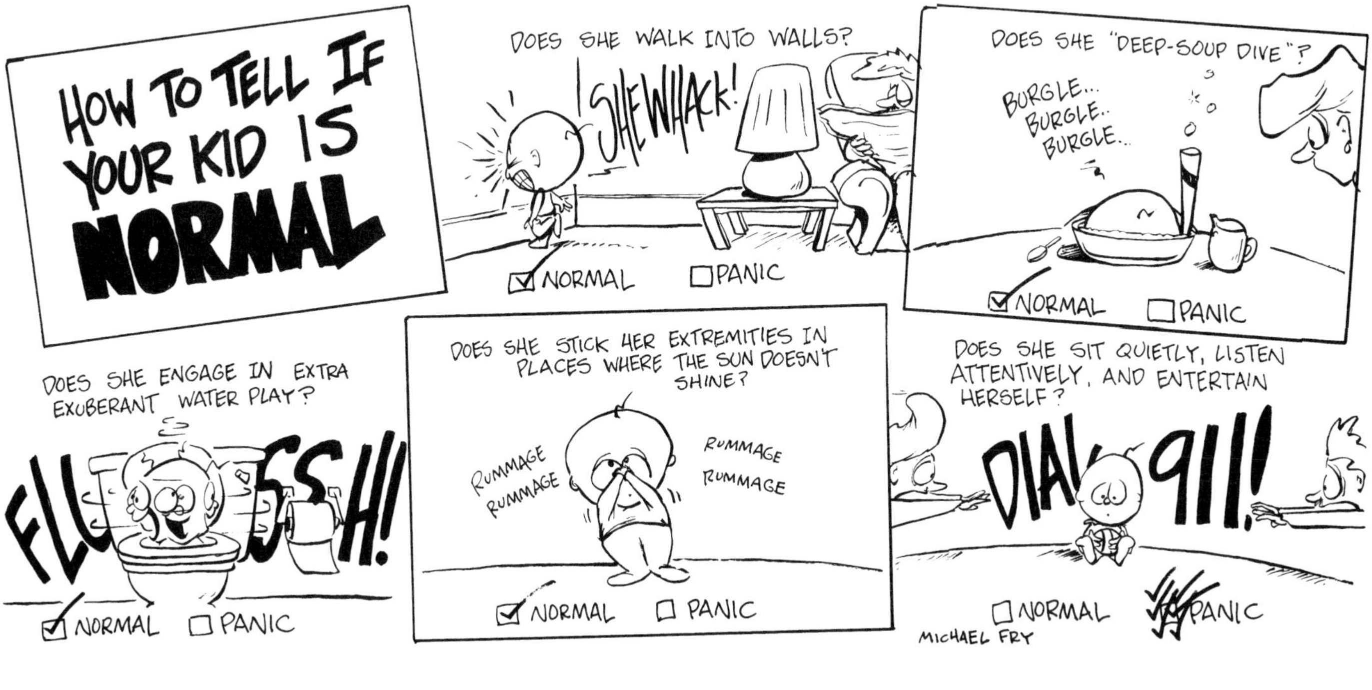

HOW TO TELL IF YOUR KID IS NORMAL
DOES SHE WALK INTO WALLS?
SHEWHACK!
NORMAL
PANIC
DOES SHE "DEEP-SOUP DIVE"?
BURGLE... BURGLE.. BURGLE...
NORMAL
PANIC
DOES SHE ENGAGE IN EXTRA EXUBERANT WATER PLAY?
FLUSSSH!
NORMAL
PANIC
DOES SHE STICK HER EXTREMITIES IN PLACES WHERE THE SUN DOESN'T SHINE?
RUMMAGE RUMMAGE
RUMMAGE RUMMAGE
NORMAL
PANIC
DOES SHE SIT QUIETLY, LISTEN ATTENTIVELY, AND ENTERTAIN HERSELF?
DIAL 911!
NORMAL
PANIC
MICHAEL FRY

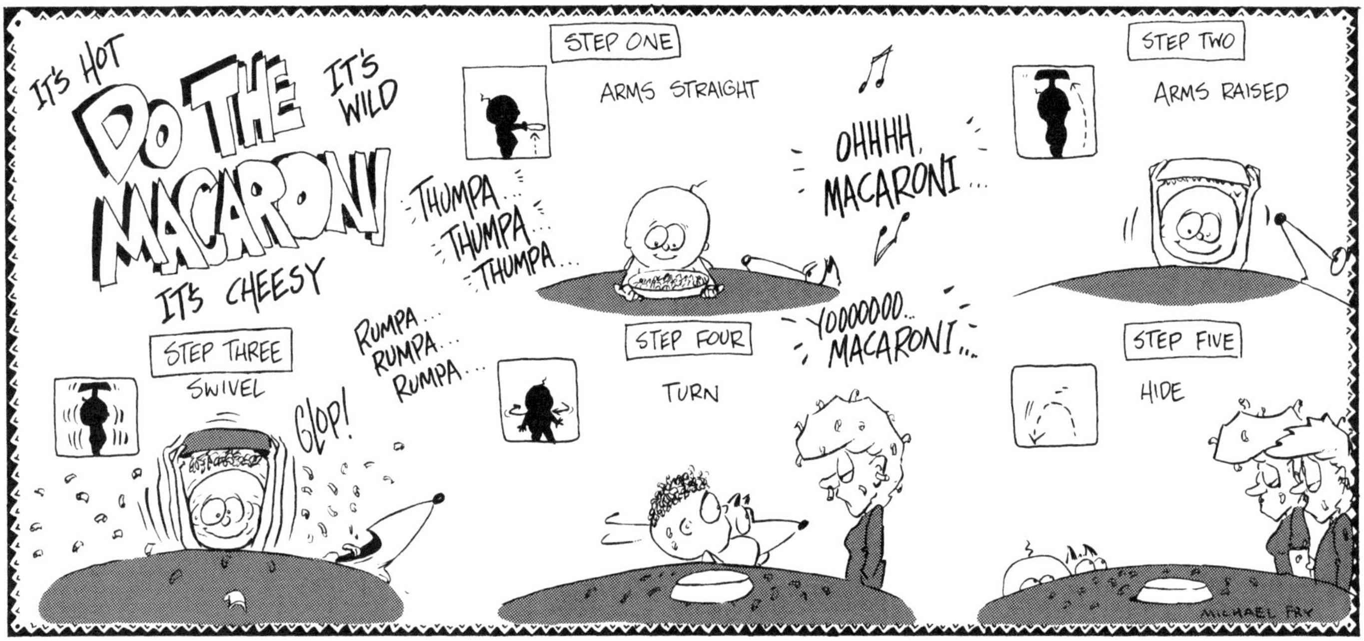
IT'S HOT
DO THE MACARONI
IT'S WILD
IT'S CHEESY
STEP ONE
ARMS STRAIGHT
THUMPA... THUMPA... THUMPA...
OHHHH, MACARONI...
STEP TWO
ARMS RAISED
STEP THREE
SWIVEL
RUMPA... RUMPA... RUMPA...
GLOP!
STEP FOUR
TURN
YOOOOOOO... MACARONI...
STEP FIVE
HIDE
MICHAEL FRY

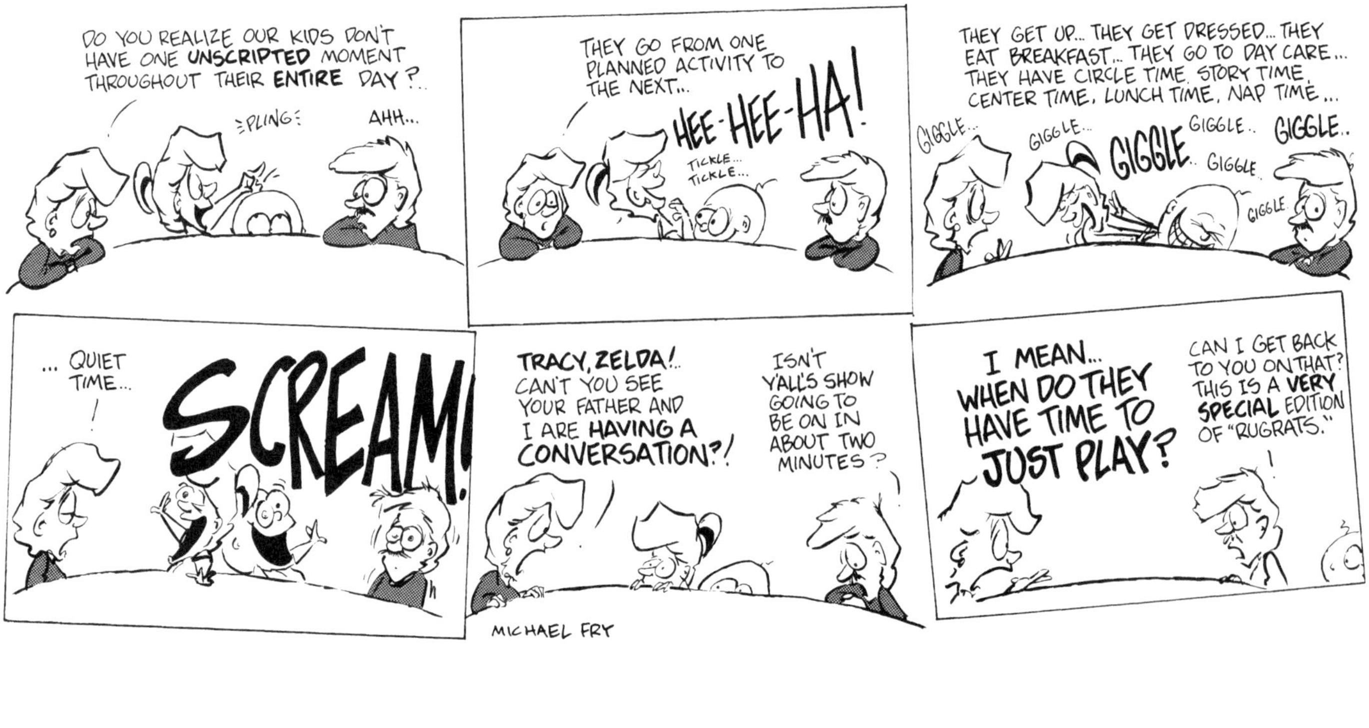
DO YOU REALIZE OUR KIDS DON'T HAVE ONE UNSCRIPTED MOMENT THROUGHOUT THEIR ENTIRE DAY?..
PLING
AHH...
THEY GO FROM ONE PLANNED ACTIVITY TO THE NEXT...
HEE-HEE-HA!
TICKLE... TICKLE...
THEY GET UP... THEY GET DRESSED... THEY EAT BREAKFAST... THEY GO TO DAY CARE... THEY HAVE CIRCLE TIME, STORY TIME, CENTER TIME, LUNCH TIME, NAP TIME...
GIGGLE... GIGGLE... GIGGLE GIGGLE... GIGGLE.. GIGGLE.. GIGGLE GIGGLE
... QUIET TIME...
SCREAM!
TRACY, ZELDA!.. CAN'T YOU SEE YOUR FATHER AND I ARE HAVING A CONVERSATION?!
ISN'T Y'ALL'S SHOW GOING TO BE ON IN ABOUT TWO MINUTES?
I MEAN... WHEN DO THEY HAVE TIME TO JUST PLAY?
CAN I GET BACK TO YOU ON THAT? THIS IS A VERY SPECIAL EDITION OF "RUGRATS."
MICHAEL FRY

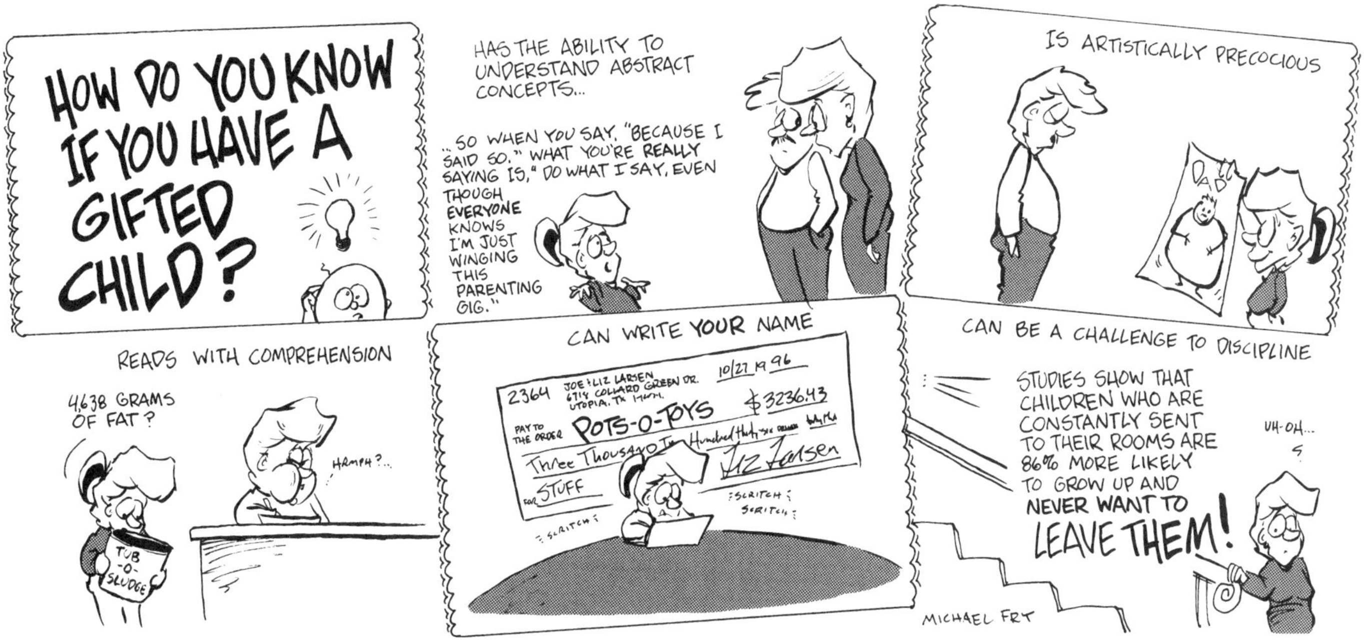
HOW DO YOU KNOW IF YOU HAVE A GIFTED CHILD?
HAS THE ABILITY TO UNDERSTAND ABSTRACT CONCEPTS...
...SO WHEN YOU SAY, "BECAUSE I SAID SO," WHAT YOU'RE REALLY SAYING IS, "DO WHAT I SAY, EVEN THOUGH EVERYONE KNOWS I'M JUST WINGING THIS PARENTING GIG."
IS ARTISTICALLY PRECOCIOUS
DAD
READS WITH COMPREHENSION
4,638 GRAMS OF FAT?
HRMPH?...
TUB-O-SLUDGE
CAN WRITE YOUR NAME
2364
10/27 19 96
POTS-O-TOYS
$3236.43
Liz Larsen
STUFF
SCRITCH
SCRITCH SCRITCH
CAN BE A CHALLENGE TO DISCIPLINE
STUDIES SHOW THAT CHILDREN WHO ARE CONSTANTLY SENT TO THEIR ROOMS ARE 86% MORE LIKELY TO GROW UP AND NEVER WANT TO LEAVE THEM!
UH-OH...
MICHAEL FRY

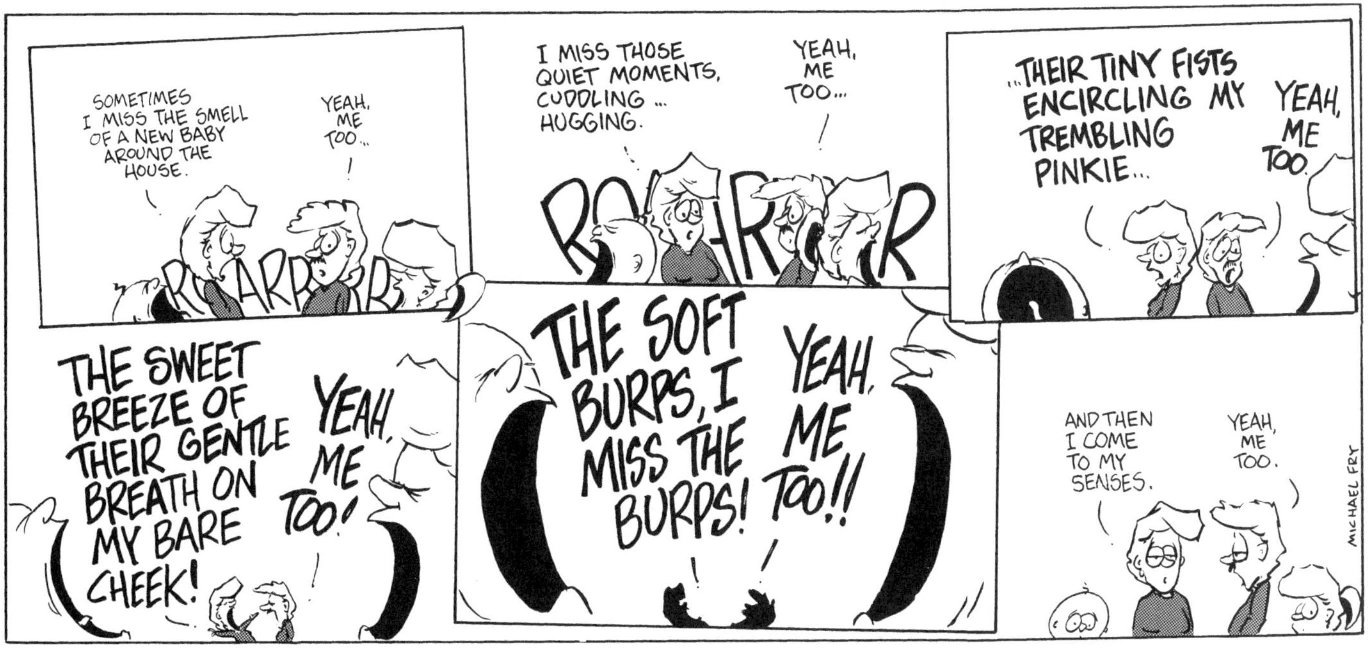
SOMETIMES I MISS THE SMELL OF A NEW BABY AROUND THE HOUSE.
YEAH, ME TOO...
ROARRRR
I MISS THOSE QUIET MOMENTS, CUDDLING... HUGGING.
YEAH, ME TOO...
ROARRRR
...THEIR TINY FISTS ENCIRCLING MY TREMBLING PINKIE...
YEAH, ME TOO.
THE SWEET BREEZE OF THEIR GENTLE BREATH ON MY BARE CHEEK!
YEAH, ME TOO!
THE SOFT BURPS, I MISS THE BURPS!
YEAH, ME TOO!!
AND THEN I COME TO MY SENSES.
YEAH, ME TOO.
MICHAEL FRY

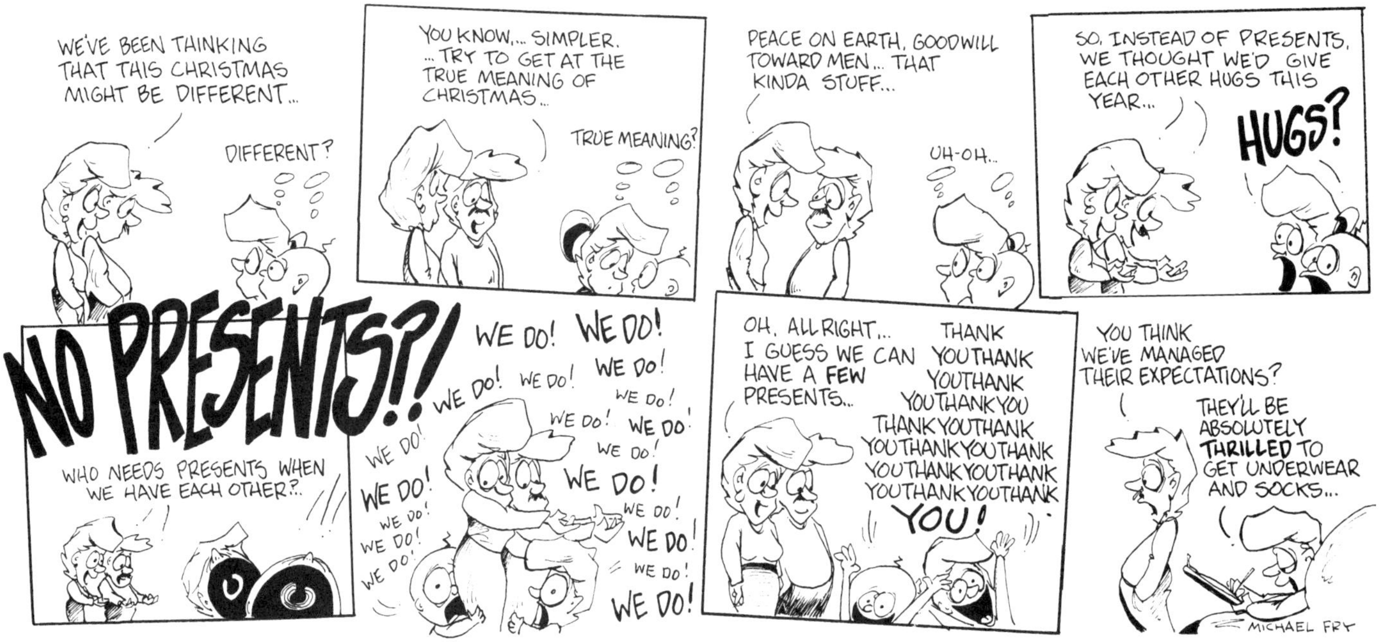
WE'VE BEEN THINKING THAT THIS CHRISTMAS MIGHT BE DIFFERENT...
DIFFERENT?
YOU KNOW,... SIMPLER. ... TRY TO GET AT THE TRUE MEANING OF CHRISTMAS...
TRUE MEANING?
PEACE ON EARTH, GOODWILL TOWARD MEN... THAT KINDA STUFF...
UH-OH...
SO, INSTEAD OF PRESENTS, WE THOUGHT WE'D GIVE EACH OTHER HUGS THIS YEAR...
HUGS?
NO PRESENTS?!
WHO NEEDS PRESENTS WHEN WE HAVE EACH OTHER?..
WE DO! WE DO! WE DO! WE DO! WE DO! WE DO! WE DO! WE DO! WE DO! WE DO! WE DO! WE DO! WE DO! WE DO! WE DO! WE DO! WE DO! WE DO!
OH, ALL RIGHT,... I GUESS WE CAN HAVE A **FEW** PRESENTS...
THANK YOUTHANK YOUTHANK YOUTHANKYOU THANKYOUTHANK YOUTHANKYOUTHANK YOUTHANKYOUTHANK YOUTHANKYOUTHANK YOU!
YOU THINK WE'VE MANAGED THEIR EXPECTATIONS?
THEY'LL BE ABSOLUTELY **THRILLED** TO GET UNDERWEAR AND SOCKS...
MICHAEL FRY

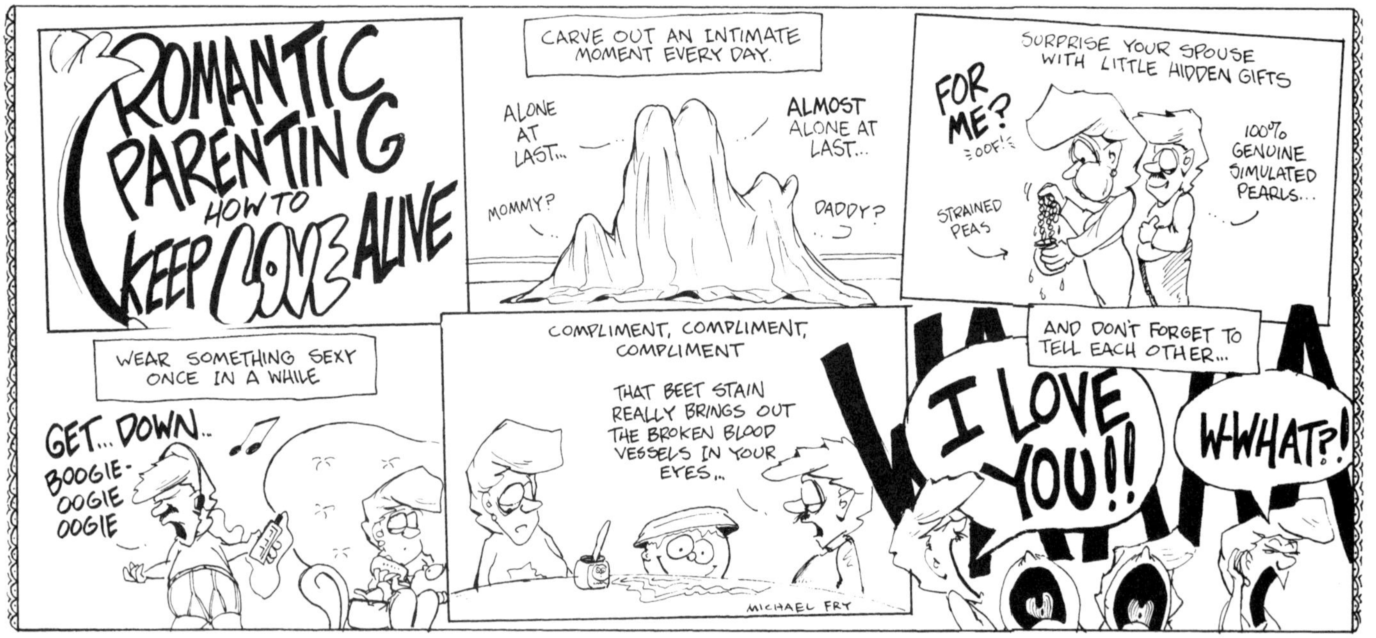
ROMANTIC PARENTING HOW TO KEEP LOVE ALIVE
CARVE OUT AN INTIMATE MOMENT EVERY DAY.
ALONE AT LAST...
ALMOST ALONE AT LAST...
MOMMY?
DADDY?
SURPRISE YOUR SPOUSE WITH LITTLE HIDDEN GIFTS
FOR ME?
OOF!
STRAINED PEAS
100% GENUINE SIMULATED PEARLS...
WEAR SOMETHING SEXY ONCE IN A WHILE
GET... DOWN.. BOOGIE-OOGIE OOGIE
COMPLIMENT, COMPLIMENT, COMPLIMENT
THAT BEET STAIN REALLY BRINGS OUT THE BROKEN BLOOD VESSELS IN YOUR EYES...
MICHAEL FRY
AND DON'T FORGET TO TELL EACH OTHER...
I LOVE YOU!!
W-WHAT?!

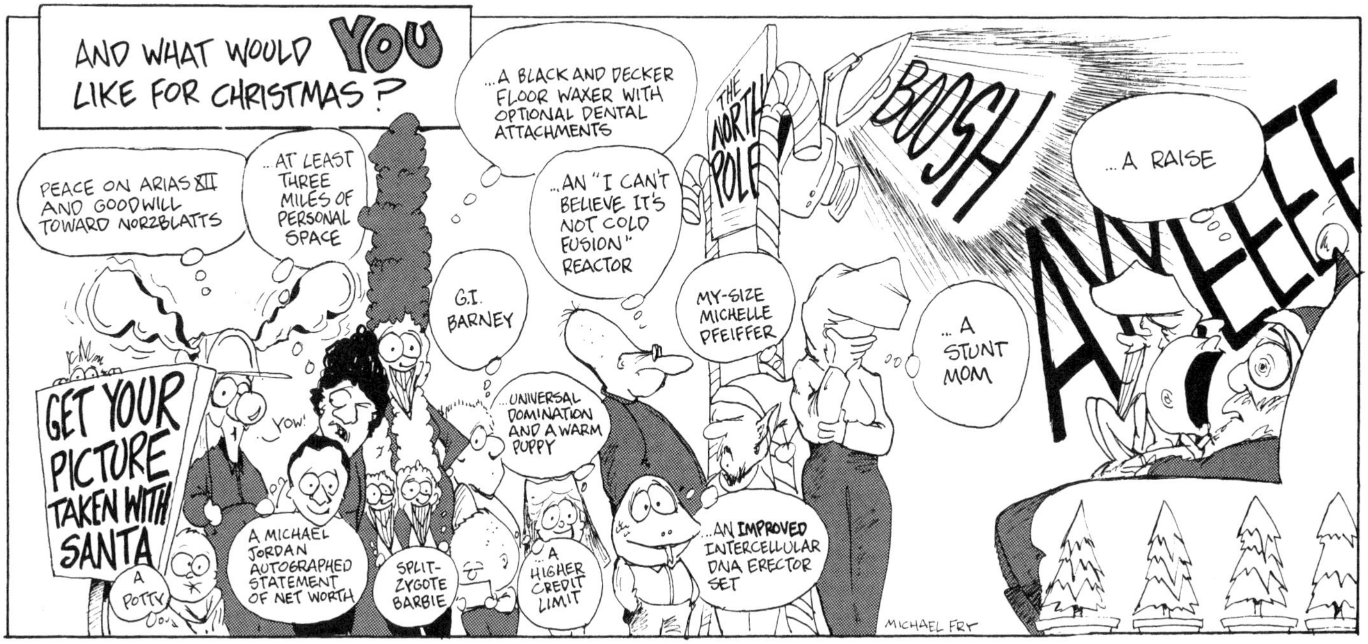
AND WHAT WOULD YOU LIKE FOR CHRISTMAS?
PEACE ON ARIAS XII AND GOODWILL TOWARD NORZBLATTS
...AT LEAST THREE MILES OF PERSONAL SPACE
...A BLACK AND DECKER FLOOR WAXER WITH OPTIONAL DENTAL ATTACHMENTS
...AN "I CAN'T BELIEVE IT'S NOT COLD FUSION" REACTOR
G.I. BARNEY
THE NORTH POLE
BOOSH
...A RAISE
AAEEEE
MY-SIZE MICHELLE PFEIFFER
... A STUNT MOM
GET YOUR PICTURE TAKEN WITH SANTA
YOW!
...UNIVERSAL DOMINATION AND A WARM PUPPY
A POTTY
A MICHAEL JORDAN AUTOGRAPHED STATEMENT OF NET WORTH
SPLIT-ZYGOTE BARBIE
...A HIGHER CREDIT LIMIT
...AN IMPROVED INTERCELLULAR DNA ERECTOR SET
MICHAEL FRY

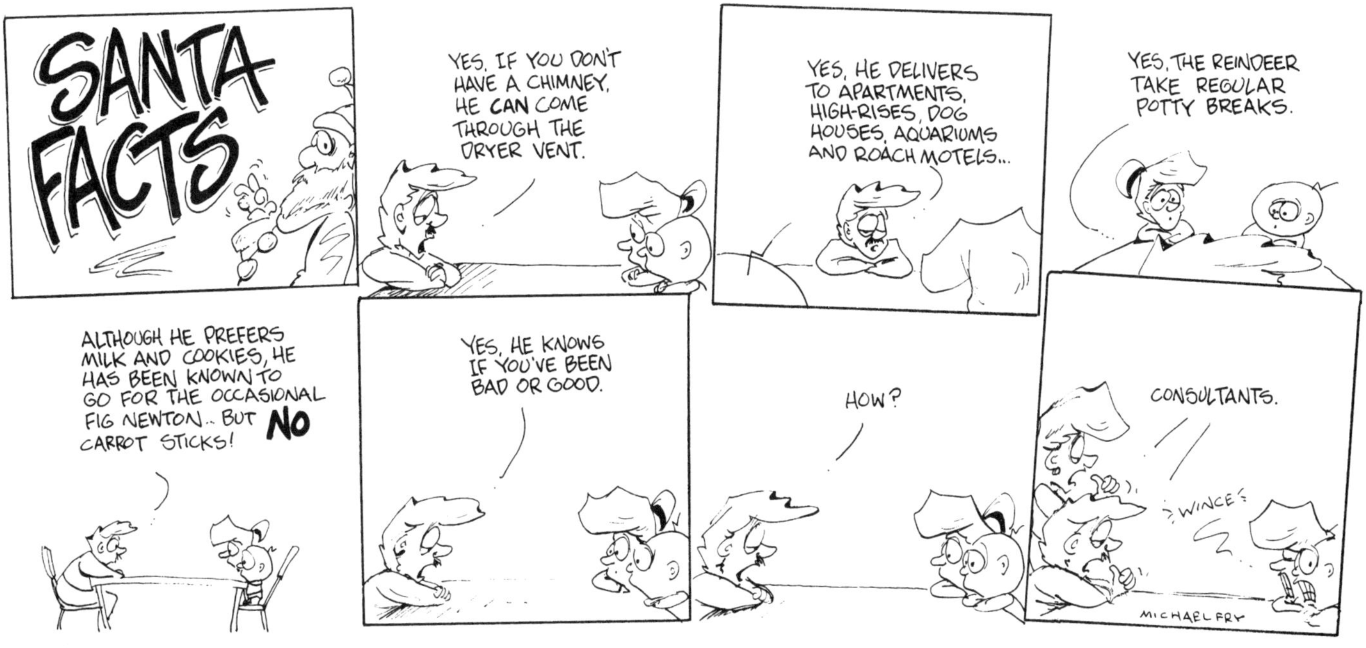
SANTA FACTS
YES, IF YOU DON'T HAVE A CHIMNEY, HE CAN COME THROUGH THE DRYER VENT.
YES, HE DELIVERS TO APARTMENTS, HIGH-RISES, DOG HOUSES, AQUARIUMS AND ROACH MOTELS...
YES, THE REINDEER TAKE REGULAR POTTY BREAKS.
ALTHOUGH HE PREFERS MILK AND COOKIES, HE HAS BEEN KNOWN TO GO FOR THE OCCASIONAL FIG NEWTON.. BUT NO CARROT STICKS!
YES, HE KNOWS IF YOU'VE BEEN BAD OR GOOD.
HOW?
CONSULTANTS.
WINCE
MICHAEL FRY

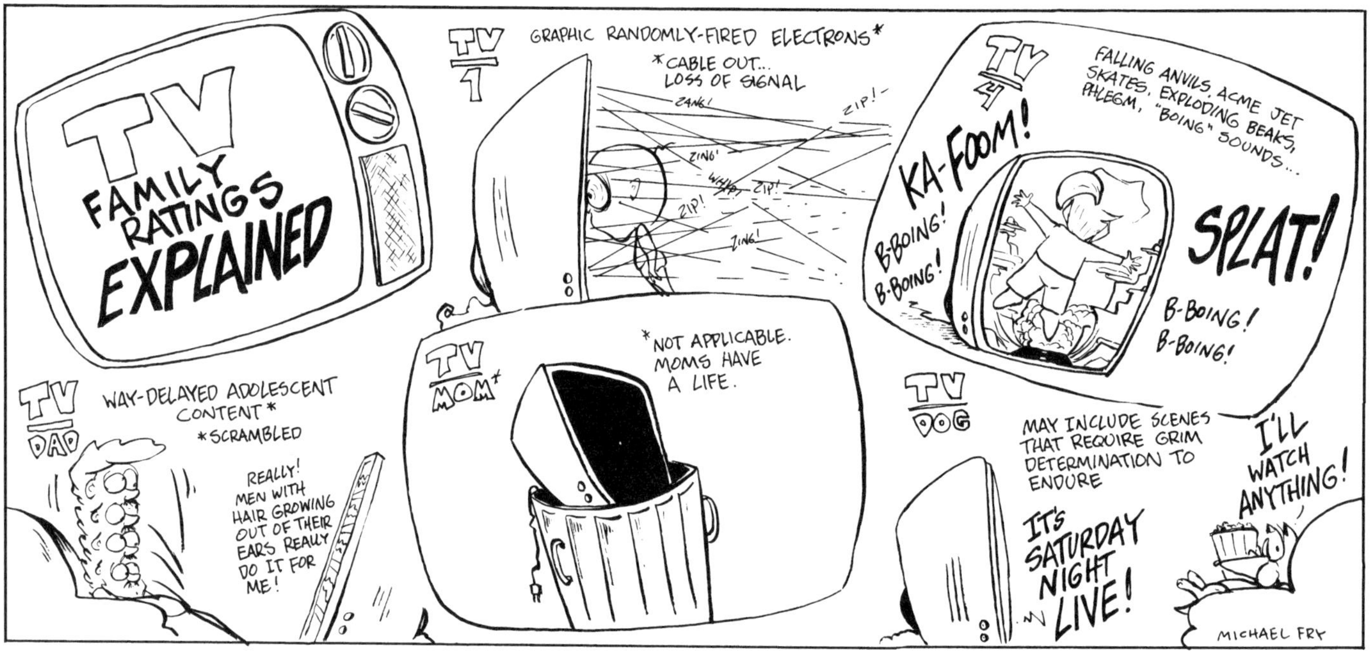
TV FAMILY RATINGS EXPLAINED
TV 1
GRAPHIC RANDOMLY-FIRED ELECTRONS*
*CABLE OUT... LOSS OF SIGNAL
ZANG!
ZIP!
ZING!
ZIP!
ZING!
TV 4
FALLING ANVILS, ACME JET SKATES, EXPLODING BEAKS, PHLEGM, "BOING" SOUNDS...
KA-FOOM!
B-BOING! B-BOING!
SPLAT!
B-BOING! B-BOING!
TV DAD
WAY-DELAYED ADOLESCENT CONTENT*
*SCRAMBLED
REALLY! MEN WITH HAIR GROWING OUT OF THEIR EARS REALLY DO IT FOR ME!
TV MOM*
*NOT APPLICABLE. MOMS HAVE A LIFE.
TV DOG
MAY INCLUDE SCENES THAT REQUIRE GRIM DETERMINATION TO ENDURE
IT'S SATURDAY NIGHT LIVE!
I'LL WATCH ANYTHING!
MICHAEL FRY

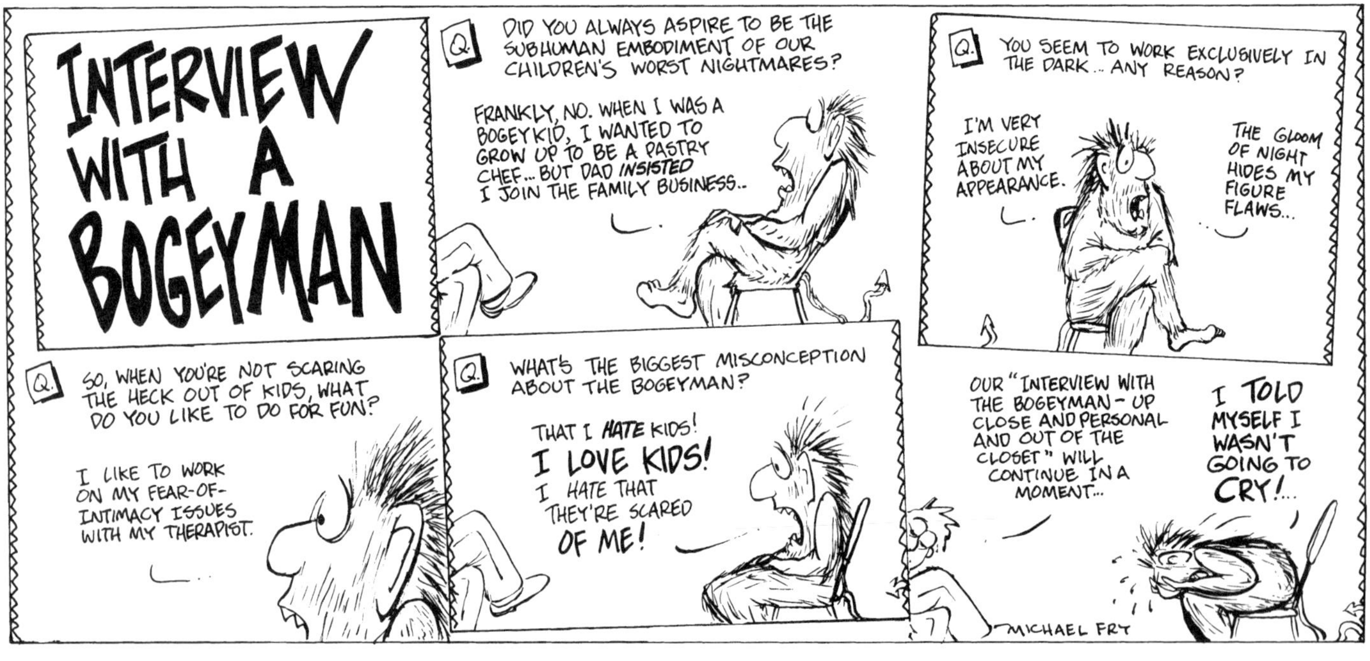
INTERVIEW WITH A BOGEYMAN
Q. DID YOU ALWAYS ASPIRE TO BE THE SUBHUMAN EMBODIMENT OF OUR CHILDREN'S WORST NIGHTMARES?
FRANKLY, NO. WHEN I WAS A BOGEYKID, I WANTED TO GROW UP TO BE A PASTRY CHEF... BUT DAD INSISTED I JOIN THE FAMILY BUSINESS..
Q. YOU SEEM TO WORK EXCLUSIVELY IN THE DARK... ANY REASON?
I'M VERY INSECURE ABOUT MY APPEARANCE.
THE GLOOM OF NIGHT HIDES MY FIGURE FLAWS...
Q. SO, WHEN YOU'RE NOT SCARING THE HECK OUT OF KIDS, WHAT DO YOU LIKE TO DO FOR FUN?
I LIKE TO WORK ON MY FEAR-OF-INTIMACY ISSUES WITH MY THERAPIST.
Q. WHAT'S THE BIGGEST MISCONCEPTION ABOUT THE BOGEYMAN?
THAT I HATE KIDS! I LOVE KIDS! I HATE THAT THEY'RE SCARED OF ME!
OUR "INTERVIEW WITH THE BOGEYMAN - UP CLOSE AND PERSONAL AND OUT OF THE CLOSET" WILL CONTINUE IN A MOMENT...
I TOLD MYSELF I WASN'T GOING TO CRY!...
MICHAEL FRY

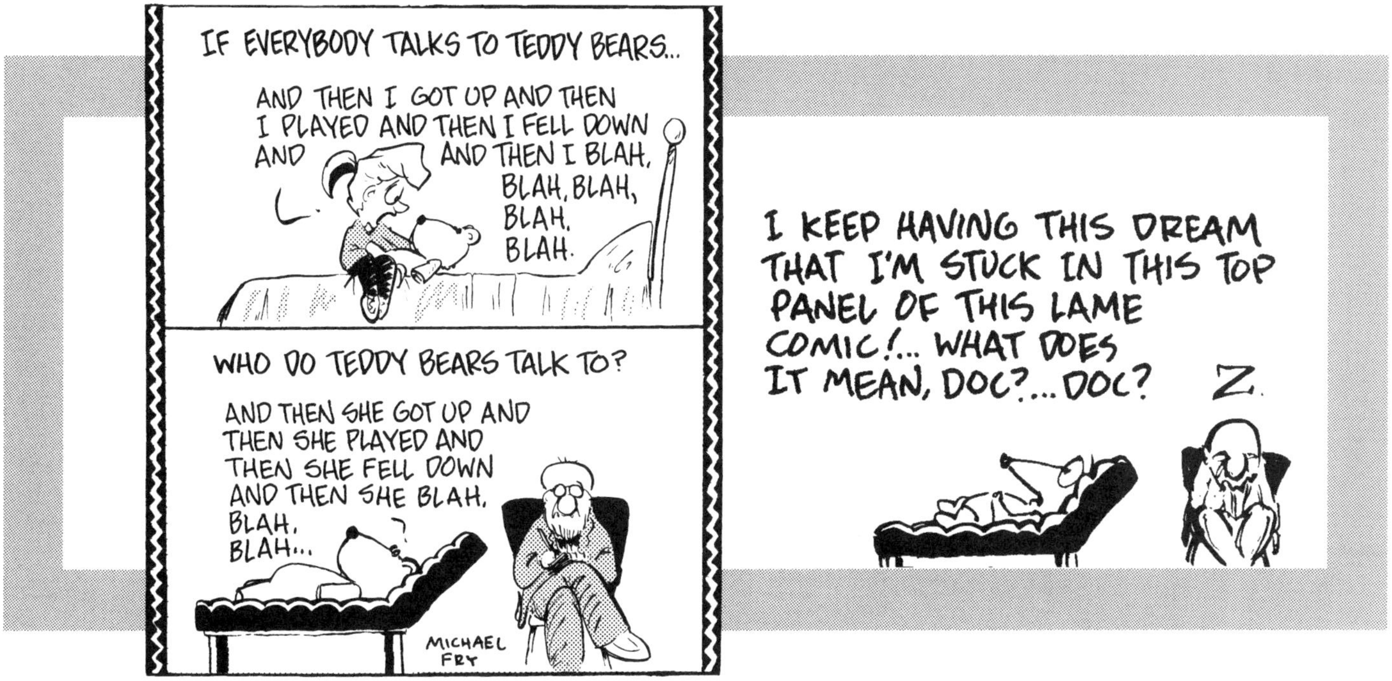
IF EVERYBODY TALKS TO TEDDY BEARS...
AND THEN I GOT UP AND THEN I PLAYED AND THEN I FELL DOWN AND AND THEN I BLAH, BLAH, BLAH, BLAH, BLAH.
WHO DO TEDDY BEARS TALK TO?
AND THEN SHE GOT UP AND THEN SHE PLAYED AND THEN SHE FELL DOWN AND THEN SHE BLAH, BLAH, BLAH...
MICHAEL FRY
I KEEP HAVING THIS DREAM THAT I'M STUCK IN THIS TOP PANEL OF THIS LAME COMIC!... WHAT DOES IT MEAN, DOC?... DOC?
Z.

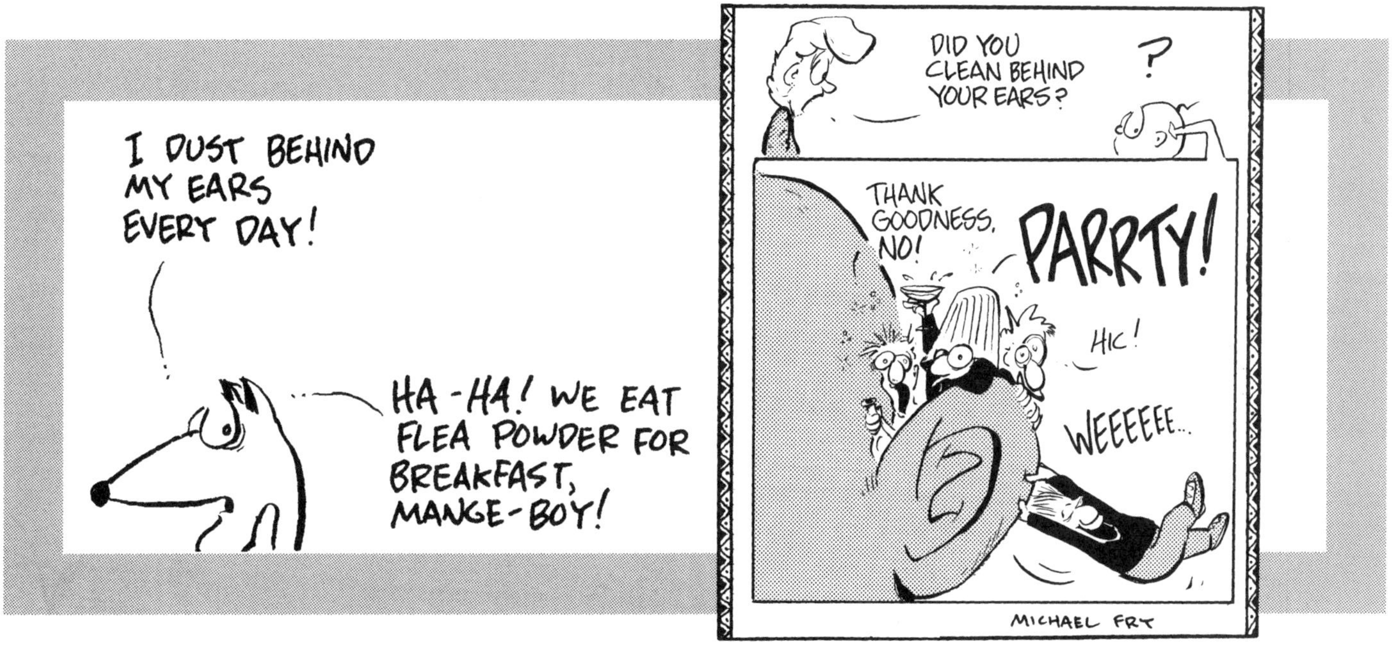
I DUST BEHIND MY EARS EVERY DAY!
HA-HA! WE EAT FLEA POWDER FOR BREAKFAST, MANGE-BOY!
DID YOU CLEAN BEHIND YOUR EARS?
?
THANK GOODNESS, NO!
PARRTY!
HIC!
WEEEEEE...
MICHAEL FRY

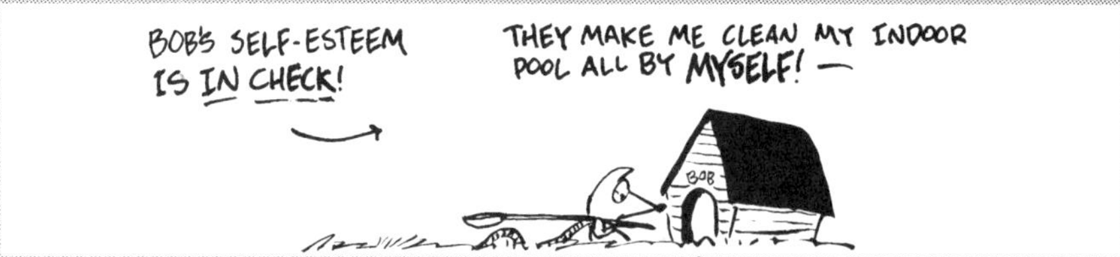
BOB'S SELF-ESTEEM IS IN CHECK!
THEY MAKE ME CLEAN MY INDOOR POOL ALL BY MYSELF! —
BOB

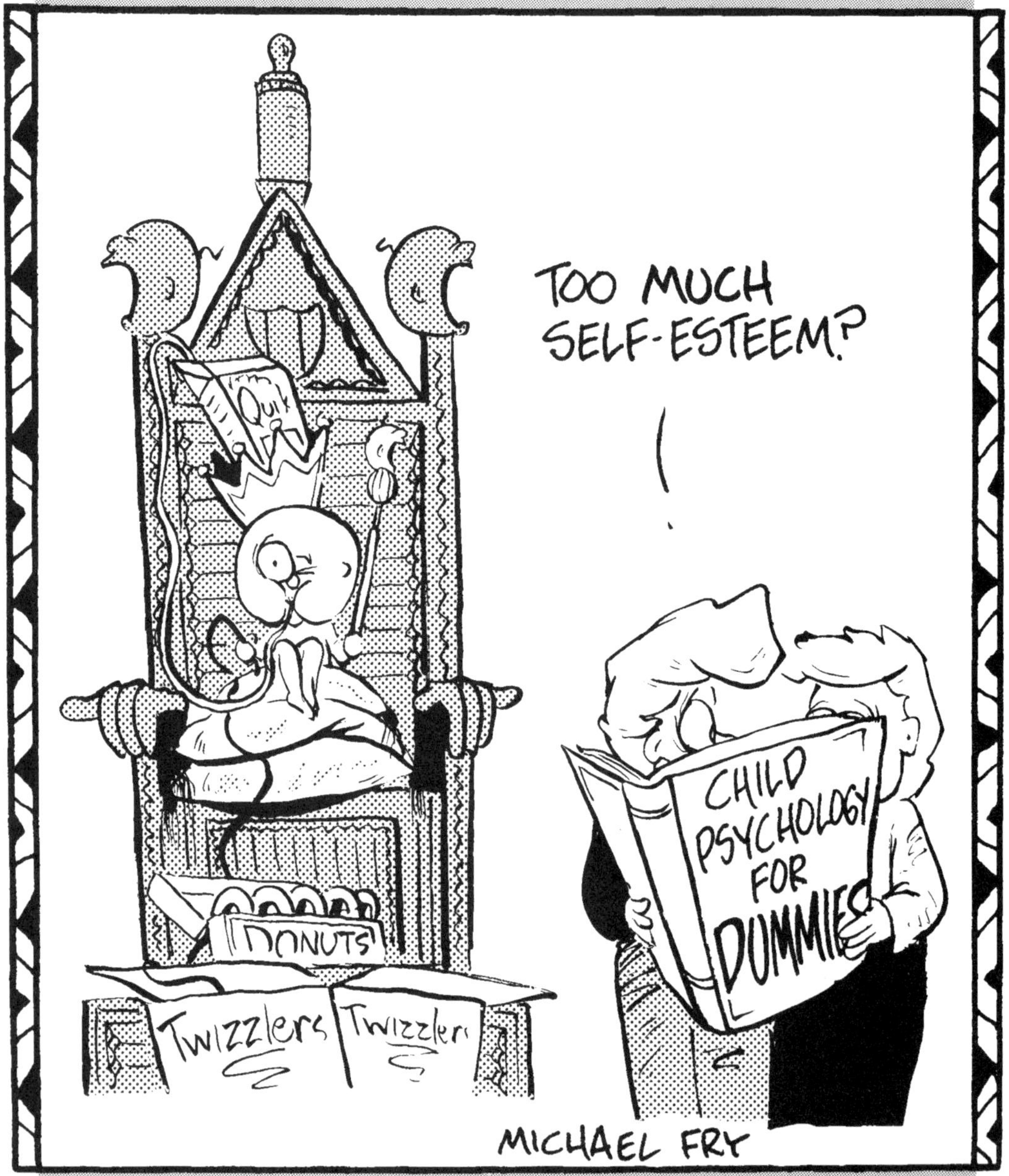
TOO MUCH SELF-ESTEEM?
QUIX
DONUTS
Twizzlers
Twizzlers
CHILD PSYCHOLOGY FOR DUMMIES
MICHAEL FRY